# I JUST KEPT WALKING

# Cass Ryder

# Foreword

## By Leigh Ryder

*I Just Kept Walking* is the true and harrowing story of a woman who has survived over 20 years of homelessness in the United States. Everything recounted in these pages is real, nothing has been invented or altered except where strictly necessary e.g. grammatical corrections or regularisation of sentence construction which would otherwise make it difficult for the reader to follow the train of thought. This is the tragic story of my own sister – educated and now in her 50s – who is still homeless, and whom I am desperately trying to persuade to come home. We lost touch many years ago due to family circumstances. Our parents are both dead, and transatlantic letters/faxes went missing due to her precarious and nomadic lifestyle. With no means of tracing her whereabouts, her siblings (myself included) concluded she must be dead. Then in 2013 I received an email forwarded from relatives who own a hotel in Wales where we used to take family holidays. Of necessity the homeless spend a great deal of their time in public libraries, and once my sister began to use the Internet she was able to track down my cousins, who then got in touch with me. The author "Cass Ryder" is thought to be a paranoid schizophrenic - though has never been officially diagnosed as such - and despite repeated offers from her family to pay for her airfare back to the UK, her conscience will not allow her to walk away from another homeless woman she met in a shelter (referred to throughout as "the Subject")

The factual account of hardships faced - sleeping rough in the open, the cold and hunger, the loneliness and extreme isolation, not to mention the ever-present threat of assault - make for disturbing reading, with graphic accounts of street-level destitution and violence, frequent arrests, bodily hi-jackings, and invasive mind-control. The central proposition put forward is that the "Vulnerables" – who include the homeless, the mentally ill, prison inmates, and those with alternative lifestyles - are being used for experimentation purposes by privately funded agencies (an "etheric neighbourhood watchdog") with feedback being consciously monitored for future control of the populace, and that these categories have been specifically targeted because they are not in a position to speak out about what is happening to them. Some of the wilder speculations concerning covert plans to economically demote over half of the current middle class to the sublevel of the homeless or impoverished categories ("New Project for the American Century") will undoubtedly be dismissed as the delusions of a paranoid and sick mind. But others going through something similar will be inspired by the writer's unique insights into the human condition, and may be able to identify with what she has termed the "invisible inquisition" operating through space and time.

The sentiments expressed by the narrator, and her musings on a miscellany of topics all come together in what is a heart wrenching - and occasionally unsettling - but compelling personal testament. Her lucid insights into her own mental state and that of others she has brushed up against in cold weather shelters or correctional facilities is explored through a blend of interior monologue and ongoing dialogue in the form of emails. The original material was sent in batches as scanned PDF documents over a period of 3 years, and at times it was like piecing together the constituent parts of a gigantic jigsaw puzzle. Due to her fear that her communications are being intercepted by government agencies, she tends to write very fast without pausing for punctuation or natural sentence breaks. As self-appointed amanuensis I undertook the task of knocking into shape and bringing coherence and order to what would otherwise have been an amorphous and unstructured mass of writing. Although I have found it necessary to edit the original script, I soon came to the conclusion there was no point in correcting every single grammatical or spelling error or it just wouldn't "ring true"

After all, someone living on the streets is hardly going to express themselves in the pristine language of an English professor. I have therefore retained many of the narrator's idiosyncrasies of expression, inventive vocabulary and inevitable profanities: of course you're going to be in a foul mood if you're exhausted through lack of sleep, risking your life on a nightly basis, and suspicious that your head is being "messed with".

Insofar as this is an authentic and refreshingly honest account of what it's actually like to be a homeless female, it would defeat the point if the manuscript were "prettied up" too much. I think most readers would want the truth - however unpalatable - instead of some sanitised version. I have obviously had to protect the identities of persons referenced, as my sister's dangerous lifestyle renders her vulnerable to attack. Although she is still clearly very disturbed and damaged by her experiences we continue to communicate via email. Even if I were not closely related to the writer, I would still be of the opinion that *I Just Kept Walking* is an important and groundbreaking work, which deserves to be read by the wider public. To my knowledge no person who has been living on the streets for this length of time has been articulate enough to write about the experience, and her journal stands as a testimony of one woman's resilience and her survival tactics in the face of almost insuperable odds.

**Special Note:** This work was published at my own expense, having been shunned by mainstream publishers who did not deem the content to be of "sufficient interest" to the reading public. Please prove them wrong by recommending I Just Kept Walking to your friends and acquaintances. It is hoped that any sales revenue will enable the narrator to extricate herself from her nightmarish existence, and to get her life back on track.

Leigh Ryder

**From: Cass Ryder**
**To: Leigh Ryder**

The night before last we were surrounded by 3 cop cars with armed men. They've got to be the most unbelievable desperate jerks alive. I told them they're cheap and dirty, just like their way of life and their relationships. The cop I spoke to basically confirmed what I had feared, that we are supposed to camp on the verge by the highway where anyone can attack us. I know they hate my guts, good job I got it confirmed. The rain and the wind might definitely be a problem, and I would not trust them not to swoop down and make an arrest based on a verbal warning. This is typical of Uncle Sam, what he does best, getting little people on the run and basking in his strength (when he's not strong) It's sad how Monica clung to me like a drowning woman hanging onto a piece of driftwood, and screamed for me to stay when I HATE being here. Sometimes I wonder whether my presence is making things worse and possibly another partner would be a good idea, because she's had this nervous breakdown. She's very managed, if truth be told, and doesn't seem to be at ease with this invisible force whose major aim in life has been to get her on her own. They're frustrated because they don't have a prostitute, instead they've got a psychopath, and I'm messing up their little management plan. I'm tired of using their libraries, they're a bunch of puerile perverts, and all they do is spy on me. The psychic domain is a place full of entities that can only view the universe through sexual acts, an intense energy field to do with coitus interruptus. People might think I'm upset because I have nothing, actually I think I did pretty well after 18 years of homelessness. I go about things differently...I just kept to myself. It's called trying to survive and I've had quite a lot of disembodied interference similar to what she's gone through. Anyway there's some sort of occult force around her and there are no Manchurian Candidate funds, and they're mainly men that make the laws that keep people like her on the pavement and me in a woodlot running like a wanted animal.

Last night a security guard attempted to illegalise us as people sitting on the benches here at night, and whether he has this authority or not I don't know, but he didn't come back and we went ahead and slept on the benches. I realise they're doing this more and more, like in Florida the homeless men are ending up in jail (I've seen homeless men who look like they're about to go ape shit) I was under the impression the homeless have rights, but perhaps the federal govt has succeeded in handcuffing this civil liberty. I'm not happy with this guard's warning because these benches provide some roof shelter from the rain. M has a weak bladder and has to hit a restroom quite often in the night so we have to be close to a 24-hour facility. Also we're women and have more assault concerns. Some areas are a lot more crime-oriented where I know I have to stay awake at night, and I think I could easily with caffeine. We kind of help each other through mutual guarding on the bench at night (which is mainly me on guard with a can of mace, but I still doze off) One cop in another state once told me they have to legally hand over a written trespass warning before they could take it to an arrest stage, but I should get clarification on that. All Americans know through visual witnessing that at least 2 million on any one night are out in the open on benches or on the pavement in full view of the public.

Monica claims her sister had "run ins" with a well-know NY mafia syndicate. She has a cousin in the FBI called Michael who she says hypnotized her. She's insufferably arrogant and often projects a sort of "mind your own business" persona while at the same time she's forcing this information on me. God, what do I care about her foul wider mafia family? But if covert operatives are involved then what they're handing her for compensation is far too cheap, and even if they're watching from unique security angles the toll of homelessness is doing irreparable damage to her psyche (like the rather rough arrest the other night) There you go, Uncle Sam, there's another one for you, and you can redeem yourself in the world's eyes, and show the poor people what losers they apparently are. Poor as she might be she doesn't have to go to banana. If I leave here I'm not coming back to witness her still out on the pavement while Uncle Sam jacks off. She was apparently dropped off at a shelter here in Sterling VA 32 months ago by someone called Liz who then disappeared, and hasn't been seen since. I managed to wrestle the begrudging acknowledgment from a social worker that Liz is a real person and does exist, so this makes me believe that some of what she's said is true. And the incidence of inheritance hijacking is on the rise, so her claim that she was "droned" as she puts it by her ex-FBI cousin may be accurate. For example, a company called CHI she had worked for in Silver Spring, Maryland with this Liz (who was her employer and friend) has now folded, and she was once told that it had merged with a government social services department. Intelligence operations often set up "fronts" (fake businesses) but the name CHI seems a clue. Chi energy in Chinese represents a sort of astral energy so it may have been an intelligence front that employs… not just physical technology surveillance but mind control techniques. She mentions the CIA and NSA all the while, as much as fifty times a day, sandwiched between references to "home invasions."

She said a black guy tried to assault her in her last job and she and Liz killed him. Whilst invoking the Castle Law in self-defence would have prohibited any prosecution by his family, it occurred to me that witchcraft is being angled at her with revenge intent and race accusations by a syndicate of this man's interests. This might explain some things. If there was also a home invasion in her former Long Island home and a close family member (her sister) was murdered then it may indicate that she herself is in danger…all the worse because her immediate family have died and Liz looked like she was scared off. And somebody might be trying to cover up something they did to her. The FBI/cop connection is there. I've read that people who worked for the federal government are often targets for research. I looked up her cousin, and he is apparently alive and kicking in New York working for the FBI. Perhaps they did intercept her inheritance (she always claimed it was him) Her father apparently had \$275,000 in mutual pension funds at the time of his demise and she doesn't know what happened to this, and M claims she's got shares in three companies, even vineyards in Italy, and if some of this is true anyone would be upset. There have been huge economic demotion actions against single alternatives and they may be trying to set her up as "unfit to inherit" (when she's clearly becoming that)

When I look back I've been in something so seedy and sicko my whole life long...like some experiment... and yes, I look bad, and my writing is never going to get published, but I wrote it partly as an explanation to some of you because I had cared about you – and partly as an inheritance – since I have nothing. I don't want your help and still don't need it except for what might transpire by means of some sort of positive energy, or goodwill for morale purposes.

Cass

**From: Cass Ryder**
**To: The Family**
**Attachment: Prelude to Homelessness**


Writer tried to go to America to find employment and then got sidetracked by various communication obstacles, but when the objective circumstances of homelessness and inability to resonate with anyone she once knew intensified, cynicism set in. She lost UK residency and therefore access to the "dole" (which exists as a safety net between the person and street level destitution) was incapable of allowing herself to be a burden to anyone, on top of estrangement from family through transatlantic residence. So there was no one to contact, which became a pride thing. Meanwhile at that time (1995) the Nat West underwent a banking scam that caused errors on peoples' accounts. Writer had not been keeping a tab on her Visa transactions and because she hadn't been keeping receipts she couldn't nail them on errors. The writer was destitute and homeless within about a year and meanwhile had not found employment in the U.S. She winds up broke back in Britain a year later, and was in a strange kind of limbo. Having decided she could not readjust in the U.S. and couldn't adjust in the UK either, at least not from the angle of having to go on welfare (something worked on a sense of guilt and shame she should not have had) she leaves for the States again. As a last resort the writer attempted to retrieve cash stored with her belongings that were sent to New Jersey, based on a misunderstanding, but when she turned up at the storage unit her items had been impounded and the cash was missing, which had obviously been stolen during a search. Writer was then cashless (some of her siblings are internationally based and a few of the others always had cash problems themselves due to struggles with investments and properties etc.) One sibling sent her a few hundred dollars and she made the mistake of taking a Greyhound bus south to San Antonio instead of going back to the UK that winter, which was the prelude to a 20 year long phase of unremitting homelessness.

She was unaware that the U.S. had no unemployment insurance or poverty safety net and got wrapped up in the 24 hour a day job of survival. There were communication obstacles from the standpoint of phone call attempts, general delivery letter interceptions etc. Writer recalls trying to make a phone call in San Francisco or LA and losing her address book (she had huge Internet problems and got misinformed a lot by librarians) Even after the British embassy confirmed that she was entitled to UK residency back then, there were documentation and fee issues... how to survive in the 3-6 months application process period. No one offered to help her in a no-strings-attached way during those years, except a social worker in Loudoun county when she was passing through much later (8 years ago) It all seemed too much of a problem. She still expected she could gain employment and get herself back, so kept going. But the day labour pool never employed her for more than a day or so at a time, and temporary contracts were usually not possible because she did not have an address or phone number. And she always found the shelters extremely hostile places. While not able to adjust in the U.S., or regarding the dole in Britain as a desirable option, she did not expect to get waylaid in one region as long as she did. Writer got stuck in a kind of "Hotel California" trap, waylaid in North Virginia and Maryland while admitting she was on a path to nowhere.

The writer also felt she was SET UP to seem like a psycho or as dangerous when she would arrive at labour pools in new cities (having walked or caught buses to other states or regions in search of work) as if materialising from "nowhere" under the critical view of local residents. She was projected as being a societal wrecker. Her younger age then and homeless status were such as to prohibit the ability to get food stamps and so she walked... literally...to secure basic food and cash cravings (soup kitchens are dominated by men, women are discouraged) Staying in one place would have been unsafe. Local food parcel referrals were often limited in allowance or non-accessible if one was not a local resident etc.

Often the writer just took to the wilderness or the trails…she could never have put up with the shelters that long with loads of others. Writer would camp just off a trail in the middle of winter with frozen streams for a water source, flossing with strips of bark, and had to walk miles into a town before she could access water to wash. She often never had money in towns where no charity was being handed out, so it was not as if she could have hit a restaurant afterwards. VERY CRUEL as the goal was not to expend too much energy by walking around.

Writer recollects during her first homeless phase winding up on her land in Kentucky and in the house of her aunt and uncle. People live risky lives so one doesn't just turn up on their doorstep, but while hitchhiking a female driver persuades the writer to call her uncle, and he lets her know that her aunt is going into hospital for heart surgery so it's not a good time to visit. Writer had inherited some land situated opposite his home, and went there for somewhere to crash, but felt that she came over as someone threatening (the homeless come over as people with viruses) Writer recalls standing on the side of the mountain swearing at the top of her lungs, and when Spring arrives she walks away from her land, leaving a note in their mailbox saying that she was in no way trying to disturb or alarm them. People, esp. if slotted in the "outsider" category for a protracted period of time, set up a "wavelength of fear", causing the fulfilment of the expectation that one is worthy of the label dangerous and threatening. The night before the writer left she experienced a huge electrical jolt, which felt like a neurological control tool, shepherding or prodding as one would a wandering sheep or cow, done to ensure she would not stray from her path. To the writer it seemed like an ether weaponry action, the key leak being the REM processes as the "gateway" through which an attack is capable. For example the usage of the enforced "bioelectrical" can manipulate the muscles and produce a chemical emission during the REM processes. After waking up the conscious will takes over and the sequence is interrupted. Dream suppressants have been developed which might block it and the statistics show a massive upswing in sleeping tablets ... though these tablets do come with side effects.

When the writer was in India before she became homeless she had an involuntary OBE after wrestling with a stomach bug somewhere near the foot of the Himalayas, at a site that is recognised as a centre of religious learning, the place where Buddha was reputedly born. Oriental philosophy teaches that the lower spinal lumbar region is representative of a kind of seat of the soul in terms of a powerful centre of emotion. The writer goes on to experience numerous paranormal assaults, one involving the line up of the planets in May 2000, at the exact same time her older brother in Mexico succumbs to a brain haemorrhage. The brother seems somehow "incriminated" for the younger sister wandering around homeless in the U.S. This is more or less proof that siblings are also the targets of physical covert interference, probably by the traditionalist crowd who seem TO WALK VERY MUCH WITH THE COVERT PLANNERS. I know my database material is surveilled. Talking about covert programmes the CIA once conducted somewhat seedy research to do with LSD in the seventies, and my older brother might have been a victim in that he had to get pulled out of university in England and goes to the U.S. for a while to get away from the "vector."

Another time while camping out in the open, the writer once woke up with deer mite bites all over her body, and KNOWS that a Cessna was flying overhead and dropped them into the tall grass embankment where she was crashed. Writer is given a forced bioelectrical whilst asleep, wakes up and leaves the woodlot, furious. Immediately a truck stops and the driver asks if she wants a box of oat cereal. Later that day in Wal-Mart lurking in the toilet tissue aisle (not the cereal aisle where you would expect it to be) is a box of oat cereal – like a seedy association linking the event with the word, interpreted as a threat or a double reminder. I befriended a cute stray dog in the Appalachians, which was sideswiped by a car right in front of me. I start crying and hold it while it was dying, then some evil jerk in a pickup truck stops and picks it up with two broken hind legs and throws it roughly onto the truck floor, claiming it was his and "it has some life left in it yet" and zooms off. I'm sure that had something to do with me wanting me to get in touch with my uncle, but because I felt it was being used to attack my uncle and aunt I didn't fall for it. They attack someone based on their sympathy or relationship with someone they care about. Basically it's like keeping a dog on a leash, a mental and emotional surveillance in step with embodied surveillance and interception (reading emails)

I am a by-product of the system in not having been able to work for years and I probably don't deserve to live, but it's a partial explanation as to why I'm homeless. At some level the U.S. authorities would say they can manage civilians, but they couldn't "manage" me because I was a weaponry in the hands of something else, and was set up to stay homeless in America to draw out in an exaggerated way the corruption in the system. Like my siblings I was born with British citizenship with an indefinite residency stamp in my U.S. passport that had to be renewed every two years. But this would work like a mental padlock, and then the process of getting clarification on the legality of my status after passing the stamp expiration date became harder due to communication obstacles, despite the Internet. So for 10 years I was led to believe I didn't have a residency entitlement but I did apparently, and mounting cynicism conspired to convince me there was no point. And thank you Uncle Sam for food stamps, petty as it sounds, and thank you U.S. civilians for the cash handouts and thank you Britain for the acknowledgment that I could have gone there and tapped into their benefits, but if you don't mind I'm going to bow out soon…unless I can see that I can pay my way and right now I can't.

Writer learned the hard way it's harder to get back up when you're down, nothing comes free, and when you have so little it's almost better to do without. Then the writer happened to bump into this woman, the subject called Monica, who seemed to confirm for her some of her worst fears, that there was no point in wandering around in the wilderness. So out of an initial concern for the subject, whom she met over 2 years ago in a shelter, and seeing the imprint of something similar occurring to her she decided to put it down on paper. The subject would be talking to herself, often while the writer was on the word processor in the library, and would pull up a chair to sit beside her. Writer now knows an awful lot about her, and acted like an impromptu therapist, occasionally a "process receiver" or walking memory bank, which seems to have been the reason for the information volunteered by the subject, who then expressed a desire that the writer stay with her. This woman is not like most of the women I've brushed up against but is probably part of a rising tidal wave of women in America who are educated yet encountering job and housing discrimination, unemployment, and criminality attacks. In 18 years of homelessness I hadn't met anyone and she's the first person I have communicated with after nine or so thousand miles of walking with a total of only five months of shelter help. Needless to say I didn't want to talk to anyone, but I've met a lot of people as brief communication channels. And considering her nervous breakdown and whatever else it might be I don't communicate with her much. She mainly communicates sort of "at me" in terms of talking back to herself. And in between writing a book, she dropped bits of her life story on me and now I've got a picture of this person. That brought it home to me what I had initially experienced ...the vulnerability, outrage, paranoia etc. all these feelings that had gradually abated through becoming inured to the state of solitary outdoor confinement and nomadism.

And I had planned on leaving the region for once and all, knowing damn well that I look strange to say the least, but then the subject was unable to go anywhere. Between that and the decision to mutually support one another for morale purposes and the liberal library services here, I stayed and am still here. I got involved with the cold weather shelter this winter which I stayed at for half of the four month open period, and was glad to acknowledge that Monica checked in almost every night for much needed warmth, security, and cleanliness. Though one is faced with a poster near the door "This is a privilege not a right" with the portraits of 2 evangelists who founded the VOA (Volunteers of America) which greatly contributed to breakouts of fear and tension, because of the constant threat of forfeiture of this "privilege". And most homeless are not equipped to be outside with a tent and sleeping bag, too heavy to carry around all day and if you leave it somewhere it gets stolen. Some states do legally incorporate the right of the homeless to cold weather shelters but Virginia doesn't. It's all pretty harsh where everyone else is in warm climate-controlled environments except for quick dashes to their car and back... harsh in this particular county with a 9pm check-in time. Overcrowding is routine in some places, and because there are more men than women the men were "sardine-can" slotted in...the county we left in December had people sleeping on the floor. This was all new to me because I've always made myself weather-fortified and slept out, and for the last three years I had been trekking to the southern regions of south and north Carolina for winter. But in reality I never had the cash resources to acquire a proper tent or backpack, or weatherproof clothing, and I've gotten caught out in lots of storms, and my lot has not been easy. I trained myself mentally not to want the cold weather shelter and while it was more comfortable even with just a floor to sleep on, as soon as the psychology issues would break out I knew I wanted to be out in the open.

I don't think I've ever met any homeless women who are doing what I tried to do or who were nomadic, but the options are really non-options as I feel women are especially vulnerable. But in the understanding of strength in numbers, two or more women can take turns sleeping, using folding chairs, tarps, string, duct tape and umbrellas etc. and it is possible to sleep out on benches in township plazas fairly safely, if also weapon-armed, watch-towered and with access to a cellphone and a nearby 24 hour facility. As a 51-year-old woman in that unique state of mental aggravation maybe what

I'm saying only matters to a few. The majority can write it off as the life of a reject, amongst others I've witnessed who are also high level mental rejects in the sense of literally being "trout pond stocked and fished" based on some kind of psychic warfare that I'm sure is going on (others are examples of souls that need revenge based on some inherited trauma they have to relive) In other words I'm not that mad, I don't transfer them that much authority by allowing myself to get upset...but we're straying. I met Monica and suddenly became reawakened again and very angry. As for all those months in libraries while homeless and day labouring, and chasing after elusive research material to consolidate some theory, while this isn't the whole story it has been much of it. It was not my intention to go back and sign on to the dole and I really didn't want anything to do with the government, so I just kept walking. I walked 9000 miles across 20 states over a period of time, and managed to survive on a shoestring.

Let's go back to where I am… destitute. So much happened to me that showed some sort of high level surveillance but was not communicable, for instance by preventing me from allying with family and never having money. Things just got worse and they got very 8888888 nasty and in all honesty I've not been doing anything too much for eighteen years, but have been on the run. Earlier I was hungry from day to day…no-one can understand what it feels like unless they go through it. I had a brief spell in Knoxville jail (I had no choice but grocery store theft because I was destitute and starving) I'm not going into detail but I ended up in jail. The only options this government and most worldwide governments are trying to promote are revolting and sexist to the core in terms of loss of self-determination, autonomy and independence (overcrowding, criminality, bad health, prostitution syndicates) and should be thrown back in their faces. I noted Monica was not the "take a boyfriend" type and this sort of endeared her to me, bigoted as it sounds in terms of belittling couples and married types. And no disrespect to women and what they feel they have to do to survive. This woman has had a nervous breakdown and needs emotional stability and physical health and to be left alone. Seems very much a survivor (three master degrees, a history of work and study of the martial arts) But for someone who has worked hard and with as much education as her, I've told her if you're going to try and kill yourself do it properly and be in control…far better to just die than suffer the mental ignominies and physical protracted ailments of destitution.

The writer only got in touch with her family because she wanted to help the subject, who once worked around really disturbed types in correctional facilities, and sometimes it seems the anger and disturbed energies of former clients have affected her. The subject is vainly trying to understand the horror of her situation, operating from a much more insecure standpoint than any woman I know, and I don't know many. And frankly the other homeless men don't go through anything compared to her or the things they've attempted on me. The writer went through a similar exposure, was very much victimized after the demise of her mother, then her father, as though something had censored her from birth as being "useless" without her parents. The writer grew up being gripped with the fear of Armageddon or a third world war breaking out, recalls taking pilgrimages to peace conferences, and being seized with dread and anxiety attacks. She was increasingly manoeuvred into a state of isolation. Something "liberal" lets her down because the wider external societal support systems were lacking, as it is for many after leaving college (job promises which never materialised etc.) while at the same time something "neo-conservative" and dictatorial seems to punish her for her wayward self. Writer feels "zeroed in on" as a pawn and gets death-threatened every night. Maybe they're going to kill me, why don't they hurry up. Sitting on the bench at night the subject often said "Someone can come along and blow me away" but it might not be that simple …a person could end up in a wheelchair, and I'm concerned that one night we're just not going to wake up or wake up in a hospital. Anyway we just take each day as it comes right now. Every day is either an arrest scenario, with the threat of an involuntary enforced commitment, or of us separating as acquaintances and her getting into a truck with a stranger (God knows to what conclusion)

I realise you can't change the world and that's not why I'm writing. I wrote this book to clarify things in my mind and because some of you had tried to communicate, and get me out of homelessness. Maybe it can be an answer to some people in my family, to help explain why I in part did choose to stay here rather than to return to England. It's a huge advancement over earlier years to just get my writing in print, let alone in cyberspace or wired out. But there's no guarantee from one day to the next my emails will be received in what is a messed-up communication thing going on. It gets to be so tiring. So far I haven't received a response back from Alex and when I tried contacting her school it didn't go through. Apparently she's got info tech obstacles to do with my transmissions, so I think I'm under surveillance and I'm probably on an assassination list somewhere. The only way to publicise these facts without any kind of academic credentials or authority, would be to produce an intellectual memoire, referencing material researched while homeless. You don't have to read what I sent, I just wanted to send evidence somewhere as I have no physical storage capability, and don't trust the library or email. I've got loads of draft material stored in a durable weather-resistant box hidden off a routeway. So far I haven't had time to finish it.

I tried to make use of my time while I was homeless. The horror of the situation that I found myself in required some positive energy to counterbalance it, as I instinctively began to understand that the environments I could have fallen into could have made the difference between psychic disintegration or not. To survive as an independent entity I just had to keep walking. M is in that situation right now and seems quite healthy (she only got influenza once and healed herself with a garlic-infused vapourizer made with cups of hot water in restaurants) but the enlarged fibroids in her cervix are prohibiting her capability to walk as freely as I had done. Not being willing to crash in a tent meant the sleep options for her have been a lot less safe. When I became destitute I was preoccupied with where to eat, drink, use the toilet, sleep, etc. I was totally paranoid and super-aware of the capabilities of an occult force (to say nothing of subliminal interference, both etheric and technological) and long ago realized I just wanted to be on my own. She's only 5 ft 1, and would wearily hang onto my backpack strap the way a child does to toddler reins. People confuse us as a couple. I'm not gay and I don't want to discredit them, but I resonate with cpink (gay) types and I get the feeling that alternative or non-married singles are the targets of some kind of psychic harassment alongside embodied attacks (possibly based on some sort of "black list") They're spooked out by us. M told the mental health care worker who visited the library the other day to "Get the hell out of here" and he did. He's not very nice and related to us in a patronising scornful manner as though our lives are worth nothing more than rats. The female welfare officers are some of the most disgusting dog prostitutes that ever lived (not all of them) and have been real foul bitches towards her.

The writer's stuff has been lost over and over again, as she has pulled up evidence from books and news articles that show that man has mind control, and just goes to show how invasive this type of action is. There is a covert NSA program called "Prism" with the permission to survey public library databases, courtesy of the Homeland Security Act. It's petty neighbourhood watchdog surveillance, specifically targeted at the homeless poor who spend large amounts of time in libraries to kill monotony and escape weather conditions. Email lifts, phone jams, database insertions, voicemail insertions…these are fairly common occurrences as far as I can see amongst alternative types and had been happening to me routinely on and off, esp. after the felon issuance several years ago. When in 2006 I threw a "golfball-sized" rock at a car, cracking a woman's windshield, and reported the incident to the police I got 3 months jail time, a felon 6 and a charge (I may also have gotten a 10 year suspension of driving in VA that I was only made later aware of) So the writer has a felon 6, but electronically it's coming up as felon 4 which is worse as a crime category, and the charge looks far more serious than the initial event had been. The defendant tried to get the writer to admit "insanity" (which she didn't) and gave inaccurate evidence, with an association of a "missile" or "shooting incident" when all the writer had done was throw a small stone at a car. The whole thing was set up, to say nothing of the jail experience, in the full understanding of how that was going to affect the writer. When the writer was in jail she thought she was initially going to get sentenced to 5 years. Her hand shook all night …she fasted for 11 days and the trial kept being delayed while one inmate stated it was not that serious at all and she'd be out in a few months. A woman called Jones cried each Wed on the phone with her mum: one night her mother reports that the electricity system in the house just got "knocked out" when no-one else's on the same road did. In retrospect the writer is certain she was being picked on through some covert angle. They tore the jail down as soon as the writer and the other girls came out of it. They've apparently erected a replacement correction facility with white and black chequers for its floor design, which gives you an inkling as to the kind of wars going on around here. This design is synonymous to the floors in Masonic clubs (the old jail had been situated on the corner of a "Church Road")

I'm an example of someone who is being character-assassinated through time even as I write. I'm certain this is going on, that psychics have a way of dowsing ... sounding out types of people even before they're born, vain as it sounds, though this could not be admitted any more than a homeowner's preoccupation with swatting a housefly can be admitted. Whether it was because I was handed a felon, or because of this specific region that I'm in (the doorstep of the CIA and Pentagon) where a kind of special skills exhibiting is going on, I really couldn't say. This is their BACK YARD, an invisible security base. It is my understanding that inmates and the homeless generally get some kind of "interference" but the kind of interference I've been getting is so monotonous, so foul, so seedy, and so non-remitting and loud. Here's an example, just last night while on the bench dozing off I wake up coughing and feeling grabbed in the throat, and no this was not a natural cough. If I could have believed it was, then it wouldn't have mattered. During research in her early homeless years, the writer came to the conclusion that there is an aspect in Western intelligence that links up with occult lodges and indirectly with the itinerant guerrilla actions of shaman type characters. And that all this forms a suppressed science - like a formula that has been passed on generationally - which governs the understanding of natural laws and how these work. And apparently it works across physical space. Their targets are the vulnerable, the prescribed gateway being REM processes during sleep. The physical dimensions are mirrored by something non-physical, complete with their "etheric neighbourhood watchdog".

Innovations that allow body parts to be remotely manipulated evolved from close up lab experimentation to current day remote operations, just as electromagnetic wave jamming is used in military technology. Few people know that machines can remotely offset a dysfunctioning, if targeted at body part areas. For instance, a man who lives near to an army base claimed that one day nobody in the neighbourhood could do any work, and their muscles wouldn't work for about 30 seconds. Cops in France apparently plan to use a "bowel opener" for crowd control in demonstrations (pretty sick and unnecessary) They have remote technology capable of arresting the heart's functioning. When those victims speak out about their exposures, they are labelled as incoherent or undeserving of attention or paranoid psychotics who are "doing it to themselves." A homeless woman I once met claimed her family hijacked her inheritance, had her sterilised and then dropped her back out onto the pavement. A black homeless guy recently died in a nearby woodlot. The cops had unfairly impounded his stuff, and the relatives can't afford to fly to his funeral. Hobos in Baltimore got trashed with the city refuse - the writer knows because she worked a nightshift in an incinerator warehouse. The homeless need an open apology, and not to be continually associated with the mentally disabled, parasites and criminals …if anything they have carried the cross and borne the burden of the sins of the over-consumers. They need vindication and the system needs to stop labelling any services they receive as "favours". The point here is that the mainstream family crowd BLOT OUT the poor, the homeless, and welfare recipients…no questions asked. The married women go back to "hubbie dearest" then go out and gratify themselves with material consumption (their vaginas resemble wallets) These females don't get that far in the long run because they can't change the fundamental systems, and it seems to cost their psyches a lot. For instance, they're obsessed with being morally righteous and clean, complete with control freak reflexes. They do a lot of cleaning, as though washing out the association of filth in terms of an alliance they'd rather not have. The wallet equals the lower female anatomy as a compensatory exchange or payoff for a compromised alliance.

Ordinary people probably won't want to read this. Great, writer wasn't trying to change the world and couldn't have if she tried, but the subject matter might have been of interest in terms of what's going on here, and what's going on is a massive attack on certain people in terms of their lifestyle. But then it occurred to the writer that it's going to be affecting everyone soon…meaning the kind of exposures she had to put up with. And what does or doesn't happen to homeless people is a minor issue. Her gripe really was with the internal psychic attacks, even less language for that. The jail experience was in fact enlightening. And the felon was worth it. They're a bunch of jerks. As for the homeless she's only ever walked away from them, because most women in this category were people she was incapable of having anything in common with. And couples just made her ill. Very few couples represent any kind of higher wavelength awareness (grace, choice, promise, mobility, freedom etc.) as is projected in the media or the movies. To continually carry the cross of other peoples' ignorance, their low-level habits and aspirations, is revolting. And maybe people in the Western world who have that overt philosophy need to protect themselves and their interests a lot more.

But the point is something is victimizing people. Writer exposed the ultimate in an attempt at mind surveillance. You and I are right now being surveilled just in referencing these materials. They're picking it up through a spirit communication as well as a physical communication and then kind of throwing it back at that person...so we have a community of silent drama viewers and judges, little monarchs in quest of the consolidation of their little kingdoms. These psychic occurrences are actually politically motivated and part of a coordinated effort with a sinister view to mind control. I am now absolutely certain that a lot of mental illnesses are mainly occult assaults and that this suppressed science is used by world governments as a front to cover up attacks on civilians. Neuroscience research has provided the insight that women have greater potential, bioelectrically speaking, and women are especially targeted (they get treated cheaply and they undervalue themselves then they service up their bodies... it's all a little desperate) The Vulnerables are increasing in number with urban sprawling and migration from small town America. I've noticed all the most beautiful places are either beset with unemployment or extremely expensive and conservative politically. The cowardly backhanded integration of different types who don't get along into less nice (ugly) environments, where they're slotting alternative types and inter-mixed races (in the context of overcrowding) is just one of an increasing list of covert actions that usually wind up affecting the Vulnerables. These people are vulnerable to a wider COITUS INTERRUPTUS AND INFLATED WOMB THAT NEVER EVER STOPS God help them. I'd advise women to boycott relations with men if they can't control procreation, which they can't, even with contraceptives which fail. And if men can't figure out their ejaculation processes, that's their problem. Women could do a lot more for themselves by shutting their legs, and the human race are going to fuck off this planet, it was designed to go extinct. All they do is stuff themselves with animal products, and compete for cars and homes. Who cares, who wants society's concept of success? I don't follow the celebrities and I don't think I'm inferior because I don't have anything.

But on the other hand I DONT BLAME PEOPLE FOR NOT LIKING ME. I'm a horrible person, it's not going to change. I don't need people to like me, and I'm not offended. Writer is not gay nor is she a het, has almost always been single and wants to remain that way. All relationships do eventually is fuel insecurity, and the prostitutes I've brushed up against in incarceration units all seemed definitely mentally ill. Women have NO FREEDOM. It's getting worse. No-one moves between the social classes. Writer grew up in the middleclass. The middleclass are nobility compared to the homeless or shelter categories. That's about as remote as someone could be from themselves in a past life. The people with money do not talk because they feel threatened they might lose their status or their money. There isn't any place on earth where childless singles can get away from the "ordinaries", and it's important for someone who is different to be in a separate community or physical proximity from those around them. I've had to change in public, go to the loo in the soil a lot when on the road. I'm always doing something wrong. I have no choice, but I was being watched. Ordinary people who slam you in the face and state "you have no right to grimace at me and complain" They're a bunch of mice who try and make themselves look big by comparing themselves against people smaller than themselves.

There is mounting evidence that there is a covert program by which to destabilise and criminalize alternative categories, with plans to extend that to 70% of the population. Things are either going to get worse or better. They can't stay the same. But as with the recent long term "getting the homeless indoors" plan and the eligibility for cash and housing etc. most people don't know about it and many who do don't trust it. For instance it is disability-strapped, when eligibility should just be based on unemployment and homelessness, not mental impairment, and it involves the kind of questions one would address to a kindergarten student. It is notable that abstinence is never promoted, nor being single, and that women are being encouraged to get married even if they're gay, preferably a church marriage... all pretty suspect in a society where no one can just be an individual. No efforts have been made to separate different types into separate bioregions, not just on racial grounds but lifestyle choices – childless versus families, or singles versus married. They've got civil liberty problems, energy and consumerism problems, and the usual employment and immigration problems, and over-procreation … which does need to be tackled radically and could be tackled without compromising human rights. But it hasn't been tackled, because the very concept is not something people can conceive, that's how brainwashed they are and have been for centuries. The kindest thing to do now would be to help people not to have children, assist them in quality of life not quantity of years, to encourage the capability to live with far less, to have different methods of transportation with substitutes for oil in planes, to allow solitary living, but in natural not sterile environments where they interface with living things (the prospects being endless esp. in the outback)

To go back to the aforementioned subject Monica, there are no plans like this right now. One could envisage that the authorities might take a violent approach (like simply jailing her to make sure she doesn't undergo another assault on the streets) But this is the tragedy because too many homeless are unjustly incarcerated, criminalized when they are not criminals. They proactively encourage rising crime rates, and have built loads of jails that stand unoccupied under a classified venture termed "Mad Rex" with one the size of a town in Alaska that the public don't know about. See Printout:

*"We are dangerously close to a situation where, if large numbers of American people took to the streets, a mechanism for martial law could be quickly implemented and carried out under REX 84 (short for Readiness Exercise 84) The Cheney/Bush administration*

*has a plan which would accommodate the detention of large numbers of American citizens during times of emergency. Through Rex-84 an undisclosed number of concentration camps were set in operation throughout the U.S.A. for the internment of dissidents and others harmful to the State (its existence was first revealed during the Iran-Contra hearings in 1987... "*

Quite a few normal non-criminal people have felons now and lots of them are just drink and drive related and almost all are alliance-related crimes in a culture where the crime wouldn't have taken place if they had not been coerced into alliances... most people would rather just live on their own and view the scenery. The jails are full of poor people who were completely set up to be poor, and the judiciaries then moralize non-stop over their criminality. Tolstoy said "A nation can be judged by the way it treats its inmates" A nation can be judged by having no inmates, it could be added.

As a transatlantic citizen I have been unable to understand how Americans in extreme poverty are punished while the Brits are handed privileges. Britain is so much more humanitarian towards its citizens on both unemployment insurance and with less workplace sexism. Americans are expected to get an alliance or marriage and at least one child before they can either get a job or benefits. The pressure is huge. Brits are made excessively comfortable so to speak, while Americans are made excessively ill at ease. In the U.S. welfare recipients are labelled parasitical and worthy of attack ...this is how they are perceived by most, and whether the reasons are fallacious or not doesn't matter (if people believe something is bad it becomes bad) The objection made by some is that if the system in America were more liberal it would be handing money to criminals who take enough advantage as it is, and that more abuses might occur if they had a welfare system in place like England's. Whether social welfare is the answer or not, some sort of answer is needed in the face of rising crime stats and the huge connection between drugs, alcohol and violent crime. An estimated 50% of homeless people never get employed, most of whom keep going from bad to worse. A senator long ago suggested "work programs and subsidised housing" as a way to get out of homelessness. They both vetoed it, democrats and republicans. Meanwhile they went on to fund a multi billion dollar homeless and failed mental health industry (via jail and hospital costs) They're disgusting hypocrites, and end up embracing what's ugly.

A brief history of mental illness yields the fact that the governments of the Western world first took an institutional approach and then a cognitive behavioural approach, then released them into the communities. Instead of doing what other developed nations were doing, such as re-routing the unemployed/homeless either into a benefits system or into employment, homelessness got much worse right after the seventies as Lyndon B. Johnson's "great experiment" died completely. Why did they unleash a lot of these people into communities where they don't belong? A possible reason being that interactions in a community and with normal people affords them a richer variety and number of contexts by which to refine their skills in terms of thought surveillance and attempts at mood control. I wonder whether that was the purpose of the homeless, the blacklisted, and an increasing number of jail inmates - extreme as it sounds - mind control on subjects who can't defend themselves, fine-tuning tactics to be used against the general populace. Mental institutions were unloaded since communities provided richer insights into behaviour, and psychic spies helped hone the blade of thought control, all this being a backdrop to covert classified research. Human crime and trauma is a productive industry, cultivated for vested interest purposes….their unconscious energies are being yoked up for entertainment like gladiators in some barbaric prehistory.

Leaving people dangling in the community without food or cash and no communication channels in some of the worst weather conditions existent worldwide seems to have been an experiment based on control weaponries, and race warring. In other words the opportunity to watch these people (using both technology and bioelectrical body channels) had obviously seemed more productive in terms of a greater variation of output and emotional response. They are psychic pawn material on an allegorical board game, whose lives are lived for no other purpose but to fulfil the requirements of the players' egos and concerns. Extremely high-level nastiness esp. on women who were expected to sustain subliminal fear of assaults without complaining. For example, what is the obsession with communal cells over single cells? In jail they purposely set up women who have character conflicts to share close spaces. Like whipping a starved beast of burden, already wired and strained through trauma exposures, to do what it can't do. Now they even have a sub-discipline of Neurotheology called "neuroamour" demonstrating how so-called "love" works …the point being that these young ladies had been targets, probably in designed cpink (gay) orientations. It's the writer's observation that certain types in vulnerable categories act like lightning rods that conduct electricity from the air, and were used to conduct dormant tension to the surface and create conflict.

These occult weapons are being used against women increasingly, and manifest as symptoms of mental illness. Behind every burgeoning psychosis is a channelling of invisible energies and forces. Society has promoted a 17th century belief which categorises childless women as witches, where men at all levels, affluent or poor, were given the green light to use women. If they don't like someone they can get at them in 50 different ways. The other day something kept grabbing my throat, as a bus was going by the county police station - like a choking. It used to happen to me in the cold weather shelter, which is right beside a lot of uniformed type facilities like an adult detention centre etc. I'd wake up with something in my throat and I knew something was causing it. But many ordinary people were also happy to kick someone like me around. The government spearheaded and set up a scenario in what seems to be a "grab your females" reflex, which is a very questionable reflex. Uncle Sam's got the world's biggest military,

Hollywood and the media, and his friends in Western Europe, with orgies on growbagism and the industrial vagina industry thrown in, so what have you got? An ego as a force to be reckoned with, and very much alive and kicking with a global support base.

IF the world is dominated by occult syndicates, which have a pattern of working for the Holy Triad (landowning, military, and clerical classes where $1^{st}$ son inherits the estate, $2^{nd}$ son becomes a general, and $3^{rd}$ becomes a priest) then I'd like to nail this syndicate who uses the Vulnerables to practise occult weaponry (or is it just modern technology?) It's logical that an ex-felon, homeless person or an animal might be experimentation material, like a deer that wanders into a hunter's camp…a power elite's "new world order" camp. But it's very serious when they can manipulate the muscles. These homeless targets are living bait, since no-one knows from one minute to the next where they are, where they spent the night, or where they're going, and man has the capability to dart them like animals on the plain, so that when they wake up they might not have any memory. Homelessness is most peoples' worst nightmare as it entails insanity, loss of dignity, illness, criminality, compromised living space etc. but it's also presenting the double-edged purpose of being yoked up to mind surveillance designed to be used against the people in the near future. The inability to even communicate reasonably on the subject is so persistent and entrenched, in the full knowledge that these people are being psychically assaulted, which is written off as mental illness and any number of other negative character defects, giving the bigots a chance to cry "devil" in a system that demonises welfare recipients. They've invented mental illness as a front to disguise occult attacks and not just mental illness but the inducement of physical illnesses, possibly as a form of crowd control ever since non-lethal implants and remote organ impacting capability became possible. And this covert agenda has been aggregating since the interception and transference of emotions was discovered in the last few decades. But it's cheap and callous, the way bigots expect soldiers to die in stupid wars and to not ask questions.

The world is about war and mainly negative exposures. Everyone is born into a potential torture chamber. There is no democracy. Democracies don't work. There is a radical covert plan and people are the losers in a losers' system. In a sense I did do this to myself, and no-one's really done me a bad turn other than that I live in a very risky society - environmentally and politically risky – and increasingly risky to all in the future in terms of a LUNATIC PROCREATION LIFESTYLE, but I've been cornered my whole life long. I've witnessed quite a few women who are intelligent and educated but who live low level lives for no reason, so don't tell the writer it's not an endless harassment and indirect crucifixion attempt. The writer may have been a surveillance target or an example of what happens to people who ask wrong questions. The writer is operating as a proactive single, and though intellectually starved most of the time didn't need that much communication. She now views the single status as a rare resource, sought after like an inner wealth. A lot of single women and the married kind do NOT see eye to eye. In fact the energies of the married procreator types are being used to justify economic demotions and other attacks on the singles and alternatives. Also I'm at war with most civilians, forget the elite, and believe me I do not want what you people have got. The mainstream crowd are a bunch of boyfriend/girlfriend repeaters. They don't go anywhere and their children are facing problems they are not prepared for. They're obsessed with sex and forced alliances and their paradigms make no sense in terms of few people having job satisfaction, time to attend to education, health or travel... and a small minority were able to see that and to communicate about it.

I'm getting tired of their communities but I don't have to live in them, and you can keep your welfare. To be wealthy is not an advantage. The writer's sick of sharing her life with a bunch of barnyard animals, psychologically speaking, and she can't, any more than a person can get shade under a poisoned oak. They messed up and created HUGE PROBLEMS like an elephant skating on ice, and no amount of current policy is helping that elephant remain on those skates (so it doesn't crash through) when ice remains ice. Then Mad REX 84 will come into reality for the purpose it was intended. Writer can't afford to be that concerned. Who cares about the poor, they shouldn't even exist anyway. The world should be looking beyond the poor, just as bible readers parrot "the humble will inherit the earth" But WHO WANTS what they have and what they are inheriting? They've got a horrible way of life. Oh I can't speak, I can only speak for myself and I agree lots of people have serene lives or whatever and that's fine, but I'd take my resonance with negativity any day. And utopia is for the young who have to absorb the risks. As for quality of life in older age, it's all relative and what is one man's medicine is another's poison. Maybe it doesn't matter. The war's been fought. As for a third world war they will all be clones by then.

**From: Leigh Ryder**
**To: Cass Ryder**

Dear Cass,

Don't fall for that cop line that you're not allowed to sleep on park
benches, and that you're supposed to camp on the verges by
highways. This would make you even more vulnerable to attack
than you already are, and it sounds as though they're just throwing
their weight around as usual. Three cop cars with armed men
surrounding 2 homeless women. My, what big brave macho men,
they must be so proud of themselves. Assholes. However, I'm
afraid you're probably right in that they are just looking for an
excuse to arrest you, so you need to get back into the overnight
shelters. With October approaching it will be very cold again soon.
I understand Monica has to be near a 24-hour public facility, but
having to stay awake all night to "guard" her from attack with a can
of mace not only deprives you of sleep, it is just not going to work
if you're outnumbered.

I've now had an opportunity to read through your "Memoire"
together with the issues surrounding this other homeless woman
you've teamed up with. Monica's story of a hijacked inheritance
and of an ex-FBI cousin caused Michael who inveigled her out of it
by means of hypnosis sounds extremely far-fetched. You suggest
that some corrupt relative took advantage of her mental state to
steal her inheritance, and then her sister was "murdered" in a fatal
car crash, adding to her considerable woes. Whatever the truth of
the matter, it's a sad tale and I can understand why you feel you
can't just abandon her. As to whether the homeless are being
targeted by an "etheric watchdog force" if I cast doubt on this
theory as being overly paranoid this will send you into a rage.
Besides, who am I to know what's really going on? Truth is
sometimes stranger than fiction, and the world is a scary place
peopled by some twisted souls.

Historically there have always been secret societies who have managed to persuade themselves and others that they have advanced occult skills, but most of it is just wishful thinking and doesn't mean they actually have any. Your theory that a lot of so-called "mental illness" is a direct result of psychic attack is interesting, but it begs the question: who would want to attack either you or M? What threat do either of you pose as homeless women? To expend so much energy seems misdirected, though I suppose your argument is that the homeless are easy prey for mind control experiments. You speak of "mental padlocks", and I couldn't agree more: the mind creates its own prison, and the world is coloured by our perceptions. I'm glad you have the sense to steer clear of drugs. I read the other day that in Communist North Korea up to 60% of the population are addicted to crystal meth. As a means of controlling the populace and keeping them in a zombified state of stupefaction – and therefore intellectually incapable of challenging the military dictatorship - this is a horrible example of deliberate weaponry by the government against its own people.

Undoubtedly people are "spooked" by the two of you: your homeless plight is not readily comprehensible to most people, and blockbuster films like "Paranormal Activity" don't help as they tend to demonise the whole area of the occult, and play on people's unconscious fears rather than furthering their understanding and compassion. In society as a whole there is an underlying fear of insanity: it is becoming increasingly common for people to go into a downward spiral after losing their jobs or getting their houses repossessed, and the reason people back away from you is because they fear that what is happening to you could easily happen to them. You must have tremendous resilience to have survived on the streets for over 18 years, but there is a fine line between self-discipline and self-punishment. You must know that your physical stamina cannot last forever, hence the reason I keep urging you to seriously consider leaving the States. The only way I can help you in any concrete way is if you would agree to accept help to return to this country. To be frank, you are not in a position to "guide her onto a better path" until you have first put yourself on the right path. People can and do get over schizophrenia, but it usually involves the support of family members.

Back to what is troubling you. M claims her sister had "run-ins" with a well-known New York Mafia syndicate, and implies that her fatal car crash was in fact a murder. I don't know how much credence to give to this but you must realise that crimes of this nature (if we give M the benefit of the doubt and don't simply dismiss it as the delusions of someone with a mental health disorder) are generally concealed from the public gaze, and are usually impossible to prove or disprove after the event. If her sister did die in a car crash this would be recorded somewhere in a newspaper archive, and to conduct an Internet search one would require the full name and age of the deceased, the precise date and location of the event. And even if I were able to corroborate that it did actually occur, in all likelihood only the bare facts would be publicly recorded. If it was suspected by a coroner that there was anything sinister about the accident, such as the brakes being tampered with, then the perpetrators would presumably be in jail. The same applies to this "missing inheritance". Those capable of perpetrating such crimes are equally capable of covering their tracks, so I don't see how someone could fully investigate this (as I think you are asking me to do?) without the right contacts and, needless to say, lots of money and time. Even if all this stuff were true, it would take megabucks and resources I don't possess to prove or disprove this. Tragedies occur and there is not always a reason or sinister motive behind them. What I do not believe is that either you or Monica is the subject of a "CIA experiment", though I am prepared to concede that the Mafia has infiltrated both the FBI and the CIA. They'd be pretty stupid if they hadn't made attempts to do so, since both organisations constitute a logical arena for their operations.

On a different note, you said I could send your document on to Maddy, but my honest opinion is that she would not be able to understand most of it, and would probably be happier with a much shorter and more personalised email from you.

Love,

Leigh

**From: Cass Ryder**
**To: Leigh Ryder**

THEY GUNNED DOWN THAT PHILLIPINES WOMAN. THEY
IN NO WAY SHOULD HAVE GOTTEN OFF THE HOOK ON
THAT ONE …they are in total harmony with the dictators of the
third world or perverted bureaucrats of Russia. They train cops and
military worldwide and are following a fascist code already there in
places like Russia, south Africa, and south America. They're evil
and Western Europe needs to watch it. England needs to pay note.
But they need to be confronted for what they are with their stinking
flies down… maybe if they could stop pirouetting in front of
mirrors and sticking their green cocks into cXXt. Loads of
examples show just how drugged these little sausages are, okay
mainly the uniformed types… but female civilians who DO NOT
want a boyfriend should not have to keep putting up with them.
He's an asshole who bullies women, he can only see through the
paradigm of selling sex, he's gross as shit.

The subject is becoming more and more traumatized …like when
her daypack went missing and at precisely that second a mysterious
blank faced man materializes on the bench close to us. She hollered
and cried non-stop, then the next day she calmly tells me that she
had given all her IDs to "Hank" for safe keeping days before. But
normally she kept these and her cash in her daypack and had
always ignored my advice to get a money belt or take her daypack
everywhere with her, including the toilet. She also said that Liz had
contacted her after two years and ensured her she was doing okay,
had married and was living in Arkansas (but M apparently got rid
of the email address) And then yesterday she tells me her cousin
Peter had called her and invited her to a reunion in August but the
voice message was on the cellphone that got stolen in the daypack.
Later that afternoon she denied that he had contacted her...but
anyway the proof is now gone. I just don't what I'm dealing with,
whether she did know all these people she talks about. I have no

idea what this all means, but she seems to have been slowly cornered into a state of street level destitution and mounting insecurity. Something is basically bragging they can kidnap her and force her into the white slave trade. Well what else is she supposed to think if her daypack goes missing after a five minutes visit to the MacDonald's restroom in the middle of the night (she's even accused me, of course she would, she's going insane)

I sent the last email uncorrected and wrote quickly because I feel that an interception will occur which used to happen a lot in the past. The subject and I no longer talk but meet up for breakfast and share a bench and a foldable director's chair at night. But if you wanted to do something for me do something for her. If not, then our communications are going to close down again soon for obvious reasons but I wanted to know if Alex had blocked communications or whether some Prism project had, as I hadn't been able to get through to her (and you didn't respond for about a month) Notice how my sister never wrote back after I called her a fucking cunt. She knows we have no-one, she knows how I crave conversation, and the other sister Alexandra is obviously being told I'm unstable, and that my writing will get her and her husband into trouble. We're not getting major interceptions? I've told you I once saw an entire page that was apparently from you, that I checked with you that you didn't write.

Another thing they're saying is that I'm interfering and that I'm taking her identity … Christ. But the money thing …she's surrounded by jerks on an occult level and also on an embodied level if what she said about her uncle and Hank is true because these men are not helping her. I agree she's expensive and there's another girl in the county who it's happening to. But I've got to go soon and I can't help her because I actually would really like to smash her in the face and walk away. These last three months are different in that she's beginning to say she despises me, wants me dead etc. but runs after me if I leave because of her feeling that the association with me can help her in some way. Help her bide her time before Hank and the mom's uncle shows up? Help her to pretend she's got a friend? I want so badly to go and live on my own again. Despite Obama's recent medical overhaul in Virginia there is no capability for the homeless to access medical health. Neither of us have insurance. As for the passport thing, I'm not willing to leave her unless she states otherwise because I'm concerned about her.

Cass

**From: Leigh Ryder**
**To: Cass Ryder**

Dear Cass,

I am emailing you from a different email address just in case someone close to you who has access to your email account and has put a block on my emails. I have no idea why your previous email account became "inoperative" (maybe you were entering an invalid password by typing in capital letters?) The reason you thought I didn't respond for a month is because I cannot reply to communications sent via a commercial printer's office (they just get bounced back to me) However you MUST change your password and not let anyone - especially M - know what it is.

I'm sorry M got her backpack stolen, but I still think everything about her sounds suspect. Like who is this "Hank" and why is she communicating with him? How convenient is it that she apparently gets invited to some family reunion but the voicemail message was on a cellphone in the backpack that got stolen? Of course the "proof" is gone because I bet it never happened and no-one actually contacted her. In fact, her daypack may not have been stolen at all but given into Hank's safekeeping, and Hank is quite possibly an associate of hers, and they are both setting you up. My instincts are telling me <u>not to trust this woman</u>. I would not believe a word she says - it's just too contradictory and implausible. You state that Monica got rid of Liz's email, which means she is quite capable of getting rid of any communication from your sisters too. The only way you can prevent anyone, including her, from blocking my messages is to keep your password strictly private.

Love,

Leigh

**From: Leigh Ryder**
**To: Cass Ryder**


Dear Cass,


I received your 42-page attachment when I logged on this morning, which you sent at 22:26pm. However, a few moments later at 22:34pm someone using your email address sent me the following message (copied below), which I do not believe is genuinely from you, especially as you would never sign off like that.

*dear leigh,*
*thanks again for the very much needed money. Monica and I are*
*very grateful for your kindness.*
*I hope her last large paycheck comes in soon!*
*She is such a nice girl and deserves so much MORE!*
*Love you always,*
*Cass*


Does anyone else know your password, or did you leave the computer without logging off? Please let me know whether you did actually receive my Moneygram, and whether it was you who sent the message above. In order that I can be sure I am communicating with you and not someone impersonating you, could you give me the answer to the following question: what is the first name of our uncle in Wales and what is the name of his daughter (our cousin)? If I don't hear back from you I can only assume you did not receive this. Please email me as soon as you get this, as I am now extremely worried, and don't forget to change your password immediately.

Leigh

**From: Cass Ryder**
**To: Leigh Ryder**

Names you asked for M------ and C-------, but the cash was genuinely received. Monica wrote that message and was just joking about. I didn't think you'd think it was me. I'm not so simplistic and friendly. I meant to email you after she wrote that but the library was closing.

She wanted to use the cash you sent to stay in a Holiday Inn. You can't begin to imagine what it's been like, as each night in a hotel room equals sanity and mental health restoration. The first night in the hotel I stayed away, then the second afternoon I stopped by to deliver some fresh produce and wash my hair, and ended up sleeping on the ottoman, then she went completely off the wall. I flung a boot at her at 3am quite forcefully and it hit her in the abdomen whereupon she did insist calmly I leave. But she had woken me up and insisted I leave and something snapped in me. It seemed extremely self-centred and selfish and I couldn't be bothered, and it's not really safe at that hour. I don't ever want any violent situation occurring between us because it's just not me…but she had been going on and on for six hours. She has this sort of cry stance (tears emerge in her eyes but don't roll down her cheeks) and increasingly she's been swearing she can't stand me and she's going to have to get rid of me etc. The verbalizations are extremely hateful in wording but there's something phoney about it, like a Dick Tracey cartoon caricature… and this can go on for hours. There's no mystery about why a person gets really upset when they're always facing hunger, cold, fatigue, uncertainty, but what isn't so obvious is that people get occult-interfered with. It's like suffering the invisible presence of someone you hate, which could be really enraging to a small person because their feelings matter and they need to be taken seriously. If they aren't then they get back some other way, so her anger takes on a sort of insincerity when she needs to show genuine hate.

We don't necessarily get along that well, we have very different views, and I don't know if she is just suffering from a nervous breakdown stemming from recent homelessness or was born slightly schizophrenic. She claims she knew a house full of people that disappeared and were replaced by look-alikes who literally took over their identities and assets, and rattled on about druggings, hypnosis etc. The freak for her could have been her cop training in Florida and the John Jay College of Criminal Justice in New York city ...the New York cops are pretty fascist. She seems to have brushed up against the most foul people. I had to listen to her glory in witnessing people who had made comparatively lame assaults on armed uniformed cops, often behind bars, being beaten to a pulp. The theory is no one assaults a police officer. To listen to this woman is to bring it all back what I brushed up against in jail, just complete victimizations in a hysterical psychopathic degree... they can't beat people in the head enough. For instance they routinely beat up innocent demonstrators, when instead they could possibly have formed concentric circles and walked in those kinds of formations, guaranteeing that if people break out in violence they sustain the impact, and that it's done in open spaces where dialogues could take place and it could be media-coveraged.

I don't pretend I wouldn't get mad if I was a cop, esp. towards some criminals, but I wouldn't have beaten them up. I understand they have difficult jobs but I just try and stay away from them. I don't even want one day with the cops, that's how much I remember that jail experience. I was denied underwear until my last 5 days in there, so only had one pair, thanks to some money I had which was used to buy stuff from the canteen. One girl fell off the top bunk bed and hurt her head (no ladder was available, it was set up like that so you had to step on a washbasin) I know all about jails: middle of the night vehicle transfers, overflowing toilets, beatings, prostitution and blowjobs in the laundry room. The cops are really foul people, afraid so, I'm entitled to my opinion. I don't like them. They build up grudges, they are ruled by an inner core mafia who then put all kinds of pressure on others. Anyway, yesterday I pulled her hair. I think we were talking about cops and I recounted an example of a recent Occupy demonstrator in New York, who was pulled by her hair across the road, and M was allying herself with those who have beaten up defenceless people. She was describing how when she was a cop or prison guard she had felt tremendous power while this guy was being beaten up. So I just told her that I hate the cops, then I grabbed her hair and pulled. She kept taunting me and yes, I'm a felon, and by her reckoning I'm the scum of the universe.

But it's sad that I feel so negative I lose control like that (what if the boot had hit her breasts?) I bought a mirror and am going to try to remind myself to look into it if a violent impulse ever occurs again. I feel sick that I did that, it's never come to blows with us, but she almost pushed me in front of a car yesterday evening so can you get a picture as to what's going on? (she's not as vulnerable as she seemed) In other words our bodies are being used, meaning something taps into dormant emotions…or is it the penis who sits in her body, an etheric puppeting done to annoy me and anyone she comes into contact with? Last night before I left the library she breaks out from about 9:30pm to 12:30pm like Adolf Hitler himself at the top of her lungs, but there is something sensationalist about it. I believe her body is being channelled, being held hostage by assholes in a spirit dimension who violate innocent people. Who the hell are these sausages? Spirits literally speak through her body, or it is a state of severe schizophrenia (but perhaps that's exactly what my deal's been in terms of seventeen years talking out loud to myself .. God I'm no standard for exemplification) She's definitely witchcraft-interfaced, and her situation is made worse by being on a pavement and indirectly soliciting. And I occasionally feel hate vibes from around her. She looks so planted, so designed. M is the most unbelievable weapon being angled at me, at my writing.

But in all seriousness if she could be used to character assassinate me and get me an indictment I don't need it. Right this moment she's trying to draw out the attention of the law enforcement. Talk about cheap (she just pulled down her underpants outside the library very briefly with no one looking, and with her back to the wall) But something is hinting that they could get her to throw me in jail and if I thought that then I would leave...but it's just fifty ways to mess with the heads of what they see as two lesbians (we're not a gay couple but we have quite a lot in common) Cashlessness gets to her, not being able to sleep properly gets to her, fear of an assault or of being aerially abducted and of things being done to her, and then dropped back on the pavement to wake up. Apparently her father had been diagnosed with "personality disorder" and her uncle used to continually say *"play the fiddle while Rome burns"* It's the most unbelievable "daughter owned by daddy" syndrome. She screams at the top of her lungs, swears non-stop, glorying in the fact that people die and are murdered, but it's the social elite thing that's unbearable. I don't see how the rich are so important. But this money admiration she has, as well as physical strength. She hails from such a fascist mould... it's to acknowledge the rapists and thugs who are in charge of America. It is a country that gets on its knees before biceps and height. She has become a complete Jekyll and Hyde and she doesn't know where she's going from one day to the next. Her soul is wandering around in a complete state of trauma.

Before she met me M was on her own, or occasionally resonated with a man the local homeless know as Bob but even he has problems. His car is overcrowded with things and she slept out in the open, which I think is a pretty poor show for a guy who's being projected as her "protector." But then again he's under lots of stress and loads of impoverished American men are. As for re-engaging with family her entire immediate family is gone and she claims she's not close to any of the wider family (she gets into cars left right and centre, or has done) People might judge her but have no idea how desperate you become when you are homeless. It's extremely cheap what she goes through, what she's supposed to do for a few dollars. Uncle Sam ejaculated while they put growbags and whores on payrolls. Anyway I'm sick of hearing her cry, of acknowledging her pain when no-one else does. She twice fisted herself in the face and I had to look on while no one else noticed. She gets quite a lot of cash so perhaps she's not as vulnerable as I thought. Just as she seems to have an invisible support network and doesn't want government benefits, but perhaps that's for a good reason. The problem with the severely "ether-used" is they will always consciously reject any channel of genuine empathy, and it's always the first thing the entity manipulating them is going to counter-checkmate on (eventually even with Liz she threw it back in Liz's face) We've practically come to blows about nine times.

It's not quite so bad now because of the comparative generosity of the locals in this state. People who hold up signs get cash. Neither of us have ever done that or would want to … not to judge those that do. I'd like to work. It's not possible, not here anyway. M's only been homeless for two and half years compared to eighteen of mine and I can't bring myself to get any closer to the federal government than accepting foodstamps. No-one trusts them. Meanwhile she apparently prefers me to be with her, and we might be better friends if we could live normally. A social worker said that together we could panhandle local housing benefit funding and probably get something. But I don't like women any longer and don't want to live in an apartment, but I don't want to live like this either. I seem to be aggravating things by being in her company. I'm a potential arrest case and I wonder whether I'm being set up, blackmailed emotionally to stay beside her here. I'd like to just walk away but I can't, my conscience won't let me. I feel like I'm linked to her and she's being set up for something seedy, and the things around her are trying to murder me while she basically uses me for a guard at night. I also think she's been planted on me so something can justify looking at me, mainly my writing, but actually I know what's going on and it's obvious. Isn't she a decoy to try and mess me up on some development I revealed in my writing? She came like a stray puppy almost literally into my presence and has hung around me ever since the moment I began writing the book. Her appearance did coincide with the writing of my book, which would have gotten me an execution in some countries. I'm definitely on some kind of blacklist.

Liz had the FBI scan her three years ago to find out if she had been mind-controlled or was a Manchurian candidate, and got a negative result, but since the character dissociation seems to have occurred at the time of homelessness when she reached northern VA, perhaps it's a further leak that weapons are used in this area against Vulnerables. I believe it is the secret societal mandate in this area to use the occult to drive out the "undesirables" The fact that it's the wealthiest region in the U.S. and the centre of the Pentagon and CIA etc. is all the more reason to believe the situation might improve if she were to leave (this area is noted for being intensely Republican and evangelist), but I think it would be unadvisable if we stray over into a more criminal area. I'll try and see if the social worker KB can get in touch with this Liz who might be able to shed some light, but you get dispirited when they don't do anything. I've gone to her about three times at least on the subject and she's told me she can't tell me anything without Monica's consent, but I'd like to get some psychic counselling for her. Everything about her stinks of an occult attack... she's impossible to be with. It seems like she's embroiled in a psychic race war ...with something that I can only describe as an African uniformed spirit force around her. There is a likelihood that this is going on and a lot of these weapons are poor man's weapons. Dion Fortune once practised as a psychic surgeon and healed patients by severing links with the silver cord (an invisible umbilical cord, which is a major gateway for occult interference) Could astral surgery be a fix...to cut off an etheric connection with a disembodied penis? I don't know if I can even take the concept of astral surgery seriously. Chopping away an etheric umbilical chord like some seaweed or crust that forms around a pipe, and then a person's alright? They're well?

You can see my dilemma, this whole thing has been forced on me so it gets on my nerves that I'm being interpreted by the authorities as "interfering." Anyway, it looks like M won't be able to go anywhere and I can't stay here, I can't stand it. I'm getting tired of risking my life and actually I'm not helping to guard her since I normally fall asleep. I wrote because I wanted you to advise me what to do with this woman. As to how much she is genuinely traumatized or whether that is just an act to survive, I just don't know. There is probably nothing you can do, but I'm sick of the way I'm used in a race war or values war and I can't afford to ally with either side.

Cass

**From: Leigh Ryder**
**To: Cass Ryder:**

Dear Cass,

You asked for my advice about Monica, and it looks like she approached you first. It's important to establish who made the first move, as the whole relationship is beginning to look decidedly suspect i.e. I think there's something shady going on. Concerning M, I have copied below are some edited quotes from your own observations (in italics) to which I have appended some of my own comments:

*She gets quite a lot of cash...just as she seems to have an invisible support network...* (where does she get the cash from? Could some agency be paying her to shadow you?) *I also think she's been planted on me ... she came like a stray puppy almost literally into my presence and has hung around me ever since the moment I began writing the book. Her appearance did coincide with the writing of my book...M is the most unbelievable weapon being angled at me ...she's not as vulnerable as she seemed* (maybe she's not really "on the run" at all but is on a mission connected with her previous cop work which involves getting close to you, and the easiest way to do that would be to play on your emotions and sympathy by posing as a homeless woman who's had a nervous breakdown) *Last night before I left the library she breaks out like Adolf Hitler himself at the top of her lungs...but there's something phony about it like a Dick Tracey cartoon caricature... I wonder whether I'm being set up, blackmailed emotionally to stay beside her here ...She looks so planted so designed...She almost pushed me in front of a car yesterday evening* (Well, that's obviously not good and you need to be on your guard in case some "accident" occurs for which she could not legally be held responsible since she is supposed to be mentally disturbed)

Oh just STOP Leigh. Now I'm getting seriously paranoid (it's definitely contagious) Anyway, I think it's pretty suspect that her appearance coincided with your writing your book. You were on the point of moving on just before she appeared in your life, maybe even returning to the UK, and it seems like she has been planted as a major DISTRACTION and DIVERSION (not only from your research) but to prevent you from engaging with family, and your meeting with her deliberately engineered, resulting in an emotional attachment and co-dependency. This is fine where it provides companionship, but it is not fine when she nearly pushes you under a car, or comes close to getting you arrested by her behaviour. So I'm wondering whether the sudden appearance of M in your life is a "set up" which is going to have really bad consequences and repercussions. Are you absolutely sure that it is M who is being "puppeted", and that it isn't YOU who are being used? Whether she is being exploited by some agency - human or occult - or whether she is using you and happens to be a very good actress is immaterial, since the outcome for you is the same: the association between you is placing you in a dangerous and increasingly untenable position. It's probably only a question of time before one of several things happens: your immune system breaks down completely due to lack of sleep and exposure to cold, you get arrested because of her outrageous behaviour, you get banned permanently from the library when access to the Internet is absolutely crucial, or worse.

You also mentioned elsewhere in a separate attachment *"The other day something kept grabbing my throat like a choking ...I'd wake up with something in my throat and I knew something was causing it"* The sensation you described might just have been some physiological reflex to do with dehydration, or a throat infection. I know that sounds lame but I really don't know what kind of physical condition you're in, and in the winter months I also sometimes wake up with a "frog in the throat" – a symptom of the streptococcus virus that usually heralds the onset of an infection. Obviously sitting up on a bench night after night, and not being able to get a decent night's sleep is going to seriously compromise your health. You can pick up all kinds of nasty things in communal shower areas in shelters.

I still think you should seriously consider the possibility of returning to the UK. Look on it as a year-long "vacation" or retreat where I will provide you with a roof over your head, and a safe and stable environment. I believe I told you we have now sold our cottage in Cornwall and exchanged contracts. The other thing we have discussed is the possibility of being able to offer you permanent accommodation on the top floor of any house we purchase. For your own sake please think very hard about what I'm saying. We are prepared to pay for your flight, and I would obviously meet you at the airport. I am trying to throw you a lifeline here, so seize it with both hands! Due to the upheaval of moving there may be a gap of 2 days when I can't access my emails, but I will still be able to receive yours in my inbox, and will reply as soon as possible.

Love from Leigh

**From: Luke Ryder**
**To: Leigh, Patrick, Alexandra, Adam**

Hello All

Cass lived with me in Wingham, Kent for 1 year (in the garden in her tent as she would not come inside) She then stayed at my house in Ramsgate for a good few months before returning to America. I also visited Cass on a regular basis after she moved to the States in the late 80s well before she became homeless. There was a definite change in Cass's personality over the years she was in Boston. At first she was very sociable but as time went on she became more reclusive. She found it hard to be in the company of people. She was reading avidly and taking in every written word, a lot of overlapping data without disposing of any of it. She didn't seem to be filtering it and the knowledge she was gaining was becoming jumbled in her mind. She appears to be doing the same now. I see her mind as a sponge that is never squeezed and cleansed. She needs a spiritual cleansing.

When she was living in her tent in the garden at Wingham, she would sometimes come in for a chat. Sometimes she made sense and sometimes not. She told me many a time that voices were talking to her. They were annoying her more and more. She would disappear for weeks on end and suddenly return. She was dealing with a lot and I didn't know how to help her. The schizophrenia and paranoia were pretty obvious. After later moving to Wales and becoming involved in Spiritualist Circles, I believed she was suffering from spirit possession, which is pretty similar to schizophrenia and can be cured. If I had known more then of what I believe now, I would have tried to help her while she was with me. I'm sorry I did virtually nothing to help her.

Anyway, after moving to Ramsgate, Cass showed up on my doorstep again. I was quite relieved as I had wondered what she had been doing. I had a spare room for her so she could have her own space. She even got a job fruit picking but it only lasted a few days. She found it near to impossible to be around people, much less work for or with them. She made a concerted effort though, which I know caused her a lot of anguish. She would disappear for weeks and then return. I believe she travelled around and basically lived in the wilderness. One time she returned with a bad case of poison ivy. One evening, I heard her screaming in her room down stairs so I ran down to check on her. She hurtled through her door so fast I was startled. I was conscious that I was standing at the top of some stairs and that I could easily be pushed down. The expression on her face and the tone of her voice was NOT CASS ! I'm telling you it was not Cass. I don't think it would be possible to consciously distort your face in that manner. I was scared out of my wits and knew if I said one word, I would be attacked. I very slowly backed up and walked back upstairs to my room.

I later understood her condition to be a form of Spirit possession. A discarnate spirit can enter a human body and operate through that body with speech. We've achieved that in the spirit circle I attend here in Wales. I believe Cass had allowed the entrance of a very negative spirit into her body and mind as she delved into the occult in Canterbury. I believe Leigh, Maddy and others in the family may have seen this spirit at No 33. but I think it was attracted by Cass's investigations back then. As I understand it these spirits can never stay permanently in someone's body, but can be there most of the time. This causes lapses of abnormality, switching back into near normality. My presumption that Cass had passed away was based on what I had been told by our circle leader, and I was wrong. I had been in contact with Daddy through meditation, and he had told me he was in contact with Cass. So I assumed Cass had also passed on. Sorry, that mistake was due to my ignorance. When I told our circle leader Rhiannon that we'd heard from Cass who was still alive, Rhiannon said that I had indeed been in contact with Cass through spirit. Whether on the earth plane or not, we are first and foremost "spirit".

The children are back from school so I have to finish soon. I send healing to Cass and Maddy nightly, I don't know what else to do. I don't believe money will make any difference. She always hated money and would try to dispose of it as quickly as she could – most of which went into buying presents for others. She needs either medical help or spiritual help depending on which side of the coin you find yourselves. She never allowed anyone to help in the past and there is no reason to believe she would now. I don't think she is in imminent danger as she is an expert in survival. She actually was surviving on the streets long before the last time she was in the UK. I of course love Cass, which is obviously the sentiment of you all. If we allow ourselves to get drawn into feuding between ourselves, we will not be able to help at all. The starting point would be to visit her. If she would allow an extended visit, she would then have to be persuaded to accept help. That would be very, very difficult. I have e-mailed her but it seems she would prefer not to talk to me. I'll try again when I feel the time is right?

Luke

**From: Adam Ryder**
**To: Luke, Leigh, Patrick, Alexandra**

Greetings,

My turn, is it? Good to see that the hillbilly practice of family feuding is alive and well! I have very little to add about Cass. I think you all know my view anyhow. I tend towards the belief that she is clinically ill and should be treated as such. I don't believe that she is possessed. I believe that she suffers from a severe form of schizophrenia (for want of a more accurate label). In the genes I'm afraid...exacerbated by environmental influences at an impressionable age, with dope a contributing factor, introduction to occultist ideas another.

I was trying to get in contact with my old friend Robert recently, and managed to track down his sister, Helen. Got a message back from her saying "How is your sister, Cass? The one who used to terrorise me at your house by chasing me around with a carving knife." She also mentions you, Leigh, who would join in the terror sessions by frightening her with your face-masks at the same time. Imagine....a 4-year old kid being terrorised by two sisters. One with a knife, the other a mask. Go figure! Unsurprisingly they did not come to no.33 often...out of fear. I used to go over to Rob's instead.

I could also go on to re-enlighten some of you about the negative familial influences on me as a kid - the fear of what terrible things would happen to my body as it changed, as explained in graphic detail by Leigh ....never mind the HORRENDOUS experiences at Wincheap Primary. Abuse (sexual and physical) was rife. The head was finally convicted for child abuse and sent away for a very long time. He used to 'spank' little boys every day in his office at lunchtime. The rough kids from Wincheap Secondary would invade the back field at lunch time and beat up the little kids. The dinner ladies would look on, laughing. I remember being given a kicking once and looking up from my bloodied nose to see Cass laughing at me. The school was a disgrace and I have never been so relieved in my life as when I was informed that I had been offered a place at Pilgrims Way instead.

I take anti-depressants now (no lecture, please, Leigh), which certainly help to take the edge off things for me. I help support a number of poor kids here in Brazil by taking them out for excursions and by buying their school gear etc. There is neediness all around and I try to do my bit. Unfortunately Cass and Maddy are out of my scope...and it is the kids that I most care about these days, anyway.

Adam

**From: Leigh Ryder**
**Luke, Patrick, Alex, Adam**

Dear Family,

In response to Luke's email, I think he may be on the right track, for too many reasons which I don't propose to go into now (maybe later) In other words, there is something more going on here than a psychiatric disorder. If you recall, there was a period of almost a year when our house in Canterbury was rented out to university students and Daddy decided to relocate the family to the States. Patrick was either working in London (?) or possibly in his last year at Kent University, I had started at university elsewhere, and the others had been enrolled at schools in Louisville, KY. I can't pinpoint the exact year – it's all a bit blurred – but sometime in the 70s. Anyway, as you know the transatlantic transplant didn't work out and the family returned to No.33. I clearly remember our mother being somewhat annoyed at the scorch marks left by candles on the walls of the top floor, and her remarking "the students must have been holding séances up here" There is no inevitable connection between burning candles and occult activity, so I have always wondered why she seemed so convinced that they were holding séances, unless she discovered evidence of this which she kept to herself. Apart from a vague distaste, the paranormal held little interest for her.

I don't agree that Cass had anything to do with starting up the frightening paranormal phenomena some of us experienced at the house later on, though it's not surprising some low-level entity might have been attracted to her natural vitality. She was not conducting any "investigations" into the occult at this point in time. She was just a normal teenager with a lot going for her: popular, outgoing, attractive, high-spirited and with a mischievous sense of humour. Her avid reading around this subject came much later on, when she was more or less left to her own devices in the house after the death of our parents, and was probably motivated by a desire to understand what was happening to her. There were a lot of books left lying around which she later picked up, but most of us had read them with no adverse affects. In any case reading literature does not cause schizophrenia. What I am suggesting is that the student tenants may well have been dabbling in the occult or witchcraft – there was a lot of this going on at the time, not to mention the heavy drug scene on the campus – and they consciously or unconsciously invited some dark negative energy into the house. It was after this year that things really started to really kick off. And Patrick should not have been dropping acid, tripping out on LSD or whatever the hell else he was doing in the family home.

Adam, I presume the remarks about Cass chasing Helen around the house with a carving knife were meant to be jocular: Cass would have been about 10 at the time, but let's face it children simply LOVE being "chased by the monster" and these games were entirely for their entertainment and at their prompting. I used to baby-sit those kids, and even at the age of 3 or 4 Helen was quite capable of administering some quite vicious kicks to her older brother when provoked. On one occasion when I was baby-sitting some Quality Streets had gone missing from Helen's hidden stash. She naturally assumed her brother Robert was the culprit and kicked his little butt halfway across the kitchen. Of course it was none other than yours truly who had scoffed the chocolates, and I had no qualms whatsoever in standing by whilst a small boy was being punished for my misdemeanours. When the parents arrived home to a chorus of wails, I calmly collected my wages and departed the scene. However I do not remember ever going into graphic detail about the "terrible things that would happen to your body as it changed" (though sadly this has come to pass) and any dire warnings I might have issued were <u>for your own good</u>, and expressly designed to keep you out of the clutches of men like Bishop G and Mr. Raynor. As for the alleged bullying that went on at Sincheap Primary, I'm afraid you brought all this on yourself.

When our mother asked what you wanted to be when you grew up your answer was invariably "I want to be a fairy on top of a Christmas tree" or "I'm going to be a womens libber" Such sentiments would hardly have endeared you to the playground bullies and "rough kids" from the sink estates. I do have a vague recollection of occasionally appearing in a white clay facemask, but certain sacrifices have to be made in order to preserve one's beauty.

On the subject of anti-depressants, I'm not sure it is an altogether good idea to "take the edge off things" like the docile citizens of *Brave New World* meekly swallowing the *soma* that was doled out to them on a daily basis. Ignorance might well be bliss, but bliss was never meant to be part of the human condition, and neither was ignorance.

Take care,

Leigh

**From: Cass Ryder**
**To: Leigh Ryder**
**Subject: Attachment to follow**

The "Stargate Conspiracy" is about a classified psychic spy
programme involving research into the paranormal domain. In it
the authors note that the "Ennead" contacted in the research state
that they're a spirit syndicate related to the ancient Egyptian
godhead (the "Nine") reputed to be very white supremacist and
neo-Nazi. The authors conclude that this syndicate are poised to
take over the so-called democratic world, using CIA and occult
lodge connections to take over Western intelligence and the
government. A British WW2 spy Aleister Crowley states in his
diary that he involuntarily contacted the Ennead whilst studying the
occult in Cairo, and claims they "held him hostage" his whole life
long. Colin Wilson wrote in "Mysteries of the Sphinx" that he had
come across the "Nine" in his research and he calls them "the
biggest bunch of conmen and tricksters in the ether". They are
understood to be extremely powerful and the theory is that this
syndicate represents a secret fraternity who pass on skills
generationally. A writer called Andrew Collins published a book in
the 90s called *The Black Alchemist.* Anyway the black alchemist is
supposed to be some godawful occultist and it is probably just a
secret societal propaganda (though the book's supposed to be
factual) and the psychic went into a coma and died. They probably
gave Patrick his brain haemorrhage in 2000 and caused his coma.
Maddy underwent a nervous breakdown and experienced quite a lot
of paranormal interference prior to this. Patrick had LSD forced on
him when he was at university. There is a red phone box opposite
the 24-hour MacDonald's here in Sterling exactly like the one that
sits at the top of Dover Road in Canterbury. Our house number was
33 (Scotch masonry 33 Degrees?) The connection between the
devils of Loudoun and Loudoun county? Diversionary material
designed to befuddle the imagination.

You might want to have paid note to the name of a private neuroscience outfit in central Loudoun with a spooky desolate barn fronting its property and what is crassly intended as a warning to alternative females okay? The institute's name is Janalia, just like the sister and her friend's name (she's not a covert operative?) Also your friend's colonoscopy was timed with my communicating with you. I think something's trying to imply that if Monica gets cancer your friend will as well...sorry. Writer's own mother's cancer was precipitated by an error, brought on prematurely by a surgical action (biopsy) by an Iranian doctor on a USAF base which left her with a year to live. She dies on Guy Fawkes' night, the writer's father dies of a heart attack on July 4th in the U.S five years later (Oh, the subject's father's birthday happens to be on July 4th) The writer travels to Iran while gestating in the womb. Okay the association is loud and clear, to do with me... I was conceived in England but born in Iran and they set it up to open up some sort of gateway. My older brother Patrick shared his desk with the princess of Iran while enrolled in a British school there. Writer's father on a nowhere ticket with the U.S. embassy and a family who lives in a big house beside a canal, and the state dept tells him he has to go back to America after a few months. Also when I was born the Kennedy admin was 'in' (probably why our father got his stupid assignment with the embassy there) I reckon they were doing some little occult experiment on me ...oh, this isn't happening? Yes it is. I'm almost certain that's what's going on. Fifty different ways to mess with your head. After WW2 they began liaising heavily with occult lodges and I BELIEVE I WAS SOME SORT OF SURVEILLANCE TARGET FROM BEFORE BIRTH.

They seem to be frustrated that I am operating as a single individual, that I survived for 20 years like a failed Crocodile Dundee without the usual trappings. The latest ploy is "You're mentally insane" They are literally using occult tactics on the homeless in this region, etheric prods up the anus, attempts at enforced bioelectricals during sleep, and a host of other things that have occurred on and off over the last six years. The writer was attacked in 1993 in a liquid magic experiment or what sounds like sub-project 4 of a MKULTRA file. She was forced out of her body and had a fluid poured down her solar plexus during an REM phase…the writer sees her dead mother protesting at the event, and then goes back inside her body. The chemical emissions during REM process are the same as in peyote mushroom-induced trance altered states. The auxiliary body (an etheric blueprint) separates from the physical body during REM stage. The writer believes this was done not by the CIA but by the occult syndicate referred to in my attachment. After which everything changed and this preceded 20 years of homelessness. That phase killed something with her relationship with her family, and she was never able to communicate about it to anyone. What initially was a "sexing" I'm not in the slightest ashamed to admit, was really sicko…flooding my imagination with lurid imageries like a gay man gnawing on the thighbone of a deceased male he was in a relationship with, an imagery which in no way resonated with any of the writer's conscious or unconscious feelings.

The subject calls me "Claudine" all the while, and is going totally insane. The daypack theft took place exactly as she was about to leave for Pittsburgh, and writer feels it was done to detain her here. They were responsible for the theft of her IDs twice, and there is the strange fact that she has no memory of an event here in Loudoun county 3 years ago, of a house fire that connotes Mob actions. Someone called Claudine was apparently with her in a house that caught fire in 2010, when she found herself back on the pavement and can't remember anything. She goes on and on about a house she lived in that belongs to her and is worth well over a million, and other things like "They had no right to involve me in that experiment at Marshal university". Back in '93 or '94 the writer had a friend who was an administrative secretary for MIT in Boston, and was given a big house to live in rent-free by the university for no apparent reason. She invites the writer to share this with her, but writer refuses. Wasn't this the context for a "rigged surveillance"? The friend's house is mysteriously taken away, and she then receives a palatial office, which is later replaced by a cupboard-sized barren room, which coincided with the writer and friend splitting up. I think the subject (Monica) was involved in a covert mind invasion surveillance program and I think she has had money appropriated. Another of her sayings: "Does anybody think I don't care what happened to her for that 362,000 dollar duplex?" She's stated before she was the victim of inheritance hijacking, and recounted how after her father died a woman comes along claiming to be her aunt, who looks like her but isn't. Look-alike relatives who then go on to intercept her inheritance? Forged letters from fake attorneys that state her money's already been given to her?

I don't think it's worth trying to contact this Liz, she sounds horrible, but then again she might have been another pawn. We're all pawns in a sort of software game or like in those gangster movies where the bad guys have things turned against them, then turn against one another. But there is always the nagging feeling that something was trying to guide her down certain routeways…definitely the feeling that she was being encouraged to wander off further in towards the Met area and to repeat the sad mistakes of countless millions of women today and in history. The subject is definitely in danger of something sexually seedy by the looks of it. But people don't need to keep conforming to those codes esp. if it's going to cost the soul that much. America has a lot of space…maybe the government could try to support the women's communities that were smoked out of their holes like animals, and have them reinstated with guarantees of future support? Susan Faludi wrote about a post 80s backlash and how women's separatist communities were busted up. A possibility might be singles retirement communities. Frankly the shelter is not going to work for her, and I feel she'd be better off in regions that are populated more by singles or maybe a security-gated "over 50s" community. M just turned 55 but in retrospect an over fifties community wouldn't work either. Singles or those with alternative lifestyles need a massive bioregion or somewhere more politically liberal, where there's strength in numbers and rednecks in the surrounding area can't attack them. Because she's influenced by people around her, and it matters what the wider community believes. Childless singles have been set up to be either impoverished and isolated with no guaranteed work, or to be high consumers and forced to seek housing in costly over-priced property zones because they don't want to share space with the mainstream crowd, where they are scapegoated or persecuted. I'm not gay, but I sure as hell didn't want a boyfriend or baby and I let people know from 14 upwards. It was understood I was a cold fish, with no breasts into the bargain.

The subject's former positive stance has increasingly changed in the last 6 months, into negative verbalisations like "You're a piece of 8888, you must obey my commands…I am more important than anyone in the entire world except Liz. I want to make it abundantly clear I do not fight for strangers, it's better your children die than Liz has a split hair. What is my job? To take care of me, my money, and Liz…" But her real fix is money. For instance, she said the other day: "If I ran a business I would choose high end real estate for the rich…I never could be bothered with scum poor and I want to stay that way." But there is something in America that proactively funds human misery, defining her psycho outbreaks as a mental illness when actually it does seem to be an etheric victimization. As soon as anyone warms to her something completely jumps in there and tries to make her look bad or mad. She talks about "spics" the whole time and the most unbelievable pornographic crap comes out of her mouth. She seems to be indoctrinated by something neo-Nazi … like generals in a jungle camp plotting the next incursion and bragging over the most recent kill etc. It's sickening the way she's always attacking people verbally, but there does seem to be something horrible around her, as well as something good that I associate with her mother's spirit. The good thing is that people around here seem to instinctively understand that and don't confront her directly, they tend to ignore it when she screams.

I checked the audiotape I made of her and spliced it, but then the microphone glitched. At the end of the 30 min audio it sounds like an animal or an entity breathing, but that might just be electronic noise. I was going to record another 30 min session but it won't record any more. She once heard her father's voice on the phone after he was dead. Could she please keep her symbolic father on a leash? At what point is it schizophrenia, at what point a pawn torn between two spirit energy worlds? She and Liz acted in self-defence when a black man from Haiti tried to assault M (they killed him) It's true M can exaggerate or lie, but it's clear a lot of it isn't a lie, and there is certainly a lot of witchcraft going on in this region. Research into spirit possessions reveal that a person can be possessed by the energies of disturbed people, either the living or by those who have died and don't realise they're dead, as it takes some time for their auxiliary bodies to disintegrate or dissociate. I just used to hit the woods if I started hearing voices. And I was functioning with voices in my head as far back as '95, not an exaggeration, and was living in a tent behind this manor house farm Luke was renting in Wingham. Then a woman and her daughter gets murdered in a pastoral meadow only 3 miles away from where Luke and I had been living in the Kent countryside (the older daughter survived) On that same day I had been working in a strawberry field nearby. The woman and her husband were both doctors, and they never found out who did it.

There is something pretty evil around her that resents the writer's observations. So I don't want to tell the government workers too much, and she is justifiably too paranoid to let a doctor look at her. Meaning that if she has inherited illnesses they could say that because she's not submitting to a check up she's a danger to herself, and use that as a reason to incarcerate her. Post 80s gay men always thought that government workers in city social service departments killed them via implanted viral dosages intended as hepatitis inoculations, and that covert operatives literally administered the aids virus through these needles, masquerading as health workers. But if mental illnesses and cancer-like symptoms are the result of treatments actually designed to weaken and destroy the immune system then doesn't she have a good reason for not going?

*"Psychiatry's solution to life's problems is the administration of mind-altering toxic drugs which according to the FDA can cause mania, worsening depression, anxiety, delusions, seizures, liver failure, suicide..."*

The above is taken from the Internet, okay? The prescriptions don't work, the diagnosis is often wrong and 70% do NOT seek medical assistance and do just as well or better without the orthodox remedy of counselling or prescription pills. The mental illness industry is a MULTI-BILLION DOLLAR FAILURE.

Cass

**From: Leigh Ryder**
**To: Cass Ryder**

Dear Cass,

My apologies. Just because I haven't been able to reply immediately doesn't mean I am not interested or haven't taken any of it on board, it just means that I've been exceptionally busy just recently. Please bear in mind that you are sending me pages and pages of your writing, all of which takes a lot of TIME to read, if I am do it justice and give it the consideration it deserves. Yes, I do remember that brutal murder back in 1996 when Maddy and I were visiting Luke (you were camping out in the top field), and how we both waited anxiously for Maddy to return after a night out with friends in Canterbury because she had to walk down a dark country lane from the bus stop and the killer was still on the loose. Someone called Michael Stone was eventually apprehended for the crime.

Much of your writing strikes me as being a desperate struggle to make sense of M's utterances whilst I in turn struggle to make sense of some of your statements, such as *"the writer was attacked in 1993 in a liquid magic experiment or what that sounds like sub-project 4 of a Macultra file, had a fluid poured down her solar plexus ... "* so that we appear to be stuck in a recursive daisy chain of claims and counter-claims, paranoid assertions and reasoned rebuttals. I honestly don't know what to think about your contention that you were the subject of a disembodied assault on the psychic plane, similar to the LSD experiments in the 70s. Naturally these types of experimental mind control programmes would play havoc with the victims' mental health, and if they complained openly would expose them to charges of insanity. Any and everything is possible, but it's best not to dwell on some of the more disturbing possibilities. I sympathise - deeply - but am reluctant to be drawn into a conspiracy theory scenario where I am supposed to believe you are both victims of paranormal assault. To take another example, *"In the Stargate Conspiracy the authors note that the "Ennead" (the "Nine") contacted in the research state that they're a spirit syndicate related to the ancient Egyptian godhead...The authors conclude that this syndicate are poised to take over the so-called democratic world..."*

Just because you've read this somewhere doesn't mean it's true. Colin Wilson wrote a lot of sensationalist literature in the 70s and 80s as did Whitley Streiber (incidentally a writer of horror stories long before he wrote about alien abductions) and a blockbuster movie was based on one of the latter's best-sellers. I'm not knocking authors like Picknett and Prince, C. Wilson, Streiber or Andrew Collins as I enjoyed reading some of the books they wrote years ago but the point to note here is that these guys are *novelists* not scientists, and what is often cited as "scientific research" or "irrefutable proof" is frequently just fiction, entertainment, or someone's paranoid speculations. C. Wilson is so persuasive he even got me hunting for ley-lines at one point and believing that standing stones are "energy gateways", but none of these hypotheses have ever actually been proved. I never used to take any of this stuff too seriously - it opened my mind to the existence of an occult plane and to the reality of psychic attacks, but at that stage I used to read widely for entertainment as well as for educational purposes. I'm surprised you remember some of these books that were lying around the house many years ago. Interestingly, you are right about "Loudoun" in that Aldous Huxley wrote a book entitled *The Devils of Loudoun*, which was about a case of hysteria in a French convent. A priest accused the nuns of consorting with the devil, and the repercussions for the unfortunate nuns were not very pleasant.

The psychic "Bernard" who features in *The Black Alchemist* did die of a brain haemorrhage in 2010, but there is no indication his demise was linked to occult activity. Fatal strokes are among the most common causes of death in older men and the culprit is likely to be high blood pressure. With respect to Patrick's near-fatal aneurysm and resultant coma in 2000, there is absolutely no connection between the two events. The very high altitudes of Mexico city and the horrendous levels of pollution makes it a risky place to live for anyone with elevated blood pressure (when Luke and I flew out to visit him we both suffered from terrible headaches) And I cannot think that your birth in Iran is **in any way** connected with any paranormal interference you later experienced, or with our mother's diagnosis of colon cancer. And although "Janalia" does sound like a composite of our two names, please rest assured the neuroscience institute in Loudoun has absolutely nothing to do with us. J's colonoscopy was arranged after an initial consultation: she does not have cancer, but had a minor operation for haemorrhoids and is absolutely fine. By the way, she says to tell you that she doesn't think she has the brains to be a "covert operative", and I think our brother Patrick would take issue with the notion that he had LSD "forced" on him when he was 19. He was a willing participant as far as I know, and paid dearly for it by hallucinating gigantic spiders. Even the drainpipes morphed into monstrous hairy arachnids, all of which were out to get him. I don't believe anybody has ever forced him to do anything against his will, any more than I "pushed" certain books on you, as you maintain. As a family we had eclectic tastes in literature. I was always a lover of classical literature and if you were drawn to occult bestsellers such as *The Black Alchemist* that was a reflection of your own propensities and tastes.

With respect to Iran, our father only had a 6-month contract with the U.S. embassy as a cultural attaché, and what precipitated our sudden departure from Tehran in the 60s was a cataclysmic earthquake. We were flown out in the middle of the night on USAF planes, and arrived back in England safely only to discover the following day the whole place was devastated – it was all over the newspapers. Of course you were only a baby at the time, so wouldn't remember the circumstances. Your belief that you were "some sort of surveillance target from before birth" doesn't make a great deal of sense. Prior to your birth there was no "you" to target

(??) Think about that. As for the AIDS conspiracy theory that covert operatives literally administered the virus to gay men through a hepatitis viral inoculation program by masquerading as health workers, I'm sure there are plenty of homophobic evangelist types out there who would like nothing better than to wipe out the entire gay population, but if it was a deliberate policy then it was MASSIVELY stupid because hey, there are tons of bisexual men and married closets who sleep with both sexes and therefore the disease is easily transmitted to the wider hetero population. So what would you achieve by this except to unleash a deadly virus which could ultimately infect your own friends and family, like the Black Death? If you stop to analyse the theory it just doesn't hold up or make any sense either logically or ideologically.

Another conspiracy theories doing the rounds is that the AIDS virus was engineered in an American lab and targeted at Asian and African ethnic groups. This rumour was actually started by the KGB who came clean after the collapse of the Soviet Union, and admitted placing an article in an Indian newspaper by an "anonymous" journalist (knowing full well it would eventually filter through to the West and percolate into the public consciousness) As a classic exercise in disinformation and deliberate anti-American propaganda, the motive was to sow distrust amongst the American people against its own government and thereby demoralise the population. This is standard psychological warfare, and nothing new. In *The Mirage Men* the author Mark Pilkington, cites various disinformation programs associated with UFO flaps, dating as far back as the 50s. Serious-minded UFO researchers suspected stagecraft behind many of the reported contactee encounters and alien abductions i.e. helicopters were modified to look like UFOs with flashing coloured lights and rotating dome etc. all inspired by pulp science fiction. At the height of the Cold War with paranoia running high about the threat of a Russian nuclear strike, these covert counter-intelligence tactics constituted part of experimental psychological warfare. The U.S. air force actually *wanted* the Soviets to believe they had captured alien spacecraft and were therefore in the possession of advanced propulsion technology. Maintaining tight security over classified projects was crucial, and with UFO investigators threatening to expose what they were up to and thereby playing into enemy hands, something had to be done. So they started to actively encourage the growing public belief in extraterrestrial visitors as it provided a useful cover for their own activities (night-time test flights of advanced reconnaissance aircraft)

This is not to say that some of the deceptions deployed against genuine UFO researchers were not morally questionable, even downright despicable. One poor guy was virtually driven insane by the "special effects" team, who were beaming signals into his house (he intercepted the signals and thought they were coming from alien spaceships) They also went to great lengths to convince him that there was a subterranean alien base under a mountain in New Mexico (even hauling up strange machinery, and dispatching air force personnel etc. to make it look like a hive of activity) All intended to distract public attention away from genuine top secret research and development projects. By these means they were able to discredit the UFO community, by using its principal spokesmen as channels through which to filter disinformation. But it just goes to show how easy it is to get sucked into a paranoid feedback loop of your own making. Just WHAT is the U.S. military DOING with all these underground facilities – building concentration camps to contain the population, developing prototype flying saucers, breeding hybrid creatures which are part alien part human - who the hell knows? Yes, there is a lot of top-secret research going on, as there is in most developed countries. Big deal. Try not to worry overmuch about things over which you have no control. My feeling is that you should leave conspiracy theories to the theorists: it is the worst possible thing to be reading for anyone with paranoid tendencies since it only serves to fuel your paranoia.

But to return to the thorny subject of Monica: it seems I am unable to express an honest opinion about your friend without getting your hackles up, so will confine myself to observations about alleged events in her previous life. The first incident seems to have concerned Monica and someone called Claudine who were involved in a house fire 3 years ago (?), and the second incident concerns an administrative worker you once knew in Boston years ago, and who was offered free accommodation because of the nature of her work at MIT, which she invited you to share with her and you turned down. An offer of a rent-free house is perceived by you as a covert surveillance opportunity to facilitate mind control techniques. If the first incident actually took place it could have just been an unfortunate accident (what caused the fire?) whilst if the second incident involving you was also a "front" (as opposed to an innocent offer of accommodation to a friend) then you narrowly escaped being used as an involuntary guinea pig. I agree it would be easier to conduct such experiments within the confined space of a "Big Brother" type house, which had been purposely rigged with surveillance equipment the tenants were unaware of.

Neither of us will never really know the truth about Monica, but given your own character and predisposition then the association between the two of you is a recipe for disaster: she is the very last kind of person you need to hook up with. You both have certain things in common, including pronounced schizophrenic tendencies and paranoia, which have been exacerbated by homelessness, social isolation, destitution etc. Please let me emphasise this is NOT a judgement (I am in no position to make such judgements) it is merely an observation with which you would have to agree if you are being reasonable. You appear to have been increasingly drawn into M's chaotic and mad inner world: a manipulative FBI cousin who purportedly hypnotised her in order to hijack her inheritance, the alleged murder of a Haitian immigrant who attempted to rape her, with M being "on the run" and so it goes on. Jesus wept. How much of this is FACT and how much the delusions of a very sick woman? She also claims a crime was committed for the sake of fraudulently appropriating a valuable property she owned, the "362,000 dollar duplex" now supposedly worth a million. It is in

72

fact very difficult to steal a property (as opposed to a cash inheritance) due to the paper trail and legal complications involving title deeds, land registration etc. so I'm afraid I can't give this story much credence.

Also, has it occurred to you that the U.S. government has better things to do than spy on two homeless women who pose no threat whatsoever to national security? I very much doubt the FBI or CIA has any interest whatsoever in either of you. Why on earth should they? You go on to speculate: *"So at what point is it schizophrenia...It's true M can exaggerate or lie, but it's clear a lot of it isn't a lie, and there is certainly a lot of witchcraft going on in this region"* I think you may have answered your own question in that it is far more likely to be schizophrenia or the projections of a disordered mind than "witchcraft." On the subject of mental illness I agree with you when you say: *"The mental illness industry is a MULTI-BILLION DOLLAR FAILURE..."* Well, you're absolutely right about that, and the closure of so many psychiatric institutions was a massive mistake. Finally, do not believe everything you read: there is a huge industry out there churning out conspiracy theories by the hour because the more bizarre the story the more books they sell to a gullible reading public. My advice is to STOP reading this stuff and instead concentrate your energies on extricating yourself from your homeless situation.

Love,

Leigh

**From: Rustlibraryvend@loudoun.gov**
**To: Leigh Ryder**
**Attachment: Scanned from a Xerox Multifunction Device**

There is emerging evidence that there are covert links between occult lodges and Western intelligence agencies. They own some occult force on earth, which has been the backdrop to my life, using me and others as pawns in that war, this area being on the doorstep of the CIA. I see it as a cabal of mainly new rich with totalitarian plans for strict mind control and a sexist class hierarchy whereby a tiny minority rule - very much wealthy elite versus commoner, male versus female. What gets me is the religious conservative or fundamentalist, and in fact they're the sleazy ones. The church is there like an invisible army with its weapons pointing at you if you aren't a believer…all those women worshipping on their knees making out to the Jesus impersonators, the master pimps and puppeteers (makes a man feel real comfortable) and it's sad the way they keep reiterating "Oh the Lord's going to take care of things" Really? The plan is to increase the use of religious indoctrination as a control tool (anyone would think it was still 1713) They're a bunch of bigots that cpink categories have to contend with daily, in attempting to ward off attacks which are emotive and not based on reason, and supported as much by women as men. For example when the recent female presidential candidate ran for office it was discovered that female religious types were very much a reason why she didn't get elected, which stemmed from a belief that "God" instructs that women aren't supposed to lead. Of course not everyone can be a prime minister or president but then again there are a lot of people who don't deserve the status or success bracket they're in when a minority are kept on a tight leash. Something watches the underlings with potential, like vampires feeding on them or like in those fairy tales where horses clad in black chain mail are let loose on them, watching every move they make….then wires the inspiration they get from them, maybe for a movie, a new science theory or political manifesto.

This subject is tricky. To go to the establishment is to be called insane and who would want to be taken care of according to their codes, since the memory of "One Flew Over The Cuckoos Nest" is all too vivid. It's about reining in the people and there never was any democracy. They can't bear any criticism...it's sad how driven they are by ego. They're heavily into civil and human rights abuses. It's arguable that the stepped-up national security quest in the wake of the Islamic terrorist threat was itself a front for covert mind control, with its attendant preoccupation with privacy issues. The national security language "database mining", "sleeper cells" might have been metaphors to cover up mind invasive technology, like a secret coded language by which to describe the actual state of affairs. Just like the Prism project and its new-found powers of public library database surveillance. And yet what are the homeless? They are people that spend endless days, even years, in libraries for cold shelter purposes. But it's sinister because of mounting evidence for an imminent state of psychic dictatorship...and since it cannot be confronted or verbalized this prohibits the capability for most to consciously deal with this information. Probably no-one is private today esp. if this kind of technology exists, and it matters for people who are seemingly more free in the West, if they're not aware of how etheric surveillance might be being used against them.

Ultimately it could be argued to go ahead with the covert plans in the interests of national security, but when they keep messing with people's heads this is a different thing, whereby one side fights with something physical the other side with something non-physical. The disreputable CIA project known as MKULTRA, which involved LSD experiments in the 70s, showed that drugs often magnify pre-existing emotional states. The major insight for young and unsuspecting users here would be not to take any drugs if they are depressed or in a bad mood. It's believed that LSD works similarly to serotonin, a neurotransmitter responsible for regulating moods and sensory perception. During REM sleep the serotonin system is switched off so that "Chaos reigns, thoughts run wild, vivid fantasies and nightmares emerge" - the way imagery in a Salvador Dali painting unfolds in a surreal way, creating the sensation of the archetypal trip. Drugs like LSD can suppress (or stimulate) the serotonin system and can therefore activate the brain's dream mode while still awake. But if altered dream states are analogous to out of body states these states could be used for ether weaponry wielding ... in this sense like viruses attacking the weakened immune system of a target who is emotionally insecure or mentally unstable, and who is more easily preyed on by parapsychological forces. In application to the homeless it would mean that the trip would be bad and make a bad situation far worse.

To say nothing of mental and physical illness through poverty, much of which is being set up, like crime. America's attempt now to help the homeless, even if they could get cooperation from home-owners, isn't going to work unless they address the need for separatist communities, because more and more people from ALL walks of life are ending up repossessed, bankrupt, impoverished and going insane. And while the goal is they shouldn't be poor the solution is psychological, and different types need separate living spaces. Women tend to get psychically harassed right after their parents or guardians pass away when they try and make it on their own. They're either manoeuvred into a state of isolation and of having to live alone, or surrounded by men who prey on them. I'm saying they need differentiation and separation from one another, some need wilderness settings and the U.S. could do this for its people. An example is the "Break Wild Horses" program in Colorado where a self-sufficient living venture is promoted for violent offenders as a substitute for incarceration. From which it can be deduced that violent offenders and criminals get better treatment than the homeless or mentally ill. The point though is that something desperately needs to be done... and that the U.S. is spiralling into a dictatorship due to problems that have been left and neglected, like bad building maintenance that now warrants a radical overhaul.

It matters how a person's self identity is associated with the kind of language used to describe them, for example the linking of poverty with moral degradation (Roman definition of class distinctions between the *honestiores* versus the *humiliores* or plebs) As just one more humiliation they are linking homelessness with mental impairment and with alcohol and drug abuse, and this is being done to character assassinate them. Who knows what twisted logic is being used to justify these covert agendas: the plan to force women who don't want marriage into impoverishment, together with the plan to widen the poverty gap and to recriminate non-religious types. Meanwhile they don't plan to LET UP on procreation, until they reach 9 billion. For example, Malthus's theory of exponential population growth is mainly relevant to the last two hundred years. Considering there were hardly any people before 1850 the implications just for survival are huge. Besides the political facts speak for themselves …that "growbagism" has been used to impose world order. Perhaps the plan should be called Spermgate, which is to keep the majority of people poor and illiterate worldwide in a global gang up. It seems to be a deliberate agenda to keep people impoverished so their lives can be valued cheaply, to make them become dispensable, so we don't have to consider their human rights: if they bug us we can get rid of them knowing there will always be millions more cropping up in their place that we can control. They no longer have a problem because they don't allow one.

This would explain the ongoing persecution of gays as they choose not to procreate, and choose quality lifestyles over disposable throwaway consumer lifestyles…the heightened scapegoating of singles vs the family orientation types. This goes on not just with alternatives or cpink categories, but also with people who are attempting to challenge the system. They're all such a bunch of clones, the ordinaries and the elites who rule them. But nowhere more than in the U.S. with its burgeoning exponential population growth. Meanwhile loads of formerly affluent middle-class are being economically demoted and faced with religious indoctrination through church-funded services to the poor, the category they now find themselves in. All tied in with the "New Project for the American Century", there are plans disclosed through foia (freedom of information act) for the economic demotion of over 50% of the current educated middle-class in the developed sectors down to the sublevel of homeless or impoverished categories, so they're as powerless as Chinese peasants and have to beg the government for handouts in order to survive. This is how a totalitarian system targets its victims: a person with different political views is punished by being consigned to street-level destitution, and the wider population is made aware that they have to avoid falling into the welfare beneficiary bracket at all costs, so the system finally gets its slave worker force. Not to mention the insights by feminists that procreation is not in woman's long-term interests, because she carries the burden of a mismanaged result in terms of compromise of quality of life, the development of her higher will etc.

Mind control is being used as a weapon, as in the recent house repossession crisis. For example the "Lord" thing is a big stumbling block as far as I can see. In the last fiscal credit crunch, thirty percent of the repossessed had been "lord inspired" - some heard voices encouraging them to buy a house even if they knew they couldn't afford it, like the instructions in a fraudulent will which they then carry out. It's possible to view the idealist as little red riding hood against the aggressor, the wolf, who is masquerading as the "Lord." But religion is definitely the opiate of the people, as Marx observed, and its interpretation has been hijacked in a way that is chauvinist and phoney like "The poor will inherit the earth" when it's a rich man's tool. The poor are not sacrosanct, they will not "inherit the earth", there is no glory in humility. Unbridled belief in God just reveals a poverty of science.

People tried to say my homelessness was the "will of God" when I was trying to point out it was a political injustice, that it was not inevitable. More cynically, there is quite a bit of evidence that the U.S. government is promoting religious indoctrination, as a smokescreen for economic manipulation. Is this an example of government acting in unison with occult actions, to make people destitute using economic routes? If so this is corrupt as anything because an actual genocide would be kinder than a slow kill in terms of deteriorating quality of life.

The authorities are more at war with their own citizenry than with any external enemy or marauding armies, and people need to watch their backs, and protect their inner spaces. The only way to access privacy, apart from a family inheritance or monetary compensation is through earning power, and if earning an income is withheld from people who have no choice but to be welfare recipients (so that nothing is one's own) then there is no right to privacy. The U.S. does have some sort of mafia working at the heart of its systems that in no way represents most of the people. In fact, aren't the few lawmakers who try and tackle something with honesty framed with some seedy sexual accusation or media scam, or death threatened? A whole host of examples too many to mention…mainly sackings and firings, all pointing to the mafia eventually. It's why the people are pretty apathetic, because they're scared it might happen to them. The current covert agenda is like a man driving a vehicle full of people over a cliff edge where they are forced to accept lower pay, liquidation of assets (house repossessions) and reduced living standards in the understanding that most will be maimed. What are all those jails that stand unoccupied for, if not to be filled with the demonstrators of the "Occupy Movement", 90% of whom were graduates and a betrayed middleclass intelligentsia ...the tip of a wave that either gets the vehicle on to a better path or heading down a worse one. A counter tactic would imply wresting the wheels from the driver, redirecting the occupants into early retirement and a revised way of living with nothing more than what they can carry on their back. Something radical does need to happen, and it would probably have to be covert in order to counteract current covert actions, but it could differ in means and intent.

A minority may be questioning what they're here on this planet FOR, and are seeing the obvious need for a radical readjustment involving a "live and let live" ethos approach to the living world, a simplification of the application of technology in a wider context of valuing the non-material. A different way of living can easily be envisioned, namely through radical reductions in population numbers, a revised sexuality and theory of abstinence, a non-anthropomorphic paradigm, a screening out of elm (electromagnetic) pollution, a confrontation with the subconscious and more honesty. The standards of success would be measured in terms of less materialism, and less compromise of quality of life for years to come. To live with far less needn't be seen as poverty, just as consumerism needn't be seen as a measure of prosperity. For example it's not inconceivable that a nomadic trailer/mobile home orientated lifestyle for residents in hurricane zones could be applied globally, enabling a person to move around. Such are the poverty projections that at current rates they won't be able to even afford a trailer. The case is there for a potential challenge and overhaul, like the overhaul of a bully in a playground. People ask stupid questions when the only question that needs to be asked is how to step around cataclysmic weather zones, how to live with less in paradigms where materialism is increasingly a burden, to live with better quality of life without the parental baby code for most of the time. People have children for very suspect reasons, the major one being consolidation of ego. But a minority with higher aspirations are tired of bearing the cross of the knowledge of there being a different way, of being a pawn in a system and a war that isn't theirs.
.

If the world is globally interconnected then a minority in the so-called "free West" now have to speak to the world, and if the world can't change then a minority have to shift over (equals "getting out") And the elites can keep their wealth, because the alternatives don't want what they've got. The benefits system in America was completely rigged to reward married or unmarried mothers. It still is, only now they're incriminating single mothers on claim applications, with a view to encouraging them to get married and remain "stable." Instead they should be encouraging them to remain single and follow a vocation. For instance, they paid impoverished women benefits they would otherwise have been denied to "lie on their backs and churn out babies" (as one black feminist put it) The Democrats were just as non-progressive as the Republicans, a black presidential Democrat candidate describing these unwed ethnic female beneficiaries as "mother madonnas." When one considers the argument for biosphere conservation then surely the government should have been positively discriminating in favour of the non-procreators? This country doesn't do people justice on individualism, meanwhile the covert agenda unravels and can be interpreted as extremely anti-women. American women DESERVE a lot better, however the writer doesn't feel they can do it on their own and it will need the support of women in Western Europe, if it occurs at all. Women are currently in a state of dormant antagonism in terms of being pitted against each other: the non-married single and non-procreator versus the wife, the mother, the whore etc. The catalyst for change would have to come mainly from women... they can either fail or win. If they win they would make radical lifestyle changes, whilst retaining control of militaries for continued border defence and promotion of human rights abroad. But women are currently controlled, and scheduled to be more controlled.

The new project for the American people leaves something to be desired in terms of privacy, autonomy, individuality... but if the poor are the rodents and the chimps then what are the wealthy? For most of the rest of the world outside the developed sectors, the simplest routes that could serve as a solution are more self-willed deaths (euthanasia), voluntary sterilizations, abstinence, and a boycott on pregnancies. The big problem is the one man has with his lower anatomy and his incapacity for abstinence, like a drug addict needing a "fix" that he can't get enough of. Though this may well be cultural propaganda: if you give a man a drink he gets drunk, the conclusion being that it's not inevitable he needs a drink. In context of the recent stats that 75% of women fake orgasms, one can see she doesn't really need it, that she's coerced psychologically into alliances where men call the shots. And she needs to be free enough to say it and those women who don't agree have no right to impose their dependency on the others. And men need to wake up to the political implications of a policy of "growbagism for empire" – to the various ways in which his semen got yoked up to control tools. Religion seems to be the rallying point around which the mainstream crowd gather - it directs and coordinates the compulsion to reproduce. The discovery of underground tunnels to brothels that historically serviced monasteries, and the fact that the church very much supports prostitution but blocks any attempt at debate on the subject of sexuality and laces it with propaganda to do with immorality associations. The church is in league with the war machines and the procreation machines, and would have suppressed any kind of information in terms of a potential "fix" for male sexuality, which might have created a more intelligent approach and might have paid off.

One idea angled mainly at men is some kind of collective spa/sauna with private cubicles for self-execution where that impulse is discharged, with a case for male homosexuals and the survival of civilization, in acknowledgment that there are now far too many people on this planet consuming far too much. Who knows what could have been gained? All that unwanted life and wrung out emotionalism. ... people on a rodent level consumed by a rodent sized habit. A recent UN publication disclosed the fact that prostitution contributes 8% of China's GNP, 4% of the Netherlands, 6% of Thailand's etc. in paradigms where some are trying to argue that it is productive economically. The indirect set ups are all too crass and obvious, alongside the over-flogged promotion of sexuality. No, there is something faulty about the way the law-makers think, that certain aspects of society are considered inevitable: that any woman should want to have babies, that kids and young women fall into prostitution, as if no other option existed. And now their attempt at linking prostitution to economic prosperity is the final palliative to the woman-hater. Profit aside, an emotive reason underlies prostitution syndicates, that reason being sexist. The exploitation of women is huge esp. in third world and LDC (less developed countries) These women have no choice and if they try to get away are "dealt with" in fifty different ways. For example, responsible outside forces could have done more for women like the "mothers of the Plaza de Mateo" in Argentina who still campaign for the right to know what happened to their missing daughters. And when women try they are often thwarted through prostitution syndicates that are connected to Mafiosi. In the West man pretends to be more "concerned" in a hypocritical cowardly way, mainly concerned that he doesn't have to see what happens to her if she doesn't put her lipstick on. Then he sets up a system of violence so someone else does violence on her, while he files his nails and reclines back into complacency status. Yes, democratic man in the developed world champions the lady, when all men knew at heart she was trying like the devil to get away from him.

But the real antagonism might be coming from the invisible realms, in terms of a double or thought form called a *tulpa* (as in Tibetan esoteric mysticism) which is apparently projected as an intense energy field which can haunt a person like a shadow, and be self destructive. There seems to be a massive "witch hunt" going on, and to get down to the nitty gritties, directed against who those are single or in some way alternative. An example is two gay men in Africa forced to get wives, otherwise threatened with fifteen years of forced labour. Certain minorities are being persecuted for the failures of the majority, who have a low or compromised quality of life but are encouraged to scapegoat those with a higher awareness (as being immoral, mentally impaired, not to be trusted, as societal de-stabilisers etc.) whilst many sociologists have openly admitted that the current economic paradigms of exponential population growth, heavy industry and over-consumption is for the most part irrational, irresponsible and destructive. The extremes could possibly be reconciled through more separatist regions (family vs childless, women vs men etc) just as one could argue the traditionalists are the real extremists and unbalanced ones, for example the incidence of child incest in the traditionalist heterosexual alliances. Assaults on girls not even nine years old goes on in Africa, which is endorsed by married couples.

To go back to the covert agenda, it's possible to see that affluence is swapping hands, and that therefore the planners are coming out of somewhere like the Levant, the Middle East, north Africa…and that male monotheisms are featuring hugely as a control tool, that these values are being promoted for the future. That not only are the poor the losers but also those who once had affluence (a falling middleclass), helping to explain how these developments are not just anti-female but can be seen as something essentially racist. These and other obvious economic actions can help shed light on why so many white people are falling into unemployment, destitution, ill health and lack of housing. There seems to be an attempt to equate the term "white trash" to an increasing number of whites, in a country that failed to provide protection against poverty, which has now reached new and nauseous heights. It's not difficult to see the signature of malice projected by third world males if they are aspiring to Western values: get rich, dress Western etc. It's noticeable that the covert planners value whiter over darker because of the association of solar with male, female with dark or lunar, in what can be seen as a robber baron elite with a whole lot of mixed racials as underlings. It's been observed that the newly empowered make themselves "beautiful", "courageous", "intelligent" etc. whilst making their subjects lesser people, just as the Huns went into battle naked, brandishing jewellery to highlight their comparative fairness. Maybe it's a physical thing. Close proximity might be a reason for race antagonism, and may be related to body mass and muscle. For example an African man might have more pronounced presence in proximity to a white or Chinese person. This might be the root cause - later embellished with value systems and race bigotry - but originally was just to do with physical differences, which were not taken into consideration in a mixed race society: the forced integration of starkly different types and the impact that would have on the unconscious, working up through the conscious mind.

There needs to be far less people, period, and a differentiation of racial types. The West might be at a point where they are overstepping some boundary to do with territory and not enough space, and that this is being used to throw dirt at an entire culture or race. An attack by the non-Nordic racial groups includes plans for over-procreation, overcrowding, increased immigration, criminality etc. It represents the most unbelievable attack on quality of life and the value of individual life. However, so does the developed world's technology and science applications. They both seem to run neck and neck in terms of which is worse and which is better. White man seems incapable of rising to a higher awareness, lost in an obsession with mechanics and muscles, and is not the black man really his master? Big physicality is another one of their obsessions, and darker pigmentation groups tend to be bigger and stronger, with greater height and bigger bones: the darker to replace the whiter in new paradigms of bigger as better. White man fools himself he set things up but seems very "puppeted" by the other races, thinks he's in control but actually isn't. But perhaps they are in complete harmony with each other and not antagonistic at all, with a pan-global syndicate or brotherhood (African/Arabic/Asian/Aryan) pulling the strings? Is there something that could act as a safety valve to release the pressure for ongoing racially motivated power competitions, a monkey wrench that can be thrown into these endless repeats from history?

With money affluence being the new flagship of civilization, the whites do look bad on their heaps of mounting trash whereas the poor in the third world look more dignified, and their poverty less polluting. Bin Laden in reverse sounds like "unladen your bins" Three days before the twin towers came down, the writer happened to be walking through the Bronx on her way up north and into Vermont. She noticed garbage flowing out all over the pavement sweltering in the late Indian summer heat, with none in bordering Brooklyn and White Plains, and had cause to reflect on social injustice in terms of neglected civic services in poorer areas. Then the towers came down – like the imprint of something sarcastic "the real issue is you and your garbage…your greed…your endless toilet visitations.." All the more reason to let up on pollution, since all it's doing is affecting quality of life. No, it's very much to do with over-consumerism. And those who deny having a problem are the ones who most have one... slightly mentally impaired happy consort and hubby dearest who reckon they don't have a problem. The weariness of these continual thought processes … the weariness of having to witness its results or the one-sidedness in it. The developed sectors are the ones with more military capacity, with the technology to effect change, while not abandoning a strong defence capability. But against that there is the probability that the ldc and third world countries would try and block anything the developed world might try to do, in their hysteria and hatred of the West. And like a parasite clinging to its host, they're obsessed with trying to reverse the whole thing, with their incapacity to do anything other than what they do on their procreation and prostitution agendas, which is to make life miserable for the vulnerable and innocent.

The Western world is imperfect but the writer feels that the Islamic world certainly doesn't have the answer. Extreme forms of Islam just want women silenced and under their thumbs, they're running in fear from the power women wield in the Western democracies. Women are major targets, based on what can be described as a gender-based global campaign against them and what they stand for. And any woman who's travelled abroad notices it in men of other countries, that they completely scorn Western culture. A global male force who wake up in the morning and hang the "cross of their grievances" on the West, the white races, females... it's like a thundercloud growing, building up into a storm that will hurtle them all into extinction. The obsession with the economy and jobs isn't the whole story, because they could easily have created jobs for the poor and homeless, instead of which they are forced into extreme circumstances. The probability is that energy, oil and nuclear power, are not the overall issues either, but economic demotion and increased mental impairment, eventually leading to fragile psyches. Whilst implying "it's too late for policy reversals" some hidden authority is promoting increased oil usage, like force-feeding someone who's trying to watch their diet when it's not too late to make adjustments. After which point they've binged and developed a dependency, and the hidden planners then have a psychological edge over the binger. It is disgusting how all this has been handled, just as the social sciences are highlighting how materialism and high consumerism are actually a burden and not an opportunity. America is full of people who think they're "free" or "enlightened" when they aren't, just as women have been fed a lot of delusions that they're "empowered" The so-called "free love" paradigms were a gimmick, like the projection of women in horrible pornographic ways as more and more fall into the difficult to defend category. It's as though they're setting up the Western female to be really immoral, which is then interpreted as a justification for endorsing very traditionalist views of women and their roles.

This country is full of really upset people, who are dangerously on edge. The mafia-led government have set up so much criminality, and the people are being set up for totalitarian mind control and then they'll really know what rape is. It's mainly men who promote religion, in other words they are promoting violence by an indirect subtle route, and women lap it up, believing it's for their own protection. They are being made to feel insecure then they go running to men. And you've got women who create their own hardships and glory in their suffering (go to banana, suck it on your knees) Most women are mind-controlled, whilst not being able to admit to their subservient relationship to the male power systems, scared of any kind of honesty. Let's just settle it up this way: could you ladies please keep your husbands on a tighter leash. And what's been going on is not in American white man's interest. He's basically being driven into a corner, in terms of an increased loss of control and having any kind of future to inherit, by a pan-global syndicate who may have conscious knowledge of a suppressed science. Occult skills might be predominant amongst the darker races, who have kept it as a weapon to be wielded like the monopoly a tribal clan holds in a region, and are a force to be reckoned with. A way to counter this would be not to "prove" it for scientific or emotive reasons, but to challenge it instead by the promotion of separate imageries, symbols of empowerment in terms of adjusted female paradigms, better quality of life and individualism.

It's time now to see life for what it is… mainly warfare on civilians taking a number of forms: famine, viral drops, female infanticide, economic demotions, shootings, house fires, bombings etc. Intelligence tactics abound like chemical ingestants that affect the metabolic rate and can cause obesity, identity thefts and replacement look-alikes, electrical grid knock-outs (they are able to knock out the power in someone's house) infrastructure non-maintenance, but also occult means like clairvoyance and using the unconscious energies of the living through disembodied energy interference and enforced bioelectricals. Men are usually too pin-holed to do anything about it, meaning essentially very drugged and controlled. The writer feels it's a covert agenda, morphing as a preoccupation with physicality and race as well as lifestyle choices on the planet. There is probably a world control plan with roots that go back centuries, and it stinks of the occult. A minority have really gotten it …what's going on, and they are NOT the 18-year-olds coming up but are now in their 50s and above (people born between these years have been impacted the most) As the current aging population passes away, the up and coming generation are by comparison mind-controlled zombies. THEY'RE INFERIOR.

The point might need to be addressed that perhaps democracy doesn't work, but that power and privilege do work and something has to take power, like having to take the wheel out of a bad driver's hand. For example ethnic and southern med types (Latinos and Hispanics) are coming into affluence and political power, whereas white women have "had it good" for hardly any time at all. One can almost see this today in terms of what it is very much an "issue for issue" attempt at revenge on the whites in return for perceived colonial abuses: black magic attacks angled at northerners seeking sunshine regions... Let's face it, the majority who live in the southern hemisphere are the most unbelievable chauvinists ....the bigotry going on in their own backyard is something to behold. They're saying "we've got sunshine you don't" and that they own their wives. They tend to be cowards and have recourse to bombing to solve problems....well you can keep the southern hemisphere and the banana that grows like a weed on it. It's actually not even possible for people in the developed world to safely take vacations in these southern sunny areas without being robbed or killed. There is a covert plan to use fairly radical means to change society while hanging onto traditional routes of religious indoctrination, and it's an appalling agenda for the women's movement or for gay males. It's a theory of the writer that the planners have a resentment of white women, that the future plans are basically a "rape standard" of institutionalised prostitution where the wife is owned like a piece of furniture. Unless the Western developed sector can rise to the challenge, it may signify the complete dominance of the white race, imminently, by other races. It's likely there will be a military dictatorship shortly and a fast track route to economic demotion through mass redundancies or firings. There have been errors but they didn't start with modernity or with the white race: it's like gunshot when someone innocent enters the scene the instigator hightails it, and the people who've been shot at get out their guns and start shouting wildly. People are desperate, they've been harmed, and now they're frantically trying to harm anything in view and calling it guilty...colonialism, imperialism. Isn't there something perverse going on here?

On the subject of contemporary injustice the U.S. lawmakers and their secret society mentors are the real criminals. They live by the code of violence and why can't they fuck off out of the uniform. Anything in a uniform anywhere worldwide has a horrible record on sexual assaults. As the uniformed trades are fond of saying "if you can cover it up it never happened" and well-dressed women who squeal delightedly "Ooh but they do such an honourable job" He's the most unbelievable thug alive, borne out by the number of vehicles and cops who turn up for "back up" when the majority of calls are either misperceptions or not serious. As for women in uniform I wouldn't trust them any more than men with those weapons...they're probably just as culpable when they get power. I don't like most people, and I don't ally with the poor either. Just one jail experience did that, really woke the writer up to human nature, which is a "dog eat dog" nature. A low level commoner will try and victimise others beneath them. The fact of the matter is the aforementioned commoners would commit the same crimes the wealthy groups are being accused of if they could, only they don't have the power. Things you learn. So don't ask someone like me to cry crocodile tears for Marxism or the blue-collar male when they took it out on women just as much as the super elite crowd. I have no pity for any of them. They presented a false gimmick of opportunity and independence whilst yoking her up to womb servitude. Even erudite women were educated to serve as mental collaborators in his knowledge industry, which consolidated the apparent intelligence of his systems. The break with absolutists was sound but then men spiralled into a kind of resurrection of their own ego, so women need to take that into consideration and understand that some absolutist resurgence involving religion and toeing the line is going to come into it.

**From: Leigh Ryder**
**To: Patrick, Alexandra, Luke, Adam**

Dear Family,

I am forwarding this monster email, originally addressed to Cass in response to another lengthy attachment she sent me, but thought it might be of interest as it contains a great deal of shared family history, including the house where we spent our teenage years. Note that she frequently refers to herself as "the Writer" and to her friend Monica as "the Subject". Poor Cass, tortured by her conscience and sense of obligation towards this sad creature, who constantly uses emotional blackmail as a way of controlling her, such as threatening to "climb into a truck with a stranger" Very manipulative, though I suppose she is hardly to blame for her mental condition – given the circumstances under which they are both living.

Dear Cass,

I'm sorry to sound so sceptical all the time, but If I disagree with some of the things you assert you become enraged and keep sending me documents which are cited as evidence or "proof", but if I agree that some of this stuff may have occurred it then places me in the dubious moral position of colluding in and reinforcing some of your beliefs – which would be highly irresponsible of me, so I cannot really win whatever stance I take. Actually I DO believe in earth energy and that strong underlying geomagnetic forces can influence the pattern of human brain waves. Do you recall a camping holiday we took on Sark in the Channel Isles around 1991 when I was working in London? On one of our numerous walks across the island we came across a notorious spot known as "Witches Corner" and became hopeless disorientated. No matter which direction we took we could not seem to leave this spot and ended up right back where we started time after time.

After hours of trying - to no avail - to LEAVE the area we were both suddenly overcome with extreme drowsiness. The energy drained from me like a battery running down, and we both stumbled into the nearest field and fell into a deep sleep or trance lasting almost 2 hours. I rarely fall sleep during the middle of the day, and this makes me think we encountered a geomagnetic earth anomaly that affected us both and which may account for the legends surrounding this "enchanted" hotspot.

There are other natural sites where the converse has happened i.e. instead of being suddenly drained of energy I have been energised five-fold, enabling me to run up near-vertical mountainsides with no symptoms of fatigue. When I was 17 I booked a holiday in the Lake District with a schoolfriend immediately after our "A" level exams. We decided to tackle Helvellyn, the highest mountain in the district. After steadily climbing for a few hours F wanted to stop for a rest and I must have fallen asleep almost immediately. I then became aware of a priestly figure in black robes walking straight towards me (he bore an uncanny resemblance to the central figure in a famous Dutch renaissance painting by Jan van Eyck called *The Arnolfini Marriage*) I couldn't move but was trying to signal my alarm to F as I thought he was going to walk right over or through me. Instead he stopped a couple of inches from me and very slowly raised his right hand in benediction, which is why I have described his general aura as "priestly". He was either blessing me or the gesture was an attempt to ward off evil spirits. F said she had seen me wave my arm feebly in the air but hadn't taken much notice. A few minutes later I saw a group of 3 teenage girls stop to talk to F, and after they had disappeared I asked her what they had said. She said she had seen nobody and was adamant there was no-one else on the mountainside, but I appeared to be in a state of altered perception where I was still hallucinating even though I was wide awake. On our journey back down the mountain, I distinctly remember being charged with a strange energy and ran all the way down at breakneck speed. I should have been dropping with fatigue after a near-vertical climb of 8 hours, and I believe the underlying geophysical terrain was somehow channelling earth energy into my nervous system.

Back in the 80s when I was living in Bristol Luke and I were visiting Glastonbury and decided to take in the Chalice Well gardens. When we approached the sacred well we were unable to get too close because, annoyingly, a young woman was lying right across the entrance to the well. She had long dark hair with a headband encircling her forehead, and raised her head to look at me. She was wearing some kind of ankle-length gauzy dress and I naturally assumed she was one of those New Age hippie types who are always floating about Glastonbury. After we had left the gardens I muttered something to Luke about how selfish it was to block the well so no one else could get close. Luke looked confused and said "What girl?" Although she was less than five feet from us and directly in our line of sight *he had seen nothing.* I later discovered from a tourist leaflet that the Chalice Well has a female Guardian spirit. I'm wondering whether I had a vision of some kind of pagan priestess perhaps connected with an ancient matriarchal religion whose appointed role through the centuries is to guard the site from profane eyes: at any rate I appear to be able to hallucinate in broad daylight in certain circumstances and in certain places. It is completely involuntary, and in no way interferes with my normal mental functioning. It hasn't happened in years, so perhaps as I get older I am less open to such encounters.

Canterbury Cathedral is a gigantic lodestone and has been for centuries, and St. Augustine's road is situated not far from the Abbey (it may even have been formerly owned by the Abbey as part of its extensive grounds) Anywhere situated close to hallowed church ground is impregnated with the residual energy of religious orders of monks and nuns, who tend to live in the spirit world more than they do in the material world and are intensely focussed on the afterlife. Moreover our house was situated *literally within a few hundred yards* of the celebrated Pilgrims Way, which has been trodden by countless pilgrims over the centuries. Many of them would have been fasting, meditating, and praying - all of which serve to increase and focus spiritual energy. What effect did this particular location have upon impressionable teenage minds, and could it have contributed to the paranormal occurrences that took place in the house? Forgive me for saying this, but you were a very disturbed teenager - even then prone to mood swings and violent outbursts. I now think that you were extremely vulnerable and susceptible to occult influences. By this time, Patrick was living on the university campus, but frequently came home. He was often tripping out on LSD and magic mushrooms, and suffered several drug-induced psychotic episodes.All the occult literature emphasises that people under the influence of drugs or alcohol are dangerously susceptible to spirit possession, because their normal psychic defences are in a weakened state and the barriers are down. Certain low-level malevolent spirits are drawn to drug addicts and alcoholics, as they are to conflicted or angry personalities, since they feed off the negative emotional energy generated. Either at this time or somewhat later I heard you were experimenting with ouija boards (which have subsequently been banned due to the high incidence of serious mental illness in young adults who have participated in séances) though they used to be sold in toyshops back in the 60s!)

At this particular point in time (the 70s) the energy forces were concentrated strongly on three members of the family: myself, you, and Patrick. I was the first to be targeted, starting at the age of 15. The pivotal experiences worth mentioning are recounted below. One night after everyone had retired and was fast asleep I went down to the kitchen to get a drink, and on my way upstairs I passed a bulky black shadow about 6 feet in height, which I sensed to be definitely male. Naturally I assumed it was Daddy, and continued upstairs to the top floor. It then occurred to me that it was odd that he had said nothing to acknowledge my presence, and the more I thought about it the more I became convinced there was an intruder in the house (Daddy was snoring loudly so it obviously could not have been him on the stairs) I was reluctant to wake our parents but felt I had no option so I crept back downstairs and woke them both. We checked the entire house. There was nobody there and no way anyone could have entered through a locked window or door without leaving some trace. To this day I have no explanation of what I saw and felt, but I was wide-awake and it was not my imagination. I don't need to remind you about the terrifying night when a horned figure approached my bed, and I had to use every ounce of my willpower to force it to leave. At the time I was a student at Bristol, back home for Christmas, and was sleeping in the same first-floor bedroom as Adam, who was just a little kid. The latter woke with a tremendous scream at the exact point I was trying to fight off the entity.

I deliberately said nothing to anyone over breakfast because I wanted to see whether I was the only one experiencing such things. To my amazement, as soon as you appeared you launched into an account of being menaced in the night by some creature whose description tallied exactly with my own experience. We concluded we must have seen a "demon" (because of the hoofs and horns) but much later I came to realise that we may have seen an embodied archetype of an ancient pagan nature spirit such as a satyr, when my extensive reading of mythological texts disclosed the association between the "Devil" and the horned Greek god Pan. This entire episode could easily have been dismissed as a hypnagogic experience if it hadn't been for your account, which I heard from you *before you heard mine.* The fact that we both experienced the same thing makes it highly unlikely that this was a hallucination. Remember Adam was in the same room at the time, and claimed to have seen me levitate a few feet from the bed!! I think he was more freaked out by me than the entity. It troubles me to this day when I think that my attempts to "banish" the creature from the house only succeeded in sending it straight upstairs to my innocent younger sister, as it obviously found you an easier target. There was undoubtedly some kind of malevolent presence in the house that night which was sensed or witnessed by 3 of us.

A few years later after Patrick and I had both left home the entities went on to plague you with greater frequency, then Maddy, who claimed to have been molested by a male entity who attempted to get into bed with her. Adam was now sleeping at the top of the house where the paranormal activity was strongest (he referred to it as "the Force") and openly provoked and taunted it. Finally they zeroed in on our father, who was not only grieving for the loss of his wife of 40 years, but also under the influence of very strong mood-altering drugs (anti-depressants, sedatives, sleeping pills etc.) on which he had developed a dependency. He appeared to be very frightened by what he perceived as paranormal occurrences and would often call me into his bedroom, speaking in a low fearful whisper, in order to point out what was happening to him. His bedside slippers would be moved to the back of the wall underneath his bed - not in a haphazard way as if they had been casually kicked - but lined up neatly in a pair quite beyond his reach (I had to crawl underneath the bed to retrieve them for him) I concluded that the drugs were adversely affecting his mental state. However it did fleetingly cross my mind that you were behind some of the poltergeist phenomena, albeit subconsciously, since your disturbed state of mind made you a focal point for any energies swirling about. Unfortunately this manifested itself in violent confrontations where you would scream at him in his vulnerable weakened state, and he would back off in horror. I suppose I was appalled by your conduct, not realising that your behaviour was not within your conscious control. I do know that for most of the time - both preceding and following our mother's death - you were in a state of suppressed hysteria which threatened to erupt like a volcano at any moment, and that Daddy was actually frightened of you: your unpredictable and hostile outbursts left him bewildered and upset, and he was in no condition to cope with the increasingly volatile domestic setup.

I have felt it necessary to go into all this because I believe this is where it all started, at No. 33. If you had received the medical treatment you so clearly needed at this stage, things might have calmed down, the schizoid tendencies might have been kept at bay, and you may not have spent 18 years of your life as homeless. When you were younger you did experiment with "soft" drugs, and it has now been scientifically proven that the ingestion of cannabis can lead to full-blown schizophrenia and extensive brain damage. People who have taken LSD can still experience hallucinations and psychotic episodes years after they stopped taking the drug i.e. it remains latent in the human nervous system. Due to chronic sleep deprivation your serotonin levels are probably very low which will affect your normal brain functioning – hence the disordered thought processes - and this is obviously taking its toll on both of you. Therefore everything you imagine to be happening may not be happening at all, you are just very tired, stressed, and malnourished and appropriate treatment is available. All you have to do is ask for it. I am going to end by presenting you with the visual symbol of Canterbury cathedral to draw upon when you need to. Apart from being a magnet for positive energies it also functions as an enormous battery which those in need or trouble can draw upon for spiritual strength. The positive energies surrounding this cathedral are some of the most powerful and protective you will ever come across because it has been consecrated and "charged" throughout the ages with the thoughts and prayers of holy-minded individuals. Although evil deeds have taken place within its precincts – like Beckett's murder - the good energies far outweigh any bad lingering in the vicinity. The cathedral is the beating heart of Canterbury (the *Sacre Coeur* in Montmartre, Paris functions in a similar way in that it has always been a place of sanctuary and refuge for the citizens of Paris during times of turbulence)

Leigh

**From: Cass Ryder**
**To: Leigh Ryder**

These last few nights were FREEZING. Subject won't put on more layers in the wind, and intuitively understands the "contract" which means you get handed more cash if you're suffering, therefore the instinctive thing to do is not get too comfortable. Heartbreaking to see her cowering under a thin fleece blanket which only covered her head and upper torso (she can't carry a thicker one in her daypack) The bench they crash on is situated 2 parking lots away from the Shell station, which is an attack trap with the restroom positioned on the outside of the building. Subject and writer always stop drinking after 5pm but sometimes the subject needs to urinate in middle of the night due to enlarged fibroids that put pressure on the bladder. Both have athlete's foot and cannot afford to change into clean socks with showers and laundering facilities being rare, both have oedema (swollen ankles) through sitting up while asleep. The subject has been like this for 3 years, the writer now for 2 (before she met the subject she always camped out) She has a right to be in a continual foul mood but she's non-focused about who or what she's angling it at, probably just feeding back what people dish out to her. Her nervous breakdown is a reaction to what feels like a betrayal, a woman who believed in society and got handed a nightmare. Let's face it, all humans are neurotic once they lose their creature comforts. I have noted that people go to pieces when their daily schedule or material comforts are removed. Their minds break down. It does seem to reflect on one's upbringing and what one is used to though, and she has far more material needs than me.

The subject wears almost no layers and I've shivered an awful lot and I can't stand it. To get a lot warmer might be the only way I'm going to be able to stay awake all night, and I should stay awake otherwise there's no purpose in us being together considering the increasing friction between us. I guess the crux is I resent risking my health and life but with a foldable stool for my feet, a stick and can of mace I can be assured I am safeguarding my life, and hers. If I try and stay awake or am sitting up on a bench it's not good, and 17 years of discipline on this subject has instructed me in the wisdom of the path I took, even though it looks like a bad path. Because I've always gotten a tent and carried a backpack (I was basically nomad before I met her) but this way I'm not sleeping. And yes I've been assaulted but not to do with where I slept. These were both early morning day labour events and none of them were too serious. But when it happens you never forget it and you know you must never take your life into your hands or take your security lightly, like non-observance of your surroundings. There's almost nothing more important than health, and if you're trying to die you should be able to take life into your own hands and self-destruct. And even then one has to be careful how one does it.

The subject threatened the writer that if she didn't accompany her to the shelter she would sleep outside on a bench all night, because she could not adapt to a tent in the woods like the writer could. Cold aside, the major consideration was assault. So just as we'd vowed to remain together at least for a little while I had to cajole, prod her (like a donkey at a stream) to get her to budge onto the bus and go into the shelter each night. I escorted her half the time and the rest of the time I hit the underpass or woodlot and got a good night's sleep that way. Why can't I just leave? Because I'm haunted with her crying and screaming about these events that no-one else has witnessed except me, and I've seen her face as she's turned to me and screamed "You ****** don't leave me in this shithole" This was back in Reston, where the homeless were sleeping on the floor and look a sorry bunch with subzero temps that make it a 24 hour job to try and stay alive (the next door county Loudoun shelter is comparatively palatial with cots, and only six or twelve women at the most in a segregated room) April 1st was kick-out day. In New York it's a legal right to get at least four months of cold weather shelter, not so in VA.

The cold weather shelter is a killer, not opening until 9pm with a gruelling wait period of 14 hours of walking around in subzero temps, or loitering in coffee joints or the library. Neither the writer nor subject ate with the other shelter clients and would have to wait for them to eat, and therefore never got to bed before 10pm. These places are surrounded by cops, and are like detention centres. Neither feels comfortable going there. One young man who was kicked out froze to death a few years ago. Writer has had her own personal spats, as has the subject, with both clients and staff leading to mysterious loss of belongings (that were supposed to have been "safe" in lockers or offices) The hot water often breaks down, and it's come under new management who are more strict, and is dominated by men. They should have a separate room for drunks, which would save the cops having to show up if someone is violent. People are continually threatened with being thrown out, with a poster of Madam and Mister Evangelist on the wall as one enters: "You do not have a right to be here. This is a privilege" Why is shelter from the elements and the right to eat when hungry a "privilege"? They should be open by 7pm at the latest, with partitions between cot areas and a complaint channel against supervisors who make personal comments and don't keep to their duties, which should be outlined. It's situated miles out of town close to an airport and they are often unable to afford the bus fares to get there. They should be situated in town centres and clients should not be punished for being late due to buses, and they shouldn't allow "throwouts" in freezing temperatures.

Shelters should also be more segregated, instead of forced integration of women with men who want to prey on them, childless singles with mothers and families, and different races that don't get along and frankly hate each other's guts. The concept of separation of race is not new and doesn't need to be viewed as racism. There should be some sort of separation of types in society to lessen the aggravation that results from differences that cannot be sustained. Religion is another big issue as in believers versus non-believers, and family units versus single individuals. So many people from so many different backgrounds/cultures are expected to coexist closely, with etheric weaponry "stirring it." I clash with the local authorities in this area, mainly uniformed white males and after that the Hispanics and other ethnics who are the norm in these places. Homeless men are increasingly turning up on a subsidized megabus…whole hordes of them, mostly African. The race tensions are there, and the black man has every right to be mad, but where women are concerned he falls down and aren't they a bunch of failed rapists? What's in it for the writer, to try and understand the "black issue" when black men have now attacked the writer on 2 or 3 occasions? The "gold standard" of all men is physical strength and the black man is their mentor, as far as I can see. They seem to have a cosy relationship with black women in terms of setting them off like Rottweilers on white homeless women, who are then thrown out into the open (it's often just done for "hate the female" or prostitution reasons to get her going to some creep) Pretty sick, isn't it.

Let's stand back and look at those swollen legs, unlaundered clothes, and the mental anguish behind her eyes…yeah what does Uncle Sam do to keep getting this loyalty from her? Approximately 12 hours out of 24 is spent asleep (our clothing gets infused with carbon monoxide exhaust fumes, which induces sleepiness) and 8 hours out of 12 in a FOUL MOOD ranging from quasi-serious murderous intent to genuine rage. I've had to witness her punch herself in the face repeatedly and then act like nothing had happened... but this may just be one way in which she gets a twenty-dollar bill tomorrow. Then she dispassionately announced "You didn't see that" and was restored to normalcy, followed by really nice smiles, humour and a natural flair for mime that is mesmerising to watch. She's such a little actress with a crescent moon profile, high cheek bones, a kind of bobble on the end of her nose, and youthful complexion despite what trials have been imposed on her, cute tiny fists that flail around as she punches the air for emphasis … It's as though she's been planted on me as the personification of a toddler, but then most American women are "little girlied" and don't seem to fight it much. It's sad how cute she is sometimes and I'm not one who believes in "cutifying"…I try and stay away from the whole parent thing. She also might have an inheritance somewhere and while she's talked non-stop about it to me I've still been unable to get any clarification, so I don't think her lost income check of 50,000 dollars is anywhere on the horizon. Maybe if I get lost someone will extend a helping hand. An African woman was here for at least five years, mainly living out in the open, but I heard someone had offered her a room. She was always sitting up in MacDonald's at night but hasn't been around at all recently, and that's kind of creepy.

Both writer and subject are continually threatened with library throw-outs (for loitering or disorderly conduct) but in all honesty where are the homeless supposed to go? Where are they supposed to eat in 50 mile an hour winds? And one sees big grown men running to their cars with their collars turned up. Heaven forbid if the breeze hits their shoulder for one moment, or if .005 dollars is removed from their income they go hollering to congress and get a hearing. Meanwhile 2 million homeless are expected to live in woodlots or on pavements for endless years, or faced with substandard Oliver Twist social services "you dare ask us for something?" In fact we were given a permanent throw out from the Sterling library last week, which I thought was inappropriate. It went from a one-day ejection for loud talking to a sudden permanent police-enforced ban. It's noticeable no other ordinary weekday librarians were in the building as this was on a Sunday. The stipulations are no admittance, even into the car park, as though they're trying to stop us from speaking to any librarians. Admittedly she and I have been noisy or disrespectful in different ways, but they were very backhanded about it. I felt it should have been a temporary suspension. Personally I'm glad to get away from it but I did value the right to …oh well, the moral is don't write a book in a library but what else was I supposed to do? I can't just switch my brain off.

The program of federal helpto the homeless is called SOAR (equals SSI Outreach Access and Recovery Program) The banana has the trade label "Dole" over here, courtesy of a united fruit company, and "Dole" is also the name of British welfare payments. The innuendo encoded here is unmistakable and it gets a little seedy esp. in context of a bird (soar) and symbol of the male anatomy (banana) to crassly infer if women don't make an alliance with men they won't receive cash assistance. Another good reason why it's NOT TO BE TRUSTED. Britain and France have rejected the idea that a woman has to go to a man in order to survive, and the Brits have one of the most egalitarian systems in the West, in contrast with the system over here with only a freezing woodlot, a public plaza, or an overcrowded soup kitchen. It's a corrupt system that expects women to sleep out in the open, and to be threatened with being stabbed to death at night. Their support system is like half an umbrella in the rain, where women are forced to resonate with men, who pick up on their vulnerability. But to offload the mentally ill and the homeless like circus fools in the downtown areas while everyone else is having a good day? To leave them dangling in the community, while servicing illiterates and criminals? To force a woman out into a shopping plaza each night and to then wonder why she's a little anxious?

Although this is a fairly affluent area we don't solicit cash but we have to loiter… all homeless do because we have nowhere to go. We try and observe the law but are being judged emotively and in a sexist way. She reacts very negatively when this happens, esp. in the context of verbal abuse and the insecurity that that produces in her. Most people who were forced to sleep out in the open and were threatened with attack would go insane. Writer would have liked to have gotten psychic counselling for the subject, but it was never available and so writer goes with her intuition and her limited research. Couldn't this be tackled with attention to basic human physical needs? (privacy, health, warmth, safety) The enlarged fibroids growing in her cervix could probably be diminished through vitamin intake or dealt with by fibrovan or oestrogen progesterone rebalanced therapies (6 months supply = $200) Lots of women today are turning away from surgery or radiation therapies (one remedy is a needle inserted through the umbilical chord and some sort of radiation is focused on it…gross) but who could blame her for not wanting to go to a doctor. Doctors create illnesses. Subject possibly has an iron deficiency due to dissolution of fibroids and likely blood loss. Has mood swings caused by oestrogen deficiency but should reach equilibrium as fibroids dissolve naturally in postmenopausal stage, but it's still putting pressure on her bowels and bladder, making it hard for her to be able to keep walking long distances.

The writer COULD NOT have left her and STILL CANNOT but things are developing towards aggression… she's getting to be a liability. Probably better that our auras didn't overlap (the aura is an egg shaped envelope stretching as far as outstretched arms either side) This might be producing the kind of closeness that married couples experience. Read somewhere recently that ideally 8 feet between individuals is better. Last night she went off for at least an hour in the freezing cold yelling and cussing but of course came back, and then insisted I stay beside her on the bench. She laid out her plastic sheet and put her blanket over herself and we both went to sleep. But I heard a voice somewhere in the ether like a theatrical prompt from the side of a stage, or a drill sergeant, insisting that she get up and remind me that she can't stand me. I'm not offended if she says horrible things about me while she insists we stay together, and I don't regret meeting her, but now I can't walk away. Earlier on she would sprint after me the few times I left her so I agreed I wouldn't leave, at least not without some sort of communication. And yet there are increasing scenarios where she's difficult to defend… I had to walk away from her the other night, and remember thinking "How could I get bothered by what you're saying, I might as well get upset by a TV set." But I have said really horrible things to her, like her father sounded foul, that this country sucks, that she's puppeted, and she doesn't like that. I think she should get away from this area that is very Republican and evangelical, but she can't abide ethnics or "white trash." Loads of middleclass females have been economically demoted to abject poverty but can't adjust in the kinds of environments they're expected to live in, and white women get attacked in multi-ethnic areas. I didn't want to contact my own sisters which could be a perceived insensitivity esp. in light of the recent death (murder?) of the subject's sister, but I was wondering if you could get some sort of psychic counselling on behalf of this woman (I realize half these people are frauds) Bluntly I was wondering if you could zero in on any large women's communities in the States, a subject I don't know much about as it's not applicable to me. I've been on a different route in life.

Meanwhile her views and her mindset is far more in tune with this area than mine, so yes I should leave but she has been adamant that I don't, so for mutual night-time guarding reasons I said I'd stay. Right now it's still quite cold but soon, say in two weeks, I'd like to help her to retrace her steps and escort her back to Long Island or somewhere she recently had a residence in. But she's on the verge of signing up for the temporary shelter for 90 days.... well that might be a good idea except for one thing, the Jekyll and Hyde breakouts. I had wanted to oversee her transition to another region, almost like an animal to its appropriate ecosystem. While I mentioned a women's community I think she needs to get behind a lock and key, with maybe a 24-hour hotline to a mental health counsellor prior to those breakouts.

Cass

**From: Leigh Ryder**
**To: Cass Ryder**

Dear Cass,

The attachment you enclosed about the cold weather shelters in VA made me very angry on your behalf. Why do they not open their doors until Dec 1st for crying out loud - do they reckon the homeless don't need shelter for the other 8 months of the year, or that it's OK to be out on the streets in sub-zero temperatures? They should be open all year round, not just for 4 months, and should open their doors no later than 6pm. And why are they kicked out at 7am in the middle of winter? I notice that another church-run shelter allows residents to stay in until 8am (Wow, how charitable of them) but only takes in 10 men and 2 women. Is that deemed adequate provision by the authorities and why the gender discrimination? I don't see why they can't provide female-only shelters where women would feel physically safer, and less vulnerable to assault and intimidation. I assume the one you and Monica use is the VOA one in Leesburg, since it opens 2 weeks earlier in November on a first come first served basis, but it's situated out of town so if you miss the bus you can't get to it before the doors close at 9:30pm (after which there's no admittance) And at what point do they have to start queuing in order to ensure a bed when there are only a handful on offer (20-25)? Talk about punishing people for being homeless.

From what you've told me of the shelters, it is imperative that you get OFF THE STREETS AS SOON AS POSSIBLE. You simply cannot go on sleeping on a park bench where you are exposed to bad weather and criminal elements. As you admitted yourself the "Shell station is an attack trap" By allowing Monica to dictate where and how you sleep at night you are ruining your health and jeopardising your safety, as well as hers. I can see why you don't feel comfortable in the shelters, and I think it is an absolute disgrace that they don't open their doors until December 2$^{nd}$, and even then don't allow anyone in until 9pm - particularly in Northern states where it must be bitterly cold at this time of year. After shivering all night on a park bench what are you supposed to do for 14 hours? I do not see why they are not situated in more accessible locations, given that the homeless are without transport or the means to pay for transport. Your earlier description of the federal-funded support systems as "half an umbrella in the rain" sums it up much better than I could. Apart from layering to keep warm, I'm sure you have the sense to wear thermals and appropriate headgear (70% of body heat is lost through the head) It's worrying that you have both been banned from Sterling Library on a permanent basis, since this is the only warm safe haven you have off the streets, not to mention the lifeline it provides in terms of free Internet access. Your writing is probably the only thing keeping you sane at this point in time, and although it appears you have been able to access the VA Tech College Library, how long before the same thing happens again? Monica's increasingly loud and disruptive behaviour - which may or may not be symptomatic of a bipolar personality disorder - will cause you to be banned from the other one. May I suggest that you visit public libraries separately and not in each other's company since she seems to become more agitated in your presence.

RE counselling, I did take the initiative by contacting psychic medium LW via her website. I stated on the contact form that I was prepared to pay by credit card for any advice she could offer. In view of the fact I didn't get any response I really don't see how I can set up a psychic consultation on Monica's behalf. I apologise if this sounds feeble, but am helpless to do anything constructive as I just don't have the right contacts, and it's doubly difficult when I'm over here and you're in the States. The issue of separatist communities has been explored before - notably by the French philosopher Fourier - who outlined an idealistic if somewhat unrealistic paradigm in which collections of individuals could live together in harmony. I agree with your idea of separatist bioregions or secure communities for women, or alternative types who just can't function in ordinary society for whatever reason. Governments always give the excuse that they haven't got the budget to accommodate these pressing needs, but they always seem to be able to throw huge resources into servicing criminals and violent offenders. There are loads of trained staff on hand and activities organised for them, "halfway houses" and employment opportunities when they get out of prison, but they won't spend a nickel on "Vulnerables" the mentally impaired or the homeless. On the subject of women's communities I've done some searching on the Internet and am enclosing a list of relevant websites at the end of this email. However, certain hard facts need to be faced:

You are not in a position to provide her material needs for the obvious reason that you are homeless and without an income. Monica's own family cannot be found, are either dead or unwilling to help. If you choose to sacrifice YOUR life in a doomed attempt to "help" her in what is a hopeless situation you are condemning yourself to a life of homelessness and danger on the streets. A drowning person cannot help another drowning person, and time spent chasing after Monica's past connections and relatives is just wasted effort. Your life COULD change for the better if you choose to accept help offered from us (which involves you leaving the USA) I've laid it on the line as clearly as I can. But as I've said over and over I can only really help you out of the living hell you are going through if you can get back to the UK. Christmas must be one of the worst times of year for homeless people: I will be sending you a Moneygram in December. Please drop me a line to acknowledge receipt of this so I know you're still in the area.

Love,

Leigh

**From: Cass Ryder**
**To: Leigh Ryder**

If it's any consolation Monica's "claw" whipped out and pocketed the dollars you sent and we spent two drama-filled days and nights at a nearby hotel. I wasn't going to cash it but she wanted to so it went to her, and so perhaps will anything else if you send any more. It was the most disgustingly cold night, we were dead on our knees with fatigue, she especially as she's got a weak heart. Except for a brief stay in a cold weather shelter 6 weeks ago the subject has not had a shower since the Marriott, courtesy of sister's charity. I am sending you another attachment tomorrow.

Cass

From: Staples Copy Centre
To: Leigh Ryder
Subject: Attachment

Secret CIA projects like MKULTRA didn't die, and later on became pork barrels for non-audited tax absorption into classified projects that practised camouflage, deception and propaganda. Naturally the whole area of invisible science opens up a huge avenue of propaganda opportunity, and a lot of mind control is coming through imagery and symbols that influence habit and behaviour. This is exactly how the law-makers set it up so they can promote their policies, just as assuredly as many of the world leaders are unaware of what's going on, whilst a covert minority is obviously speaking for them. Whether that involves physical technology or some sort of occult facet I don't know, but down through the ages there have been cases of political leaders having their minds messed with, the U.S. president no less. Before the Iraq war it is noted that Blair was very much against the Iraq war, then visits the U.S. and has completely changed his mind when he comes back (his mind was conditioned?) The UK Prime Minister Cameron is forced to toe the European line, but is not conscious of any interference or mind control. Some occult force is being used to influence the minds of high-level VIPs, and those responsible are trying to hang the blame on the CIA, but as conspiracy theorists point out it's more likely the CIA is split within itself. In "Beyond Secrecy" Marrs drags up evidence that the downing over Lockerbie, Scotland of a jetliner had been an attempt to suppress evidence being forwarded by some CIA members on board about secret societal alliances (in this case the Italian P2 lodge which was accused of misrepresenting the Vatican's interests) And read the news, NSA staff are resigning in big numbers, meaning perhaps a difference of opinion on core means/intents?

Two thirds of the female victims of the witch craze were in Germany, further reason to see the connection between this historical persecution and an inherited vendetta by a syndicate of covert planners who could be seen as the face of the rising Nazis. Since these plans look quintessentially anti-female and anti-individual. In Strasbourg they are the most unbelievable control freaks, the last 2 millennia culminating in totalitarian charades like Communism or German National Socialism (Nazis) And these inherited systems of corruption all bear the imprint of secret societal warring, with the insights of parapsychology being consciously employed as weaponry. At the turn of the 20$^{th}$ century the royal British name was changed from Saxe Coburg to Windsor, the reason given so the public can pronounce it better…but possibly the real reason is to detract attention from the royal lineage in terms of increased intermixtures of a Germanic line with a British nobility bloodline. The evidence of something Germanic in the British Empire is better covered up. The UK then joins the EU, and something Germanic can be seen to replace something British, in step with more traditionalist totalitarian systems on earth. Queen Elizabeth in Britain looks like a gimmick, just like in the Chinese fable: the wolf makes sounds to lull the pig into a sense of false security then moves in for the dispatch. German imperialism is written all over the one-time British empire, and it's not difficult to see a Catholic German link, with a plan formation dating back at least to the 13$^{th}$ century.

In the dispute that eventually ends in the Reformation, German princes side with the papacy against the German king. Are these the "black nobility" described by conspiracy theorists, the "Judas force" who are in step with something covert in contemporary U.S? (60% of Americans believe in and pray to the "Lord" whereas in Britain it's only 30%) It's noticeable that Catholics divide on issues like gay rights and women's rights in quite stark ways with Protestant denominations, who are more liberal. It's also noticeable that Europe is 75% catholic … almost exclusively on the continent, apart from Scandinavia and the UK, who have constitutional monarchs. Apparently the early founders of America disputed as to whether to put "In God we trust" or "In reason we trust" as part of the grand seal....all looking like the forerunner to an ongoing faith versus reason war. Linked in with this is the conspiracy theory that a "man in black" mysteriously materializes on Thomas Jefferson's estate and gives him the idea about choosing the grand seal that is put on the dollar. Another "man in black" materializes at the Philadelphia congress during the pre-Independence war vote and makes a speech that decides the vote by a very slim margin in favour of going to war with Britain, then just as mysteriously disappears. An agent of Catholic France or Spain or imperial Germany? Men in Black started materializing in the post seventies in Britain and America, and most of the subjects of these materializations felt threatened: some American researchers sum it up in terms of operatives that they reckon are coming out of a facility in northern Virginia (unless the entire book is propaganda), but based on the case reports the subjects were also visited by some "psychic component", which is interesting because the "man in black" symbol looks like their emblem through the centuries.

Conspiracy theory suggests that government intelligence is LINKED IN with occult lodges and hired witchcraft operatives like the *Brujos* (mainly male sorcerers) in central and south America who have knowledge of suppressed sciences, and whose job is to consolidate power through a controlled and vested interest. How that knowledge got hijacked and held onto as a monopoly represents by far the bigger story behind mind control, just like the fiscal credit crunch conspiracy theory that federal government agencies are in cohorts with private syndicates - now globally coordinated through secret societies – in order to bring about the *novus ordorum seclorum*. Possibly the U.S. military literally put witchcraft practitioners on a payroll like taking on a bounty hunter to "sound out" and watch people who might be on an alternative wavelength. Perhaps modern day governments are a cabal of witchcraft operations, with psychics on government payrolls for gender or race related vendettas. If the conspiracy theorists are correct then the U.S. government is transferring them too much power...they are the Frankenstein experiment, the new world order gone astray. What isn't a given is what actually stands at the apex of power in that new world order they're creating? Who takes second place, who takes third etc? Perhaps it's time for the populace to grow up and take sides in a war where in the long run there is not going to be a lot of choice.

The Wall Street journal recently did an article about the fairly high volume of *brujos* who presumably operate on a kind of "neighbourhood watchdog" level. "Oh those are just the boys in the back room" one UK white witch said. Does she just mean energies? No she means more than this...she described the current military industrial congressional complexes as a projection of occult force - sorcery on a high level - more dangerous because it's much more powerful and operates through numerous folds of deception. How moral are the means being used for this new world order? A book was published in the 90s about this powerful syndicate based in Switzerland and the theory is they're trying to take over the U.S. government by using a series of occult actions and connections with high-level government officials, who have offshore Swiss bank accounts. It's been speculated that economic forums are just smokescreens or fronts, that there are definite business connections between secret societies and increasingly corporate-owned conglomerates. For example hardly any presidents were able to "get the ticket" who were not a member of one of these "round table" Bilderberg conferences: the secret societies are globally presenced and help keep the alliances between a super elite and government power brokers running smoothly, and block any challenges to that relationship.

Britain's under attack right now ...the writer has a theory the covert planners plan to isolate Britain, which represents a higher aware wavelength, and that's what's on the cards. Something's going on behind the scenes that's leaving them far behind. Women are better off in Britain and Western Europe (though France and Germany don't have the comparatively generous benefits system that Britain and Scandinavia have) Unchecked immigration in

England means non-whites gaining advancement in almost all areas except the highest echelons, with snubs on poor whites, who don't get nearly as much social welfare income or housing. No, something is working against democracy. The former UK PM Thatcher contracted Alzheimer's, then a blockbuster movie is made which seems critical of the symbol of the British female…hinting the former prime minister deserves her fate. What you have is a kind of broken-down personification of this "Iron Lady", the coded message being Western woman might as well forget it. Something secular and British is coming under judgment. Like a woman who is tossed aside as a rose no longer in bloom by some seedy male who then moves on to other women and more usages. Even if the Brits are not destined to reap the benefits of the new world order, it has to be admitted they did take up arms and pirouette in front of mirrors a lot, they seeded their colonies worldwide, and their global image does look pretty bad.

From: Staples Copy Centre #1094
To: Leigh Ryder
Subject: Attachment

What possibly isn't being said enough is that Western governments
and even the U.S. military bark to the orders of an invisible
authority, which very much promotes religious fundamentalism.
An article on remote neural monitoring (RNM) states that it works
remotely in order to read and detect any criminal thought taking
place inside the brain of a possible perpetrator. After 50 years of
involuntary experiments, microchips can now be implanted that can
influence thought, performance and behaviour. And this is probably
fuelling human conflicts. In light of the Monroe OOB experiments,
if a person's auxiliary spirit can chat with that of a friend or
relative, then what else could be witnessed on the astral plane? If
someone is thinking about someone else negatively, it would be
like heavy breathing down a phone line and might be enough to put
them in a bad mood or cause depression without them being
conscious of what's caused it. Perhaps astral bodies might get too
close to one another due to physical proximity and aura overlap,
like family and friends crowding in at the bedroom door of a
couple's wedding night with full implications of privacy invasion.
See enclosed Internet printouts on neurological surveillance
technology and MKULTRA subprojects, which proves that mind
control is being exercised.

**Printout – Psychotronic Weapons**

*In March 2012 the Russian Defence Minister Anatoli Serdjukov
said "the development of weaponry based on new physics
principles: direct-energy weapons, geophysical weapons, wave-
energy weapons, genetic weapons, psychotronic weapons etc. is
part of the state arms procurement program for 2011-2012" (Voice
of Russia) The world media reacted to this hint on the open use of
psychotronic weapons by the publication of scientific experiments*

*from the 1960s where electromagnetic waves were used to transmit simple sounds into the human brain. However most of them avoided saying that since then extensive scientific research has been carried out in this area throughout the world. Britain's Daily Mail wrote that research in electromagnetic weapons has been secretly carried out in the USA and Russia since the 1950s and that previous research has shown that low-frequency waves can affect brain cells, alter psychological states and make it possible to transmit suggestions and commands directly into someone's thought processes. High doses of microwaves can damage the functioning of internal organs, control behaviour or even drive victims to suicide.*

*Transmitting human speech into the brain by means of electromagnetic waves is apparently one of the most difficult tasks. It must be much easier to control the human emotions that motivate thinking, decision-making and actions. People who complain to be victims of these experiments, aside from hearing voices, complain of false feelings (including orgasms) as well as aches of internal organs which physicians are unable to diagnose. In November 2000 the Committee on Security of the Russian State Duma stated that capabilities enabling remote control of the human nervous system, or the remote infliction of health impairment are available to many modern governments. It is rather evident that these technologies are used, in conflict with the Nuremberg code, for experiments on unwitting human subjects.*

*The ousted Honduran President Manuel Zelaya – whilst under siege in the Brazilian embassy in Honduras - complained that he had been subjected to an "electron bombardment with microwaves" which produces "headache and organic destabilisation" (The Guardian, October 2008) During the failed putsch against Mikhail Gorbachov in 1991, General Kobets warned the defenders of the Russian White House that mind control technology could be used against them. (Komsomolskaya Pravda, Sept.7th 1991) After the putsch the Vice President of the League of*

Independent Scientists of the USSR published a declaration in the *Komsomolskaya Pravda*, where he stated: *"As an expert and legal entity I declare that mass production of psychotronic biogenerators was launched in Kiev...what are psychotronic biogenerators? It is electronic equipment producing the effect of guided control in human organisms. It especially affects the right and left hemisphere of the cortex. This is also the technology of the U.S. Project Zombie 5."*

When the construction of the American system HAARP was launched, with the system supposedly being able to target large regions of the planet by vibrating the ionosphere in brain frequencies, Russia declared its willingness to ban mind control technologies. A similar bill appeared in the U.S. congress, but only for a short period of time. The bill was then changed, and neither the U.S. congress or U.S. president ever made an effort to ban mind control weapons. The testimony of the American author of the book "Angels Don't Play This HAARP" Nick Begich, apparently convinced the European parliament of the possible use of this system to manipulate minds of whole populations. In the report by the European Parliament's STOA (Science and Technological Assessment) panel on "Crowd Control Technologies" it calls for an international convention and global ban on all research and development, whether civilian or military, which seeks to apply knowledge of the chemical, electrical, sound vibration or other functioning of the human brain to the development of weapons which might enable any form of manipulation of human beings, including a ban on any actual or possible deployment of such systems" But apparently at the same time the European countries resigned on this intention when accepting the NATO policies of non-lethal weapons.

## Printout - MKULTRA

Project MKULTRA consisted of 149 subprojects, many of which appear to have some connection with research into behavioural *modification, and testing or administering drugs surreptitiously, including as follows:*

*6 subprojects involving tests on unwitting subjects*
*8 subprojects involving hypnosis, including 2 that also used drugs or chemicals*
*4 subprojects used the "magician's art...with surreptitious delivery of drug-related materials"*
*9 subprojects studied sleep deprivation and psychotherapy's influence on behaviour*
*6 subprojects studied the effects on human tissue of "exotic pathogens and the capability to incorporate them in effective delivery systems"*

*The CIA lost or destroyed all records of Project MKUltra...almost no records remain of the 10 years of covert activity. As Senator Kennedy noted: "Perhaps most disturbing of all was the fact that the extent of experimentation on human subjects was unknown. The records of all these activities was destroyed in 1973, on the instruction of the then CIA Director Richard Helms" Some records were overlooked during the destruction because new records were found in 1977 on Project Bluebird/Project Artichoke detailing research on interrogation techniques, truth serum and brainwashing, electronic implants, the discovery that hypnosis can cause "alternate personality", the use of acoustics and/or brainwave "synchronizers", the use of frequency and amplitude variations to produce mood swings, the capability to remotely target and dysfunction an internal organ.*

Didn't women at the Greenham Common peace camp sited at a USAF base in the UK complain of headaches, dizziness, uncoordinated speech, temporary paralysis etc. when walking up to the fence? MKULTRA subproject 14 describes something called the "liquid magic experiment" In 1993 the writer had an OOB where an etheric liquid was forced down her solar plexus, after which a host of communication channel interferences and mood swings occurred, just as the family residence was sold and writer was about to take a visit abroad. What is certain is that covert actions are going on and the players are split within themselves. They obviously plan to survive and to play these board games into infinity.

**From: Leigh Ryder**
**To: Cass Ryder**

Dear Cass,

There is really no point in sending any more transmissions via the Xerox machine as I cannot reply to them: I tried but my messages were just bounced back to me so the only way we can communicate is via email and I have made a note of your latest email address. I honestly don't know why the other one became inoperative. However, the lengthy attachments you previously sent to me and Alex did get through so you don't need to worry about that. On the subject of electromagnetic weapons and their use in the remote control of the human nervous system, I read with interest the extracts from the Internet article in your attachment.

It is common knowledge that such technologies have been available to government intelligence agencies since the Cold War era. I don't know if you recall whilst we were holiday in St. Petersburg, Florida (1990?) there was a notorious female serial killer (Aileen Wuornos) on the loose who was targeting lone white middle-aged men whilst posing as a hitchhiker. All the law enforcement agencies were out actively hunting for her as if she were the spawn of Satan, when they can't be bothered half the time when it's a male serial killer targeting women. Years later I watched a British documentary about her after she had been apprehended and was on Death Row awaiting execution. Her motivation for performing sex acts with men whom she picked up on public highways was to earn money to support herself and another homeless female with whom she was in a relationship, and she claimed she only shot men who became violent with her or who threatened her life - in other words she acted in self-defence. When the British program-maker interviewed her in jail she complained that the prison authorities were messing with her brain with some kind of ultra-sound frequencies similar to the ones you refer to, resulting in a continual buzzing in her head. Although certain people were attempting to get her death sentence commuted to life imprisonment she was adamant that she did NOT want this i.e. that she wanted to die. She was extremely angry with these interfering do-gooders, as she saw execution as being the only way out of her nightmare existence. All the time she was talking she was staring into the camera in a really scary way, and it occurred to me at the time that she was *being made to look like a mad woman* so that her claims (of being electronically interfered with) would not be believed by anyone. So yes, I agree with the concept of "weaponry angling at a certain category of women" and am pretty sure it does take place. Females who kill are perceived as monsters and are demonised whereas the murder of women by men is so commonplace that it is almost perceived as normal, and they are often released back into society after serving the most derisory prison sentences.

I did some digging around on the highly secretive Bilderberg Group: the main objection by conspiracy theorists seems to be that these "high priests of globalisation" are trying to impose a one world government or New World Order. They are said to have Nazi roots, but other researchers seem to think that they are actually "paving the way for world communism" Though this is just a question of semantics since fascism and communism are flipsides of the same coin, in that they both aim to impose a totalitarian system of government where ordinary people are powerless, and individual liberty and freedom of expression is stamped out. According to Daniel Estulin (who has been investigating and researching this group for many years) the BG's grand design is for "a One World Government with a single, global marketplace, policed by one army, and financially regulated by one World (Central) Bank using one global currency." The Trilateral Commission, founded by David Rockefeller, is a similar group that brings together global powerbrokers, and *"plays a vital role in the New World Order's scheme to use wealth, concentrated in the hands of the few, to exert world control"* their motivation being that they were fearful about *"the increased popular participation in and control over established social, political, and economic institutions and especially an increased popular reaction against the concentration of power of Congress and of state and local government.* " To address this, media control was essential to exert *"restraint on what newspapers may publish (and what TV and radio may broadcast)"* The Rockefellers apparently loathed competition and relentlessly strove to eliminate it, the result being a shrinkage of the middle class and plans for its eventual demise. The Council on Foreign Relations (CFR) has stated that leadership must make *"an end run around national sovereignty, eroding it piece by piece, until the very notion disappears from public discourse"* Bilderbergers, Trilateralists want *"an all-encompassing monopoly over government, money, industry, and property that's self-perpetuating and eternal"* I pulled off the following from a web page that lists their overall objectives:

*Centralized control by controlling world public opinion*
*Manufactured crises and perpetual wars, and making NATO a world military force*
*Control of education to program the public*
*Using the UN as a de facto world government and imposing a universal legal system*
*Imposing a UN tax on "world citizens"*
*Expanding NAFTA (North American Free Trade Agreement) and WTO globally*
*A "zero-growth society" without prosperity or progress*
*No middle class, only "rulers and servants (serfs)," and no democracy*
*A global "welfare state where obedient slaves are rewarded and non-conformists targeted for extermination."*

After one key conference, Estulin obtained a 73-page report from an "insider" who was uncomfortable with what was under discussion.. He noted that *"One of Bilderberg's primary concerns...is the danger that their zeal to reshape the world by engineering chaos toward their long term agenda could cause the situation to spiral out of control and eventually lead to a scenario where they are overwhelmed by events and end up losing their control over the planet.* " It's notable that the European Union and NAU (North American Union) share similar common goals:

An economic and later political union
The blurring of borders and creation of a Superstate
The creation of a common currency and eventual global one
To get the Lisbon Treaty passed for EU open border trade
Fewer worker rights and social benefits
Increased militarization to suppress civil liberties

To quote Jean Monnet, French architect of the European Union:
*"Europe should be guided to the Superstate without the people understanding what is happening. This can be accomplished by successive steps, each disguised as having an economic purpose, which will eventually and irreversibly lead to federation"*

When Blair was in power, he signed up to the to the European constitution (Lisbon Treaty), acting entirely alone and without consulting Parliament. It has been suggested by conspiracy theorists that the PM was the subject of an electronic implant or some kind of hypnosis in order to explain his robotic and slavish adherence to European diktats, despite mounting evidence that membership of the EU is detrimental to British interests and erodes national sovereignty. This sounds far-fetched, but in actual fact it isn't. Whilst attending conferences in Brussels leading politicians are accommodated in expensive hotels where they are routinely subjected to electronic surveillance, so why not subliminal suggestion or implants without their knowledge, to take things to their logical conclusion? Witness the recent scandal over Cameron's aides being supplied with free USB plug-ins for their laptops whilst in Russia to enable the Soviets to capture sensitive data. British diplomats are of course amongst the most sophisticated on this planet, having been in this game for a long time, and are simply not that naive (we hope?) so the dastardly plot never really came off. But it does serve to illustrate that the most implausible-sounding scenarios are a real possibility in the murky netherworld of espionage and counter-espionage.

I believe I read that the HAARP program mentioned in your previous attachment, which is "able to target large regions of the planet by vibrating the ionosphere in brain frequencies" was subject to an EU ban on all research and development which might enable any form of manipulation of human minds. However, given what we know about the inherent corruption and secretiveness of the European Parliament, and its propensity to say one thing and do another (publicly endorsing a ban whilst unofficially giving it the "green light") isn't it more likely that certain agencies have made use of similar technologies to persuade political leaders to "come on board" With respect to the EU it does rather beg the question as to why certain prominent politicians are so eager to embrace this nightmare scenario. Of course financial incentives can be just as persuasive as any posited "mind control" technologies, and the answer might just lie in a number of bloated Swiss bank accounts. Just supposing, for the sake of argument, certain high-ranking politicians were persuaded into making a colossal investment in the Euro – so that if the Euro sank the personal fortunes they stood to gain also sank. The sums involved would not be trivial. Would that explain their eagerness to see the federal Superstate known as the EU succeed at whatever cost, *no matter what the cost*, to the United Kingdom? It just might. If you wanted to prove that such a connection existed i.e. that political manoeuvrings were linked to currency investments, how would you go about it? In order to find evidence of vested interests, bribes offered and received, political leverage and so on you would have to search for the paper trail that such investments inevitably leave in their wake. The reluctance of European Commissioners to submit their accounts to an independent audit, the overall secrecy and unaccountability, and the punitive measures enacted against those investigating corruption and fraud (they are invariably hounded out of their jobs) would also seem to indicate that there is much going on behind the scenes that ordinary people are unaware of.

I don't know what Lockerbie was about, but I wouldn't necessarily give credence to the wild speculations of some best-selling author who has a vested financial interest in making his conspiracy theory as sensationalist as possible in order to generate sales. It's what the tabloids do all the time: the truth can be somewhat boring and commonplace so they invent tall tales in order to sell copy e.g. "My mother-in-law gave birth to an alien baby". A lot of the stuff you wrote about enforced bioelectricals is reminiscent of Wilhelm Reich's discovery of "orgone energy". According to his son, Reich was horribly persecuted by the U.S. authorities and ended up being incarcerated in a mental institution. They obviously felt very threatened by his findings: he claimed orgone energy could cure cancer, and more pertinently he may have been one of the first people to discover how to control weather events (his experiments with cloud seeding resulted in thunder storms) The CIA would have been extremely interested in exploiting his discoveries - dangerous knowledge in the wrong hands - one reason for shutting him up. The psychic "Bernard" mentioned by Andrew Collins in his novels was insistent upon keeping his identity secret, because such people are proactively hunted by intelligence agencies who would like to recruit them for their own political agendas.

Just recently I find myself returning to the classical authors like Thomas Hardy, who remarks of one of his characters: *"...a vehement gloomy being who had quitted the ways of vulgar men, without light to guide him on a better way."* If character is destiny, then one's unique personal makeup will have contributed to produce the events and circumstances in a person's life. Depressing to acknowledge that to a large extent we still remain prisoners of our own mind - the "mental padlocks" you refer to. The corollary of true independence is a solitary existence, but I don't think this is good for anyone. The complete absence of social intercourse drives most people insane, and in the long-term causes irreparable psychic damage. If the human soul is a battleground between the forces of good and evil, then make sure that you back the right side. People with real strength of character, like the great spiritual leaders, naturally gravitate to what is good, and only weak characters gravitate towards evil. As a guide to living this may sound simplistic, but corrupt souls only have their way for a short time because ultimately they are defeated by a force which is much stronger, and which has all the best people on its side.

I've attached an excerpt on "The Magical Battle of Britain" by Dion Fortune in order to make the point that not all occult activity is malign. In fact the most talented psychics and mediums tend to avoid dark energies; they usually have a highly developed moral sense of right and wrong and work towards what is good. The number of people with genuine psychic skills is very small (as opposed to the huge number of frauds out there) and amongst that small band the number of "white" practitioners vastly outnumbers those who practise the "black arts", despite sensationalist media accounts of devil worship. I also believe someone is looking out for you on the spirit planes (possibly our parents?) otherwise I just don't see how you could have survived all these years. I get the distinct impression there is something protective around you that persists despite the obstacles you've encountered, and that this has somehow "guided" you back into communication with family members.

Love always,

Leigh

**From: Cass Ryder**
**To: Leigh Ryder**


I've nothing against Britain but you're not being sincere when you write all that stuff about World War 2. It's a little sentimental. The reference to the EU as a prelude to the "new world order" is a perceptive point. While people try to understand the complete mismanagement of latter day governments, a few have grasped that it's not mismanagement or incompetence, but that it's planned: that 200 men own the world, are a mixmax of commerce, military, government, and new wealth nobility, allied to a minority of totalitarian weapon-holders. Considering how the federal government has been empowered through the bailouts of banks - wasn't it all designed? For example, the Cultural Revolution in communist China and everything it represented: the theft of capital assets and properties by gangs of thugs, the beating up and slaying of the educated bourgeoisie who had not been "roughened" by endless working the fields, or down the mines etc. The poor were not supposed to keep hold of what they gained, no matter how hard they worked, and isn't something covert in the West doing exactly the same thing today? And like Judases to Jesus when he prophesies that the disciples will betray him at the hour of his lynching …these elite males would betray the middleclass (as well as women and alternative minorities, it might be added) Writer agrees that the covert agenda to demote the middleclass looks like a global communism, and while the middleclass is very imperfect the writer has observed that the very poor classes and very wealthy classes are more corrupt because they just go along with the plan and are not likely to challenge it. OPERATION CHAOS IS GETTING OUT OF HAND.

And we come back full circle to the covert plans in the West and what is being promoted as a justification for a domestic military takeover and REX 84, if only in terms of increased criminality. Meanwhile its obvious that while the empowered are almost always the wealthy super elite, history demonstrates that wealth can be stolen. In such a scenario the wealthy become absorbed while a kind of totalitarian code operates through them, and that's often where women and a minority of males meet unhappy fates. Increased weather cataclysms and attendant chaos will be seen as the raison d'etre that will justify it. Physical weaponry and hardware matter. What's the point of trying to do anything unless one has the backing of a powerful military, and those peace camps of the seventies did look kind of ..stooopid. The "Occupy Movement" were 90% graduates. No efforts were made to restructure demos, such as to set up campsites in an outer met area, to say nothing of a gathering cop force (if a cop gets beaten up by a crowd of thugs then naturally the cops are going to come back a hundredfold and beat up everything that moves) As laws came in forbidding them to demonstrate in inner cities and in government centres, effectively disbanding them, one authority complained that "their tent cities were encouraging rats" Writer noticed that stacks of hay were positioned at intermittent ten or fifty yard spaces along an Alexandria bridge leading into the southeast district of DC, which she suspected was set up as a river rat enticement (not visible because construction made it impossible to walk the pedestrian way and the writer accidentally found herself on it) She noticed seriously HUGE RATS around a market called "the fresh fields."

I notice you didn't comment on the printout about the scheduled opening up of the metropolitan "silver line" extending the metro into Loudoun county from the inner city areas. This symbol has come up again and again in a secret societal encoding. For example, in occult literature the metaphorical umbilical cord that joins the physical body with the etheric body is called the "silver cord" and is a sort of gateway into the astral realm. I don't expect you to respond, or to understand that the silver colour code was chosen as a symbol or a sort of pledge of counterattacking, which is what the metro line represents, and I just joined the dots. Now consider what I said about the silver line being a sign of a counter-weaponry being picked up by an evangelist-minded syndicate that have allies worldwide, and I can swear to you the occult is being used very audaciously. I have a theory that it's to do with the CIA and the Pentagon and M is like a sort of trusting deer that's roamed into the camp of a bunch of hunters. These are occultists who are used to working on the minds of government officials, and something in U.S. covert policy today is very rightwing, militaristic, religious fundamentalist, and anti-female. Anyway to go back to the invisible energy attacks, this is a form of terrorism, a high level form of mental violence on her. They're the CRAP of the universe.

In true paranoid fashion one could argue that patterns of weather extremes around which political events are moulded are being orchestrated, with the possibility that an understanding and control of weather processes is held in a monopoly by a minority of knowledge holders. As for Wilhelm Reich who discovered orgone energy, he was murdered before he got a chance to extrapolate from his researches, which were potentially dangerous in terms of a suppressed science. It has even been theorised the Great Depression was manipulated, to mean the moulding of events around an imminent western dustbowl, with anticipated grain price rises: silver iodide seeding and an early Lindbergh type Cessna could have been used to precipitate and worsen drought conditions (droughts can be caused by drawing away clouds to other regions, in the known application of "cloud seeding" which Reich wrote about) How long has weather weaponry been used? After all, anyone with a Cessna and a fistful of silver iodide tablets, or with oil drilling technology and a map of fault-lines, can cause earthquakes or storms. Man might be able to sort of "snooker ball" a cyclonic wind pattern into a certain "pocket" and destroy an entire area.

I had always wondered even then whether people's emotions weren't being somehow manipulated by physical technology. I received a cat scan in '85 courtesy of a minor back injury (a slipped disc) I incurred while on a welding job working for a Pentagon defence contractor. I later read that cat scans are employed for brainwave soundings, like a "fingerprint" or tabbing. Then years later I run into the aforementioned subject and experience an intense emotion but realize it's misapplied. Coming back from the restroom in the library, this paragraph just appeared on the computer screen "Some people need to rein in their emotions and keep within their space" It's almost 100% certain no-one in the library did this and I don't ever speak to anyone, so this looks like an example of an interception... eerie because it betrays knowledge of innermost emotional "reading" Though it's possible that the database doesn't have knowledge of people's inner emotions but that some other invisible force does, done to make the person really paranoid. While physical implants are obviously possible in a range of functions like robotics and cochlear ear implants that can help a deaf person to hear, this is different from telepathy or perceptual interference, involving a system of deception inserts after which the ordinary processes of the psyche can be relied on to consolidate its own sense of tunnel vision. The secrecy and uncertainty is conducive to paranoia and insecurity.

Only a tiny minority of people in the West know about non-lethal implants, and remote neurological and brainwave "fingerprint-like sensings and transmissions." One weapon is called "disassociation of memory" another uses "pulsed microwaves in the form of audiograms." Writer recalls hearing a distant voice in her head when she alights from a Greyhound bus in Boston saying "You're dirty" or "Fuck off". I get told to commit suicide all the while and heard what felt like audiograms on and off for 8 months. They can get you through the occult if it works like LSD, in altering perceptions and emotional states. Non-verbalisation is how they get away with it, because it is difficult to put into words something which the ordinary complacent man in the street will understand. Let's face it Western man is so pin-holed (that's my expression for sex-drugged) he colludes in it because all the while they're "pigging out" in her skin as they sit in it. Actually I'm not so certain the latter is going on so much as a manipulation of the subject's verbalizations. But that's exactly how I see these spirit entities, and they are having a BUFFET on Monica. For example she kept saying "I'm superior, I'm an alpha male god" the way a little child proclaims they're superman wearing a toy costume. There is something forced and mechanical, drilled about the reiterations. Based on my observations the spirit domain does exist, there is an etheric weaponry set of skills that a minority of embodied men on the earth can use, what the writer calls the "invisible inquisition."

They're such a bunch of old bastards and I don't have to carry the cross of their bigotry any longer, and I know you go through it but less than I did. I've never told you what went on here in the States. I was thrown into the Jennifer Road Detention centre, Annapolis on a false charge, for a stone throwing incident ON EXACTLY THE SAME DAY I received a letter from you 7 years ago (when we probably hadn't communicated for 2 years) So are you starting to get the picture? I never got to read it. Your letter got sent back a day after it had arrived when it should have been held for me. I was told it had arrived over the phone one whole state away and when I turned up in person it wasn't there, after travelling for miles … always on an empty stomach with strained back and feet. You lost your job on another occasion as soon as you received my letter. I am attacked, almost raped and murdered exactly seven days after you and Alex send initial faxes to me. Alex is obviously made to think that I am somehow "stalking" her when I call her when I happen to be in Vermont at the same time she's landed a teaching job there. She doesn't understand that in the first few years of homelessness I used to spend time camping there each summer in the national forests, and then day labouring in a labour pool in Burlington. That's what my schedule had been before she arrived, because I knew I could get work with this particular employment agency and not with others. In fact I'm sure I saw her husband Jeremy in Burlington just off the university campus one early June day before they both leave for the Virgin Islands.

In one phone call Alex reminded me that I had "wasted a small inheritance" and that the "federal govt gives all kinds of assistance to help the homeless" Neither of these statements were true. I was criminalized and had all kinds of communication obstacles with respect to my residency status, let alone getting employment. As for federal govt funding at that time they did absolutely nothing. And I lost any savings I had within a year while trying to survive. Each winter I had been wintering in the southern states but I had not planned on turning up on Alex's doorstep. Writer sensed she and her husband both felt threatened, so volunteered not to meet with her sister and bid her farewell, and has been homeless ever since. Because I come over as very strange. I agree I look weird and I haven't tried that much to adjust but I NEVER had a drug or an alcohol problem (except for a very brief earlier marijuana habit) And I never laid my problems on any one. An evangelist here in Loudoun county sent me info that Alex is now in Atlanta, on her own initiative (I hadn't asked her to) The writer has credits almost equivalent to a BA, but got knocked off her humble pedestal a long time ago. I resented being thrown out of college at 19 and left the following year to salvage my ego and try my luck at employment in America. In 1994 I turned up in New York with $30 in my pocket. Then after the family house in the UK got sold I took possibly 10 airline journeys in a year (including Australia, Mexico, France and Crete) with the intent to settle somewhere, but lost almost all my money within a year while on the move (and due to a rip off by the bank) and so couldn't use my Visa card. Between that and 5 semesters of self-paid college I became bankrupt. The local education authority didn't come up with the financial assistance they had promised if I completed the first year, which I did. This was cash that could have been sunk into a property, a home base that I needed, and all the rest is history...I've been floundering around like a homeless impoverished idiot ever since. It took me ten years before I found out I can go back to England legally courtesy of a passport stamp renewal, a three to six month process involving a fairly sizeable sum of money. None of you know what

I've been through. You never had to spend one night out in the open and have never been hungry.

Cass

**From: Leigh Ryder**
**To: Cass Ryder**

Dear Cass,

When I sent an aerogramme to a *poste restante* mail delivery
address in 2006, I remember including all the information the U.S.
authorities required in order to issue you an airline ticket, and
providing a guarantee that you had a home with us as long as you
needed. I waited anxiously for a reply but never heard from you
again, absolutely NOTHING until 2013. I didn't know whether you
had received my letter or whether something had happened to you,
but none of us had any way of tracing you or knowing whether you
were still alive. Even a private detective would have found it
impossible with no bank account or social security number as a
starting point. It's heartbreaking to think that you trekked all those
miles across state to pick up a letter from me, which they didn't
even hold for you. And then being thrown into jail. I note from the
transcript you sent that your felon charge in 2006 has been
recorded in the official documentation as "Shoot at Motor vehicle"
when you merely threw a "golfball-sized" rock. Presumably the
driver provoked you in some way but was not injured, and you
actually reported the incident yourself. This is a highly misleading
account of what actually occurred and implies a gun was used: a
misdemeanour has been made to look like a felon and whoever
swore and testified to this at the County Sheriff office has
committed perjury, which is utterly disgraceful as it affects your
criminal status. How can the bastards get away with that?

The fact you were missing for so many years has affected all of us
in different ways: I had countless dreams in which you would turn
up for a few days, and then declare that you were going off again
despite my pleading with you to stay. In the dreams I was in often
in tears, and would wake under a cloud of heavy depression, almost
like a bereavement. I had no idea that the last time we met in

Bristol in 1996 was the last time I would see you. You never actually told anyone that you were homeless or what you had gone through (you managed to conceal it very well) I had NO IDEA. I knew you were moving around with a backpack, but I thought this was your choice. I assumed you still had money from your inheritance: after all you had been backpacking around India so I thought you still hadn't got the *wanderlust* out of your system and that you would eventually settle down to a permanent place of residence. And just because I "never had to spend one night out in the open and have never been hungry", it doesn't mean I am totally lacking in insight or have no understanding of what you have had to deal with. You don't have to personally experience something like war or physical assault, to know it must be deeply unpleasant.

In connection with the "silver cord" which connects the astral body to the physical body, rest assured there is no sinister connection between the scheduled metro extension line into Loudoun county, the "Silver Line" and the astral silver cord. The human brain is hard-wired to discern patterns and connections, and to attribute meaning where there may be none. As a species we would not have mastered language if this were not the case, and most creative and scientific endeavour would be impossible without this faculty: the recognition of odd-seeming coincidences - termed "synchronicity" by Jung - is yet another example of this e.g. no sooner do I read your email than I pick up a newspaper article about Esther Rantzen setting up a "Silver Line" to provide a telephone support system for the elderly. Just a naming coincidence, since senior citizens who avail themselves of the Internet are termed "silver surfers". We look for meaning everywhere - we cannot help ourselves! I agree, however, that the bioelectric components of human physiology make mind-invasive technology a distinct possibility. The latest TV sets incorporate spy chips which record peoples' viewing habits, but it's mostly about targeted advertising and not about Big Brother snooping (though of course it could be, in the wrong hands) Google is one of the worst offenders in terms of the invasion of personal privacy, but what can you do about it? Don't sunbathe nude in your garden, and don't switch on the webcam on your computer just in case there's some pervert out there watching you brush your teeth through your laptop screen. We are all liable to succumb to screaming paranoia if we pay too much attention to this stuff because that's the kind of world we live in, and the technological capability is there for endless spying and the acquisition of personal data. I regard it all with much the same weary insouciance that I regard media celebrities who discourse at great length about matters of no consequence, namely themselves.

At the same time you mention federal cash for housing assistance is being made available for the chronically homeless in the States, the welfare system is being severely curtailed in this country as public sector expenditure is reined in, due to the system being abused by fraudsters and "health tourists" who continue to pour into the country in order to take advantage of the generous welfare handouts, free NHS hospital treatment etc. The cuts are absolutely essential if we are to survive economically as a country, but an unfortunate by-product is that those who are vulnerable and in need, such as the genuinely disabled, the homeless or mentally impaired are being caught up in the clampdown. I actually think the world is getting worse and that each successive generation is less intelligent than the previous one. Reproduction for the sake of reproduction is insane and maybe it's time to seriously consider a system of benevolently administered eugenics (as did WB Yeats, GB Shaw and many others) though I suppose one would be considered fascist these days to propose such a solution. In the misogynistic world in which we live any artificial attempts to control population would tend to result in baby girls being aborted and males outnumbering females, leading to yet more violence and aggression. The world was probably not created with human happiness in mind and appears to be under the control of a malign Demiurge who is no friend to mankind, and whose mechanical workings are responsible for most misery on the earth plane. The Demiurge may not be actively malevolent but just insentient i.e. unconscious of its general tendency and evil productions. An agricultural threshing machine can hardly be blamed if a farm labourer accidentally falls into its path and is caught up in its blades.

As for Monica's story about being on the run because she apparently shot someone who threatened her relatives after a home invasion, and that her FBI cousin stole her "inheritance" frankly, it sounds like the plotline of some third-rate soap opera such as *Dallas* or *The Sopranos*. Often, when people are lonely or powerless they make up fantastical stories in order to sound more interesting or important to other people they meet, or they suffer from delusions of grandeur. It's an unconscious mental process and a desperate plea for attention (and let me make it perfectly clear I am not passing judgment here) but I would take everything Monica says with a pinch of salt. I find it highly improbable that a petite female of only 5' 1" would be capable of fending off 2 male intruders, shooting one of them and actually getting away with it - particularly if they were Mafia gangsters! The latter are professional hitmen who plan their operations meticulously. She wouldn't have stood a chance, and if they were really after her they would have tracked her down by now and killed her (you too, in all probability) Besides, if Monica's story were actually true, how much danger would she be putting herself (and you) in, if you were able to track down her only living relative and claim her "inheritance"? Her whereabouts would then be immediately known to those she claims to be on the run from, and how long do you think either of you would survive? If she *is* telling the truth then the stupidest thing you could do would be to return to her home territory, so put that thought (of escorting her back to the Long Island area) right out of your mind. The likelihood is that no-one is after her, and that she is delusional. It sounds like a load of bull to me, and Liz probably concluded much the same and eventually got tired of hearing the same old story - like a record stuck in a groove - and disentangled herself for her own sanity.

The mentally ill are very wearing to be around for any length of time, and the only people who can go the distance are parents and close relatives, or professionals such as counsellors or psychiatrists who are paid handsomely to listen. Focussing on Monica's problems all the time is not only obsessional and unhealthy, it doesn't achieve anything. But what comes through loud and clear is that she knows how to look after her own interests, since it appears she was the one who benefited most from the moneygram we sent. I would wholeheartedly agree with you that anyone who has experienced homelessness and extreme isolation for any length of time would either suffer a nervous breakdown as a consequence or have mental health issues. The fact that you are still able to write and do research is testimony to your strength of character and resilience. Most other "normal" women would have broken down years ago, that's if they survived. If you can get hold of your passport Luke and I will liaise to get you back to the UK where you will be safer, happier, and more secure. But in order for that to happen you need to be willing to let us help.

Love,

Leigh

**From: Leigh Ryder**
**To: Cass Ryder**

Dear Cass,

Did you receive my previous messages? (I haven't heard from you for well over 3 months) It is important that you reply to this and let me know, because if I don't hear from you I will assume the worst i.e. that my replies to you are being intercepted. There is no logical reason you shouldn't have received my messages unless someone else who has access to your account is reading them and deleting them before you get a chance to. And I have a good idea who the culprit is. Let me repeat, if Monica has access to your password and is able to read your emails you need to change it immediately and do not let her know your new password. She is desperate for you not to leave her, and feels threatened by my offers of help to get you back to the UK. As I have portrayed her in a less than flattering light by communicating my suspicions to you, she will not want you reading my messages. Which means the only person to read this email will probably be Monica herself, but at least I will then know exactly what's going on.

Cass, if you do receive this please email me back as soon as possible.

Love,

Leigh

**From: Leigh Ryder**
**To: Matt Ryder**

Dear Matt,

I'm really sorry to have to approach you like this out of the blue, but as I currently reside in England you're probably the best person to shed some light on our predicament. Luke gave me your email address.

As you may or may not be aware our younger sister Cass has been homeless and missing for many years. We only found out last year that she was still alive, and managed to re-establish contact recently. I desperately want to get her off the streets otherwise I cannot see her surviving such a dangerous lifestyle for much longer. Anyway, she has a simple request: she wants to claim the land in Kentucky left in Granddad's will. According to Luke this was never subdivided properly, but it looks as though it appears to have been surveyed in 1992 (is this correct?) I know the land we each inherited doesn't amount to much but she is welcome to my share in addition to her own if it could be sold. We are trying to ascertain its current value and whether it is still the wilderness it once was or whether any development has taken place since Luke last discussed this with you.

Your cousin,

Leigh

**From: Leigh Ryder**
**To: Patrick, Luke, Alex, Adam**

Dear Family,

I actually spoke to Cass last night! She had recently sent me another lengthy attachment in which she casually mentioned she had managed to acquire a cellphone with the number scrawled at the bottom. I dialled the number and left a voicemail message, praying she'd pick up at some point. As she is too paranoid to set up another email account (convinced her emails are being intercepted by shady U.S agencies) I have been unable to communicate with her: in other words I am the unhappy recipient of various faxes sent from impersonal print/copy centres in Loudoun county to which I cannot respond by email.

I am copying below Matt's replies to my queries about the land in Kentucky. So far Adam and Luke have indicated they are willing for a survey and a legal subdivision in order to determine ownership of our respective "parcels" of land. No point in contacting Matt again yet as we don't have an estimate of what it is going to cost (survey, legal fees etc.) but presumably that cost would be split between all willing parties so should be bearable. I won't be hanging onto my parcel but will either deed it to Cass outright or sell it, with proceeds of the sale to go to Cass. Until we have further info from Matt including a realistic price per acre none of us can really rush into this. I doubt whether any of us can or would wish to contribute to the cost of a common access road through mountainous terrain, unless Matt could organise it cheaply through his engineering firm. The reason I'm trying to expedite this affair is because her lifestyle is just so dangerous - I have nightmares about her ending up in a body bag as just another nameless and faceless "Jane Doe".

Leigh

**From: Leigh Ryder**
**To: Cass Ryder**

Dear Cass

As you can see I have set up a brand new account for you under a fake identity, and you should be able to use this now as I've tested it out. Obviously if you're reading this then you got my voicemail informing you of your new email address and password and I suggest you do not give this to anyone. It's OK to keep sending me documents via Xerox attachments, but for personal communications (and especially if you want a reply) you should use the new email address I set up for you. I will wait to hear back from you before I write more.

Love,

Leigh

**From: Cass Ryder**
**To: Leigh Ryder**

Thanks yes I can access this address. But this will probably incur a communication glitch soon enough. Despite my criticism of the SOAR program to help the homeless this is comparatively thoughtful, whereas under the Bush administration one just got a toilet roll.

I agree the cousin Matt probably doesn't want a communication from me. You're wrong about an access road. I've crashed on it briefly when I was homeless. And a hireable backhoe would be the only thing necessary in order to facilitate levelling of terrain. You're also wrong about the land, it wouldn't be that hard at all. Lots of Americans have cabins and live with outhouses and sometimes just a mechanical pump, and with non-electrically powered light and cooking. This would have to be brick in case one boarded it up and left it, otherwise I wouldn't doubt that someone would try and burn it down. Also I would create further storage by building a couple of storage cellars underground. Anyway it would only have been for 6 years until she gets a pension, and I would never have thought to do it on my own. I think I can get a stupid job for one day a week at least... preferably 20 hours 30 of labour. I do have critically strained feet but I learnt while doing community service for 5 weeks after jail, that if I drink enough soya protein each day (like almost 200 ounces a day) I can deal with the pain.

The social worker said she was trying to get a 2-bedroom apartment for both of us...I'm not waiting around. I'm going to sign up for winter work, anything I can get, but I usually don't even score on that. I get the feeling this area doesn't want to employ me. Last winter at the mall where we'd while away endless hours, I got the feeling they were going to help if I applied for part-time work as a cleaner, mainly because they seem to want to help HER. She does have a psychic impairment and she cannot or will not take benefits so this is a human rights issue. Maybe the writer can jumpstart the manuscript in the next month.

Oh, I didn't tell you a black person almost killed me the other day in Baltimore, three or four men ganged up on me in a street.

Cass

**From: Leigh Ryder**
**To: Patrick, Luke, Alexandra, Adam**

I have just set up a new email account for Cass and left the username and password on her voicemail. She picked up the voicemail message and emailed me this morning successfully so for your information her new email address is -------. Along with her request for Matt's number was the following throwaway remark

*I didn't tell you a black person almost killed me the other day in Baltimore, three or four men ganged up on me in a street...*

which is truly alarming. If she's still in Virginia what on earth was she doing in Baltimore - are the two near each other?

Leigh

**From: Patrick Ryder**
**To: Leigh, Luke, Alexandra, Adam**

Dear All,

A couple of points:

The city of Baltimore and the state of Virginia are contiguous.

I fear the land may have been confiscated by the county many years ago for non-payment of taxes. I don't think Daddy ever had legal title to any land to pass on but count me in for surveying and dividing if it seems feasible - my guess is that surveying costs exceed any market value.

On the subject of Cass, there's not much to be done except to send money if you can or want to. I don't because I can't afford to. And a quarter century of homelessness for a decently educated, healthy white female in an overall affluent society that has not been in recession for most of those years drags up an unsettling thought: the possibility of a degree of complicity in her own circumstance. Sounds like Cass might find Prozac of more use than Colin Wilson. And what is it about "Monica" which provokes such sight-unseen hostility?

Will write properly soon.

Patrick

**From: Luke Ryder**
**To: Patrick, Leigh, Alexandra, Adam**

Dear Family,

That sentence from Cass has a 12-year old mentality. Are her other communications anything like that one? And emotional blackmail comes to mind. Matt doesn't live in Pineville or even in the state of Kentucky so hopefully she cannot contact him. I'll emphasize again that money won't help Cass and I don't think building a road to wilderness in order to camp out is a plausible survival alternative. She or someone else is picking up on your emotions Leigh, so be careful in what you say to her as I'm starting to think that you could have been right in that "Monica" is playing a part in all of this. Patrick, what does contiguous mean? Can we catch it and will antibiotics help?

Luke

**From: Alexandra Ryder**
**To: Patrick, Leigh, Luke, Adam**

Dear Family,

Have been communicating via phone with Cass & managed to call her back last night so the conversation lasted until my battery bleeped, so at least we were able to say good-bye before it cut off. The call lasted about 2 hours. More like a monologue a good part of the time. She did lose control at one point and screamed down the phone that I didn't care, that nobody cared, that I shouldn't pretend....it was agonizingly vicious and desperate, but she regained a normal tone shortly afterwards and carried on in a more normal vein (which is to say not normal but calmer) Thinking about it, I feel like she's almost like a small child, desperately upset and angry that she's been wronged. Of course it's a warped perception as none of us inflicted this on her, but when she gets like that, she blames us all (Leigh a little less) and it is an expression of hurt, deep and terrible hurt. The gist of most of the monologue is that she needs to help her friend, Monica. This is what has prompted her to make the contact and try to get the money from the land – to give it to Monica because Monica won't accept handouts from the government. As for what she was doing in Baltimore, she had gone in search of Monica who had run off to Baltimore.

On the subject of Matt, I said I didn't have his phone number but that I had an email address, which I gave her. She wants to ask if he would offer her something for her share, even without knowing its value. She's also under the impression it's worth about $10,000 and it was no good trying to explain that we have no clue what it's worth, which might not be much. I said we were all trying to figure this out and that it would take a while. I'm sorry if you all think it was a bad idea to pass on his email address, but I had to make a judgement call, and of course I pretended not to know his phone number.

So that's it for now. I need to get something to eat as I was up at 5:30am to take Jeremy to the airport, then went straight to work and have just got back. I see an email has just come in from Luke ....this is all somewhat draining as in my heart of hearts, I don't think the KY land will solve anything for Cass. She needs medical treatment if she is to function in a world like most us function in, yet I don't know that any of us have the legal or moral right to impose it on her. Well, we don't have a legal right but if we did, do we have the moral right? These are agonizing questions that will remain regardless of land, cash injections or whatever other temporary "relief" we can give.

As for contiguous, I think it's where the cheese is next to some rather sad looking salami in my fridge door, which I am about to pounce on....

Love,

Alex

**From: Alexandra**
**To: Patrick, Leigh, Luke, Adam**
**Subject: Slippery Slope**

Received another quick call from Cass…don't think she had much credit on her phone as it cut off. We phoned back & forth a few times to reconnect. She asked me to send some more cash as they haven't got any money for food. I think she's spent any spare cash on phone credit, who knows. So I've just transferred another amount, but don't get any voicemail option on her phone when I tried calling…it probably needs topping up.

However, I'm not going to keep sending money as this is not a solution, and I don't want her to just phone and assume money will come. It's expensive as it costs 10% commission just to do it. I have to use Jeremy's card as the website won't take mine. It's stressing me out as this is how I've been spending my weekends and evenings recently, engaging in long conversations with her, or in tricky online money transfers which don't always seem to work first time. Jeremy is away in Qatar. I asked him to write down his card details in case I needed to use it again so luckily I was ready when she called. Thanks for the new email address, Leigh. Much better to use this for communication purposes than phoning, which takes its toll emotionally.

I just don't know what we do. Of course it's absorbed all of my thoughts over the weekend and I've been researching on the Internet for ways to help, but I feel burnt out already. It sounds crazy to say that, but it's intense, as you know. I tried reading some of the attachments she scanned & sent.….I could probably recite the whole thing I've heard it so many times. Nothing has changed from her rantings last year.

Oh well, better go. Got school work to catch up on now and need to eat…..will try to forget about it for the time being but just thought I'd let you know the latest.

Bye for now,

Alex

**From: Leigh Ryder**
**To: Patrick, Luke, Alexandra, Adam**

Dear Family,

Another very quick message as I know neither of you has the time for all this. Alex, it probably wasn't a good idea to give her Matt's email address but she is determined enough to find it out for herself soon enough. As I've stated before the only way I can help her is if she can get to the UK, and if she breaks the tie with Monica who evidently has expensive tastes and is milking Cass for all she's worth. It was her idea (not Cass's) to spend the money I sent on hotel rooms. I'd hoped she would buy a good tent, sleeping bags and some warm clothing. J and I are happy to help Cass out with cash when we can afford it, but I am not prepared to subsidise some stranger who will happily take everything we give to Cass. So I understand where Alex is coming from RE "Slippery Slope" However, because neither of us can control how Cass spends any money she receives, does that mean we should therefore not give her anything, and deprive her of any financial help whatsoever? A gift with strings attached is no gift at all, and we either agree to help her in a concrete practical way, which will inevitably involve some hard cash, or else forget the whole thing.

I suspect Patrick may be right about the land being confiscated by the county if no-one has been paying the taxes. If an equitable land division and ownership is eventually determined does that mean we'll all be clobbered with a bill for back taxes? The game is probably not worth the candle. Let's wait and see how much this all might cost. Hopefully Matt will get back soon with an estimate for a survey. I'm feeling somewhat emotionally drained so will sign off here.

Leigh

**From: Leigh Ryder**
**To: Cass Ryder**

Dear Cass,

Sorry we got cut off the other night. I guess you ran out of money. You can't imagine how relieved I was to hear your voice again after all these years. Please understand I am unable to respond to attachments or faxes sent by Xerox machine: any replies I send just get bounced back to me, which is incredibly frustrating, as you must have thought I was ignoring your communications. Be assured your emails are not being intercepted: the reason your email didn't transmit to Alex was because you spelled her email address incorrectly. You should also avoid capital letters as this can also cause problems. When you're using the Internet in a public library, sometimes the previous user has accidentally hit the CAPS LOCK key on the keyboard, which means when another user comes along and types in their password it is not recognised. If you're unable to log on this could be the cause, so the remedy is to hit the CAPS LOCK key again so it reverts to lower case.

There is a reason why your documents might keep mysteriously "disappearing" when you are using a word processor like WORD. At the bottom left-hand corner of the screen there are a number of small square icons: if you click on the rightmost icon whilst holding it down at the same time with the mouse it acts as a slider, and will slide all the way across to the right margin. As an experiment type in a few paragraphs then click on the icon at the bottom of the screen, and "drag" it to the right. It will look as if what you have written has mysteriously disappeared (actually it hasn't, it's still there) To make it reappear drag the slider back to the leftmost margin. Occasionally, if you are typing fast you can accidentally hit the slider and the screen looks blank because you're way over by the right page margin. When this happens just drag it back to the left margin and your text will reappear. It's far more likely this is what is happening rather than anyone intercepting/deleting what you've written.

You can email Matt if you like but the reason I advise holding fire for a few days is that any delays are definitely not being caused by him: in my experience lawyers, surveyors etc. take their own sweet time and you can't hurry them up. Providing the costs of the legal process don't outweigh the value of the land it looks as though our aunt would be willing to buy people's shares, once ownership has been determined. So we just have to be patient and wait until Matt can provide an estimate of what it's all going to cost. When I say I honestly don't see how I can help Monica, it's the truth. Why would you expect members of the family to squander hard-earned cash on a complete stranger whom they know nothing about? Put yourself in our shoes. Would you give money to a friend of mine you'd never met if I asked you for it? We sincerely want to help YOU, but you've made it abundantly clear that any money sent to you goes directly to Monica. Frankly, none of can understand why you think we would be willing to do this. I know you weren't asking me for financial help, and I applaud you for not wanting to be on the dole. All I suggested is that you agree to let us help you to return to the UK for a **temporary** period, only until such time as you can stand on your own two feet. I would ensure you have a roof over your head and sufficient income until you can find some means of supporting yourself.

There is no shame whatsoever in accepting help for yourself, if it gets you out of your homeless predicament. But if you refuse to leave Monica then I don't see how anything is going to change. It's probably a waste of time to keep labouring this point as you don't seem to get it, and the last thing I want to do is upset you. But Alex is not happy about giving you cash when she knows you hand it over to Monica, when it's YOU she is trying to help. What's the point of any of us giving you cash if you immediately give it away to someone else? It's kind of like kicking us in the face, and makes us feel that all our efforts are wasted. I love you no matter what, but you cannot expect me to feel the same about your friend: I don't wish her any harm, but J and I simply don't have the kind of wealth that is needed to keep her off the streets in expensive hotel accommodation. Whatever your land may be worth (and it certainly isn't $10,000) if you sell it and hand over all the proceeds to M do you SERIOUSLY think she will hang around? Forgive me for being so cynical, but I predict she will do a disappearing act one she's cleaned you out for all you're worth, and you'll be left high and dry.

I have to say this even if it offends you, because I have to try and make you see sense. You are far too emotionally attached to M and therefore not seeing things clearly. Even if she herself isn't just hanging around you for what money she can screw out of your relatives, the likelihood is that there are other people in the background who are using HER in order to get their hands on hard cash. I think you're being played, you are the one being set up here. Be very careful who you talk to about any land or money which you hope to come into, because you are putting yourself in physical danger. At the moment you are useful to them as long as there is a prospect of forthcoming cash, but the minute you hand it over then you become expendable and someone could just kill you to shut you up and cover up their crime.

Love as ever,

Leigh

**From: Cass Ryder**
**To: Leigh, Alexandra**
**Message: Very Angry**

Frustrated jealous green penises watching Cassandra. Good, we killed him okay and his homosexual pan-racial electronic surveillance force. We murdered them both we murdered their plans. It's sad how they ejaculate and they love their dog. They are completely frustrated at me, at who I am and the fact that she even chooses to resonate with me. M is their GODDESS....they ejaculate to her in unison. They're desperately trying to murder me every other moment. All she did was try and get me to stay with her. They're extremely frustrated that I might have any influence over her, that she might have a friend. I'm convinced a mafia dick watches her electronically, her every movement. It's either an audio recording that they drilled into her brain or a channelling. It seems something takes her body. I hate you and I hate the lot of you and you're going to understand just how much I can't stand the human race ... away from the king, away from the general, away from endless pregnant cunts, women who splay their legs for a living. Well they are up against a force to be reckoned with. I don't give a fuck about politics. There is no war. The war is over. They're degenerate and they're controlled by little old dicks through space and time. I'm sick of feeling like they're inside my soul looking out spying.

Yes but what's more important, essential facts or being able to work a damn caps lock key. You're not sincere at all. I'll accept though that our sad transmissions are being intercepted. I stated overall and specifically that this woman Monica is GENUINE ...what else could they do but try and cast her as a sleazebag...and that someone like me is going to have lots of enemies, that she is being interfered with, and it seems like a colour pink attack. This woman has had loads of money stolen from her by 88888 mafia.

But as you are "white man" that explains why you NEVER respond on the subjects that are relevant.

Islamic state ISIS in the news... forcing impoverished women up to what the writer calls "old man daddy wars" Poor women around the world shouldn't have to put up with that shit any longer....but isn't this a typical "Nine" language gesture leak? The authors of The Stargate Conspiracy state that the CIA involuntarily contacted "the Ennead" while psi research was under way, and the authors' interpretation is that the "Nine" are based on the Egyptian godhead and ISIS who are a syndicate of occult practitioners currently linked in with covert intelligence and poised to take over so-called democracy. I tend to think occult syndicates are linked in with higher government authorities and act like paid hired assassins, but in this case their work was on the astral plane.

I resent the way I'm always so truthful to the point of being a loser because NO-ONE'S listening. I was drugged on a few occasions. I think they were using it as a prelude to kill me. I've told you I was attacked in '93 you didn't respond. It sounds like what is described in the MKULTRA files as Subproject 4. I was dragged out of my body and had a liquid forced down my solar plexus, followed by 20 years of destitution and homelessness, and that's what happened before I knew it. I lost my UK residency (or it wanted me to think I had) and lost fifty thousand dollars or whatever it was I had. The writer was half British and got endless flak for being yoked up to the Queen of England "why don't you go back to Britain?" and she's been flailing around on a loser's ticket since the moment she arrived. You write I have suffered enough. What do you know? Alex is getting this as well. I don't like you or her or any of you. I'll come back to England if I want to and if I don't want to I won't. You have no idea what I've gone through. Every day in a library .. every day forty mile an hour winds ...every day stinking cops lurking in the background. You have no 8888888 idea. All my stuff right now is being surveilled.

They're messing with my work as I write. I just wrote some stuff and that got edited. They're penises I can't take it. I know 88888 is watching... You're such a 88888 you're going to get it you stinking little fasc88888. Uncle Sam tries to torture me, the US govt is so stinking black magic occult lodges. WHY don't you 8888 off why don't you 8888 off. Alex didn't respond back because she feels death threatened. I'm so sick of being watched by those invisible stinking 88888. You're a bunch of jerks.. the truth is my prayer so keep on trying to mess with what I'm writing. They waste a lot of time and energy watching an apparent nobody .... for instance, the database just lifted sentences I mentioned to make the reader miss the message and see me as some foul bitch. Done on purpose, sly as anything. They're deeply jealous to focus this closely on a woman and the way they go about it.

Wire back to me last ten lines of my message very angry but if you don't forget it its not important

Cass

From: Leigh Ryder
To: Cass Ryder
Subject: RE Very Angry

Dear Cass,

I am relieved that you are emailing again from a computer, and have copied in the last 10 sentences of your "Very Angry" email below as requested so you can see whether they have been tampered with or not) I'm sorry you feel I'm insincere but I can assure you I'm not. And as for me being "white man" Jeez I don't even have the appropriate lower anatomy! Though I confess to being white, like you. I really didn't mean to anger or upset you by my remarks about Monica. My conjectures about her being a possible "plant" were triggered by a few of the things you mentioned i.e. how she can suddenly switch from hysterics or tears to a state of apparent normalcy in seconds, which could indicate one of two things: 1) a genuine bipolar disorder or 2) a well-rehearsed act where the "mask" has inadvertently slipped. I agree it's not for me to judge as I don't really know her, but in the context of covert ops, which you suggest she may have been involved in as a former cop, why is this such an improbable scenario? Agents who have been assigned missions such as infiltrating drugs cartels sometimes have to go undercover for literally years: in order to avoid being "rumbled" they have to be pretty damned good at what they do, which in turns means the people they are practising the deception on are usually 100% convinced they are genuine.

For the sake of argument, let's say M had been instructed to keep you under surveillance (though of course this begs the question WHY) The only way she would be able to get close to you would be to pose as another homeless woman. But as it's known you don't talk to many people, she would first have to obtain your trust by pretending to be the victim of occult attacks or by displaying schizophrenic symptoms in order to make you feel you both have a lot in common. Appearing vulnerable and on the edge of a nervous breakdown would be another surefire way to arouse your sympathy. Although you are not gay you are sometimes perceived as such, so another way to gain your trust would be for the undercover agent to pose as a gay woman. As you pointed out back in the 70s and 80s the women's movement was infiltrated by a lot of fake feminists at the instigation of the FBI for the sole purpose of keeping tabs on their activities. Yeah, I know, what a bunch of sad wankers, but it goes on. I'm not saying this is what Monica is, but it's something to bear in mind. She may be completely innocent of any of these charges: if she is a genuinely homeless gay woman with a mental impairment then she deserves a lot of compassion for what she has been through, but if she has been planted on you with the object of doing you harm then of course I'm going to be hostile towards her. That's only natural. I hope she's genuine, for your sake. But for the time being, keep the subject of this email to yourself.

Love,

Leigh

**From: Adam Ryder**
**To: Patrick, Leigh, Luke, Alexandra**

Dear All,

The sooner that we all begin to realize that Monica is most likely not a real person, but more probably a delusional creation of Cass's the closer we will get to realizing that her life can only be improved by professional evaluation and life-long treatment. It is not helpful to continue along the lines that Monica is exerting a malevolent influence over Cass, as Leigh keeps suggesting, without STRONGLY considering that she may well be another of Cass's personalities, uncomfortable as that may be for some of you to accept. Leigh, both you and Luke were sure before that Cass was dead...further that Luke had been in communication with her through the so-called spirit world. You were both wrong then. There is but one avenue to pursue for Cass, and it involves one or more of us physically going to where she is and spending some time with her, with a clear plan of action.

Alex, you say that you have the money, but not the time, and Leigh you say that you have the time and not the money. An obvious solution would therefore seem to be for Leigh to go to USA and for Alex to pay for her trip. As I understand it, Jeremy has now gone back to Qatar to earn another shed load of money. It's time for someone to put up or shut up. If nobody has the bottle then I will go; but not until I have the time, and not without financial assistance to help pay for the trip. In the meantime focus on someone that you CAN help. Maddy. She is non-violent and also requires evaluation and treatment as we all know. She is recoverable. Help her if you can before she finally decides to put herself in harm's way. A lonely council bedsit, on top of the pain that she believes that she has suffered through the years, may eventually push her over the edge. Her world is a fragile one.

Adam

**From Leigh Ryder**
**To: Alexandra**

Dear Alex,

Cass must have called me just before she called you last night as it was close to midnight and we were fast asleep. She said it was urgent and that Monica was getting worse, and made me to listen to a tape recording she had made of a recent argument they had had, presumably to demonstrate that this woman is possessed (or "channeled") I couldn't make out what was being said, but I did hear raised voices and another female voice (not Cass's) screaming "I am a white god" or something to that effect. The woman sounds pretty far-gone, and I guess part of the fascination for Cass is that she has encountered someone who is more disturbed than herself, and this is the basis of their relationship. She and Monica don't even get along very well and argue a lot, but for some reason Cass feels morally obliged not to abandon her without at least seeing her settled somewhere. Therefore any money we pass on to Cass goes straight to Monica, and I agree with you this cannot continue. Monica is not our responsibility and we have offered a lifeline to Cass in that we are both willing to fund her travel to the UK, and I would personally see that she is fixed up in this country with a roof over her head and an income. Before we were cut off she insisted angrily that she doesn't want to be on the dole in England, or to be a financial dependent.

Adam's self-righteous comments were less than helpful. He appears to suffer from chronic envy of anyone who has more money that him, hence the snide digs at us to "put up or shut up" and your husband going off to earn another "shed load of money" in Qatar. If anyone is delusional it's him. *"There is but one avenue to pursue, and it involves one or more of us physically going to where she is and spending some time with her…"* What a brilliant plan of action, got to hand it to him. One of us heads off to Virginia in the hope of finding Cass who just happens to be homeless with no physical address, and then we happily squander thousands of dollars on expensive hotel accommodation for possibly months whilst we try to persuade Cass to have "treatment" – which as you point out we cannot legally coerce her to have. She's a paranoid schizophrenic and won't go near a shrink. Or alternatively we investigate the possibility of having a valid passport re-issued for her (a bureaucratic nightmare which could take up to a year) but hey, who's worried? Good ole Alex and Jeremy will pick up the tab. And as for him offering to meet Cass if you fund his airfare, easy for him to say. If we called his bluff and said fine, go ahead, he'd run a mile. He's never made any effort to communicate with Cass so far, despite having email addresses and now a phone number. And presuming to lecture us on Maddy when we have both have hosted her in our homes for extended periods is a bit rich. As it happens it is always me who sends her something on her birthday and at Christmas. If he is so concerned what's stopping him from doing the same?

STOP PRESS!!! Adam has just been unanimously voted Personality of the Year by the inhabitants of Loserville.

Nobody expects Patrick to be able to do anything much since his stroke (I know he and Susie only have a small pension to live on in Mexico since he was forced into early retirement) and I'm sure that remark of his about Prozac wasn't meant to sound callous but it shows an astonishing lack of insight into her circumstances. A female sleeping out on a park bench at night and in imminent danger of being attacked cannot afford to be heavily sedated. She needs her wits about her the whole time, and Cass is savvy enough to realise this. Back to last night's telephone call. I tried to hint that the conversation was only supposed to be 5-10 minutes, and that I did not want her wasting all her dollars on phone calls (for some reason she didn't pick up when I called her back) but couldn't get a word in edgeways. In response to my observation that I honestly don't know how I can help Monica, she retorted "I'm not ASKING for your help!!" I knew that if I said a word against Monica she'd blow up, so I held my tongue. The fact that she seems to think it's perfectly OK to ask family members for cash to help her friend out is somewhat irritating. However, I cannot get mad at Cass because she is so unworldly and one has to continually bear in mind the following facts: when you or I are stressed out we can do any number of things, such as soak in a hot bath, have a glass or two of wine, have a good night's sleep in a comfortable bed, talk it over with a supportive partner, watch some TV etc. She can do none of these things. She cannot even get a decent night's sleep and is now suffering from a dislocated left shoulder and bruising from the attack in Baltimore, so for these reasons I cut her a lot of slack. You cannot help but pity her in her predicament.

But as long as she insists on hanging around this woman she is lost. Admittedly it's her choice, and she is her own worst enemy, always has been. Now that M is fully aware that Cass has family who are capable of sending her sums of money she will continue to hang around until such time as this KY land thing has been resolved in the mistaken belief that she will come into $10,000 or so. Once she's cleaned Cass out she will bugger off, leaving her high and dry. From an earlier communication I gleaned that Monica and a former colleague called Liz accidentally killed a black man who tried to rape one them. I don't know whether to believe this or not. OK I know horrible things happen but this sounds like the overblown plot for some 3$^{rd}$ rate crime thriller, what with the Mafia involvement. M is supposed to be on the run and in hiding because of this alleged murder. Personally I think the woman's a drama queen and prone to hyperbole. Maybe she invented this cock and bull story to add a little drama to her otherwise drab and monotonous existence. What do you think?

Leigh

**From: Cass Ryder**
**To: Leigh Ryder**

Just one more surveilled day in the library with something gathering information on my thought processes. Fifty ways by which to "grab" the alternative female. You have no idea do you? There's an ongoing congressional enquiry into the abuses of power (the homeland security database stuff) and people claiming their emails are intercepted. They in no way have the right to do this. We're taking liberties in the library? It's not exactly taking a liberty when one doesn't have any choice but to go to a library. No they invade my privacy FIRST just like they set me up to be a homeless idiot. Done to attack the "*humiliore*". Wow they got a real criminal they got a real bin laden. They're upset that I'm NOT in a bad mood, and I'm not really ugly or obese, or with my forehead on the ground in a minimum wage job.

We're leaving the library and waiting for the plaza restaurant to clear in order to crash there. The subject is dozing off and continually berates the writer with comments like "they're all a bunch of shit" Last night a black man walks by our bench (M doesn't wake up) and writer readies the can of mace. He walks on by, so she falls back to sleep then wakes up to notice him walk by closely again. Writer felt like it was a deliberate set up to point out "You don't protect her. We could do anything to you" Subject had been saying the word "nigger" continuously before falling sleep, and earlier at the library had been loudly whispering "…cocksucking motherfucker" When she does that she sounds like a rap artist, or a channelling by a black entity to piss off people in the library. Later in the evening when she started again with the racist verbalising it sounded like some white supremacist. Writer's theory is that occult forces use her body to attack the opposing race group with, and the man walking by seemed like "revenge" for her reiterating the n word, which was specifically angled at the writer. They're basically saying "We would kill you and leave her all alone" She's scared of being attacked… it's there like a chill. Every night we're threatened with assault, I already have been 3 times.

This society spends far more on criminals in jail than on homeless vulnerables. They set up crime and over-procreation like an overstocked fishery and then stand back, casually picking them off as bait for sport. Weren't they fed as bait like a tuna fish to a killer whale? The national psychiatric association stated that more than 6 weeks solitary confinement is enough to do irreparable mental damage. Many homeless people have been in isolation for much longer than that… most homeless don't talk to anyone. For her it's already been over two and a half years….anyone would go insane. The recent federal efforts to get the homeless indoors are insincere in terms of a psychological block to stop people tapping into those funds. For most of them homelessness did a large part of the damage, after which they're then picked on and persecuted for being homeless. And consider how they can come from vastly different backgrounds, can be seen as "pawns" on a board game who get pushed around by egotistic players.

Mental illness is the hallmark of the modern era. Most people aren't ill they're solar plexus silver cord assaulted. M doesn't want to see a doctor. She adheres to a fairly good diet, doesn't drink or smoke, is hygienic (we both are and use wet wipes to keep clean) Her body is a vocal mouthpiece: screaming to the cops "You just aren't getting this…I am perfection, I am superiority!" She literally comes over as somebody puppeted, a recorder with someone's else's voice coming through – in this case a furious man just spitting violence and revenge intent… "Let karma take care of it…let it crash in on itself…let things rip. They're dirtbags and their children. I was not meant to live like a piece of garbage" Any positive energy coming from her – like her singing or smiles - would quickly evaporate, replaced by something extremely hostile, cussing in the most disgusting crude and offensive way. Something vulgarises her, and in this way they alienate her from people who are sympathetic towards her, and a women's community are going to wash their hands of her.

They manipulate her in a cartoon caricature way to be extremist and white supremacist, like mocking an old lady, to make her look crass or gross in order to put people off so no-one wants to help her. The average male on the street is shocked, and seeing her openly associated with criminality, illness, and insanity react to her as if she is this – a caricature projection. The spirit world sets up a false personality for character assassination purposes to discredit a person and everything they say. They control the emotions which are then like red flags to a bull causing the person to go to extremes. The person is judged, and then splits off and defends the extremist self in what manifests as an excessive egotism blocking off ordinary channels of communication. The spirit entity consolidates its hold this way because a person loses friends. Anyone who expresses an interest in her is "blown off" as they see a reason to lose interest. And yet a higher self seems to be trying to hang on to some kind of awareness of what's happening, but it looks like she's subject to "soul twists" and has no defences against this kind of disembodied attack. For example the writer's personal observation of "soul floods" is that they are usually wired into something sordid: on one occasion I had a lucid dream about experiencing feelings of amour with Pekinese dogs. I would invariably be dreaming when it occurred…it's disgusting, it's as though they're literally "milking" an animal.

If M is in the wrong neighbourhood and is confronted by people who don't understand her, her perceived racist views are going to be received with hostility. But in all honesty I don't think this is even HER. Sometimes it's like listening to a tiny baby mafia "I'm going to get them, I'm going to cut their throats" But if a person's symptoms are an example of an involuntary channelling, does one blame the person for what comes out of their mouth? Any more than one beats up a computer because one doesn't like what's on the screen, or a parrot that's been taught swear words. No, I don't think it's her speaking but in certain circumstances I could actually envisage her "going for them" and then what have you got? She can't carry a backpack or get lost in the wilderness and be in some sense restored like I've done. She often talks about home, wants to "go home". There is no home for her to go to and she doesn't cooperate on anything and is in danger of jail or a mental institution. A cop asked me yesterday "Do you feel she's a threat to herself or the community?" I said no. I've done my homework. The law no longer institutionalises but if a person is perceived as a threat to themselves or someone else they can be forcibly incarcerated. But people get abused in institutions. Some perverts who work in hospitals would take advantage of a woman with a psychic impairment. A Japanese researcher once said in response to a question about his views on psychiatric commitment "what are the various definitions of rape?" Okay what are her other options …oh the bench where we crash at night. She could get bustled into a car trunk, drugged and put on a plane, she could be roped into the white slave trade or just smacked in the face or worse, and then be a wheelchair-bound homeless person. Loads of innocent people have been done in recently and we're always in danger of being considered as soliciting, loitering, trespass or being accused of disorderly conduct. It's all bad in terms of dependencies, but the final worst dependency is compromise of health. I just try and stay positive.

Last night was awful. The writer said something to the subject she wasn't at all proud of "Hurry up and go to that mental home you're headed for" But she would practically hit me in the face if I said anything at all, even just to murmur agreement. It sounds like it's a man coming out of her and he's the one the writer objects to. It's just a never ending "You're a piece of shit and I'm superior" She let on her father would punch her in the head as a child or teenager, and if that kind of thing went on? The liberalization of foodstamps has been useful, however last month this was knocked down from 7 dollars daily to 5.50. There's a warm office in the town that stays unlocked and if I could get a portable bolt… I don't know if such a thing exists… then we would feel safe. It's much more of a crime trap on the bench beside a 24-hour MacDonald's where we are. The cold weather shelter opens in two weeks. Subject barely managed to turn up when it was just as much her right as other peoples, and I had to escort her right up to the bus stop. It's hell during the day, to mean 14 hours of walking and loitering about between 7am and 9pm when the bus picks us up. The occupants on the bus are often a bunch of loud partying men. No wonder she's scared shitless. I would rather be on my own, and had no problem with crashing in a tent at night in woods, but that's also how I know about covert actions...deer mite drops, swine flu virus drops, sometimes the apparition of men who look like they are trained Manchurian candidates.

Last night the subject said "if Claudine's involved I'm going to have her gutted like a pig and her neck slit" She said it to upset the writer. "Gut their children like pigs and kill all soldiers. I am a God. Get the picture?" The writer's impression is that the subject is definitely under the influence of something, and that this is being done to make an association of lesbians with dangerous sadists who want to kill people, and to promote a phoney response in mothers in defence of their children, when there is NO THREAT. She's like loads of women, her back is against a wall and she's saying exactly what they're telling her to, but maybe she's being used to fuel their agenda, and her laughing is why the slaves sang in the cotton fields. What they are also trying to do is pit me against her, and I'm tired of feeling like an entire nation gangs up on me every day. What gets me is the unbelievable swearing, resonant of what you'd find in a hard-core porn mag or what in Britain is called a "video nasty" Another thing she said "David Smith will get shanked and fucked up the arse in a New York jail. Going to take these perps back to NY for processing" (rehashing in her head memories from when she was a correctional facility officer?) The New York police are known to be fascist and it was sickening to hear this endless "they deserve to be beaten and killed etc" (the perps) and it just seems a little extreme for a normal person's prejudices, but it could be a self-protection mechanism to seem to be in step with the police...the cussing as a kind of psychic self-defence, the way a turtle curls into its shell or the way a chameleon camouflages?

To say a Mr. Hyde takes over is an understatement, she's literally vowing she'll cut peoples throats and make them go to a New York jail etc. and has recourse to really uncouth language. The aggressive vocalisations seem representative of an entity "droning" (her term) and she sees nasty red rings materialising around her neck whilst she's singing. She appears to segue into "fascist mode" at night-time or early hours of the morning: "America should keep out people who aren't American" and she is totally obsessed with "can't stand niggers or spics" but apparently trained with lots of African men at John Jay Criminal College of Justice. She seems to very much walk in the path of a rightwing Republican, you couldn't get more patriotic shit coming from her mouth, whilst another side to her very much rebels against that and is for womens/gay rights. She was much more open-minded in the 80s, and then in the 90s it all changed, but as I keep saying to her in response to her extolling the virtues of the CIA: THE CIA PUT YOU HERE. To hear her speak half the time is enough to make a person sick. For example, "The homeless need to be rounded up and shot. They treated me for 3 years and had me screaming in the street. They're going to get rid of your brain chemistry with testosterone poisoning. Their jealousy is just soldier's green cock. Men deserve to be imploded" As though she was the Queen of Hearts in *Alice in Wonderland* "I'll have them deposed. They are beneath me" and "The NSA had no right to involve me in their scummy experiments with green cock for soldiers who are living waste, when I have to live on a bench like a piece of scum and they've got a life because they have a cock. It's their world, let men take care of the problems they create. They're going to pay. I want them dead. I'm not a piece of garbage, I'm a god and I've known gods. The NSA are going to pay. It's all going to be rescinded. I am perfection, I am superiority"

There were no women's communities the subject could have fled to. As for the website info you sent on the "lesbian enclave" in *Carefree Blvd* they look a little mind-controlled themselves or intimidated, put it that way. There are a lot of dirtbags out there like Bob and his harem of hookers… bigots who totally endorse WOMAN GIVING IT AND HIM TAKING IT and the projection being given is that they chose this. No prostitutes choose their clients or pimps, they have no choice most of them. Meanwhile, her mental state has gotten a lot more non-clarified (unless it is an act) with encroaching deterioration of the psyche. She used to be fanatical about going to day shelters at least once a week for a shower, and was a lot more robust and enlivened when she came back from Baltimore (when she left she was getting to be like a living corpse) Another thing she once told me, she was sitting on Long Island beach reading *Mein Kampf* but it occurred to me that they have been calling her a Nazi for a long time, when they set her up to be extremist or white supremacist. She needs to get the hell out of here or GET INDOORS. She can't keep living on the pavement (and the daypack theft made me nauseous because I went through something similar many years ago) I lost things a lot, I'd come back to my tent in the middle of the night and find it stolen, along with my sleeping bag, and it definitely felt like things were blocking my capability to trace my steps back home. I see it as a kind of invisible hostage-taking supplemented by electronic surveillance. I know I could go back to the UK. I guess that's where I was headed but don't particularly want the dole either. And I can't live with you or with anyone, I have to have my independence.

But I'm tired of living in this Dick Tracey cartoon, like I'm sick of not showering or laundering. And I'm tired of feeling threatened by the worst jerks alive and females that I wouldn't even think of spending one second of my life with. "What one doesn't have one doesn't miss" and the snob cats and fussy pet types get help, the others don't. Lots of women hate me because I'm not a prostitute. And it's astounding how women try to fuck up the kinds who don't go to banana, and their deep frustration over our independent status. They're jealous, just like most women who sold cXXX on planet earth to survive. They fool themselves. Who isn't fooling themselves today? Who isn't nurturing their ego like some unbelievable wound? They're obsessed with suffering, it's an obsession, watching them undergo assault contests – those women out there in the open - using the writer as a viewfinder. Women's unconscious energies are turned against one another gladiator-style, and loads of women can't scheme enough to get a boyfriend. They pirouette in front of the world's media as a moral force, they're like Dorian Grey and the stain of their true appearance is daily beginning to show as they frenetically try to cover it up. And women really didn't take things very far despite four decades of feminism. Women do not have to be on the level of barnyard animals because of the view of some old bastard in power worldwide. If radical covert changes are being made for reasons that are pretty gross and sexist it doesn't matter to me as I'm getting on and will die before the full effects of these actions transpire and the biosphere collapses. In a way I totally can empathise that the super-elites need to defend their interests but their interests aren't mine, nor are most women's interests mine. I don't have anything in common with people. But I believe that you just keep going through something ..it doesn't get easier it gets harder…and I'd like to see changes while I'm alive.

Cass

**From: Leigh Ryder**
**To: Cass Ryder**

Dear Cass,

When you refer to M as the "Subject" (much like a psychoanalyst refers to a patient) you come close to diagnosing some of your own mental states: *"...cussing in the most disgusting crude and offensive way....The spirit world sets up a false personality and does it for character assassination purposes to discredit a person.."* This could well apply to you, in that when you are disturbed or angry about something your language and sentence construction collapses completely, to be replaced by a torrent of foul language. Further on you state: *"The person is judged ... then splits off and defends the extremist self in what manifests as an excessive self-egotism blocking off ordinary channels..."* This is spot on, and is an illustration of how your "extremist" self continually undermines and sabotages your higher or rational self, often succeeding in thwarting normal communication channels, leaving you further isolated. Some of M's unconscious utterances *"I'm a god and I've known gods..."* are probably just typical self-defence mechanisms, an attempt to bolster her ego against the constant attacks on her psyche. Something inside both of you is determined to "mess up relationships", and if you are aware of this aspect of the psyche you will be better equipped to challenge it, and to put it in its place. You should not allow your lower self to achieve dominance over your higher self, which requires constant vigilance and self-awareness, and I believe that putting it in writing is helping with this process. Given the right circumstances, I think you might have found a rewarding career in the field of psychoanalysis, as you seem to have an intuitive understanding of the mental processes at work.

You appear to have doubts yourself as to how much of what she says you can believe: *"... her mind state has gotten a lot more non-clarified (unless it is an act)"* Which begs the question, if it *is* an act and she is not as disturbed as her bizarre utterances would lead one to believe, what would be her motive for acting - to gain your sympathy or some material advantage by playing on this sympathy? You say that she is always threatening to get into the back of a stranger's truck, which I see as a form of emotional blackmail because she is aware of the effect this has on you. What does she do when she is not with you and who does she talk to? I hope your intuition can be trusted because right now it is the only thing that will keep you safe. The reason I included gay retirement communities was because I couldn't find any women-only ones advertised on the Internet, and I thought it might be a starting point. The trouble with trailer parks is that they tend to be populated with low-income "welfare families" - often the worst sort of "trailer trash" as Maddy discovered when she left the U.S Navy - and I know you couldn't and wouldn't WANT to fit into that kind of community. I agree that you both need an alternative community where you won' t be judged or hounded because you happen to be different.

The aggression prevalent in overcrowded urban areas is directly linked to the lack of personal space and invasion of each other's personal territory. I've outgrown cities, and have little tolerance for out-of-control youngsters on drunken binges vomiting and urinating on your doorstep at all hours of the night. The nightly mayhem people have to endure is a direct result of the relaxation of the licensing laws. City centre pubs which used to close at a reasonable hour now stay open until 4am, and because of all the screeching, brawling and shouting, nobody gets any sleep. The widespread violence and public disorder endemic in English cities and towns is now such a normal occurrence that the police literally cannot cope, and no longer even bother to respond to complaints from citizens.

Take care of yourself,

Leigh

**From: Cass Ryder**
**To: Leigh Ryder**

The subject cannot get away with moving me to tears out of
concern, and then forcing me to listen without expecting me to
make an appraisal. Agreed I'm not her mom but if a person feels
another person is completely at risk, whilst giving out "help me"
signals, and has a conscience they have to do something to help
them survive. However these spirits, and that's what they are, do
not own her. Something is channelling the subject like a
shuttlecock that goes back and forth across a net. She's got a red
sore spot in her eye (I suggested she get eye drops, she won't think
of it but then again she probably feels she can't afford it) She's
crying right now loudly. On top of that I actually pulled her hair
today pretty viciously. That's why I have to get out of this
situation. She kept putting fascist violence on a pedestal as if to
annoy me... it's just a matter of time before I get implicated for
doing violence on her I didn't do. And I don't need any more
problems with the law. I'm going to have to leave soon. And I'm
not good for her, I think I aggravate her and she stays silent when
she's on her own. She's unhappy three quarters of the time, crying
and screaming. No-one does anything, no-one can. She mentions
Liz like a drowning person clinging to driftwood. The social
worker KB said she's not authorized to talk about it. Personally I
think this Liz used Monica because M had been employed by her
for some social service outfit to do with rehab drug and alcohol
types, but if she saw encroaching mental impairment in M the
kindest thing would have been not to resonate with her for 4 years,
and she should have dropped her off back where she's from in
Long Island. After conferring with the social worker, Liz, another
woman and two men just drove off and left her on the pavement.

I just got interrupted. She had been crying loudly in the library
entrance lobby. The staff called the cops. After an inquiry they
advised her not to stay in the library. I was advised to accompany

her. I'm now back in the library. The subject told me she would occasionally get cash for a hotel and self-execute under a showerhead, then she's back out on the pavement again, destitute and homeless. She actually did this under a shelter showerhead and I would bet that her earlier self would have been disgusted. Pretty fucking weird…loads would beg to differ but I think it's weird (unfolding like a new form of prostitution?) I think that's shady considering her mental impairment. I don't want to detract from cpink and its cause or quest, but the context seems a little seedy, as though designed and surveilled by the forces that try to disempower her. It's sinister, using a woman's body as a viewfinder or interactive video by which to "sound out" and view other cpinks who then become a focal point for attack. Maybe in the psychic domain sexual energy is like "enriched uranium", and they can possess your body in a really sicko way. Anyway she dropped all this information on me (I in no way asked or was interested) literally as though some part of her was disgusted at what was transpiring. I'm mentioning it as an indication of what is helping to destabilize her. I think her body is being exploited in some sort of psychic war based on values, gender issues, race etc. And they're attacking people who they consider "undesirable elements" in the region.

The death threats angled at me are outrageous. The writer experiences endless assault targeting by something invisible, like being in a story she's able to read but is not allowed to comment on. She also experiences mild paranoia and definite mood swings that are objectionable…but if a soldier in battle who swears and yells is something to be objected to, do people in white garb walk up to him and put him in a straightjacket? No. Oh they manage it through drugs? No they don't, just like they can't fix a homeless person's muscle strains overnight. The writer recently incurred a strain in her left shoulder after a 3-man assault in Baltimore, and also has a strained back, aggravated through carrying backpacks for years. One thing I found researching the MKULTRA project is that the chemical secretion of serotonin occurs at the onset of shamanic altered states, as a result of ingesting peyote mushrooms or LSD, but also occurs during the paralysis that sets in during the REM process dream function, the latter acting as a channel for an invisible energy force which the Chinese call "Chi" and Hindus call "Prana". Further, the auxiliary or etheric body separates during the REM process, providing a major gateway with the capability to induce hallucinations. These preset conditions are a big part of ether weaponry attacks, the paranormal domain being dominated by men.

The weapons and tactics they have are a scarce sought-after resource, like a company with a monopoly, perhaps operating like engineers in a sound recording studio pulling levers and pushing buttons with respect to invisible media. The astral silver cord acts like a phone line, and the dream function like a sort of generator that powers a transmission. Or perhaps it all works like Voodoo based on likenesses, and the rigging of a person's number in context of another number or symbol, somehow connected with how the memory works, archivist-style, using associative coding. The job of an occult practitioner is similar to that of a software programmer. Writer tends to think that's what "mind control" is and all the rest is just disinformation…helping to explain mysteries like "I can't understand where it went". It didn't go anywhere (the key, the purse, grocery bag, the spanner) the person just perceived that it went missing. A person's perceptions can be altered by a skilled operative, acting through the astral dimension. But the main targets are the vulnerables - inmates, the homeless, the mentally ill - all seen to be in the "reject" or "loser" category who have nobody to turn to. The research on high school shootouts reveals some interesting things. A Saturday night brawl or relationship feud is one thing, but the reasons given for why they take up a gun are really extreme and non-grounded in reality, providing examples of possible occult manipulation. The apparent reasons are that they are made to feel inadequate so develop an inflated persona to compensate, but it seems a further indication that some occult force uses it to mock these young men by stereotyping them as machismo contenders and failed ones at that. Media personifications aside, the social systems are designed to cause mental disassociation, and nuclear isolation encourages non-communication and distorted information channels. Further reason to believe these are psychic assaults, though it might also be involving remote neural technology, all of which bear the signature and imprint of the covert planners who seem to have made use of the U.S. as their stepping stone.

It's almost certain that enforced bioelectricals occur during the REM dream phase, but I've fought this, I've more or less proved that this can be obstacled. Don't cringe. Yes, insert an object then "fine-tune" its size. I noticed the channel opens out at the back so it was important to make the object firm and with a wider slightly hammerhead-shaped tip. It would be good if a kind of expandable tip could be devised because this is not a nice thing to have to do and can be quite painful. This would bang up against the muscles, and at the slightest movement cause the sleeper to awake. I was then able to mentally prevent the process from "sequencing out". My second sense warned me when it was going to happen, and it started to slack off when I began doing this. In retrospect urinal pads would have eventually been necessary. Naturally I would bag the thing and have plenty of wet wipes on hand. It would put pressure on my bladder, and my bowels would need to offload early in the morning. Being crashed somewhere out in the open and not close to a flushing toilet, I had to dig a hole the night before as I had no choice but to shit by the side of the road. I realised I had to pull it out before I woke up in case of stumbling and injuring myself. But enforced bioelectricals can be counter-attacked. I proved a woman could do something about it mechanically by an insertion and muscle blockage. Whoever they are can't bear the thought of women overcoming it, and before leaving my crash site I would stick up a kind of "fuck you" poster for any kind of spirit world looking on.

Another woman in the county called Claudine, who we last saw 2 years ago when she invited us to her apartment over the New Year, disclosed she was taking a fistful of pills each evening to help her sleep. And this might be in response to a similar attempt made on her, but she seems too mind-numbed and kittenish to make any effort to counteract it, obviously wrapped up in the 24 hours a day job of surviving. She said she heard the couple on the floor below each night as though she was between the sheets, and witnessed paramedics carry out the corpse of a woman who had threatened suicide (one wonders whether was she on pills too) There are drugs that cause deep sleep, designed to suppress REM functioning, but they come with side effects and I proved it can be fought without pills, and maybe something could be patented. It's being practised on men as well, just 50 different ways by which to control human beings. I believe it's a shepherding tool employed by an elite minority who have hijacked this knowledge and used it to slot women into being growbags or prostitutes. At some level men are really pissed off by women, by the engagements they got involved in…but why take it out on women when they probably instigated those engagements in the first place? Anyway, it's karmic justice that women can fight it mechanically and easily. He thinks he can do violence on her soul. What a bunch of sad mice when you get a man trying to victimise and violate a female remotely. Very cowardly, getting at people when they're off their guard as it's intended to be confused with a dream, when minds are only in a subliminal state of awareness.

Cass

From: Staples Copy Centre
To: Leigh Ryder
Subject: Attachment

The hostility against white women on earth is pretty damn huge.
Her media image looks bad...she's been set up to look like a shady
theatrical piece. The message is that she's the "devil" meaning
she's simply more complex and eludes the linear definitions of
male language. But white woman is increasingly difficult to defend
in terms of her consumerism and stumped agendas. Some feminists
have reasoned that the ancient matriarchies were not always an
example of good governance, and that this was used as a reason for
male violence towards the female, and that these actions turned
competitive and increasingly gender-antagonistic over time. There
is evidence of a fundamental parting of ways at some point in
prehistory between the female goddess symbol versus the male. In
step with mythological research are psychology insights about the
dormant power of the goddess in man's subconscious, coupled with
increasingly neurotic reflexes in terms of a conscious denial of the
power of women. For example, ancient Sumerian artefacts have
been stolen from archaeological sites in Iraq by professional
syndicates. They are not being sold for cash so it's possible that
some group "hogs" and assimilates this information, and uses it to
project a censored reality that endorses the current systems. If the
highly-organised plunder and looting of these dig sites in former
Sumer city state had been about suppressing artefacts and texts
which shed light on the birthplace and common roots of the three
male monotheistic religions (Christianity, Judaism and Islam), the
synoptic gospel would also be seen as a challenge to accepted
religious dogma. The story of the gospel of Thomas the Agnostic is
recounted by employees in the Jungian Institute in Bern,
Switzerland: the gospel is transported by special courier, who
reports several near losses, inferring invisible forces at work (which
might initially look like a Vatican-sponsored manoeuvre)

What has been recently unearthed by researchers, linguists and interpreters presents a threat to current dogma and belief systems, and it could be that the theft is being done to keep back evidence which yields a different interpretation of the deity e.g. Gnosticism implies a goddess who is not a wife or consort, but in this context a teacher imparting instruction (Sophia = wisdom) The value of the Sophia-centred religion of the ancient Semites and Sumerians provides a different interpretation of the allegories in the Old Testament. According to the Gnostic gospel the serpent had wanted Eve to eat the fruit (because knowledge is good for mankind) and the "fall" was supposed to have been a creative act, not a sin. In light of this the New Testament could be slightly altered to accommodate the new evidence while still retaining much that was valuable, as in the Dead Sea scrolls. But in terms of the HUGE role played by religious indoctrination and mind control by male monotheisms in bringing about world order, the obvious conclusion is that such reinterpretations of spirituality would not be desirable.

It is a historical fact that two renowned centres of science and learning, including the library at Alexandria, were razed to the ground somewhere around AD. The Romans probably used the information to claim certain applications of science as their own discoveries and held back others in secrecy. But aren't most men hypocrites with their lunar goddess fixation, rejecting women on a conscious level whilst being deeply influenced by the power of women on a subconscious level. He's a hypocrite and a coward because if he claims women are worthless why does he invest so much energy in destroying and covering up the evidence of female empowerment? If women have no value or power why is he running scared? Bluntly speaking, the world's got a problem with women and Islam specifically does, and they're a bunch of smelly bastards most of them…No? It's gender-based war, it's not based on religion, it's based on man's emotions and his deep-seated fear of women. The Freedom of Information Act reveals that in the seventies the women's movement was under surveillance as a security threat. While half of the feminist literature was garbage and in fact anti-women, men felt threatened by the feminist movement - not so much by the research uncovered, as at the idea of women *communicating* with other women in a meaningful and intelligent way: they had always been comfortable with pitting females against each other in the ploy "divide and rule". When women started to see a common enemy and began to compare notes, sharing experiences and observations, this is what scared the shit out of them.

For example it's noticeable that contraceptive instruction is targeted at younger and younger women, at teenagers who are more naïve and who are psychologically coerced into male alliances by using shepherding control mechanisms and ongoing stereotypes like the glamour girl/glamour boy imagery as being worthy of emulation. The solution might lie in older women not repeating the cycle of their recent ancestors, that a positive projection by older women helps younger women to see a different route to one of compliance with males, and if that means having no relations with him or with his systems then so be it. Against this insight lurked the continual fear by the male that this might be the goal. Meanwhile one would think he would have the integrity to want to sidestep his total dependency on women. Men hang onto women like babies onto a mother's teat. While most women might complacently retort that they had freely chosen their husbands, there had always been this ongoing insidious system of affirmations or reprisals angled at them that they would not admit up to, that they had been. The latter group can't bear to see that some other group might have something they haven't got (like self-respect), or that they have been indirectly coerced into something (a male alliance) that the other group simply doesn't want. And the woman of the non-developed sectors is jealous because white women did have something she didn't have (more freedom) so she takes it out on white woman. Because a lot of it is just about ego, and who wants a lot of women lording it over one, even if she is charismatic?

These contests between females matter in an age where man has the technology for close-up surveillance. Women are the major victims in paranormal phenomena, proof of huge energy absorptions to do with high-level mental assaults. They could be trying to take possession of women to a higher level with plans for mind control by trained occultists and remote viewers capable of flipping a switch, exercising techniques that have ramifications for the lives of the common people. They are using homelessness and mental illness as a smokescreen by which some pretty vicious persecution is going on, and the astral dimension that Dion Fortune wrote about is coming to the fore in new science paradigms of bioelectricity, morphic resonance etc. All this represents a dawning awareness and insight into the psychic domain, involving a threat to the Holy Triad, which might shed light on upswings in fundamentalist religious indoctrination. The Islamic terrorist is an example of the character deficiency of a certain type who will not "remove the veil" – the veil being a metaphor to indicate deception and cowardice. As an Islamic feminist pointed out, the imposition of Sharia law is an example of a global conspiracy by a bunch of Arab and African dicks who feel threatened by women, in particular Western women. Which at the same time is checkmated by Western powers in an ironic attempt to apply these same forces to stave off the dominance reflexes of the Holy Triad, so as to ensure power remains with the present power brokers, which is where things are at now.

Parapsychology and anthropology indicates that over time men tend to dominate the "harmful" occult side while women, if involved, tend to be students of "white magic", the healing side. The roots of all this lie in shamanism. Man in prehistory and in certain cultures possessed a spiritualism known as animism, a belief in the soul of animals. For example the caves of Lascaux in France have depictions of stags etched on walls, now known to have been an instinctual or intuitive understanding of the connections between imagery and the psyche. A similar example was revealed by the Dutch explorer Van der Post in his explorations in and around the Congo. His observations of how pygmies draw a diagram of a deer in the sand, aim at its heart with their bows and arrows, then stand back and watch the deer show up and become deer meat, might be an early form of sympathetic magic. The Maori are known to have done something similar with sea mammals. When flute music is played upon the shore as a lure they "fin" their way onto the sand as though offering themselves to be butchered. The seventies bestseller series of Carlos Castaneda were based on the phenomena of shamanism in Mexico ... skills which in a modern business context could earn one loads of money but which are traditionally associated with a higher spiritual self and non-attachment to things material.

Many animal species have been used in experiments to increase knowledge of etheric weaponry wielding, an example of something originating from shamanism that has turned bad - turned away from healing and spiritual guidance, which had been its original purpose. In the 70s the CIA experimented with chimps whereby electrodes were inserted into the hippocampus, which were then stimulated and machine monitored for neurological feedback. They have also been used in the context of induced orgasms. Why? THE THUGS MOVED IN WHERE THEY ALWAYS HAD BEEN. Sick enough that it has been employed on animals, but the idea that the usage has graduated to remote manipulation of the human nervous system is even more sick.

From the foregoing it can be extrapolated how animal exploitation is all tallying up like a debt which ultimately backfires on homo sapiens. Insights produced by the Monroe experiments ... in this case between human and animal energies...suggest the existence of an auxiliary cross-communication channel which might be received by man in uncomfortable ways that erode his confidence, like a nightmare or an agitation state, with an animal projecting resentment or disapproval. Psychiatric case studies reveal incidents where people are apparently possessed by animals, and this might be a connected with revenge and inherited negative energy fields. One case history about a man who felt compelled to kill his wife, reveals under hypnosis a story of a bear that had been tortured with fire by a group of men in a cave, and further analysis revealed that the man is possessed by this bear's spirit. It's ironic that what is causing the stepped up $co2$ warming (heavy oil usage) is said to be the calcium carbonate remains of the living organisms of the pre-Neolithic past. The dinosaur is even now "reaching out" to vanquish the species that was destined to go before. It has been speculated that man was selected as an agent to close down all biodiversity, because as a mechanism or way of life it is inherently weaker than the dinosaur mode. And a future resurgence will be about very little biodiversity, in the context of an anticipated imminent extinction of the human species and reversion to clone status.

In the Koran it states "In the beginning was the ray" and this may be a reference to electromagnetism (to do with energy wavelengths and frequencies?) A parallel reference was thrown up by a British researcher Lethbridge in a book entitled *The Power of the Pendulum,* who goes onto explain there is a vibrational rate and an electromagnetism underlying all things. Lethbridge goes on to speculate how a sleeping person's auxiliary or astral body separates from the physical body and journeys through the astral plane. He claims that the dream world is not a fantasy world but an alternative reality in another dimension. The composition of the physical body prohibits survival across time in terms of space travel unless one can accept the Star Trek notion of wormholes. But time travel might make sense in the context of an etheric body, leading to a different concept of travel …not physical travel across cosmological space but astral travel, which might shed light on the ability of "ghosts" to dematerialise and rematerialize. Can the etheric body affect another person in terms of a sympathy wavelength they both are on? The influence of the invisible realms on biological, neurological, physiological systems in humans is taken very seriously by occult practitioners who argue that there is a proven link between emotional thought forms and energy fields that can traverse time and space. The psyche creates its own realities and if a person feels targeted they are in a sense targeted, since mind and matter influence one another (the perceiver affects what is perceived) the key component here being heightened emotion where the human psyche acts like a tuning fork in a constant state of vibration, tuning into other electromagnetic wavelengths.

In the field of Neurotheology they are now beginning to understand how emotions are capable of being influenced both by electromagnetism and bioelectricity… and it's now known that elm pollution interferes with concentration and thought processes, producing nervous or agitated states, eventually destroying the brain barrier. There are mechanisms or techniques that can be utilised to transmit or pick up on these frequencies, and this can form an ether weaponry realm using skills similar to those needed to operate modern warfare aircraft like remotely-piloted drones. Rupert Sheldrake, who wrote about morphic fields as constituting part of a new biological discipline, is on the tip of a revolutionary wave that is either going to do a nosedive or usher in a radically different way of living (at current rates it's doing a nosedive) However, if his research is accurate and emotional energy is capable of working across space and time then maybe it's even possible for people's energies in a past time continuum to resonate with others in a contemporary space or time continuum, in terms of providing empathy. It could work both ways, in that traumas are inherited through the collective unconscious (the past affects the present) Morphological biology and Gestalt psychology both suggest that people are influenced through inherited energy fields, quite separate from DNA. Where woman's nature has been misunderstood and then proactively persecuted during a collective exposure over the last few millennia, these traumas and animosities have been inherited through morphic energy fields that resonate across time and space. These are powerful energies that come back through time like a debt that remains unpaid and keeps accumulating interest. There is the possibility that re-engagements like "unresolved karma" do make sense, and that the modern era is an example of the reaped harvest of earlier genocidal actions and a rebounding of these energies which, if not challenged, bode badly for the future.

Neurological research has recently referred to the notion of separate male and female brains with distinct differences along gender lines. If women's brains have greater comparative complexity, then it's possible to extrapolate in terms of a kind of separate emotional or mental faculty in the latter. And if emotional energy is a powerful force field, then it could be harnessed to further specific ends. This leads on to the possible use being made of higher female bioelectrical capabilities, through which to maximize a certain kind of interface/surveillance. It has to be remembered that attacks on women are largely on their unconscious energies, and that an objective process of natural laws has been overlooked, namely the presence of an invisible emotional energy and the probability of a connection with other living things. The success of a sorcery attack is based on the existing mindset or emotional state of the victim. Possibly the only way to counter this would be to "fight fire with fire" with psychic self defence tactics. What has transpired on earth in terms of man's behaviour to woman and to the planet may require an energy transfer, and this may be what's taking place right now with the increase of unpredictable and violent weather-related phenomena. Floodwaters and mudslides are the inevitable spin-off of deforestation and logging, highway and industry construction, and the destruction of fragile ecosystems. Female emotions are inextricably linked in with a collective unconscious and comprise a HUGE ENERGY FIELD that broods in the subconscious like a volcano. The destructive weather forces unleashed with increasing regularity, and the damage of the biosphere may be a manifestation of all that suppressed negativity, an act of revenge set in train by (female) earth energy.

Subjective attacks on individual women aside, man has messed up, like a father who mismanaged his household in a feudal system. It may be time to realise she's very upset, and time to gently assist in re-channelling her viciousness and dormant violence due to states of suppression imposed on her. Ancient Vedic texts describe how men and women lived in separate societies. A radically different type of existence experienced at a much earlier time phase could possibly be "tapped into" in terms of a kind of invisible covenant of sympathy and power resource. The triple white goddess of the former Celtic or wherever isles had not been anything other than a male consort, so in terms of something separate from men women would therefore need to go way back in history. But it should be possible to get beyond emotion in terms of an earth science which could provide a conscious plan of action to counter the current covert plan, which not only embodies a "fang and claw" race/gender war, but a lifestyle or values conflict. It can't be denied that most people on earth have a really horrible concept of quality of life and horribly limited expectations. Most people work in pointless jobs that serve to prop up a pointless way of life...and these ways of living are like invisible wires attached to horses in film footage of old cowboy movies, which are rigged to trip up the horse. The systems are pre-set and designed to trip up women and her unconscious energies. A new paradigm would have to mean women stop having children for at least three generations, people consuming far less, and doing something about the rest of living creation ...such as substituting soya-based foods for animal products, the immediate stewardship of all animals in the understanding that man has no right to transgress on their evolutionary niches, and promoting the awareness that eating into the biosphere to the current manic degrees causes psychosis, criminality, madness. And showing consumer materialism for what it is… unintelligence. Dull ways to live and die.

Maybe all women will just go into a state of singularity and indifference, deep freeze or whatever….but they need to refocus on who their problem is since they seem to be so obsessed with the fact that they've got one. The pan-global brotherhood have messed up so severely it's just a matter of time now before they and the people they attempted to rule are going to self-destruct, biospherically speaking. They had a problem all along in terms of womb dependency, the warfare clashes and weather cataclysms that their relations with women invoked. He was a loser in history, he's a loser today. Yes, while all along he took an awful lot from her soul and then tried to turn it around it and say she was the problem. However he's the problem and if the world wants to keep on taking it from men with their brains in the tenth century holding up a cross, that's their problem. And souls go to where souls resonate if they survive at all, and those without a problem essentially just don't come back to have to re-encounter it. And women are forever being blackmailed with the crying of children. That's like a putting a caged bear on someone else's property and blaming the property owner. The answer is to stop having children, and whatever they do or not do on the sad subject of you know what, pregnancy is the point and not the other thing. People are a little perceptually distorted on the subject and think it's inevitable. Go forth and multiply....why? Do people today have to listen to the dictates of a bunch of old men (drug takers at that) who were roaming about in the Judean desert 5000 years ago?

And some of us saw the corruption in it all and didn't want to repeat the mistakes of recent history, and for that are expected to have to put up with a lifetime of mental assaults and economic impoverishment. And haven't an intelligent minority been proactively YOKED UP TO IT like pouring salt into a wound? But half the people should not have to put up with the warped philosophy of the other half, hence the need for separate communities. It's not uncommon for a Japanese man to also have a Korean whore alongside his wife. Well, if the wives are allowed to speak they should point out what fucking assholes the husbands are, and when they get a chance they should fight it and try to figure out why procreation happens. One big reason is superstition, survival of the soul through the bloodline, consolidation of a dynasty or estate to pass on, or a reincarnation belief running through the world. The writer always found the concept of reincarnation suspect. What it does is galvanize people into growbagism, esp. in the Orient as it developed into a direct "survival of bloodline" through the rebirth of a recently departed ancestor. Man seems to have definitely inherited an obsession with procreation in terms of inherited archetypes via their genetics. A fear of physical or material loss at death does shed some light on this obsession, but perhaps the tribal feeling of influence from another person's energy field resonating on the same wavelength comes into it. But individuals are essentially different like a fingerprint or DNA is unique, therefore if individualism matters procreation is not that important, but if everyone is serving a group or tribal interest then it does matter due to the perpetuation of an energy field. Any progress then meters out - the bitches win, men are drugged-out pinholes, and all the rest is capital in motion. In consideration of this kind of razor edge competition it gets a little sickening in context of where it's all going.

There has been a massive scapegoating of people whose lifestyles are different or alternative, and punishment meted out in terms of increased poverty, illnesses, accidents etc. And a lot of people post-sixties seem to have been caught up in it…an ageing minority who hailed from the middle and rising lower classes, mainly confined to the north western developed world and who have about 30 more years or so to live. The former ageing groups are the only ones who can speak, and the up and coming so-called "educated" younger generation have no MEMORY or knowledge and are probably not going to be capable of the challenge. There is a collective amnesia and the world has maybe about 15 years for this information to be made public before it is totally suppressed as it has been throughout history. America is either going to get better or worse, and based on what I know it's not going to get better and good luck to the brave new world coming up. Far better to anticipate it, get a "north face" and learn to live with it. More realistic and intelligent ways to live might involve death with dignity, solo living and scaled back technology with the capacity of living much more simply. It's the dream of lots of people to live simply but qualitatively... a new economic paradigm that leaves behind materialism as a gold standard, and that liberates a lot of men in terms of an awareness that they are being controlled a by tiny cabal (a clandestine fraternity who hijacked suppressed knowledge) and by acknowledging that they are actually quite burdened and don't have much power.

Most trade on earth, the so-called free market, is conducted between the developed world and third world nations on a par with a bunch of fat men running up the bill at a gourmet restaurant, and a semi-starving waitress who has to pick up the tab because they hightailed it. It's mainly being taken out on women and she is being made to pick up the tab in the same way Buffalo Bill took his mum along for the ride, but her ongoing support cannot be counted on. Which come full circle to what I've seen in my life and what I've brushed up against….increasing revenge attacks on the "restaurant eaters" (equals the developed world) Oh, and women are attacked by the restaurant diners too. If a man attacks another man what does he do? He runs off and attacks a woman. But in terms of who the revenge attack was really angled at it's misdirected. Nordic male had an orgy recently through his dominant global position but didn't see what was going on overall. It would have involved an entire overhaul in terms of inherited gender interpretations and actions. But just like his non-cooperation on women's rights he also proactively "blacklisted" the alternative female, whilst clinging to his harem of whores and wives in a way that makes him look very weak. White man did this cowardly "throw off" of anything that truly challenged him, and I guess all races do it to the females within their race, then try to make women focus on the outsider as the enemy.

**From: Leigh Ryder**
**To: Cass Ryder**

Dear Cass,

I've been re-reading some of the earlier stuff you sent and I am of the opinion that most of this should be published. However in order to make this viable as a project the material needs to be organised into a more readable format - and there are some things that would be off-putting to a mainstream audience. With your permission I would like to try and organise your writings into a more publishable medium, which would involve a certain degree of editing and fact-checking, though I couldn't guarantee to find a publisher at the end of the process. Needless to say IF it did get published all proceeds would be entirely yours since it is your life experiences and your material. I feel I owe this to you.

Your last email was heartbreaking to read: *"I've fought this, I've more or less proved that this can be obstacled...don't cringe. Yes, insert an object, then "fine-tune" its size..."* the lengths you went to protect yourself from what you perceived as attempts at bodily hijackings, and what you've had to go through on your own. But the fact that you were camping out in the open means that you would have been doubly exposed to electromagnetic interference, which could be coming from overhead electricity pylons, cellphone transmitters and receivers - any number of sources. It is obvious that you are especially sensitive to elm pollution, and this can interfere with your brainwaves and sleeping patterns, not to mention the biological effects. Do you recall an incident when you were quite young, visiting me in Bristol back in the 80s and I took you to an underground nightclub? There was a strobe on the dance-floor and the next thing I knew you had keeled over as stiff as a board, completely rigid, with your eyes staring like someone in a catatonic trance. Two men had to carry you out of the club where you recovered as soon as you were away from the flickering lights, but you had no recollection of what had just taken place. It was quite scary to witness, but there are a significant number of people who react in this way to strobes, which can bring on an epileptic seizure. And yes, there are drugs that induce deep sleep and which suppress the REM phase - but as you rightly point out they come with undesirable side effects leaving you groggy, and you need to be mentally alert the whole time if you are to survive. Those with a drug dependency don't last very long on the streets, and soon become the prey of criminals. Another thing I noticed when you were a teenager was that it seemed to take you a long time to wake up in the mornings: most people "snap to" fairly quickly but you appeared almost drugged, with glazed eyes. You would sit on your bed for a few moments in a daze, as if you were finding it difficult to adapt from the dreamworld back to reality.

An increasing number of people are prone to electromagnetic hypersensitivity (EMH) and I think you may fall into that category. Apart from physical symptoms such as headaches, tiredness etc. there are a host of psychic symptoms as these low frequency waves interfere with the brain's functioning, and can manifest as paranormal phenomena. In other words exposure can affect mental health as well as physical well-being. We are bombarded with invisible electromagnetic waves from mobile phone masts, overhead electric power lines, WIFI hotspots etc. Before we moved to our present location, J and I lived in an old stone-built cottage on the edge of Bodmin Moor. For a while we thought the cottage was haunted because we experienced a number of inexplicable occurrences on a regular basis, some of it quite frightening. Most of the stuff that occurred centred around interference with electronic equipment e.g. my laptop would switch itself on even though it was properly shut down with the lid closed and not plugged into any power source, the battery-operated smoke alarm and alarm clock would go off even though we had **removed the batteries** (which seemed physically impossible) And on several occasions whilst we were watching TV the (locked) front door would open quite loudly with the door handle rattling – and someone would be heard to enter the porch: as were sitting only a few feet away form the door nobody could have entered without us seeing them.

Whilst J was working outside in the shed she would hear the car radio start playing, although the doors were locked and the ignition switched off (again, seemingly impossible) All this phenomena started to escalate in 2013 shortly after one or two of the mediums in Luke's spiritual circle told him you were now "on the other side." I was distraught at this news and maybe my depression contributed to the frequency and escalation of these occurrences. J thought it might actually be you trying to communicate on the spiritual plane, and then – out of the blue – we heard from our cousins that you had sent an email to the hotel they own in Wales, and discovered you were still alive! This was back in March 2013. Strangely, the paranormal phenomena tailed off after that. It has since occurred to me that someone else (maybe one of our parents?) was trying to attract my attention by alerting me to the fact that you were still alive, and not to give up looking for you. Anyway, based on the above I would not discount any of the incidences of occult activity you have experienced, but it's worth mentioning there were overhead power lines crisscrossing our garden, and of course I had broadband for my Internet connection (though there was certainly no more ELM pollution than most people have in their houses in this technological age)

I was interested by your research into Neurotheology, i.e. that emotions and moods can be influenced by psychic as well as technological means, and your theory of an "invisible watchdog" utilising this knowledge and skillset for mind control and surveillance/harassment purposes. The notion of an ether weaponry operated by a syndicate of trained occultists is really not much different from subliminal advertising, or media distortions of the truth so I don't know why people find it so hard to accept. As for the "Liquid Magic Experiment" where you were attacked in 1993, I am still left wondering whether your interpretation of this could have been coloured by your circumstances and mental state at the time (insecurity, vulnerability, isolation, paranoia etc.) By the time I was 17 I had quite accidentally acquired the art of astral projection - I never wanted to, it just happened - and had had several OBEs. One night I floated out of my body up to the ceiling, and clearly remember feeling the rough texture of the plaster mouldings with my fingertips. I was on the point of floating out the window before I was returned to my physical body with a jolt. This happened on several occasions but I never became adept enough to travel very far or to explore the astral plane. No doubt my rational mind or superego called a halt and shut down this capacity, maybe in the interests of preserving my sanity. On another occasion I was taking an afternoon nap (unusual for me but I think I was revising for my "A" level exams and therefore quite tired) I was half awake and saw what appeared to be an Egyptian "mummy" figure wrapped in white bandages. At least this was how I described it to people, but later on I realised that I may actually have seen my own astral body swathed in white light unwinding from my solar plexus.

I don't doubt that you underwent some physiological process that involved bioelectricity, as this is a well-known phenomenon. For example, J suffers from backache associated with cartilage wearing away and on more than one occasion has reported that whilst half-asleep in bed she felt a strong current of electricity flowing through her body, as though "charged" or plugged into a socket, and that when she woke up her back felt much better as if someone had used the energy to heal her! I used to sometimes experience these same electrical charges, accompanied by physical paralysis and a sense of terror during hypnagogic states when I imagined something paranormal or ghostly in the room, and I've read that it can occur following extreme bodily fatigue or stress. It is the body's mechanism for releasing tension by relaxing and contracting muscles, and the electricity is actually neural impulses firing off in sequence i.e. an electrical discharge by the central nervous system. However, if you don't find this explanation satisfactory and are convinced that an occult agency was involved, has it occurred to you that any spirit entities might be benign and not malign? Maybe the next time it happens, instead of trying to "block" it you should just go with it, meaning surrender to the energy surge, and observe how you are feeling in the morning (obviously if you feel worse then this is not the solution)

In connection with the above you suggest that certain occult practitioners could be trying to take possession of women, and if this is the case women need to find effective counter measures and go on the attack. They need to equip themselves with psychic self-defence techniques and tap into their own power. Women are in general emotionally more intelligent than men, naturally more in tune with their intuition, the psi factor and the invisible realms, and therefore don't need all the technological weaponry or gadgetry which men have recourse to. Every village once had a "wise woman" versed in herbal lore and healing, but of course it is a suppressed science. That science could become readily available to women again by first making them aware and conscious of what's going on behind the scenes (much like the "consciousness raising" that went on in the 70s) and then deliberately invoking the unconscious female energy forces which surround us. I don't believe all men want to control women, but I agree with you about male hypocrisy in that they consciously reject the idea of intelligent or powerful women (whilst at the same time being deeply influenced by female archetypes on a subconscious level)

You mention that many of M's aggressive verbalisations appear to occur at night-time when she goes into "fascist mode"- so your conclusion is that this is somehow connected with REM process interference, and that she's being "puppeted". I agree it is very worrying if they can also manipulate her vocal chords and muscles, whether by electronic means or by thought transference. On the subject of neuroscience and muscle manipulation, there was a celebrated tennis match between Billie Jean King and the tennis pro Bobby Riggs in 1973 - termed the "Battle of the Sexes" - which was supposed to definitively prove men were superior to women, and that a female tennis player couldn't beat a male tennis player (or so Riggs kept bragging prior to the match, which was widely televised) BJK won the match, she really wiped the floor with him, and he suffered a humiliating defeat from which he apparently never really recovered. However, shortly afterwards she succumbed to this strange paralysis of the legs and ends up in a wheelchair (a super-fit top athlete?) I have since wondered whether BJK's paralysis had natural causes or whether something more sinister occurred whereby she was deliberated targeted, but I guess I shouldn't voice this doubt as it will only fuel your paranoia.

I suppose that logically it makes sense that the mentally ill, the homeless and prison inmates should be the chief targets of this kind of experimentation since they are the most vulnerable. Being stigmatised by society ensures that they are not listened to, which gives the perpetrators a free hand. For many years there have been conspiracy theories surrounding the large number of mysterious cattle mutilations, with claims of UFOS and alien involvement - when it is most likely to be the military - and it is quite feasible that they have since moved on to humans (as long as they believe they can conduct their covert experiments in secrecy without causing a public outcry) Nobody likes to think of this kind of thing happening, but whatever may or may not be going on, I wish you could focus your mental energies on more light-hearted literature, so that you are not overwhelmed by all the negative things out there. I'm not suggesting you read shallow or mindless garbage, but that you follow Monica's example by perhaps listening to music you like when you're in the library, since this appears to put her in a positive frame of mind. The world can be an evil place, but we are what we think and to a large extent we mentally manufacture the world we inhabit.

Love,

Leigh

**P.S.** We recently drove past our previous cottage and noticed it was up for sale again: our previous neighbours informed us the woman who bought the house put it on the market shortly after moving in, and is no longer living there, which makes us think the paranormal activity we experienced may have driven her out.

**From: Cass Ryder**
**To: Leigh Ryder**


They're getting stingier, enforcing compliance to working 80 hours a month in order to get foodstamps. I just went to the foodstamp specialist to enquire about a government program of cash help involving employment. It's only open to women with babies. Keep the job OK. I said they all needed to be sterilised including the wealthy womb, and why don't you get to it by the New Year? It's obvious what's happening. Provisions are being made to allow the chronically homeless to get social security payments, but it's funded through the emergency services/mental health depts so they have to state they are permanently mentally disabled to get it, when it should just be related to unemployment. And when people are DESPERATE for cash they have no option but to comply if they want benefits, which might have a sinister glitch attached, so they end up being dependent and possibly have it withdrawn. Instead they're actively thwarting a potential work guaranteed programme with subsidized housing attached, and single childless people are being discriminated against from getting employment. It matters for people who have worked, like the writer, but NOT ENOUGH to gain eligibility for the basic pension. In other words they're denied the right to earn a pension and those earnings go forfeit.

In the library just now a little suburbanite Christian with tears in her eyes promises to come back and provision us with showers.

Cass

**From: Leigh Ryder**
**To: Cass Ryder**

Dear Cass,

I did some checking on the Internet and I'm pretty sure they cannot terminate your foodstamps, particularly as you are homeless and without an income. I re-read the eligibility criteria:

*"a chronically homeless individual is someone who has experienced homelessness for a year or longer, OR who has experienced at least four episodes of homelessness in the last three years and has a disability...."*

which means you definitely qualify as you have experienced homelessness for much longer than a year. The disability clause is a red herring as it is preceded by an OR: in other words if you fulfil the first condition you don't need to fulfil the second condition. It's not just for women with babies - that doesn't make sense. You may not qualify for extra cash assistance targeted at single mothers, but they are definitely obliged to provide foodstamps for all homeless people. Go to see your social worker and ask her to clarify what is meant. You were probably so enraged you didn't fully understand the regulations. If they are now enforcing an 80 hours a month compulsory work in order to qualify for foodstamps then surely they would have to pay you a minimum wage for your labour, as anything else would be illegal. It sounds harsh, but maybe you should seriously think about it, because any type of paid work would help to get you back into normal employment, and at least you would be under shelter during your working hours. If you are earning wages then you also might be in a better position to get a cheap rental somewhere. As for the "permanent mental disablement" criteria, homelessness is a set of circumstances which may or may not be associated with disability. Conversely disability is a medical condition which may or may not be associated with homelessness. There is no inevitable connection between the two, and if this is what they're telling you they are talking complete bullshit. It makes about as much sense as saying that the homeless have cancer, or are clinically obese. Homelessness has **absolutely no logical connection with any form of disability**. I can't believe the assholes you have to deal with, but unfortunately most government employees who administer welfare payments are not very bright, and have massive chips on their shoulders.

I spent several hours going through the various batches you sent me over the past year, but couldn't find any printout of your earnings and tax paid covering the period 1996-2013 - are you absolutely sure you sent this to me? I don't remember receiving it. Your social security number alone should be ENOUGH to prove any earnings or taxation within the specified period, since it is all recorded on a central database against your SSN. That should be all they need to verify your income or lack of income: all they have to do is contact the IRS to get any information they need relating to your earnings. I don't know enough about the rules to comment further, but IF they are saying you have to work 80 hours a month without being paid a minimum wage - which I seriously doubt - and they cut off your foodstamps I don't see how you can possibly survive! I know you don't want to return to the UK right now, but if it's a question of survival then you will have to compromise. J and I are both fine with you living here with us as long as you need to.

Love,

Leigh

**From: Cass Ryder**
**To: Leigh Ryder**

I mentioned M occasionally self-executes under showerheads and recently relapses into this habit a lot and I just wonder whether it's a control channel... the kind Dion Fortune wrote about in *Psychic Self Defence*. Can you get hold of that book and see if there are any psychic surgery techniques? I tried to order it from the library but couldn't because I have no address. But it would be good if there was a way to nail that dick in the subject's body. Witchcraft is being used and continually watches her, what I call "faces crammed at the Monica window pane" Cop work didn't suit her at all, and only seems to have contributed to brainwashing her. She's on a rough path that is all the more backhanded, just as it is potentially scary since her immediate family went into recent demise. Anyway it's typical you didn't respond on that. I also sent an email about insertion of a candle or a lime to thwart induced bioelectricals, but I notice you didn't mention the "fuck you" sign I would put up. Sorry, but I'm tired of talking about these subjects. Why I think it's happening to M. If a person self-executes, euphemistically speaking, an invisible energy channel or conduit opens through the pertinent chakra, when a "sexing" interference takes place. Like gin given to a baby to stop it crying, as once done by impoverished women. Maybe you should pay note to the following:

RNM or remote neural monitoring – supercomputers are being used to send messages through an implanted person's nervous system in order to influence their behaviour

AIDS and Ebola viruses bioengineered in U.S. laboratories says Dr. Leonard Horowitz.

See extract from the Internet on fluoride, which may have given our mother cancer.

*"Fluoride is another major intellect suppressant that is being added to drinking water supplies and toothpaste. Sodium fluoride is one of the basic ingredients in Prozac and the Sarin nerve gas used in the attack in the Japanese subway system. Independent scientific evidence has claimed that fluoride causes various mental disturbances, and makes people stupid, docile and subservient, besides shortening life spans and damaging bone structure. The first use of fluoridated drinking water was in the Nazi prison camps in Germany (done to sterilise them and force them into quiet submission) thanks to the Illuminati's notorious pharmaceutical giant I. G. Farben, the company that ran camps like Auschwitz, and it still exists as its constituent parts as Bayer. Charles Perkins, a chemist, wrote in 1954 "repeated doses of infinitesimal amounts of fluoride will, in time, reduce an individual's power to resist domination, by slowly poisoning and "narcotising" a certain area of the brain, thus making him submissive" and referred to it as a "convenient light lobotomy"*

To go back to conspiracy theories in the early nineties, much of that stuff may have been a mingling of propaganda and truth … the "men in black", UFOs etc. all look like decoys in a prelude to world event deceptions (some of those authors might have been unconscious or conscious agents) Post 9/11 conspiracy theory states the fbi did the twin towers: the three pilot hijackers looked just like three others who had been cultivated over the years and were paid agents (who later testified and admitted culpability in court) who are then are removed and replaced with the lookalikes. The initial Logan airport plane is filled with agents then removed in the air and replaced by an un-manned drone and permitted to smash into the wall of the trade tower. Sometimes it feels like they are not fighting an enemy, and that the "Taliban" are an acting troupe. There is evidence through personal testimonies of actions by private syndicates, which are not necessarily connected to transgressions by intelligence agencies. For instance, a U.S. female civilian is given life in Peru for apparently consorting with the

"Shining Path" while she was on vacation abroad as a way to punish her father who was a liberal type spokesperson in New York at the time. George Bush apparently went to Peru to plead for her extradition, which is reason to believe that the CIA are being interfered with as well, otherwise why would the president intervene? I guess I shouldn't write any more on these subjects in a public library but something to do with their government really hates me and I hate them and I want OUT of this place, and frankly I don't want to witness her being murdered. This woman M seems as though she is a sort of whetstone on which the post-9/11 crowd are honing the skills of their trade.

But that's the GLITCH I'm always in a foul mood. I was going to ask the social worker if she could provision Goretex type hats, socks and long johns (we've never had coats – M has a threadbare polyester 5 dollar blanket over her at night, one hood for her head and usually this IS IT) She sleeps on a metal bench and only recently allowed me to provide her with an aerobic exercise mat. The area is a well-known wind trap at the base of the Appalachia range and the temperatures are often well below zero most winter nights. She doesn't move despite being in the path of the wind, and I get the impression she is not in control of her shivering. It's either a conscious condition she invites or she is under some coercive influence, as though they're literally telling her to suffer, but the main issue is safety and what could happen to us. With respect to unnecessary shivering she once said to me "They make me do this, they make me shiver like this" It's as though something's dictating to her, but the writer is also aware that you're less of an attack victim sitting upright on a public bench than a lady who's wrapped in loads of blankets snoring peacefully.

The cold weather shelter is not a good idea, nor is loitering in restaurants or walking about in the cold until 9pm each evening, which is really exhausting. There would always be quarrels for a full sixty minutes up to two hours, when her verbalizations are megaphone Adolf Hitler style. Behind that was the perennial fear that she will have an altercation with the shelter authorities, ending in us being thrown out or being put on a charge. She has NO tolerance for the other homeless people. Writer may try and get a job since a store in the plaza where we crash is advertising. This way maybe I could save some cash by next April. I feel bad because I know at some subconscious level, she's expecting me to come up with some cash. Although donations from the public are enough to get us through on food and basics we walk a fine line esp. when she breaks out in the library or in MacDonald's in the morning with teenage boy type sicko innuendos in a loud whisper, which the subject often was NOT AWARE of doing. Others in the library heard her (I got feedback) proving I'm not hearing it in my head. They literally puppet her to say things that are not really her, causing her to attack people in her local environment...sorcery by which the Brujos do their little witchcraft tricks. Writer feels it's like a mediaeval style inquisition, accusing an innocent woman who then becomes a kind of witch. The sorcery is black man's thing mainly ...white man does it in other more backhanded ways, but it's something African channelling her...black people definitely shadow this girl.

Writer thinks the murderous verbalisations would seriously diminish in proportion to satisfying comparatively basic human needs, like an apartment and cash for groceries. But with thin walls in shared apartments loud argumentative voices carry, and frankly it's not going to work if M keeps exploding in rage. But one can get acoustic diminishing devices that form sound barrier boards, even portable "whisper rooms" which are popular amongst people learning a musical instrument. But these apartments paid for by the government seem pretty bleak, and it's a shame they couldn't have provided work. Actually the homeless work hard at just staying alive. Let's look at it this way, society spends a comparative fortune on jail inmates who committed a crime, so what's this obsession with a little bit of charity for the homeless when no-one does anything about bringing down the crime rates or reducing the cost of jails. There's loads of government-funded assistance for growbags who produce at least one baby. Men can't reward procreators enough with job and housing opportunities. The subject went on and on about this, how they couldn't get the whores, girlfriends and mothers indoors quick enough .. many of them live in very nice detached homes, not just apartments. She doesn't get anywhere unless she salutes sausage or his system. Yes he is such a pimp, a male femme fatale who uses credit or favour to blackmail them into his bed. It can get so low, this trading and coercion …I've actually witnessed a pretty young black girl being blackmailed over a second helping in a soup kitchen to smile and chat with men, otherwise there's not going to be any more food for her.

Quality of life for all is being seriously compromised by over-procreation, and the rest is history – rising poverty, overcrowding, escalating crime. Separate gender-based societies would be more in woman's interests, as would options for abstinence, and a subtle non-health-impacting programme of sterilization. As an Indian feminist remarked "Abortion is just another violence, and who wants it for a liberty?" A plan for sterilisation is probably not going to work in the present day U.S. For example, Indira Gandhi's experiment (didn't they call it "ball taking"?) backfired in the form of her getting assassinated. For it to have worked it needed to be covert and under another label. Stupid people are going to keep on cramming junk food in their mouths, and you can't force them to stop. But you can improve the quality of the food, or take away the stuff that's bad for their health. What could work would be a covert program, sugar-coated with a white lie…perhaps a pregnancy viral epidemic not interfering with the capacity to have a good day and applied across all races and across all social classes in a proportionally representative way.

The most recent thought the writer had was to get a ventilated cabin delivered to a woodlot with a portojohn. Another thing I was going to do was make a bicycle rv which would include a tent that could be used at night…. build a small shed on top of an elongated trailer pulled by an industrial cargo type bike which could be fitted with temperature control devices…and pretty much stay on the bike paths and move around on the edge of a met area. It would have to be 10 feet in length by 4 feet wide to carry indoor foldable equipment, and convert into a study in the day and a bedroom at night, and could be biked to one's work or study place. Make it big enough for 2 people sleeping in opposite directions, and put a roof rack and ladder attachment over its edge with a 200 watt generator on the roof capable of charging a heater and fan. Paint the outer walls with fire retardant and make it lockable and chainable to a fixture during the night. Add a portable deodorised camp toilet … the contents released the next day in a park. Probably could have made the whole thing for $1500 including the bike. These are selling today for twice that much. But she needs something stationary that looks normal, and you're right about her as the kind of person who needs a certain standard of comfort.

Writer feels FBI surveilled and that Monica's purpose was partly that (to watch the writer) Who the hell are these sausages? I can write what I want and I'm no God and if I offend someone so what? Possibly it's a prelude to get the subject into an inner city area and into the prostitution trade, or by which to surf in on her energy. She's obsessed (like I was when I was first homeless) with complete hatred of other people, scorn for white trash, snobbery over Africans and "spics" as she puts it, total belief in the educated over the non-educated, the wealthy as being better...and just seems brainwashed, but one man's medicine is another's poison. Her body sometimes seems like a piece of interactive video… no, more like a car that something else drives. I've tried to bring it to the attention of the local authorities but they don't do anything, and she won't accept help because she says she is not a "client" but eats into my foodstamps and takes cash from me. But I'm beginning to wonder just what's being expected of me? Based on what I now know about the spirit dimension and "ether weaponry wielders", they're like movie producers. All these negative happenings (like being thrown into jail) when my sister and I communicated I can now see were designed like a movie set, to create a scenario of a shady or mad person by which to manipulate the perception of people around them, who then think she's weird and treat her in this way.

I'm sending you 10 more attachments. Respond immediately if you get them. I KNOW I'm being surveilled, and something is trying to steal my work. Anyway control freaks are watching and this isn't going anywhere. I don't mean to offend you … a spooked out sister (the one who gets harassed by psychic coverts and remote technology) who's forever going to relate to this younger sister like one would relate to an alarm bell sounding. Based on what I've observed she's extremely dated, she's another apparent John Lennon. Oh well I better send this before it blips off.

Cass

**From: Leigh Ryder**
**To: Cass Ryder**

Dear Cass,

Sorry about the delay in replying but we've been busy outside doing work to the front of the house which we couldn't get a builder to do. Most builders have morphed into property developers and won't get out of bed for less than a cool million. First off, stop worrying about your manuscript. I have taken the precaution of backing up your work onto a secure flash drive (just in case my laptop was to go down) so your writing is secure. Secondly, do you have the email addresses of any individuals e.g. social workers who are in a position to proactively pursue your case for cash and housing assistance, and can confirm whether this assistance is tied in with mental disability? (I agree the definitions you sent are self-contradictory and illogical, so clarification is needed) I don't particularly wish to get involved in red tape and communicating with U.S. bureaucrats, but I will if it helps you, and I therefore need the email addresses of whoever you think is best placed to obtain federal assistance. On the subject of on-line surveillance, it may be helpful to put things in perspective. Cyber attacks are on the increase and are a daily occurrence for many, myself included. It's easy to become paranoid and imagine you're being victimised on a personal level, but this type of activity is actually quite commonplace. I am subject to a constant barrage of fraudulent attempts to empty our bank account by fake emails purporting to be from my bank, requesting I verify my details for "security reasons" My work is being pirated on the Internet, with illicit websites offering my books for free download, which not only violates my copyright but deprives me of an income e.g. my satirical fantasy *Albion Imperilled* ("Narnia for Grown-ups") has been downloaded well over a thousand times, and I've lost an estimated income of circa £15K. This kind of intellectual theft is rife on the Internet but what the hell can you do? As soon as I make a complaint to Google requesting they block the unauthorised content, yet another website pops up in its stead. I suppose the only consolation is that the book is quietly achieving cult status without me having to lift a finger.

Secondly, what M does under showerheads is her private business, and nothing to do with me (or anyone else for that matter) which is why I haven't commented. Indira Gandhi's experiment which backfired in the form of her getting assassinated – a program of sterilisation mainly using vasectomies - was actually spearheaded by her son Sanjay. However, I agree with you that impoverished and ignorant females who keep churning out babies should be sterilised, and the men given vasectomies. They're treated like sacred cows by the system, given financial assistance and free housing – for what, their contribution to over-population? The standard and quality of life for all is getting worse due to over-crowding and the strain on finite resources. Reproduction just for the sake of it is mindless and anti-social, given the overpopulation of this planet. I'm afraid it's the much the same in this country. The benefits system sends out approval signals to people who are basically mindless baby-breeders, whilst penalising single childless adults (taxing them to the hilt so that married couples can claim child benefits) What's even more sickening is the punitive attitude taken towards the homeless, whilst the State proactively mollycoddles and panders to the criminal classes. I must confess I no longer have much faith in the democratic process because it presupposes that the majority are able to use the franchise wisely and are able to make rational decisions. Unfortunately the average person in the street is pretty ignorant with no interest in politics or any real understanding of the issues involved. There's a good case for people not being entitled to vote until they are at least 25, since the young have little experience of life and are too naïve and easily manipulated by politicians. Your solution is far more intelligent i.e. a program of sterilisation which is applied proportionately and equitably across all social classes and races.

I get that you need some kind of cheap accommodation that provides stability, but I must say the notion of a bike RV with something like *"a small shed on top of an elongated trailer"* sounds wildly impractical. Not only would you need a hell of a lot of muscle power to haul it (by pedalling?) but if it's to have a *"portable toilet and tent and fitted with temperature control devices including a 200 watt generator on the roof, and also convert into an office during the day and sleeping quarters at night"* then this would be a pretty sophisticated contraption which would be a prime target for thieves. It sounds great in theory, but the security issues surrounding such a vehicle would mean you wouldn't dare leave it untended if all your gear and belongings are stowed inside. People who own these type of bikes probably have secure garages to lock them up in, and can afford to parade their expensive "toys" on the streets secure in the knowledge that at the end of the day they are locked up out of sight on private property, and not left in public parks or on cycle tracks.

The second point I want to make is, given how harsh the welfare system is in the States, and how you think someone is intercepting your communications and trying to get you thrown into jail etc. isn't it time to get the hell out of there? I understand that you want to help Monica, but you can't. Why on earth would you choose that life for yourself when you could escape from it all? I think you should take immediate steps to get your passport re-issued, and I can provide the authorities with an assurance, if needed, that family members in the UK are willing to accommodate you. I can pay for your flight ticket, meet you at the airport etc. but there is no point in me wasting my money and time unless you indicate you are WILLING to leave. If I sent you some more cash to buy warm clothing would you use it for this purpose, or would you just let M spend it all exactly how she wishes? You see my dilemma. I am not a rich person and cannot afford to keep sending cash, which is immediately snatched by M and gets swallowed up in a few nights at a hotel. And I feel increasingly uneasy about the fact that "she's expecting you to come up with some cash". Are you expected to provide financially for her, in the same way she eats half of your foodstamps whilst refusing "on principle" to claim her own? If she's prepared to help herself to your entitlement there is no principle whatsoever involved here, just plain selfishness. It has to be said the continued association with her is seriously jeopardising your health and your safety night after night, and the fact that you allow this woman to completely dictate how you live means that I can't do a damn thing to help you - but perhaps that's the whole point. Maybe the ill-fated alliance with Monica is MEANT to destroy any chance you have of bettering your life? Perhaps the point is to drive a wedge between us - with me becoming increasingly frustrated and with you becoming increasingly angry at what you perceive as "attacks" on your friend.

You mention in passing that a man recently handed you $70 of which you took $10 and Monica took the rest. If M is such a nice person how can she possibly think this is equitable or fair? If you weren't so emotionally involved you might stop seeing her through rose-tinted spectacles. I have never once implied she is bad or evil (just someone with a serious psychiatric disorder, and in urgent need of medical and financial assistance) but she is certainly no paragon of virtue, and from what you have let slip in your unguarded moments I am convinced she will always put her own interests before yours. I don't think your concern for her is in any way reciprocated. At which point I'm going to sign off here since I don't seem to be getting through to you. Seems you prefer to listen to little Miss Adolf Hitler who (in your own words) "has no tolerance for other homeless people"

Much love,

Leigh

**P.S.** I've just ordered a copy of *Psychic Self Defence*, and will forward anything that may be of assistance.

**From: Cass Ryder**
**To: Leigh Ryder**

I'm sorry to hear your manuscript is being stolen. Isn't there some viral safety device you can purchase or is it too late?

Writer is worrying because M now goes DAILY to the local authorities and mental health dept and sometimes spends 2 hours there ... what are they talking about? It's good that she's talking, it's just that if she's not careful it's all going to come out, these extreme projections and feelings she has about people around her. It could lead to an enforced psychiatric evaluation and she would likely end up in a communal setting with a revolving door relationship with the street. No, she's on a bad path and lithium and government housing would make it worse. The subject has severe psychosis symptoms but it doesn't necessarily mean it stems from mental impairment. She apparently had a compulsory medical, after being picked up on the pavement before she met the writer, and was diagnosed with 3 different illnesses. She also said she had some cranial compression at birth, which can lead to neurological difficulties later. I brought it up with her once, offering to fund an MRI with sister's cash and she attacked me. She rattled off these two words *dementia lupus* and went on to explain her father (or stepfather?) had it. Writer now wonders whether the lupus diagnosis was correct. M seems to have had a different father from the individual who brought her up, so there is cause to be cynical about the diagnosis because if she's not his real daughter then it's likely she doesn't have what he had.

The subject was hovering uncertainly on the county line when she first invited the writer for coffee. When the writer met her she'd weep a lot, and was terrified of men picking her up. Writer knew she felt insecure and threatened by some of the other homeless men. The subject once said in Sterling that things "were holding her against her will." Another thing she would say in the throes of an argument (when the writer would be trying to get away from her) was "that's what they want, for me to be on my own" and she admitted to feeling "preyed on" by the law enforcement (cops) when she was on her own. Which shows how predatory and spooky the wider external system that she lives in is. Her life is an example of running from the Bogyman. But God help her if an evaluation revealed what are really murderous vocalisations, which makes it inevitable there be a court-enforced commitment. One of the health workers said she is going to try to get an apartment for the subject, and said she didn't realise the subject had been diagnosed with lupus, which is pretty strange. Writer feels perhaps the subject is being set up for a premature end. This medical diagnosis may be correct, but isn't this how they "get" at women covertly? A book by Stan Gooch entitled "The Origins of Psychic Phenomena" is about the links between mental illness and the parapsychology realm. They assault with hidden weapons, and the medical establishment just categorizes it as mental illness.

In an Internet article I attached this woman called "Babe" is put on a treatment plan of anti-psychotic drugs, having been diagnosed as a schizophrenic, and the treatment makes it worse. Then after 10 years a neurologist scans her and discovers a pea-sized brain tumour, which grew to grapefruit size. It only became evident when screeching headaches drove her to the emergency wards: the record on misdiagnosis is pretty bad, and it's much easier to misdiagnose a mental impairment than a physical illness because there's no tangible proof. Meanwhile the evidence is pretty huge that diet can cause a tumour to go into remission or an immune dysfunction to go into reverse (which is what lupus is, immune deficiency) As for diet, if we had the money we could hit Tropicana and try out one of those Greenleaf veggie juices. Dion Fortune, who was a psychic surgeon in the fifties, wrote that she had attempted to cut away a client's "silver cord" and therefore the link with a telepathic harasser, but the link was re-connected, the client relapsed and DF had to acknowledge she couldn't help her. But possibly she could be helped today. Perhaps it is to do with the will and some aspect within M is giving up.

The subject also mentioned that her sister and former colleagues were mysteriously putting on loads of weight, esp. around their breasts, while working at Catholic charities in New York....the really diabolical thought occurred that there may have been a viral or pathogen that slows the metabolic rate so that whatever you eat you get fat. There's an occult force surrounding her, managing her like centaurs in the presence of royalty. She wouldn't be around for 2 or 3 weeks at a time, when she was normally there every day...where did she go? EERILY the concept that something is setting her up to sound dangerous and to get a jail sentence. There's a lot of mind control around here to do with religion. Gays (if there are any) are as timid as mice and certainly aren't communicating too loudly. I'm almost certain they are able to "GPS tag" alternative types - in this case cpinks - then as with a cattle earlobe tag keep tabs on where they are. I think she's "trout pond stocked" (my expression for being set up like a lab animal experiment) then they have the liberty of cat and mouse games with her.

The head of emergency services provisioned the subject with a fistful of MacDonald's cards and a one-way ticket to Pittsburgh after a $70 cab ride from Leesburg to the Greyhound bus station in Fredericksburg. They know she's mentally impaired, so why would they do that? That's the other thing, a really bad bruise appeared on her arm before she left for Pittsburgh; a few nights beforehand she was twisting my head and neck so I exerted some pressure on her forearm to release her grip. But I honestly can't imagine I exerted enough pressure to cause the really big bruise on her forearm. Anyway the social worker casually asks "How did you get your bruise?" whereupon she responded "Cass did that" This is the most amazing attack to try and throw me in jail. And this teen who gets gunned down in an otherwise Postman Pat town up the road on 24th May, exactly the same day she leaves for Pittsburgh, is wearing a black and white checked pattern tie in the news picture

(the checkers pattern is on the floors of masonry clubs, see below)
So maybe it's a CHURCH VERSUS MASONRY thing. His name
was Christian Sierra.

*The Masonic checkerboard is one of the most important symbols to
the Illuminati, and used in ritualistic ceremonies because black and
white is a symbol for duality, or the base of consciousness
(important because it is where all other states of mind arise)
Duality patterns such as checkerboards, stripes or zebras are also
commonly used as **triggers for mind control slaves***

Cass

**From: Leigh Ryder**
**To: Cass Ryder**

Dear Cass,

RE the Masonic Checkerboard/Duality Symbolism and the photo of
the young man who was gunned down: are you suggesting the
murder of Christian Sierra was triggered by the symbol represented
by his checker-patterned tie, and that the cop who shot him was
some kind of "mind control slave"? Who were the controllers
meant to be here - the Freemasons? Or were the latter meant to be
the victims because the victim just happened to be sporting a
prominent Masonic symbol? And what on earth was this alleged
crime supposed to achieve? Frankly, this stuff is enough to do
anyone's head in, and you need to keep away from all this Internet-
fuelled conspiracy material. And I suppose the photo of the models
posed on a gigantic checkerboard (captioned Amy Winehouse) is
supposed to signal that she was another *Illuminati* pawn. The
Internet is crammed with all kinds of lurid allusions to Satanist
groups e.g. I came across a website which suggested that the late
singer songwriter (who recently committed suicide aged 27) was
part of the "27 club", and that she had been ritualistically murdered
as a sacrificial victim by some sinister group to which half the
celebrities in Hollywood and the music industry supposedly belong
to. On the website it stated that a close neighbour heard screaming,
howling and drum-beats coming from Amy Winehouse's house on
the night of her death. If that is so, how come it was never revealed
in the police report and that no neighbour came forward to report
what they had heard at the time? It reminds me of the urban legend
doing the rounds back in the 70s that Paul McCartney was dead and
had been replaced by a "look-alike", and that the other Beatles had
deliberately concealed his death in order to go on making records.
Sorry, but it's horseshit.

I don't know what *lupus dementia* is but it sounds like some kind
of horrible werewolf syndrome, lupus being the Latin for "wolf".

Actually, I just looked it up and amongst other physical symptoms the neurological ones include cognitive dysfunction, psychosis, and in some extreme cases personality disorders. If this diagnosis can be confirmed then it may explain why M's conversation is increasingly disordered, and why you have witnessed such a marked deterioration in her clarity of thought and behaviour over the past 2 years. In other words, there may be nothing "occult" about it, no sorcery attacks: it could just be the natural progress of an inherited disease. When you say *"There's an occult force surrounding her, managing her like centaurs in the presence of royalty"* I presume you mean sentinels i.e. guards. Lupus may or may not be curable, but either way you **cannot** help her, so let the medics treat her if they can. It sounds as though she has voluntarily submitted to a psychiatric evaluation and medical diagnosis, indicating that she prefers a measure of comfort and material security to an "independence" which equates to shivering on a bench out in the open. She is not like you and creature comforts are obviously far more important to her, so if she can get the treatment she needs and an apartment at the end of it then maybe this is the best outcome for her in the circumstances. So perhaps you shouldn't interfere, assuming of course that this is her will and what she wants. I get the impression she has a much cosier relationship with the health workers than you do and my advice would be to let them help her if they can.

This brings me on to the second observation, based on the following quote from you. *"That's the other thing a really bad bruise appeared on her arm before she left... the social worker casually asks "How did you get your bruise?" whereupon she responded "Cass did that". This is the most amazing attack to try and throw me in jail..."* I have to agree, and would go so far as to say that this is a really dangerous situation for you to be in, because she is causing the authorities to believe that you are an aggressor when the complete reverse is the case. She is the actual aggressor not you, and it seems to me as though she is acting as an *agent provocateur* so that when you retaliate in self-defence she goes running to the social workers, who are supposed to conclude you are psychotic and dangerous, which will give them the legal ammunition they need to get you locked up and silenced. Who knows what she is telling them, and who knows what is being recorded about you on official records. And when you say elsewhere: *"Writer feels FBI surveilled and Monica's purpose was partly that"* it's immaterial whether what she is doing is conscious or unconscious, the point being (IF she is being used as a pawn in order to get at you, the target) YOU will be the one who ultimately suffers for it.

However, I'm not altogether sure it is unconscious and I think you are far too trusting. For example, the following sounds quite suspect to me: *She wouldn't be around for 2 or 3 weeks at a time when she was normally there every day...where did she go?* Reporting to her superiors, quite possibly, and staying in a comfortable hotel before returning to her undercover existence posing as a homeless woman. No agent would want to be sleeping outdoors in the cold for too long - even if it is part of the job - hence the reason she would insist upon staying in shelters as much as possible and insist that you accompany her (so she could keep you under surveillance) and when she got fed up with the discomfort the "sweetener" would be that she gets a break from time to time: this would be when she disappears and resumes her normal identity. So are you being duped here? It is also significant that at times she commands you to look at her and "stares" intensely at you. This is a classic control technique used by people who have been trained in the art of hypnosis. If this happens again, refuse to make eye contact and tell her in a firm, loud voice to remain silent (in case she is actually being channelled by someone who is an adept at mind control) You are a lot stronger than she is anyway, both physically and mentally. Keep in mind that she is five foot nothing, and is incapable of dominating you.

The danger in continuing to associate with M is that if the handler or agency behind the scenes becomes frustrated at the fact they're not getting the compliant responses they want from you, or if they find it too difficult to control the situation they might decide that it would be a lot easier if you were picked up from the street and incarcerated. And the way to do that would be provoke you into violence (using Monica as the goad) and if you refuse to take the bait they then get M to manufacture an excuse to get you jailed, such as self-inflicted bruises. If I recall this is not the first time you have been falsely accused of this type of behaviour, and Monica seems to be at the bottom of it. I think you are being SET UP, and you need to get the hell away from this woman. You do not need to concern yourself about her welfare because a) if she's putting on an act and is NOT who she says she is nothing bad will happen to her because she's just an undercover operative who will be given some other task more within her capabilities or b) if she does genuinely have mental health issues and is not practising an elaborate deception on you, the welfare workers have already begun the process of providing an overall assessment and will ensure she gets medical care and gets off the streets. This would be more in her long-term interests than continuing to hang around you. Either way the best option for both of you is to let the authorities take care of her, and for you to sever the links completely so that you are no longer under her influence and in a situation where you could be picked up at any time by the police and blamed for her provocative behaviour.

The following article may shed some light on the mysterious weight gain M's sister and colleagues experienced while working in New York. I watched a recent documentary about U.S. farmers who were faced with an over-production of corn; a deal was struck whereby the surplus was bought by the government, and U.S. citizens were putting on vast amounts of weight as corn syrup was surreptitiously added to virtually every foodstuff, causing the obesity epidemic.

*In the 1970s, Nixon's Agriculture Secretary realised that farmers were harvesting more corn than they knew what to do with thanks*

*to more efficient, industrialised methods. His answer was to
champion increased production and use of high-fructose corn
syrup – now nicknamed "devil's candy" in the U.S. – which was
cheaper and sweeter than sugar. By the 1980s, high-fructose corn
syrup (HFCS) was the favourite substitute for sugar worldwide,
and the subject of a new BBC series called "The Men Who Made
Us Fat". A growing body of research suggests that fructose has
strong links to obesity, as it suppresses the action of the hormone
leptin, which tells the body that the stomach is full. The substance
is used widely in the U.S., especially in soft drinks, for flavouring
and to improve shelf life. In the UK it is found in a range of
products including McVitie's Hobnobs, Jaffa Cakes and Classic
Rich Tea biscuits, Carte D'Or ice cream, Lucozade, Kellogg's
Special K cereal bars etc. Laboratory research by Princeton
University concluded that long-term consumption of glucose-
fructose syrup resulted in "abnormal increases in body fat,
especially the abdomen".*

The other night I tuned into a documentary about "Extreme Brat
Camps", an example of numerous boot camps springing up all over
the States, ostensibly to deal with children with behavioural
problems. What struck me as sinister was that most of them appear
to be run by ex-military types, who treat the kids like prison
inmates, complete with orange jumpsuits, long hours of enforced
labour, sleep deprivation etc. None of the children featured looked
very old or as if they constituted much of a problem (one mother
complained her son spent too much time on his computer, big deal)
I didn't see any obnoxious behaviour except from the adult camp
leaders, who were well over 6 foot tall with tattoos etc. and
intimidating their tiny charges by yelling in their faces like sergeant
majors bawling out raw recruits. At least 2 children looked
completely traumatized and were sobbing in terror. Once the
parents had signed the form giving their consent these aggressive
"transporters" were given *carte blanche* to take kids forcibly from
their homes to remote and isolated locations such as "Camp
Consequence" Whether they got to go home or not was entirely at

the discretion of the camp leader who even boasted he could keep them "shackled" if they defied him.

I found this really objectionable for a number of reasons: 1) they were going for soft targets - vulnerable children instead of hard-core offenders such as older teenage gang members who engage in real criminal activity and who are an altogether tougher proposition 2) children shouldn't be treated like hardened criminals, and in any case research has proved that countering aggression with more aggression only makes it worse 3) the minority of girls at the camp felt extremely intimidated being bossed around by these huge muscled guys with shaven heads who looked and sounded like thugs 4) what is to prevent these children who are placed in complete isolation from being brain-washed or experimented on in the way you write about? Who is monitoring these camps, which are not licensed in any way? Having been in the military does not qualify them to have complete control over a bunch of children, whose (mostly single) mothers seemed pretty ignorant and far too trusting. Apparently there have been numerous complaints about kids being abused. This smacks of military dictatorship on a small scale, and Americans really need to protest strongly and ensure they are shut down. In any case it seemed to me that the children were being punished for their parents' failings. One mother complained that her 8-year-old "controlled" the household. Well, whose fault is that? If she can't control a little boy then she must be a really crappy parent, and it's the parents who should be sent to boot camps to learn parenting skills. Another horrible bitch, who was obviously some kind of control freak, expected her kids to say "Yes, Ma'am" every time she spoke to them over the breakfast table, and wasn't satisfied unless they were responding like little robots. Jesus, what does all this tell you about American society?

I understand you might feel it is not practicable to return to the UK at this point in time esp. if the offer of an apartment might be forthcoming. However in view of the fact that it normally takes a lot of **time** (literally months) to process a new passport application,

I still think it's a good idea to start the process now and get the ball rolling. This course of action does not commit you to jumping on a plane but it means you would then be in a position to take off if the situation became intolerable. I'll pay for the admin fees.

Love,

Leigh

**From: Cass Ryder**
**To: Leigh Ryder**

I got 2 passports stolen – at Phoenix airport and at a Chicago day labour pool. Had to get an identity check in person at the state dept in DC: a Miss Grant authorised the re-issuance, but held it back in her files in the fear that it would go missing again based on my lifestyle, and agreed to release it when she could witness a UK-bound airline ticket. I had no choice but to agree.

It's very obvious what's going on here. Okay let's cut the crap, something is trying to get her tabbed with a "terminal illness" leading to a chemical prescription. I feel like the witness at the scene of a crime, but ironically I'm in danger of being indicted for leading her onto a "wrong path" For an entire year now she has insisted I stay beside her and I've been insecure about leaving even for a few weeks, in case she might not be there when I get back (she threatens rebelliously almost the way a young teenager does that she will walk off and do something bad) Another thing I heard around the subject one night on the park bench was a woman's voice from nowhere "We've caused you a lot of discomfort" I distinctly remember that woman's voice, almost like a horse's neigh: "We've put you through quite a lot of anxiety, but we could put you through more. It's going to be okay" At the library I've witnessed people complaining about M's loud whispering, and later I've tried to bring it up with her "Do you realise what you've said?" She exclaims "I in no way know what you're talking about." The other day she was whispering "between the arse…yes, yes" (that's the kind of stuff she's saying) Outside the government centre while waiting for a bus she said in a soprano intonation "I just do this" (she makes a sweeping motion across her pelvic area) "and the problem fixes itself"

There is almost no information on this on the Internet, but it seems an example of sexual exploitation on an invisible level, taking advantage of a woman's mental impairment. It's fine while we're out in the open, but if it happens in the library then what? On the subject of what I euphemistically call self-execution (which health guides advise is normal) in the last two years of homelessness she has relapsed into that habit while in expensive hotels paid for by well-meaning strangers, but my point is don't invisible male entities basically participate and secure some greater hold over her? It's the context that gets me…the nice hotel thing I can just about understand, but under a homeless shelter's showerhead? Now that really is weird and seems another example of someone who is being manipulated or coerced at some level. And in defence against the accusation it's private and "none of my business" she forced the information on me. Writer also notices the subject's language is extremely sex and violence orientated, set up to create this false image of her. The subject may be committing self-bio in the can, and the writer's observation is that this relapse is obviously in step with an increasing conversation disorder that runs like an audio recording. Writer intuits it's NOT a good idea - isn't she consummating with some disembodied entity, and isn't this a prelude to complete psychic disintegration?

Last night she said in a rambling incoherent way "Some things are telling me not to touch myself, some things are telling me to touch myself". For the last couple of nights when they hit the "Giant" at 10:30pm one of the cubicles was non-accessible so they had to visit the restroom in single file. The subject was taking forever and whispering to herself, so the writer hesitated then stood on the toilet rim and looked over the stall. Too late, the subject was folding her immaculate shirt under her trouser pants. Writer felt nauseated that she had actually peeped over the stall and doesn't ever want to do it again. Subject comes out of the restroom kind of reinvigorated and says things like "Liz is going to get you", "Love Liz in the toilet", "Going to turn it around in the toilet" etc. It feels like something is being milked (like a snake for its venom) For instance, if orgasm is like car fuel which gets a vehicle up a road they then use this energy of hers that they've "collared" as a means to propel her vocal chords, and in this way coerce and condition her behaviour. Apparently it's none of my business, but it was when she'd come out of the restroom and say "Liz is going to kill you" Maybe it is an incubus. She chimed out musically one morning "kiss me on my heini" She was in a kind of "baby toddler mode" when she said it.

But let's go back to her family. Her father called her and her sister "barren whores" This is the kind of mindset of the male members of her family. Once she said that a nanny apparently abused her and her sister, so it seems like something that stemmed from her babyhood. If occult attacks work using symbolic language translatable as imagery, this is sicko as shit, they're "surfing" in on some kind of guilt/shame association to do with something in her past, and the self-execution they force on her in the Giant restroom, shower cubicles etc. Like yesterday she was dancing break dance style while waiting for the bus…her egoism is off this universe. There's so much intrigue around her, one side can't get her dead quick enough (they are now trying to hint she has a terminal disease and shrouding it with honour) Couldn't you have tried to get some sort of psychic counselling based on what I've told you, which is that she is puppeted by the occult and held hostage against her higher will, and they are using her homeless circumstances to compound her state of discomfort so she cannot communicate in a normal way. I know because they have done the same thing to me, one reason why I instinctively took to the green belts and the trails, something she can't do…remember she's got fibroids that are causing bladder weakness, muscle strains in the lower back, and swollen ankles from sitting up on benches at night. Things start to straighten out after the menses for a lot of women …oh you just sent me an email so let me go read it.

Cass

From: **Leigh Ryder**
To: **Cass Ryder**

Dear Cass,

I am sending you some cash, which should be ready to collect
tomorrow. Please buy some warm clothing for yourself, and goosedown sleeping bags until such time as the social workers can sort
out some housing. Sorry, I don't know anything much about
"sexual exploitation on an invisible level" but practitioners of black
magic or "the left-hand path" such as Aleister Crowley, practised
sex magic in his rituals. He was a notorious abuser of women, and
an altogether unpleasant character. I would strongly advise Monica
to stop allowing herself to be used in this manner, as it makes her
even more susceptible to harmful occult influence, but only she can
make that decision for herself. And the reason I responded "it isn't
my business or yours" when you asked for my opinion was because
if there IS an attempt to "draw you out" onthis subject this could be
another way to entrap you. Since they couldn't provoke you into
violence, it could be they're dumb enough to think that this type of
stuff might interest you, particularly if the cubicle in question or the
entire restroom is wired and fitted out with concealed cameras.
This is a well-worn tactic used for years against gay men by police,
many of whom were imprisoned for offences which only amounted
to acts between consenting adults.

I don't blame you at all for looking over the cubicle wall, esp. if
you can hear "whispering". Maybe it's a cellphone she's whispering
into, or she may have a microscopic earpiece and microphone
hidden on her person and that's what you're hearing. Quite possibly
she is being coerced or controlled - as you seem to think - and has
no choice but to continue with this, and receives her instructions in
the restroom, along the lines of "Has she taken the bait yet?" or
"You're going to have to try harder, we want something juicy so we
can get her picked up on grounds of public immorality" etc. and in
the meantime, smile you're on candid camera. And M puts on a

seedy little show to keep them happy until they can get what they want from you. Women are definitely used in this way by men, and I have come to the conclusion that sharing an apartment with her would be a very bad idea, in that this kind of provocative behaviour would only escalate. Also, it would be much easier to rig up an apartment for surveillance purposes than a bench outdoors. You need to think very seriously about where all this could be taking you, and that's why I advise you to be totally neutral whenever the subject arises. So if M starts acting under this kind of compulsion again just IGNORE it. Don't comment on it, don't get involved or show the slightest flicker of an interest. This is your best defence. There is a strength in spiritual purity which corrupt minds cannot fight, since corruption of the soul is based on a fundamental weakness of character.

Stay strong and focussed.

Leigh

**From: Cass Ryder**
**To: Leigh Ryder**


The Best Western is associated with the military, so I wonder why she chose to go there since one thing she's famous for is she hates soldiers. I wondered whether something in the hotel was setting her off - she's asleep right now. The hotel is really nice except she was cussing loudly all the while (the same things over and over again like a mental drilling) I'd like to have bought a recording device to tape it. We got a cab to the hotel and as soon as we get there she turns on the TV and zeros in on "The Godfather" like she's being mocked for some kind of Mafia association. While she was in the shower I became riveted by this "Lizzie Borden" documentary, then horrified. There was a graphic shot of the axed caved-in face of the father (writer checked the TV guide and didn't see it in the guide) Earlier in the hotel we had a spat and in retrospect it looked very much designed, and what was seen on the TV was probably a "beaming" Some covert group or criminal syndicate (it's probably the govt) masquerade as CNN and 'beam down' a picture, a piece of film or news item. They're now so audacious they're manipulating embodied pawns to enter businesses or hotels where a TV screen is positioned on the wall, and then doing the beaming to time with their entrance. The subject experienced "chills" (writer just described it as an electrical wind) which make your innermost soul cold and static...electricity starts sticking to you as one clamours to get warm.

The writer mentioned in an earlier email she looked over the stall to see why the subject was whispering aloud. When they visited the restroom the next night, the cubicle adjacent to the subject's cubicle is wrecked, seemingly to prevent her from standing on the toilet rim to look over the wall. Writer just had a sick thought – writer and subject's energies are somehow being overlapped? Writer's observation that divide and rule ploy is being employed, using designed auxiliary spirit overlaps. Coincidentally we were just offered a two-bedroom apartment that apparently Monica is willing to co-sign on. While living on the pavement is not good, I agree it might be an excuse to "rig" the apartment. It feels like some sort of criminal syndicate is WATCHING the whole time. Maybe they intercepted your email and wrecked the cubicle to cover up something. You still don't get it do you…hours and hours, sometimes half the night, of tears, screams, with me just standing there forced to listen …shit, something doesn't expect me to accompany her for years like this? But what gets me is this continual reference to the NSA and FBI. She reiterates "masters of the universe" and when I queried her the other day she claimed that had been a reference to the CIA. The subject was always saying "they had no right to involve me in their experiments of green cock for soldiers" and referred a lot to the Marshals Institute which the writer had looked up and does exist in Arlington county (and DOES LOOK like a CIA or FBI front)

Two nights ago she rattled on about having been kidnapped on one occasion in Long Island. Her sister was accused of being lesbian by her ex-boyfriend, and she and her girlfriend were both shot. The subject remembers having to confirm the identity of her sister's corpse and that her eye had been blown out. Sometimes the writer wondered if these were clever camouflage self-protection ploys: "Keep away from me, I'm mafia" and "this is why I'm a loonie". She once said her black cop friend Bob died in a subway attack in NY (when he was alive and kicking) She said "He never left a forwarding address" and threw up the imagery of his head rolling down the subway. But she's a spectacular exaggerator, and uses the word "dead" as a metaphor quite a lot. For instance, coming out of the Safeway restroom she exclaims "I had to kill him" (meaning the guy she met coming out of the restroom) We're in room 308 at the Best Western if you want to call.

Cass

**From: Leigh Ryder**
**To: Cass Ryder**

Dear Cass,

It looks as though you did receive the cash I sent yesterday, or you wouldn't be in a hotel. The "chills" or "electrical wind" you describe was probably just the air conditioning in the hotel, which you are not used to. It shouldn't be on in the winter but maybe it was switched on by accident. I don't know what kind of experiment M might have been subject to - I suppose you are referring to the "enforced medical" at Marshall Institute in Arlington? I understand you care about her but not why you feel you owe her so much, and am somewhat aggrieved that all you got out of the money I sent you was a measly coffee and sandwich. Having said that, I am actually glad that you still have her companionship, as it's not good to be completely alone.

Long term it's pretty obvious you two are not going to be able to share a close living space, in view of her increasing hostility and verbal attacks, and the possibility that you are both being watched. It's good news about the apartment offer and potential SOAR cash funding, but I'm still concerned about the potentially criminal types hanging around Monica (though I think the "Mafia" connection is just a figment of her imagination) However, for the short term I think you have to take this on trust, in that it is being offered with good intent (I hope) So if the social worker has managed to obtain permanent housing for you both, **don't turn it down**, since it is preferable to being on the streets and will serve as a stable base where you can both recuperate, and she can begin to tackle her medical/health problems. If it doesn't work out you can always leave at some future point, but in the meantime it will provide you with warmth and security, as well as your own kitchen and cooking facilities. So I advise you to accept the offer as a huge opportunity to change your life. If you're worried that you wouldn't be entitled to any cash assistance if you accept the housing, explain to the social worker that you have been misinformed before and request that they provide you with an official copy in writing signed by an appropriate authority, which clearly states that you are entitled to both forms of assistance. Do you have access to free legal advice? In England there are Citizens Advice Bureaux which the general public can avail themselves of, and I'm wondering if there is something similar where you can get independent clarification in order to put your mind at rest.

I didn't log on until late last night so didn't get your email until this morning, and I guess you will be checking out of the Best Western at noon your time (?) so there's no point in me calling now as it will be the middle of the night there and you will be fast asleep. I repeat, M should **definitely** accept the apartment and you should definitely accept the SOAR cash offer (AND the apartment so long as it doesn't affect your cash entitlement) but get a second opinion before signing. Try and get it sorted out today if you can, because if you delay too much the offer might be withdrawn or given to someone else on the list.

I'll be in touch again soon.

Leigh

**From: Cass Ryder**
**To: Leigh Ryder**
**Subject: Looks like a set up**

They're full of shit. The workers told me I could get a back
payment of a year or two, that's bullshit. They both made out that
the process could either be expedited or take three months. That's
injecting false hope in my expectations. They make me sick.
They're complete mind-control freaks, they're communists. God
are they perverted. They seem to be frustrated over how we
survived with a certain amount of dignity and sanity despite it all,
and are obsessed with trying to prove we're idiots. Subject talks
down her nose at them, and they don't like that at all. In a New
York study professionals posed as homeless, who were then picked
up by mental care health workers who labelled them all as mentally
ill, when they definitely had not been. Permanent supportive
housing PSH is linked in withmental disability, when it should only
be linked with homelessness. Writer cannot see why the homeless
Path Programs were linked in with the Mental Health Programs.
Homeless people are somehow encouraged to be seen as mentally
impaired, and the association is not a good one. The homeless shy
away from benefits and feel it's not to be trusted, because they get
contradictory information and are made to feel humiliated for their
circumstances, and then exaggeratedly grateful for any help. THEY
HAD NO RIGHT TO LINK PUBLIC ASSISTANCE HOUSING
IN WITH MENTAL HEALTH. It's an anti-gay or anti-single
thing. Possibly it's an anti-white or anti-middleclass attack. They're
a bunch of jerks. Pretty desperate jerks when you consider all they
did was service up opportunities to people who had babies and to
immigrants, and yes this country should deal with it.

The worker basically lied about the permanent supportive housing,
stating that it's based on a "time duration of homelessness in the
area" when as far as the writer can research, it is a mental health
connected housing program that is available to anyone who has

been homeless for at least a year (as the printout I sent states) and that definition might be applicable nationally not just regionally, so M would probably be eligible for this somewhere else. I've said NO to the permanent supportive housing. If it's approved you still have to give a third of the rent to housing costs. If I can't get a job and no-one will give me one, how can I pay a third? They get you dependent on the housing then they threaten and blackmail and coerce. To be a govt beneficiary is to invite in all kinds of problems. The sister Maddy in Britain is an example of what seems to be an ongoing mental assault, and comes over as someone totally dependent on welfare. Exactly, who wants the dole. Meanwhile there's usually no other option for affordable housing. M's not going to have any cash at current rates, and the point about regular visits is not clarified .. does she mean each week or each month? There might be friction with other people in the housing development and one of the workers who she can't stand, will probably turn up each week to spy on her. It's on the ground floor, and the windows are huge... I doubt whether they'll pay for wooden shutters (although they have agreed to furnish it) I know she feels unhappy about that and doesn't feel it's safe.

The social worker said they in no way enforce chemical prescriptions. That's total BULL. They do, in fact what they're doing is giving people a voluntary "option" first on the general psychiatric commitment law basis, those perceived as dangerous or danger to themselves etc. I'm absolutely convinced that they're coercing lots of homeless who are NOT in that category to take it... like a kind of "advisory" option which is essentially a threat in the context of housing benefit removal (so if a court order goes in they have to stay in that area which can lead to endless years of waltzes with the authorities) Then people either get stiffed on payment checks, which are held back for whatever reason, or on protracted rental agreements. Not to mention enforced medication in the case of "violent orientation" Better not to have the dependency. Not only do I think she would be worse after those prescriptions (and they do want to put her on those, but they're not saying it to me

234

though) Like the latest comments from the social worker that the subject "could do with a bit of lithium"... her exact words. And lithium dulls the senses, causes overweight and other side effects and produces dependencies... things you especially DON'T need if you're asleep on a pavement. Wouldn't she be WORSE off as a result of their so-called "treatment"? It's all being done as a prelude to inventing a terminal illness, and they just move on from there. They're actually coming out with enforced two weekly injections that are often administered on the inside of the thigh just to make sure they take it – what is their obsession with needles? They can't bare to admit they've got good incomes for doing an evil job. They're used to completely lording it over people on a rodent level, they can't bare my criticism. They're assholes. You asked me to give their names to write to them. Don't bother. FIRE WILL BE MET WITH FIRE.

I'm beginning to wonder whether quite a few of our messages had been intercepted (respond immediately to receiving this and yesterday's 40 pages) For example, in an email sent by you dated two days ago you actually advised NOT accepting an apartment offer. I was definitely of the same opinion. The reason I think it's a setup: the reps seem especially sensitive to the fact that I am to be "included" in co-signing for the apt, and that it is done under my signature. Which seems to go beyond the reasons that they are giving, like I'm first on the list and Monica isn't, based on a criteria of time homeless in the area. But because the apt is NOT under section 8 and since my name was never on a Section 8 wait list .. why on earth would they therefore include me if that were the major criteria for eligibility? THEYRE FULL OF SHIT

Cass

**From: Leigh Ryder**
**To: Cass Ryder**

Dear Cass,

I did get the 40 page attachment, so I don't think our communications are being intercepted. However as a precaution and an experiment I have attached a password-protected document with this email containing one simple phrase. If you are able to open it successfully, then, if necessary, I can use this means to communicate with you in secret. The password you need to open the attachment is the *first name of the teacher's son* (you will know who I am referring to) If you are successful in opening it then email me back the phrase contained in the document.

Although I don't think living in an apartment with Monica long-term is a good idea I nevertheless think you should accept it as a way out of homelessness - what have you got to lose? I definitely think M should accept the offer of an apartment as she needs comfort and security, and if she were settled not only would her mental/physical state improve but you would also feel freer to leave her if you wanted to at some future point. Her condition sounds pretty serious, and it would obviously NOT be treated with lithium (that's just your paranoia speaking, probably triggered by some ignorant remark from a social worker) You appear to be talking yourself out of accepting any federal assistance, but this is crazy because you both desperately NEED it. So accept what's on offer, and if you later find out there are strings attached you can walk away. I'm going to sign off here as I don't want to be on the computer all night, and need to wind down. Take the money and run, you crazy girl, OK?

Love,

Leigh

**From: Cass Ryder**
**To: Leigh Ryder**

I think her family were under some kind of perverted influence.
What mother sews on the butt of her daughter's trouser pants "Sex
makes you come and go?" and she always complained of being
"yuhindied"(feeling sexed – a term for a chemical African natives
take on hunting trips) I get the feeling there are definitely African
spirits around her. While training to be a cop in San Francisco she
complained of 2 weeks missing time. How does one miss 2 weeks
of time where one is alert and time-conscious in context of job
training? She trained with a bunch of rapists and harem-keepers,
the kind most people would vomit over, including a black cop
called Bob who called ordinary people "dirtbags". While residing
in Liz's apt (some time between 2006 – 2008?) she was picked up
on her way to the store in Laurel, Greenbelt or Bethesda MD and
doesn't remember what happened after that. She ended up getting
in touch with her old friend Patty some time later after most of her
immediate family had died. The mother of Patty, a wealthy
German/Jewish woman in Florida deeds her $15,000 so she's able
to live in a motel for perhaps a year on this. Writer guesses Liz
called the authorities who forcibly committed her, then dumped her
back out on the pavement. She had spent one FULL YEAR
sleeping out on public benches in shopping plazas on her own
before she met the writer. She might have been assaulted, and I still
don't know what happened in Pittsburgh recently when she took
off. I sent a letter to the head of the gender department at the
university of LA by certified mail but NO RESPONSE.

They obviously think I'm a bad influence. The worker thinks I feel
rejected and I'm trying to wreck things, but I AM THE ONE WHO
REJECTED THE APARTMENT she was willing to share with me,
OK? I told them I didn't want the apartment and won't co-sign, but
she's desperate to get indoors. They're trying to insinuate that I
coerce or influence her, and that I'm misrepresenting her. Just like
they set her up to drop her wrath on me, and see ME as the

problem. The theory is I'm "interfering", I'm jealous, I'm ego jilted...they have dirty minds and can only see through the 22 lettered parameter. We were NEVER an amour couple...I thought about that one but no that's not the reality...I was only concerned for her almost like a guardian towards a little child, not without a healthy dose of ego vindication at seeing her go through something I went through. I wouldn't be surprised if she's back out on the pavement soon. She was MANOEUVRED down here to Loudoun county... someone needs to confront that person, grab him by the collar, fist under chin. This is all the information on housing and cash assistance you asked me to send through.

**Rapid Rehousing** - it's only available for 6 months, after which if the person hasn't got a job and can't sustain themselves they get forced back out onto the street. Requires utility service payments, plus landlord's refs etc. so really unhelpful. Not adequate for homeless people who need the assurance of permanent housing.

**Section 8 Housing** - permanent housing, but which involves the client paying 30% of rent. This is not good enough for someone who doesn't have any income or job.

**Permanent Supportive Housing PSH Program** - linked in with the Mental Health Programs, whereby one has to state they are disabled. There is NO reason why the chronically homeless should be associated with disability (the latter should be left to another determining body) Application eligibility on condition of one year's uninterrupted homelessness might make it difficult to apply for this immediately if settled somewhere else. Can supportive housing be transferred across State lines?

**SSI Outreach Access and Recovery (SOAR) Program** - only relevant to the "chronically homeless and the disabled" so not an option for people who don't accept they're disabled. Writer is not disabled but has been homeless for 18 years

**SSI = Supplementary Security Income** - SSI benefits for homeless individuals. Can SSI applications interfere with getting housing (are deductions made? No answer was given) The SSI admin in Baltimore had contradictory definitions about temporary or permanent disability, therefore preventing the prospective client (the writer) from applying earlier (who had a temporary not permanent physical impairment – strained feet and lower lumbar region) The Mental Health dept stated the Emergency dept deals with it, the Emergency dept stated the Mental Health deals with it.

Writer's conclusions are that the federal government is not sincere about funding an initiative to get the chronically homeless off the streets by 2015 because they're still denying the right to access all three at once (housing, food and cash for income)as basic needs. None of the housing options involves cash assistance, or recognises that people need other things apart from just housing and foodstamps. The SOAR program offers cash but is a little shady. What's their obsession with calling them disabled? Why can't they just be defined as unemployed and homeless? According to the definition of chronic homelessness both clients were eligible for housing in the last 2-4 years but this was denied, further injuries were incurred (the writer has a strained shoulder due to a recent assault) an ingrown toenail so bad it was oozing pus (writer had to razor out the root problem but never got out a splinter in top of toe) and loss of potential income through a back payment case she could have pursued but which is now too late due to time restrictions. The subject's psychic impairment symptoms GOT WORSE proportionate to the time spent crashing on a bench and being touched up by men walking by at night. Mental illness is not so much the problem as assaults and trauma exposures due to homelessness. In fact don't the homeless deserve injury damages for being assaulted on the street, and guaranteed work programs? Writer acknowledges that one client said she was grateful. Writer wants to reaffirm that she is NOT grateful. Pretty cheap considering what they put a person through. The shelters were never adequate. There are psychological complications to do with different types of people who don't get along and should NOT be integrated in neighbourhoods where they feel insecure…some of these low-income housing options meter out as jumping out of the frying pan into the fire. A little Mexican shit is watching me in the library as I write this... please send cash for a microphone.

Cass

**From: Leigh Ryder**
**To: Cass Ryder**

Dear Cass,

It's disappointing you've turned down the apartment offer, as I think you are whipping yourself up into a frenzy of paranoia when you need to keep calm. I don't know why you're so convinced it's a "set up" Sometimes it just seems like you are your own worst enemy, and when someone does try to help it's rejected. I think they should have offered you both **single separate** apartments instead of a 2-bed apartment. There is clearly a lot of very negative energy surrounding Monica, which was why I didn't think sharing an intimate space with her long-term is a good idea. I would rather not hear any more on the subject of Monica. Actually J and I were pretty annoyed - not at YOU, let me emphasise, but at the fact that every time we send you our hard-earned cash, it seems that she dictates how it is spent and you're left with nothing to show for it i.e. you're no better off and we feel like our generosity is being abused by this woman. I thought you said you needed warm Goretex clothing, so why didn't you use some of the money to get what you need? Was staying at the Best Western your idea or hers - couldn't you have chosen a less expensive motel? I honestly don't see how you could have spent all the cash I sent ($400.00) so soon! I guess it has all been swallowed up in hotel bills, but a microphone recording of M just isn't important at the moment. In all honesty, who would want to listen to it? (in any case it breaches her privacy) I hope to be able to send you a bit more around Christmas, but please understand that nobody else in the family is helping us financially with this.

I did read all the information about the types of housing/cash assistance available in the printout you sent, including your questions to the social workers, and your conclusions. Unfortunately, bureaucrats are the same all over the world. They disseminate ambiguous and misleading information, and when you attempt to get clarification they place obstacles in your path, or are too damned lazy to chase up the answers you're looking for. At least accept the SOAR cash assistance if it's still on offer, as this will give you a measure of independence. I would pursue this proactively if I were you, and once you are in receipt of income get yourself a good tent/sleeping bag. If the social workers are such assholes, which I can well believe (though this Donna sounds OK) why don't you take steps to leave the USA? You don't need this kind of aggravation - has it occurred that something might be trying to trap YOU there, and that M is the crucial link that is being used? It seems whenever I voice any criticism of her, you get really defensive and take it out on me. I hope for your sake you eventually part company, since she is preventing you from moving on with your life, and her presence acts as a barrier to communication with your family. I know for a fact that the reason Alex refuses to help is because she thinks anything she gives you goes straight to Monica.

Anyway, that is all for now. Hope this doesn't offend as it's not meant to, but I somehow don't think you're getting the point.

Love,

Leigh

**From: Cass Ryder**
**To: Leigh Ryder**

FUCK OFF. As for Alex, don't expect me to listen to your explanation or excuses for her. She never ever sent ONE RED CENT. And I don't want her sad help. I don't need your help with publishing the book. I hate you, I hate her>>I esp. hate her.

I think we're receiving interception difficulties .. I thought I saw on one of your email messages that you advised me to get any benefits that Im eligible for? Not that I was going to listen to that but I was curious if that was something you sent or not Write back immediately you get this. Write back immediately to confirm those messages were in your last communications .If not then Im going to block a capability for you to transmit anyway .Im under unbelievable stress as usual>YOURE EVIL. YES YOU ARE SO WAS ALEXANDRA KWEEP THE HELP I never wanted it SONMETHING FUCKS WITH US . ITs obvious youre one more stupid bitch on the run youre head is coerced by hags and growbags and whores

Cass

**From: Leigh Ryder**
**To: Cass Ryder**

Dear Cass,

Your reaction to my email was a little over the top. The way you react to any criticism, however well-meant, strikes me as being a manifestation of some negative and hostile energy which has taken root in your psyche, and is not any way representative of your higher self, which is much more thoughtful and rational. Considering how much information I have been force-fed about M (rather in the same way she dumped her life-story on you) it's somewhat unreasonable to expect me to not to respond, or to venture an opinion of my own. However, it should be possible to disagree without resorting to verbal abuse. For instance, Patrick and I are at opposite ends of the political spectrum, but that doesn't mean we have to hate each other. It's hardly surprising you find it so difficult to relate to people if you cannot tolerate an opposing opinion or viewpoint. There are always two sides to a story, and the version you've been given is not necessarily the true one.

I wasn't making excuses for Alex, I just felt you were owed an explanation as to why she hasn't been more forthcoming with cash assistance. I'm not looking for thanks, any more than I ever get an acknowledgement from Maddy, despite the fact I am the only one who makes the effort to send her anything on her birthday or at Christmas (all I ever get in return is FUCK OFF) Still, I guess that's my role in this family, and no matter how hurtful it is to receive an email like that I certainly don't hold it against either of you. The untimely death of our parents ripped the rug out from underneath your feet - leaving an enormous vacuum - and seems to have triggered a lot of the subsequent problems you have both had to deal with. And the only reason I want to help publish your book is that if it were to achieve some commercial success, then I would ensure that all the proceeds went to you since it's clear only a very large cash injection would be of practical help to you. I wasn't going to all this effort for my sake (what's in it for me, except months of painstaking and time-consuming labour?) I was doing it for your sake, and will continue to work on this in my own time. I feel I owe it to you.

I understand M has now accepted the apartment offer, which doesn't surprise me since you have observed before how the "Subject responds very well to cash" However I sincerely hope you are not going to be suddenly dropped like a hot potato if she decides she has no further use for you, after all the support you've given her (guarding her on the bench at night while she sleeps, sharing your foodstamps, treating her to hotel stays courtesy of our money etc.) If this is what happens don't say I didn't warn you, but it really sickens to me to hear that she is now ensconced in a warm furnished apartment while you are left with NOTHING, and are supposed to sleep rough out in the open. I am extremely worried about the safety aspect of how you are coping on your own at night. It's a shame you couldn't have been offered a separate apartment each in the same block, because it must be very lonely for you all of a sudden, having spent so much time in her company. However, this does seem to be what she wants - at least for the present - and you will have to accept it. Bearing in mind what you've told me about some of the compulsive behaviour she's engaged in, maybe it's best if you keep your distance for a while. You definitely need some space and time apart from each other, so it's not a bad thing, though it may seem that way right now. Sometimes there is a higher wisdom in taking a step back and letting things take their natural course. There is nothing you can do about it, and it will make you ill if you keep focussing on all the negatives. You can punch through this if you don't allow your defences to become weakened.

I would advise you NOT to forward any of your observations about M to any of the government workers, as they were written when you were very upset: it makes you look bad and full of revenge, and this could be used against you. Although your intentions are good it looks as though your continuing concern for her is being seen as unwonted interference, and they could get you on a harassment charge. Maybe the thing to do is to monitor Monica's situation, and see whether her condition improves or deteriorates as a result of being placed in secure accommodation. If her outlook seems a lot more positive, and her general health seems to be improving then that would be a signal for you to go back to the workers and say "Look, I've changed my mind and would like an apartment" And the process needs to be expedited on the grounds that it is just not SAFE for a female to be sleeping out on a public bench on her own. But you should definitely be entitled to cash assistance: it is their legal obligation to provide clear and unambiguous information to you, and it needs to be in a written form so that there are no misunderstandings.

Love,

Leigh

**P.S.** Did you manage to open the password-protected document I attached, and if so what was the phrase contained in it? The book you asked me to order has just arrived and as soon as I've had a chance to digest its contents I'll pass on anything of relevance.

**From: Cass Ryder**
**To: Leigh Ryder**

Yes, I opened it, the phrase you sent was "white horse". I was composing this the other day and an African American man opposite began vocalizing what I was texting, so I then began writing anti-NSA things which I could see just made him more angry. He loudly vocalized a Google search about "mind control and western intelligence and genetic testing" I began vocalizing also. He then attempted to get the librarian to make me move which was annoying because I wanted to challenge him on abuse of surveillance powers. Which he MUST have been doing otherwise he could not have known what I was writing, as I didn't say anything out loud. I guess that is his job, to spy into people's personal communications. I do not feel he had any right vocalizing my text in my presence when he and I both knew NO-ONE else knew the meaning behind what he was saying. It was done to make me paranoid (which came over as an attempt at physical intimidation) Who cares, soon I won't have to come to this vomit place any more.

I'm currently in the apartment with M, which is under her name. The apt was offered to me at first because I had been seen longer on and off in the region, but I refused to sign and they put Monica at the head of the list based on more acute need. I am perceived as a "guest" and will probably go back out in the open very shortly and we will meet up during the day. I'll try and get Christmas work but they never give me work. The apartment offer was so sudden and there was no indication prior to this that we would be offered one, because despite the new federal rules this county refuses grant money as part of a "deter the homeless" policy. So I went through with the social security application and it's still being processed (next week I'm scheduled to see a chiropractor) The social worker Donna once let on to the writer she was diagnosed with breast cancer 6 years ago, and doesn't get along with her Sicilian husband that well. Bluntly speaking, isn't this further reason to believe M is being set up to have a terminal illness, and that Donna represents the other pawn in our pawn usage scenario? Maybe they plan to kill them both. Donna is the only nice one (she once broke down and cried in front of us, I guess because she felt sorry for us). Maybe she just needs a divorce, and if she's as liberal as those vehicle stickers suggest maybe she needs to get out of the mental health industry if it can't change.

In the meantime if we continue to be on bad terms I can't escort M anywhere. I don't really belong here and I don't want to live here.

Cass

**From: Leigh Ryder**
**To: Cass Ryder**
**Attachment: Psychic Self-Defence**

Dear Cass,

I am relieved to hear you have been crashing at M's apartment, but this arrangement is only temporary as you are perceived as her "guest". However, I wouldn't advise moving off anywhere soon if you have a stable base, besides which you would need multiple chiropractic sessions if they are to have any appreciable effect. With respect to the guy in the library doing Google searches and vocalising what you were texting, you should have IGNORED him: don't rise to the provocation, because this is exactly what it is – knowing what buttons to push. By rising to the bait and engaging in retaliatory slurs, you are playing directly into his hands since his object is probably to get you banned from the library, thereby making it difficult for you to communicate with me. The last thing you need right now is to be thrown out of the library, so if it happens again either leave the vicinity immediately or move to another computer.

I am now starting to think M may have been used by some agency to watch you, so you possibly made the right decision to turn down a shared apartment, and things would have come to a head eventually. The type of psychiatric treatment offered to those who claim to have been the victims of occult attack is completely inappropriate and inadequate. In-depth Jungian psychotherapy would achieve better results, but who can afford this, apart from the wealthy? The problem is that any government-funded treatment is bound to be the cheapest option i.e. chemical prescriptions, since they refuse to invest any money on the homeless or the mentally ill and couldn't care less how badly they deteriorate over time. I am attaching another lengthy password-protected WORD document at the end of this email called "defence" which you need to open by means of the same password as before. Don't forget to ALWAYS log off/sign out of your email session to keep your emails secure.

**Psychic Self-Defence**

If you're reading this you managed to open the attached document. From my reading it would appear there are two major gateways through which occult attacks or spirit possession normally occur, and both involve strong emotions: 1) desire or 2) fear. When something or someone attracts us we naturally feel desire and when we sense danger we experience fear. However, you need to ensure that you are not a slave to your emotions, that you are able to rein them in instead of allowing them to control you. A man who kills because his ego has been wounded obviously has no control over his impulses or emotions, and is weak in this respect. And I have long suspected that many random murders are actually the result of evil "suggestions" which weak or corruptible people are peculiarly susceptible to. Some murderers are "instructed" to kill, and the excuse given (that they were "hearing voices") may have some basis in reality. Soldiers can be programmed to carry out assassinations, and weak types with criminal propensities can be easily hypnotised to attack or kill another human being whom they have no personal animosity towards.

Many people do not realise the extent to which we subject ourselves to our own telepathic suggestions (by our choice of reading matter, the thoughts we dwell on etc.) DF observes we can be mentally poisoned by our own negative or revengeful thoughts, in the sense that cosmic forces tend to be cyclic and recurring, which is how anger and negative energy can rebound on the unconscious sender. Whatever thought-forms we project into the atmosphere are likely to return to us. The most effective form of self-defence is therefore to *refuse to react* to an attack, thus turning harmful suggestions back on the sender. Although we cannot prevent other minds (whether embodied or disembodied) from transmitting telepathic suggestions, you can strengthen your own mind so that these suggestions don't take root and flourish. And the way to do that is to keep your mind as pure as possible, which means blocking out negative thoughts (hatred, anger, revenge, lust, greed etc.) and avoiding evil people and evil thoughts. Easier than it sounds when you're permanently in a foul mood due to sleep deprivation, constant insecurity etc. but something to bear in mind is that if a discarnate entity is attacking you, it may not be malevolent – it may simply be desperate and miserable and deserving of compassion, as in the case of a haunting. In fact DF cites a case of severe psychic attack where the attacking entity, a rather sad and lonely earth-bound soul, had to be "treated" (i.e. sent to a higher realm) before the victim of the haunting could be successfully treated.

Where disembodied attacks are concerned, there can be no entrance to the soul unless a person's aura is pierced, or their etheric envelope has been weakened or damaged. If a person is kept in a state of fear/anxiety or is unable to inhibit their emotional responses, then the aura can be pierced by an entity seeking a gateway into the psyche. The key is to keep your aura strong and impenetrable, which may entail shutting down your emotional responses to whatever is bugging you. If a social worker infuriates you by being obstructive try to keep calm instead of reacting furiously; if someone is deliberately trying to provoke you or taunting you, again remain calm. Avoid knee-jerk reactions, and don't respond without taking the time to think things through. Walk away from the situation if you can, and do not give such people the POWER to upset you or to pierce through your aura, which you must hold in front of you like a shield. When someone is verbally abusing you, try visualising yourself as encased in armour from head to foot. Alternatively, folding your arms across your chest and remaining expressionless will also signal to the other person's subconscious that you are not a weak person, and that you are a force to be reckoned with. You can also protect yourself on a psychic level by visualising yourself in a pyramid of white light or surrounded by an impenetrable force-field: by using your imagination you are creating an invisible psychic barrier, and combating "dark" energies with the opposite.

You are correct in recognising how symbols and word associations can be manipulated. The human subconscious belongs to an earlier phase of evolution, prior to the development of speech, so in order to influence it a skilled occultist or marketing executive has to resort to symbols, signs, and pictorial representations. All you need to do to protect yourself is to be aware of such ploys, e.g. when presented with negative images or associations that imply something sordid, immediately focus your mind on something else. The impression you want to convey is that nasty or unpleasant suggestions are of no interest whatsoever to you, and therefore have no power over you. The other point to remember is that discarnate entities cannot operate directly upon their victims; they work through an **operator**, normally another human being in the close vicinity of whom they wish to target. I think that M may have been chosen as an operator, her task being to provoke you or draw out emotional responses in order to enable a "gateway" into your psyche for control purposes. You do not have to cooperate or allow this to happen. But if you have a weak spot in your own nature then it is easier to fall victim, as M seems to have done. A weakened immune system can also make a person vulnerable to attack or mental suggestion. Fortunately you are not an alcoholic or drug addict, since these are the classic weaknesses by which people lay themselves wide open to occult attacks.

In your discussion of REM processes, it's generally acknowledged that many people involuntarily project their astral bodies during sleep, and conflicts or fights sometimes occur on the astral plane of which the person has no conscious memory, but they may awaken with bruises which were not there before they went to sleep. Another sign is being grabbed by the throat – which you mention as having happened to you. I don't like to think it's remote technology causing physical effects, but either way your observation about "overlapping auras" where you both spent so much time together on a bench - compounded with her mental instability, the frequent arguments between you and so on - could have led to conflicts on the astral plane you were both unaware of. It can occur wherever there is an emotional co-dependency or morbid attachment between two people (parent/child, husband/wife, close siblings, friends or sworn enemies) There is usually a dominant partner who may actively resist separation, but sometimes this is necessary if a pair of people are adversely affecting each other. Another thing to be on your guard against is *folie de deux*, in which two people intimately connected share the same delusions, and can influence each other through the power of suggestion.

DF cites a case of "vampirism" early in her career where paranormal occurrences were plaguing a teenage lodger in a boarding house. Every evening at the same time his bedroom window would fly open no matter how many times they got a locksmith to lock it or barricade it, accompanied by cold draughts of air, the frenzied howling of all the dogs in the neighbourhood etc. It turned out he had been asked to sit with his wounded cousin, a young man who had been invalided home from the Western Front allegedly suffering from shell-shock: it transpired that the latter had been caught red-handed in the act of necrophilia, but due to family connections he avoided a military prison and was placed in the care of his family. While his nurse was off duty his teenage cousin was employed to sit with him. It also emerged that on one occasion the invalid bit the boy on the neck, drawing blood. The latter believed he was being attacked by a ghost but feared no-one would believe him. DF was not qualified to deal with the case so called in a more experienced adept who was able to successfully treat both victims by means of a specialised occult technique. His opinion was that the boy's cousin was not a primary vampire, but himself a victim who had been exploited by the earthbound soul of some other soldier (I know this sounds like utter bullshit, but bear with me) Eastern European troops had been brought to the Western Front, amongst whom were certain individuals with knowledge of black magic. After being killed on the battlefield "they knew how to avoid the Second Death i.e. the disintegration of the astral body and could maintain themselves in the etheric double by vampirising the wounded" i.e. attaching themselves permanently to living soldiers. After the case was closed, DF theorised that the entity had originally attached itself to the first cousin through his depraved practices, but once his energy was depleted was able to alternate between the two cousins due to the intimacy of their relationship (she hints at something homosexual)

All this may sound pretty crazy to people unfamiliar with how the occult works, but to my mind there doesn't seem to be a great deal of difference between spirit possessions and so-called "vampires" in that both entities operate on the astral plane and feed off the energy of living human beings. DF makes the distinction between vampirism (which is deliberately willed) and parasitical behaviour, which is involuntary and unconscious. In the latter case a drowning person who drags his rescuer to his death is not motivated by malice but pure panic. Nevertheless, at some point the rescuer may need to let go if they are not both to drown!

Love,

Leigh

**From: Cass Ryder**
**To: Leigh Ryder**

The admin dept never commented back about that contradiction on the disability connected cash assistance. On the one hand it's defined as "at least 12 months of serious disablement" on the other hand it's defined as a "permanent disability" THEY REALLY ARE NASTY AS ANYTHING THEY NEVER COOPERATE AND THEY'RE FULL OF THEMSELVES. THINK THEYRE GOD But that's the impression I get of all social service workers, they obviously feel they're better than the people they serve. Bunch of hypocrites and inflated despots. What they plan to do is GLITCH it electronically. Also the workers are now saying there's no need for me to go see a chiropractor and that a brief physical evaluation would suffice. Rather strange really when I have critically strained feet and lower back …and that these were caused through homelessness and having to walk with a 60-80lbs backpack for years and years (to say nothing of the recent dislocated shoulder, courtesy of a 3-man attack in Baltimore) Anyway after the pinched nerve in my back which occurred while working welding ships for a Pentagon contractor in 1985 I was told by the chiropractor I'd never run again. Within 4 years I ran the London marathon and 6 more miles in one afternoon = 33 miles in total.

It's all morphing as multiple dependencies and to take the housing means to take less SSI cash. The cash may have been helpful for a transition to a different area but it's doubtful the subject would want to do this. Go into the wilderness and nature? Even that's not accessible unless one has transportation, and if you're a woman expect to be assaulted. Otherwise I was happy to be on my own (I don't even want the food stamps) but I can't readjust to living in a wood. I used to pass on through places, but it's not a good idea to do this on a long-term basis. A white woman in the town who is homeless showed up at our bench in the plaza one night and told us she had been hit in the face at her tent crash site. It's not safe. I never used to stay in one spot, but that's a huge hassle to have to move around and around in small circles. I just used to walk on through fairly large territories.

If we ever hear back from the cousin Matt I'll make an effort to sell my land then I can provision Monica with a lump sum. In the meantime I don't see why I can't score a job in terms of at least one day a week. We need at least 40 dollars a week as supplemental cash. Subject gets food pantry, detergent and supplemental support like bus tokens and Wal-Mart cards as part of the permanent supportive housing, but it's not enough. They don't want to give this to me, they never approved of me, but I only stayed here because of her. She's worked with the most unbelievable douche bags. She offended sausage, who then tried to assault from the invisible energy angle. They've been hammering her on the head since the moment she hit the delivery table from her mother's womb. It's as though a woman is being beaten up in full view of the public everyday and no one does anything about it. Something is definitely trying to involve the subject in something like bondage and they seem to resent my so-called interference. I'm not interfering, if anything she interfered with me.

I lost some work recently so now I carry my backpack into the restroom with me and everywhere I go, and do not trust leaving this in her apartment where I have my camp mat in a corner of the living room. Subject has a mattress against an adjacent wall. The rest of the apartment is empty, which is fine with her because she doesn't consider it a home or as a long term stay. It's a lot better than the street or the cold weather shelters, however. Subject is a good little chef. We are working with paper plates, bowls, cups and towels and plastic knives and forks and one aluminium pan and one microwaveable deep bowl. Writer knows she has to put that heavy backpack down but doesn't trust any avenue for storage, with her intellectual property in it. She's going to offload some of it into the soil once she gets money to buy an appropriate metal vault which would have to be weather and termite proof, not to mention gopher and mole teeth that can razor their way through just about anything. Yes, send more dion fortune defence tactics please.

Cass

**From: Leigh Ryder**
**To: Cass Ryder**

Dear Cass,

I strongly advise you don't leave your daypack or any valuable ID documents at the apartment, since you don't know who M could invite into her apartment in your absence.

Psychotherapists posit three basic human instincts: 1)self-preservation or the ego 2) the reproductive or sex instinct 3) social interaction or self-expression. If one of these instincts is thwarted e.g. by years of loneliness and isolation the ego will try to compensate by manufacturing artificially what it lacks. After a while the mind will actually prefer its own created world to that of reality, which is where a form of insanity sets in and normal judgement and self-control go by the wayside. At the same time displacement of emotion can occur e.g. an obsession with comparatively irrelevant issues. Repressed emotions erupt in fits of crying, screaming, even muscular spasms as they act as safety valves to relieve tension. What you view as an "enforced bioelectrical" may really be the body's natural method of relieving tension through the muscles.

I am sending you some more insights gleaned from my reading Dion Fortune's *Psychic Self-Defence* (you should be able to open it with our agreed password)

Love,

Leigh

**More Psychic Self-Defence Tactics**

As you are aware, emotion radiates out from a person forming a magnetic field which those with occult knowledge can link into, all the more reason to cultivate an attitude of calm. Emotional states can also alter the electrical conductivity of the body. The more robust your physical condition, the more control and stamina you will have and the better equipped you will be to defend yourself against psychic attack. DF also mentions 2 important psychic centres: the head and the solar plexus. One way of relieving tension in the solar plexus is by means of a hot water bottle placed between the pit of the stomach and the ribs, but in the absence of a hot water bottle a firm pad held in place by a belt can be used as a substitute. All these tactics enable you to put up a more effectual resistance, the idea being to endure or "sit it out" even if you can't prevent it happening. Psychic attacks, even by experienced adepts, use up far too much energy to be maintained for very long, so someone in good physical condition with endurance and stamina will always win through. Conversely a person who is very sick or whose immune system is severely weakened can be more easily controlled through whispered suggestions.

With respect to the use of emotion as a magnetic force field a trained occultist can concentrate and direct that emotion into a beam of energy, by focussing their attention. The energy can be used for good i.e. spiritual healing or for evil - destructive attacks. In order to "desensitise" yourself and make yourself less vulnerable not only should you strive to be less emotional and less suggestible, it may mean you have to avoid reading any material to do with the occult. Your aim should be to keep the psychic centres *closed off* from attack, so apart from avoiding complete solitude make sure you have food in your stomach i.e. don't fast or go hungry as this makes you more open to occult forces. One other way to close down your psychic centres is to avoid a completely vegetarian diet, as this can make a person hypersensitive. Chronic malnutrition - which can occur when you are eating enough for sustenance but not enough quality food – can lead to hypersensitivity and in turn to psychic disturbance. Finally, try to focus on more mundane matters. Witchcraft practitioners despair of working their occult attacks on someone who is watching a comedy or engaging in physical activity.

There are three factors in a psychic attack:

Telepathic or hypnotic *suggestion*
*Reinforcement* of an initial suggestion by the use of invisible agencies or "triggers"
Employment of some point of contact, rapport or magnetic *link*

I have explained how a trained occultist can concentrate the magnetic energy or force field produced by emotion. In order to direct this at his target, he must form a rapport or point of contact in order to pierce his victim's aura. Sympathy is a very powerful means of establishing an immediate rapport between two strangers so if M is being used as an "operator" her sob stories would be an ideal way to gain your sympathies (sister killed in car crash, inheritance hijacking, house fire, Mafia persecution etc.) What I find suspect about the disembodied female voice you claim to have heard on the bench "instructing" M is that entities from the invisible realm do NOT communicate via words to humans on the physical plane. They can cause physical phenomena e.g. move objects and make inexplicable noises such as footsteps, groans, crashes, and they can also render themselves visible as astral thought-forms, spectral figures, balls of light, columns of luminous mist etc. But they CANNOT use human language. DF says: "if actual words are heard, auditory hallucination should be suspected, for in the absence of a medium, spirit messages are given to the inner ear not the auditory nerve" Bear in mind she was writing well before the era of wireless remote technology which leaves another possibility. So if you clearly heard a voice coming from M on the bench it signifies one of two things:

1) You were suffering an auditory hallucination. It was entirely in your mind, and is a symptom of schizophrenia or

a dissociated complex – in other words it can be explained in terms of a psychiatric disorder

2) You did hear a voice and were not hallucinating, but the voice was human and came from a small electronic device similar to a cellphone through which M receives her instructions/commands and acts accordingly. You were obviously not meant to hear it (or perhaps you were, to further convince you M is subject to occult interference, or to increase your paranoia)

Either way if you heard clear articulated words you are definitely NOT dealing with anything disembodied or occult, and it is far more likely to be either your own psychosis or covert communications taking place between her and some other human agency. If you recall, I posited the same theory RE the "whisperings" you heard in the toilet cubicle, and it does seem rather odd that the adjoining cubicle should be wrecked right after my email warning you of possible cameras. I'm afraid it comes full circle to Monica, and if you wish to continue with this alliance you should be very much aware that she is being used to target you, and that all of her utterances and behaviour are to be taken as a form of deliberate provocation designed to work upon your emotions (to incite sympathy, rage etc.) At first I thought she was doing all this consciously and practising a deliberate deception on you, which explains my distrust of her motives. I also thought some accomplice was possibly using her to obtain cash, a not uncommon scam directed at relatives. I'm still not convinced this isn't the case, but even if it is unconscious being around her so much and within her sphere of influence is not good for you.

The other problem with living in the same space is that she can easily get hold of something impregnated with your personal vibrations (nail clipping, strand of hair, a soiled handkerchief or article of clothing habitually worn) which can then be used by someone versed in the occult to establish a magnetic link with you in order to target you more effectively. These are well-worn tactics used in witchcraft. Alternatively, a symbolic object or talisman magnetised or "charged" by magic ritual can be hidden and placed in a room occupied by the victim, or even buried in the ground so the victim has to pass over it frequently. These talismans can then serve as a focal point of concentration for the sorcerer to work his harmful effects on his victim. For instance, in *The Black Alchemist* the sorcerer buried stone flint-heads which had been inscribed with magical symbols/formulae and charged through ceremonial rituals in sites specially chosen for their potency like church graveyards or pagan sites, with the object of weakening the aura of Christians who worshipped at these sites.

So far I've described how psychic pressure can be exerted on an intended target so that he or she comes under the complete influence or domination of the operator. Now I will touch on an etheric operation known as *congressus subtilis*, which has a direct bearing on M's compulsive behaviour in toilets. Sexual union can take place on the etheric as well as the physical plane, hence the well-known phenomena of people being troubled by nocturnal visitations from entities held responsible for erotic dreams (succubi or incubi) These entities are usually low-level elementals or artificial astral thought-forms created by adepts. I don't know quite how it works, but you were probably not far off when you suggested that this practice can be "milked" by those who have occult knowledge, which is why some witch covens indulge in degenerate practices. DF suggests such activities are "used systematically as a means of obtaining occult power" which is why what M is doing (or being coerced to do) is so dangerous since it increases the power and influence of those who are using her sex energy. There is a parallel to this energy in Tantric yoga or philosophy, which is one of the manifestations of *kundalini* - the symbolic serpent that lies coiled at the base of the spine. The control and concentration of this force is used in occult ritual, and Aleister Crowley made use of it in quite a sick way for magical purposes, in order to conjure up demons and other elemental entities. I came across the following quote from the Internet: *There is a sacral chakra that stores sexual energy, also known as "kundalini" or life energy. Abstinence allows you to redirect your life energy from the sacral chakra to other parts of your body, so other chakras esp. the one around your throat become enriched. This empowers your body as well as your mind.*

## Warding Off Psychic Attacks

If you have trouble maintaining an emotional distance from someone who is unduly affecting or influencing you, imagine they are separated from you by a sheet of glass, so that you can see or hear them but their magnetism or force field cannot affect you. And if you suspect someone is trying to "hypnotise" you by gazing intently into your eyes don't stare back or return their gaze, but look at the spot just above their nose between the inner ends of the eyebrows. Whatever mind-power he or she thinks they possess, they will not be able to dominate you if you do this and will soon give up. In the case of someone whom you suspect is sapping your vitality, or who makes you feel uncomfortable or vulnerable, interlace your fingers and place your folded hands on your solar plexus, keeping your elbows pressed against your sides. At the same time keep your feet touching each other. By doing this you have made your body into a closed circuit, not allowing any of your own vital force to go out of you. This is a very effective technique and the other person is likely to accuse you of being unsympathetic, but that is the point. Any nauseating or revolting images that are presented to your consciousness have been put there by someone who has used their imagination to create thought-forms (film-makers do it all the time in order to influence the viewing public) But you can use your own imagination to picture such images out of existence by visualising the image shattering into fragments, being dissolved in water, or going up in flames. Anything that has been thought into existence can be thought out of existence.

## Nation and Race

Countries or regions develop a "group soul" over time, which can take on the aspect of a distinct personality. DF later disassociated herself with the Theosophical movement because she felt it was too overshadowed with Eastern mysticism, whereas she considered herself more within the tradition of Western esotericism, in accordance with her Anglo-Saxon heritage. Whilst training she came across an Indian occultist who tried to persuade her to join his lodge. He told her he wanted to "pour the regenerative spiritual force of the East into the group soul of the British empire." His central idea was that England must acknowledge the supremacy of India and take its inspiration from the East. DF instinctively distrusted his motives, and the more she thought about it the more uneasy she became about what sort of spiritual force was going to be poured through the channel the meditation group were constructing. Concluding that something sinister was being attempted against the group-mind of the British, she invoked her spirit guides for direction, and the man eventually returned to India.

She also believed that there is an occult group called "The Watchers" who concern themselves with the welfare of nations, and that part of their job is to "police" the astral plane (she appealed to this group of Watchers during World War II when Britain was under attack) These Watchers operate through various lodges: other nations avail themselves of different occult lodges. In addition to the Watchers there are groups of occultists who have banded together in order to combat the "Black Lodges" or harmful occult forces (who are operating contrary to cosmic laws) She observed that the Watchers appear to possess alliances in unexpected quarters and can pull strings. Because of this ongoing psychic conflict it does mean that ordinary unsuspecting citizens are not completely at the mercy of dark forces, and that there is a measure of protection afforded by their astral adversaries (our spiritual guardians)

**From: Cass Ryder**
**To: Leigh Ryder**

The psychic self-defence thing you sent isn't coming through, oh it's too topical their minds CANNOT take it. The medical mafia information that disappeared as soon as I tapped into it, the stuff about how they kill people with treatment …the problem with them is they can't BARE it if someone is not so ugly and stupid as them, and who doesn't bark to their orders. They're going to try and give her chemical prescriptions which cause mental illness, they're trying to hide the evidence of what they did to her in her disorientated state. Not only do they plan to bump her off, it seems, but the two stray hound dogs by the roadside with electrical plugs for collars around their necks in Frederick MD were supposed to represent her and me. Writer had a confrontation with an animal control unit worker who had to pick up a baby hound dog, while the adult dog ran into the woods. The baby hound dog was almost certainly put down in two weeks (equals "the procedure") and that right there is an indication of a set up. Lupus dementia is an autoimmune thing like AIDS and was diagnosed 3 years 6 months before I met her. Lupus does mean wolf and is the symbol of the Roman empire (2 brothers suckling from a she-wolf) They are able to get away with this kind of encoded symbolism because absolutely nobody understands this language, any more than anyone in the 40s could have understood PASCAL or COBOL as emergent software languages. Just learnt yesterday there is a massive underground town beneath DC, which sports a Scottish masonry temple construction.

The subject feels "chills", her word to describe something which writer also feels and can only be described as an "electric wind" – like an internal cold wind or enforced shudder. The fact that it happens to them both at the same time is significant, and seems an example of "bad electricity", which writer had always associated with criticism, like something judging her. Got dragged out of my body a few months ago (enforced OBE) and my breast was tortured. The area was manhandled and squashed agonizingly. I guess it could have been remote technology but I tend to think it wasn't, and I'd never experienced anything like it, the flesh area was red afterwards. The attack was completely off the wall but writer was able to sublimate it. All people have an etheric body, and they can torture you in the ether. They did it to me once in Sterling about a year ago, I'm not going into detail here, okay? SICK OF THIS LIBRARY, AND I'M NEVER COMING HERE AGAIN, AND THE WAY HE TRIES TO FORCE CAPITAL LETTERS ON ME WHEN I'M WRITING (sister said I'm accidentally hitting the caps lock key, NO I'm not, how does that explain the small lettering in certain key words and it keeps changing back) I just complained about the NSA jerk in the corner. The little old lady at the desk couldn't bear the complaint and ignored it, but then what else does he have propping up his system but an endless army of little old ladies and Barbie doll look-alikes. That sausage has the MOST PATHETIC JOB ALIVE SINCE HE SPENDS HIS LIFE INVADING OTHER PEOPLE'S PRIVACY.

M didn't "break out" after dinner, and it seems they compensate by making her break out in the middle of the night. I ignored it, but am wondering if the people next door can hear it… I heard a couple making out in an apartment above a few nights ago, so it's likely they can hear her but I wonder if they could hear the content. She doesn't realise anything's wrong, and will attack you if you try and talk about it, but where is all this going? Is she going to be thrown out on the pavement again soon? This is what I dreamed last night: I see her sitting between the legs of some man and I say "Why do you allow yourself to sit between his legs?" and then there's an image of loads of panicking English people as though they're running to get out of the country like from a sinking ship. The man in the dream was significant? What's noticeable is she's involved in a layering of psychic influence. For instance, the presence she describes as a Catholic priest is actually a very nice man and seems to be concerned for her, exactly as a father to his daughter. But there's something else seriously powerful interfacing with the subject, who are the most unbelievable dirtbags....one thing you can count on them doing is unleashing something African and threatening on white Nordic racials. They did it through shelters, jails, and they're now doing it through their sad little NSA jerk in the library, who's the ugliest piece of shit alive. God what a bunch of fuckups. I'm not coming back here tomorrow.

Just the other day in punching out "mafia and mind control" on the Internet the writer undercovers an interesting file about the rock and roll industry in terms of how many of them had been set up or assassinated. Alexander Constantine (the author of "Psychic Dictatorship in The U.S.") just came out with a book called "Covert War on Rock" describing what he calls a massive attack on people in the entertainment industry in the last few decades: *the agency and organised crime have, for over 30 years, engaged in a program to silence popular musicians whose influence subverts the cynical thought control tactics of American government and media"* Joan Baez was apparently experimentation material as a child and fish-baited through time …her father worked in research with reference to Operation Chaos at Stanford, CA. What was Operation Chaos? *"The promotion of widespread drug use in anticipation of chaos and criminality"* Loads of people in the rock industry have been roughly dealt with or assassinated, the list is just too long to cite here. Bob Dylan has a motorbike accident the same time a relative of Joan Baez does, and the latter dies. Bella Abzug the women's movement leader who said "Women belong in the house…the House of representatives" ends up in a wheelchair. Whilst the writer feels he's courageous and making honest points, he's tripping up on the major conclusion about what's going on (though Constantine does make the point about the links between occult lodges and Western intelligence and mafias) Recent freedom of information disclosures reveal there was a deliberate agenda pursued by the FBI amongst others to make rock stars look depraved. But some rock musicians weren't all that nice. For example they easily became yuppies, and tended to view women as "chicks". What's so heroic about continually lighting up a marijuana stick? A man who's now working in Starbucks (retired from working in the White House) says "The government are mind-controlled, the executives are mind-controlled" (his eventual conclusion after decades of observation) The system is corrupt, but do you tell someone with a weapon in his hand that he's wrong, when he's got it aimed at you?

The meal M cooked was really good but it was unhealthy, and I doubt whether I'm going to be able to persuade her to go for orthomolecular tailor designed diets. She can't stand men and hisses angrily at them like a wounded feline in bus queues and cafes. Writer had always felt she should stay close like a sort of umpire over a tennis match. We argue a lot then she says "That's it, you're out" and I say "Fine, I didn't want to be here anyway" On top of this the feeling that someone is watching and listening. I told her she's possessed when she started "Slit their throats. Crack their heads on the pavement. Make them suffer and die. Kill them" Her latest continual reiteration is "rape them up the arse, I hope they get raped up the arse" It sounds like a man speaking, it doesn't sound like her. I'm not allowed to speak to her, but am expected to stay beside her. She clings to me and at the same time projects her grievances at me like it's my fault. She calls me "Claudine" and blames me for something this other woman did to her. I don't like to say it but she increasingly wants to get hold of those firearms she was used to carrying, or trained with. Apparently she killed Robert in self-defence, when he and Sal were coming after her and her uncle and aunt. He had already killed her sister and friend earlier in a home invasion (which was some kind of lesbian accusation feud against her sister) these facts could probably be checked with the local town records. This character Sal is apparently the brother of the FBI cousin Michael, so Robert must be another cousin (there are cops in her wider family) She talked about 2 weeks of missing time while training to be a cop in San Francisco. She failed the training and ships back out to NY.

Subject needs extra grocery cash (for instance she has to have fresh cilantro garlic peppers, which can't normally be obtained from the food pantry) and cash for cellphone, wifi, buses, toiletries, coffee. She seems to have a real problem getting foodstamps...right now she's dipping into cash the writer's older sister sent her, but it shouldn't be spent on food. If it was just possible to get work...I'll keep trying.

Cass

**From: Leigh Ryder**
**To: Cass Ryder**

Dear Cass,

If M's condition was diagnosed over three years ago then it's not surprising that it should now have deteriorated to such an extent. However, the sadistic and homicidal things she's coming out with are just not normal for a woman (sounds more like a male psychopath) I mean, how many females fantasise about "raping someone up the arse"? If we assume that the conversation disorder associated with a disintegrating psyche is similar to the conversation disorder associated with prolonged alcohol or drug abuse (which also results in brain cell damage and cognitive impairment) then the symptoms will also be similar. For instance, drunkards lose all their inhibitions and will act on impulse according to their nature: someone with a nice or generous personality will become very outgoing and sociable when drunk (loud, singing etc.) However, someone who has an unpleasant personality or violent inclinations will act on their anti-social tendencies when drunk, showing no moral restraints whatsoever. In other words someone under the influence of drugs or drink usually cannot help *revealing their true nature,* which is normally repressed. Therefore this indicates one of two things about your friend:

a) She is actually quite a sadistic and intolerant person, with psychopathic tendencies - these impulses being normally repressed - but her deteriorating condition has brought these aspects of her character to the surface, as there are no longer any conscious mental restraints in operation, the disease acting like a "truth drug"

b) She is, as you suggest, being channelled by some malevolent male spirit like a demonic possession and now no longer has any control over her thoughts or (more worryingly) her actions

In either case, this is a very DANGEROUS situation, and I wonder whether you are right in keeping this from the medics as she may break out in actual violence and could end up stabbing someone in a frenzy, possibly YOU, as she is obviously losing control. I recently watched a documentary on Broadmoor, and it's notable how many of the inmates claim to have "heard voices" in their head, and seemed almost bewildered at the crimes they have committed. They admitted responsibility for their actions but had no explanation as to WHY they had been driven to murder. One black inmate said his father had been a "complete bastard" who repeatedly raped and beat his mother, believing that every time he abused the poor woman this gave him more power, enabling him to "conjure up demons" For me this illustrates a dark aspect of certain African belief systems, and people who generally dismiss this stuff as primitive superstition really ought to pay more attention to some of the more evil aspects of certain rituals such as Voodoo: the dismembered bodies of young children who have been mutilated in voodoo rituals have been brought to the attention of the police in London and other major British cities.

Although women are far more vulnerable on the physical plane for obvious reasons, I believe men are more vulnerable on the astral plane and are more susceptible to occult influence - either from disembodied entities or from embodied human agencies - who are able to manipulate their thoughts and behaviour, directing them to kill and maim. The reason they are more susceptible is because many men are naturally more prone to violence than women, and are therefore much easier to corrupt. Eventually a corrupt and degenerate lifestyle has the effect of weakening the protective psychic barrier, enabling malign influences to take advantage of their weakened state. To take a couple of recent examples in the British press: a schoolboy stabbed a female languages teacher to death in front of his class. There was no apparent motive as the teacher in question was universally loved by everyone who knew her: this particular boy had developed a pathological hatred for her, and was always boasting to fellow classmates that he would "kill the bitch" etc. using the most foul sexist language. Nobody took much notice, and then one day he acted out his murderous intentions, brutally butchering her in front of a shocked class of students. It later emerged he was addicted to sadistic interactive video games such as "Dark Souls" and "Grand Theft Auto" which are specifically targeted at a male audience, and one has to speculate whether there is an element of subliminal suggestion going on here. Without wishing to sound overly paranoid, this leads on to the suspicion that the teenage male mind is being deliberately "messed with", through suggestions being implanted in the unconscious via unsavoury websites and online gaming. It makes you wonder just how many zombified young men walking the streets imagine they have free will and are free to do as they wish, when they may actually be doing what they are programmed to do (like brainwashed "Manchurian Candidate" assassins who can be activated by a given trigger)

The second incident involved a 29-year-old Englishman living in Hong Kong who had a highly successful career in finance, and was recently arrested over the double murder of 2 young Asian women whose mutilated bodies were found in his apartment. It emerged that for some time he had been addicted to orgies, and had spent a lot of his considerable wealth on clubbing, drinking to excess, hiring prostitutes etc. In the photograph of him being led away by police, he looked bloated and overweight with lifeless "dead-looking" eyes, and bore no resemblance whatsoever to the good-looking, slim, smiling young man who had gone out East a couple of years ago. His former girlfriend said he was virtually unrecognisable as the person she knew, and that he had always been thoughtful and kind, the "perfect gentleman" (she was adamant that he had never been violent towards her)The "before" and "after" photos in the paper were such a contrast that everyone was left wondering what on earth could have happened to change a relatively normal person into such a homicidal maniac. My own theory is that once he started to drink heavily and became addicted to prostitutes this provided the opportunity or gateway for something horrible to take him over. From then on he no longer had any control over his increasingly violent behaviour.

As for the alleged astral attack *"Got dragged out of my body a few months ago (enforced OBE) and my breast was tortured"* this may be symptomatic of some underlying medical condition. I prefer to seek a natural explanation before resorting to supernatural explanations so I looked up breast pain (mastalgia) and discovered that cyclical breast pain is quite common just before a period. Do you still have periods or have they stopped? There is another condition called costochondritis which may be experienced as a "burning sensation" and can be connected with poor posture (sleeping upright on a bench for over 2 years?) On the subject of health I think it's a pretty poor show that the apartment is not equipped with crockery and cooking utensils. Paper plates are a false economy as they cannot be washed and re-used. Whilst you are staying at M's apartment, I am going to suggest a couple of inexpensive and nutritional meals:

**Breakfast - Porridge**

Apart from being a good way to start the day in cold temperatures, it also has the advantage of being cheap and easy to prepare. The only ingredients required are water and natural unprocessed oats. The proportion of oats to water is one cup of oats to 3 cups of water. Put the oats into a saucepan and gradually add the water as the saucepan heats up. Keep stirring as you bring it to the boil. The consistency should now be porridge-like, and you can turn down the heat, letting it bubble for another minute or so before serving.

**Dinner -Vegetable Stew**

The ingredients you will need are a selection of raw vegetables, such as carrots, potatoes, onions or leeks, swede or turnips, something green like sprouts, cabbage, etc. plus a couple of stock cubes for flavouring and a tin of chopped tomatoes. Cover with water in the saucepan and let it boil. Add the vegetables in the order of those that take longest to cook e.g. sprouts or swede first, then crumble in the OXO cubes, stirring occasionally. Allow it to boil for a few moments then turn the heat down to just above simmering, replacing the lid. Allow about 25-30 minutes for the vegetables to soften and cook properly. Finally, stir in the tin of tomatoes.

In the meantime, you should remain on your guard in case M suddenly goes berserk and lashes out at you. Maybe you should talk to a trusted social worker about some of her vocalisations and ask for advice.

Love,

Leigh

**From: Cass Ryder**
**To: Leigh Ryder**
**Subject: youre going to fuck off**

I KNOW YOU TAKE ADVANTAGE OF THE FQACT THAT
IM NOT TAlkjing to anyone i dont have to listen to you much
longewr ,,.and your lame .. attempt to get <me annoyed > you re
backhanded >> and youre a liar .. like your occult knowledge TO
SPREAD your little disinfo in yoiur emails…YOU DONT LIKe
ME AND YYU NEVER HAVE

youre so cheaP ITS NOT TRUE EGO PENIS HURT THE LOT
OF YOUU iD HAte to have your life and live where you do ..The
things .. you writeare obscene OATMEAL  Oh but I should be
grateful for your recipos because Im am an american dunderhead
who knows nothing?  keEP YOUR CHEAP CHRISTMAS CASH

mY STUFF HAS BEEN INTERCEPTED ALL ALONG NOT
JYST READ BUT INTERCEPTED INOTHERWAYS >>i HEArd
a voice the other night saying 'my family is gpoing to be murdered'
.. Youre not my family anymore but I guess something means 'you
people ' You took total advantafe of the faqct that you were the
only one I was communicating with..Yourer not doing anything
withmy book Im not sending you anything else ./ The brits dont
want to read it anywaty theyre too stiff too jealous.. they do not
have openminds LEAVE my writing alone ugly bitch ....

I think people are disgusting . i DONT HAVE TO PUT UP WITH
P[OVERTY6.. youre go(ing to fduck off as my sistewre youre
going to fuck offd  yopure going to fuck oiff youre going to dfuck
off ypu P-0ERVERT5 .. KEEP0 YOUR SAd family love ..YPOU
DONT GET IT . iM NOT AT ALL THREATENED BY HER ..
yOU ACT .. LIKE IUM complaining too you
YOU bnevwer .. ever commented wqhen I talked about political us
corruption nor did..and he sits on your face and youre noit even
aware of it.. the drug addicts of the earth rthe control freak drug

addicts HES CSO >> JEALOUS OF ME .. SO jealous he gets black men rto iwatch me on the sly You st5inkingt jealous lkittle jerks

he s .. a friusatratred little driug addict if anything hes the drug addict on this earth .. he has no powqer .. and .. hes a little sex pervert

YO(U&R#EW ALL A BUNCH OF FUCKING PERVERTS

THE POINT ABOUTY .. mentiuoning the person vocalizing what I was texti8ng is that he didnt see what I was texting .. okay .. so he was electronically surveilleiying while he was tryiong to physically intimidate . You didnt respond on that as usual . Youre so srtupoid .. You talk about black voodoo ytoure all perverts

Shes far nicer than you projhect and you.. purposely ..do that and one reason is you idont like me ande nwever have and youre not honest about it .. MY FAMILYARE NOT VERY NICE but I agreee we were hounded by somethingt ..

I HATE AMERICANS BUT I DONT HAVE TO COM<E OVER TO BRIT . AND KEEOP YOUR STINKING SMELLY DOLE >> THERE was .. a covert war on single females and lesbian\s.. but its not going to come out the occult is a reality

the penis ..squaSHED MY BREAST AGONISIGLY IN THE Astral plane .. we were .. ALL BORN INTO POTENTIAL TORTURE CELLS >> YOURE all so stuopid and ugly

**From: Leigh Ryder**
**To: Cass Ryder**
**Subject: No I'm not going to fuck off**

Dear Cass,

Did you write the message I've copied below? If so, I cannot understand your rage towards me. Looking back over what I wrote I realise some of it does sound rather patronising, but I wasn't trying to imply you were a "dunderhead" who knows nothing. After 20 years of homelessness I doubt whether you have had the opportunity to cook anything - and since you now have access to an apartment I genuinely thought you might appreciate a few tips on some basic meals which would keep you fuelled up on a tight budget. Apparently not, but I don't see why a harmless reference to oatmeal should be "obscene" or why it should annoy you so much. When you're up against the wall, sometimes it helps to focus on practical issues - which may seem trivial - but they are an intrinsic part of survival.

And of course I am not taking advantage of the fact I am the only one you are communicating with! I cannot prevent you from communicating with whoever you like, and wouldn't want to. You are completely wrong when you assert I "don't like you and never have" That is completely untrue –just who is drilling this garbage into your brain? You keep judging me as though I were the same person I was 20 years ago, and yes we've had our differences (you weren't the easiest person to get along with) but I understand a lot more now than I did then about what you've been through, and what has triggered the problems and setbacks you've had in life. There have been times in my life when I have been stupid and selfish, and moments I deeply regret, but I can't change the past. All I can do is admit up to it and try to be more compassionate and understanding. Obviously I must be failing somewhere along the line, if you imagine I would deliberately do or say anything to upset you.

I mentioned the incidents about Voodoo and spirit possession in order to illustrate how someone who is basically a decent and normal person could be controlled or manipulated to such an extent that they could be directed to commit atrocities, without even being consciously aware of what is going on. Hence I felt you might be in real physical danger, and I just wanted you to be on your guard. I realise you have not felt threatened by Monica so far, but that doesn't mean she might not constitute a threat in the future. If, as you maintain, her vocal chords are being "puppeted" and that someone else is speaking through her, then why is it so farfetched to assume that her **actions** might be the next thing which are manipulated - either by occult forces OR remotely via electronic means. I did not say your friend was evil, I implied she might be under the influence of something evil, and as you have implied *exactly the same thing yourself* on many occasions I fail to see why you should take such offence if I conclude that you might be right. The natural progression of the disease *lupus dementia* would explain the disordered conversation, but it does not wholly explain the sadistic nature of some of her verbalisations. God knows what's going on here, but if someone or something is seeking to increase its power over M, the next logical step is a complete bodily hijacking where her body could be used to carry out some horrible crime. Yes, I am frightened for you and I don't mind admitting it. Why do you insist on telling me about the things she says in a "man's voice" like "slit their throats" etc. unless you want me to believe in some kind of possession? I have stated all along that this may be nothing occult but could be some kind of hypnosis or remote manipulation using technology. Whatever the case it IS a dangerous situation esp. when you are living in such close proximity, and I refuse to apologise for warning you to be careful. It is the right thing to do in the circumstances.

And as for not "doing anything with your book" I have been working on it constantly for about 6 hours a day with no let-up. If you want me to leave your writing alone I will (after all, I have not asked to receive all these lengthy attachments, you are literally bombarding me with the stuff) but is this really YOU speaking here or is it someone else who feels threatened that we might actually succeed in putting your writing into the public domain, thereby exposing how the U.S. treats its homeless citizens? I think it deserves to be published, and I am in a much better position than you are to attempt this. It will stand as a written record of one woman's experience of homelessness and it is a pretty remarkable testament. Also, it is the only way I can see to raise some cash for you, since you seem determined to stay over there.

I have not commented on American political corruption, which I know to exist (just as it exists everywhere) because this is not about me or about my opinions, it's about you. Constantine's book about the covert war on rock musicians was interesting, but didn't reveal much most thinking people didn't suspect anyway i.e. that LBJ and Nixon were paranoid bastards and that many musicians who were involved with civil rights or took a stand against the Vietnam war were bumped off or silenced in other ways. The totalitarian mindset cannot bear challenge on any level, and will naturally seek to stamp out and eliminate anyone whom they perceive as a threat. Lennon was well aware his phones were being tapped, and as a vocal critic of the Nixon administration he also feared that he would be assassinated (for the same reason Socrates was made to drink hemlock, because of his popularity and influence on young people) I don't propose to waste any more time commenting on the obvious as I would rather concentrate my energies on doing what I can to help you.  These entities feed off hate and paranoia, so try and keep your shadow man on a leash.

Love,

Leigh

**From: Cass Ryder**
**To: Leigh Ryder**

Yes I wrote that, not ashamed or proud, and agree I'm a horrible person. Proof that there was an interception, your voodoo message has just disappeared (been lifted from my inbox) Last night M sprang into an agitation state that lasted for hours, an angry and vitriolic soliloquy (to the room presumably, as writer was under the covers in the corner trying to sleep) then in literally about 10 seconds fell into a deep sleep, like something switched her off or pulled a plug. That right there is further proof her body is channelled. To be gesticulating wildly and then suddenly to be snoring like someone pushed a button? Half the time she's not even aware of it. When I question her later "does she remember the pornographic comments she's made out loud in the library etc?" she doesn't know what I'm talking about. Sorry to sound racist again…trying not to…but the African people upstairs were having a party, and when they started shouting she shut up immediately as though they have some influence over her. When she walked towards me the other evening I saw white energy coming out of her left eye. In the last 3 weeks she has been hissing really loudly at men in bus queues, cafes, store aisles, you name it, and the men are sidestepping it as fast as they can once they acknowledge it's angled at them. Subject calls me Claudine and reiterates "that filthy act we were made to do together" Once she complained her inner thighs were blackened and also black on her backside area, and her underpants torn…. sounds creepy as anything, but they medicate people this way esp. if they're perceived as aggressive. Liz is a like a drug to her (even soul mates don't harp on about a person 100 times a day) and seems to be the wolf in grandmother's clothing.

Being on basement level is not conducive to security or safety. Both of us thought we heard men tapping on the window a week ago. The front door in the entrance foyer isn't lockable and there is a 2nd floor stairwell alcove which is basically an assault trap for an attacker to hide behind. The entire building complex is 90% ethnic, predominantly African or Hispanic and mainly het couples/families (most have fully grown sons with loud boom boxes and threatening demeanours) and as usual we're made to feel uncomfortable as white women who stand out. The subject won't use the food pantry c/o Loudoun county "faith-based initiative" church - one reason is because end date codes are not adhered to. They should start up a transportation service from the local pantry back to the permanent supportive housing units (perhaps operating 2 times a week at certain hours) However, her immune system seems strengthened, her jaw is less inflamed, the red spot on her sclera disappeared, and her athletes foot is better (they give her money to do laundry once a week so she can keep her feet cleaner) Overall she's better rested, and getting more protein. Writer didn't go to the chiropractor, would rather not have anything to do with the social security crowd. The new contract struck with the subject this morning was that I go to the apartment at 7pm, with no meals, and "hit the mattress" (not engage in any mutual conversation with her) Subject basically relates to the writer like someone does to a service animal "Shut up, don't talk back, it is your job to listen and obey" I have to walk behind her and to the right. Pretty bizarre, but that suits me fine. Writer always gives her half, if not most or ALL of any cash donations she received (not to mention her foodstamps which she shares with subject)

Cass

**From: Leigh Ryder**
**To: Cass Ryder**
**Attachment: Security**

Dear Cass,

Are you sure my last email was "lifted" from your inbox? If you get a lot of spam or junk mail arriving every day then it's easy to lose sight of former messages. If you scan backwards through your messages you should be able to find it. In the meantime it's good practice to delete incoming junk mail so as to make it easier to search for previous emails that you want to retain. Just in case there are any interceptions or electronic surveillance I have enclosed another password-protected attachment at the end of this email.

I think you should voice your security concerns to the welfare workers: the fact that it's basement level and the communal front door is kept unlocked, tapping on the window which you both heard etc. They are unlikely to grant any requests for acoustic diminishers, which would be perceived as an unnecessary luxury, but they should take safety issues seriously. And by providing insecure accommodation they are putting you at risk and thereby failing in their duty of care. Also the fact that the apartment seems to be unfurnished is disgraceful. Even prison inmates have basic furniture (a proper bed, chest of drawers, chairs and table etc.) The provision of housing seems very poorly administered - it sounds more like a squat to me – surely this cannot comply with federal regulations? They could be in breach of the law, banking on your ignorance to get away with it.

What also concerns me is that you are being treated like a "service animal" in relation to M with the new "contract" between you specifying that you are not allowed into the apt until 7pm, and expected to "hit the mattress" as soon as you come in, and not even allowed to engage in conversation. Now that you are no longer any use for guarding purposes, you are being treated like a doormat. And as for you having to "walk behind her and to the right" this is how Arabs treat their women in Muslim countries. Considering how you have generously shared your cash and foodstamps with her, the relationship is totally one-sided but you don't need me to point that out. Let me know if you were able to open and read the attached document.

**Security**

You mentioned that back in her cop days M was in the habit of "relaxing" with Bob (the black pimp with his harem of whores) but I share your puzzlement when you ask "what did she really have in common with this Bob?" Quite. Why would an allegedly gay woman choose to spend her off-duty hours with such a douche bag? In connection with the two weeks "missing time" window when she was training to be a cop in San Francisco I am beginning to suspect that something traumatic occurred, though it is now too late to investigate this, given the amount of time that's passed. You say that *"she once noticed her inner thighs were blackened as were her backside area, and her underpants were torn ... sounds creepy as anything"* OK here's what I think, based on the information you've given me. Have you heard of a "date rape" drug called Rohypnol? Typical scenario is at a bar or party where a would-be attacker buys her a drink spiked with Rohypnol. This causes temporary paralysis and leaves the victim completely powerless, in that she cannot fight back or even remember what has happened, though she may later experience flashbacks. To casual bystanders the victim will look as though she is simply drunk with slurred speech and uncoordinated movements, before she is hustled away by her attacker and assaulted somewhere private. There is a huge black market in this drug, which is sold over the Internet. I don't think that medical procedures provide an adequate explanation: although an injection might be administered via the backside I doubt it would be administered on the inner thigh area, nor should there be any "black" bruising such as she describes, or torn underwear. Even with no conscious remembrance of what occurred, a traumatic experience such as this would be enough to trigger a mental breakdown, as it would register on an unconscious level.

Whether this theory is correct very much depends on whether this is a factual account, or whether she is just reiterating symptoms of sexual assault she has come across or heard about in TV programs, and ascribed the same symptoms to herself due to her confused mental state. Have you seen any evidence of this bruising yourself? Another thing, isn't there a minimum height stipulation for cops? In this country it's 5'4" for female police officers, and as M is only 5'1" this would automatically disqualify her for active duty. When police need to apprehend criminals well over six foot tall it would be absurd to employ someone so tiny. There are an awful lot of inconsistencies and improbabilities in her stories, which makes me question much of what you have been told. Since you think she appears to be surrounded by a benign spirit presence in the form of a Catholic priest, I would agree that spiritual counselling may be appropriate esp. in view of her religious upbringing and background. The Catholic faith is one of the few denominations that takes demonic possession seriously, and a priest might understand what's going on here. It's worth a try.

I have just started to re-read *The Stargate Conspiracy,* in order to refresh my memory. Will comment in due course on anything relevant which you may have forgotten.

Love,

Leigh

*Unshackled: A Survivor's Story of Mind Control: Kathleen Sullivan (Foreword by Michael Sweeny)*

*Most victims of mind control are not assassins. Many have been used less dramatically to infiltrate and manipulate the development of corporations, foundations, agencies and other socially influential infrastructures. Many more seem not to have been used at all; as sleepers, they may simply be awaiting some future event requiring them to be triggered into action. While historically the CIA has been the most significant developer of programmed operatives, today it is clear that the same technology has been widely used by other groups, including intelligence agencies of other nations, various mafias and occult groups, select "elite" families, and perhaps most frightening of all, certain churches and fraternal organisations. What makes the latter so frightening is that many of them operate networks of hospitals and clinics that specifically involve themselves in the creation of programmed victims, as well as the recapture and reprogramming of those whose control mechanisms seem to be slipping.*

*In my first book, The Professional Paranoid, I listed over 400 CIA fronts and CIA-influenced companies and institutions. Fully half of these are involved with mind control. Half of those seem bent on convincing us that mind control does not work, and that complaints of ritual abuse are nothing more than false memories induced by bad therapists. I'd rather that was true. But in point of fact, nearly a third of all my clients turn out to have suffered ritual abuse and/or programming, though when they initially reached out for help, they generally had no concept of what lay behind their problems. Virtually every one of these people has had some exposure to cults, military intelligence or the CIA. None had been to therapists, except those belonging to these groups – their programmers.*

*Mind control is a covert crime perpetrated by covert means. There are organisations which have been established to rush in and ensure any exposure of the crime is dealt with quickly, and effectively covered up with disinformation. It thus remains the perfect crime, reduced to nothing more than a mysterious bump in the long, dark night of our political and social nightmare. Victims of mind control often do not realise they are victims. They are even less likely to wake up to their own reality if there are people deliberately put into their lives to ensure the secrecy – people disguised as friends, relatives, or co-workers – their handlers and programmers. In my book MC Realities, I offer a long list of symptoms and clues to help identify such unhappy states, as well as advice on how to fight back. It is not a hopeless journey, but it is a perilous and difficult one. This book is testimony that success can be had.*

*Unshackled will cause many readers to question whether we are being told the truth about the political and social landscape of our world. If you value the purpose of our laws and our constitutional rights, if you treasure free will and the pursuit of happiness, you will realise that these rights are in jeopardy for all of us, when they are denied to anyone.*

**From: Leigh Ryder**
**To: Cass Ryder**
**Attachment: Stargate and beyond**

Dear Cass,

Our communications must have coincided in that I was just about to send you this, when I received yours. I started to read the photocopied extract by Kathleen Sullivan which sounded interesting, but I couldn't read more than the introduction since the rest of your message was handwritten and I can't read your illegible scrawl. Why have you stopped using your email address? Actually, after re-reading this it appears that the foreword is actually a commentary by another writer called Michael Sweeney and not an extract from K. Sullivan's book.

The connections between paranormal research, the intelligence community and new technology are nothing new, as any intelligence agency worth its salt would be interested in remote viewing, psychokinesis etc. for defence purposes. The way the military mind works is "if the enemy's doing it, we need to be doing it too" I don't think the Cold War ever went away, and like it or not mind control research is part of modern warfare. Britain is faced with a huge problem in that our avowed enemies (chiefly Islamic terrorists) have British citizenship and live legitimately in the UK with housing and generous benefits provided by the government. Given the opportunity they would happily bomb us all to extinction, and impose a reign of terror where Christians, Jews etc. were indiscriminately slaughtered, all females forced to wear the veil and deprived of their basic liberties. A significant number of them are now clamouring for strict Sharia law to be imposed on the rest of us against our will.

Given that this state of affairs exists, what are the governments of democracies supposed to do – sit back and allow them to destroy our civilised way of life? I don't subscribe to some of the more extreme conspiracy theories, which cast all agencies like the CIA, NSA, MI6 etc. in an evil light. Although such agencies undoubtedly include corrupt individuals (as do ALL organisations including schools, hospitals, charities, care homes, orphanages) most of the people who work for them are probably quite ordinary, and their brief is to keep the citizens of their country safe (which frequently involves the use of electronic surveillance techniques) The criminals and terrorists are the real problem, and if peoples' civil liberties are encroached upon as a result, the fault lies squarely with the psychopaths who have brought about this state of affairs and not with security agencies who are trying to combat the spread of evil and intolerance in our society. I have now had an opportunity to re-read *The Stargate Conspiracy*, and have summarised its findings in the attached document (to be opened by the usual password)

Is shadowman still troubling you in the library? It's interesting how the physical manifestation of "shadowman" in the library acts like a symbolic metaphor, and mirrors the shadowman lurking in your own psyche.

Love,

Leigh

# Stargate

The unfortunate corollary to psychic surveillance is *remote influencing* (which the CIA and other defence agencies naturally seized upon, since this would confer an obvious military advantage) Another author (Constantine) remarked that the Pentagon's enthusiastic research into remote viewing was "more concerned with beaming information into people's minds than information gathering from distant locations" The possibilities for mind-control over the general populace are ripe for exploitation, and since the 70s these techniques have advanced to such a stage that ordinary people who know no better tend to ascribe this phenomena to "occult" interference when it is nothing of the sort. Only occult perhaps in the literal meaning of the word i.e. "hidden" but the source of much paranormal interference is terrestrial: the chief puppetmasters are human. Of course this doesn't explain phenomena like spirit possession etc. but once you accept that human agencies are at work, everything else pretty much falls into place. Since all psychic processes are 2-way the victims can protect themselves if they have access to counter techniques to block mind interference (like "radar jamming")

The authors of *The Stargate Conspiracy* argue that the feverish promotion of the existence of a "Council of Nine" (allegedly the Egyptian godhead called the Ennead) - coinciding with the appearance of several best-selling books in the 80s and 90s about the pyramids of Giza and the so-called links with the "Face on Mars" - appears to be deliberately orchestrated. As was the widespread belief that contact with extraterrestrial beings had been established, since this would make it easier for gullible people to swallow the hidden agenda: if an advanced race of beings were responsible for "seeding" (genetically modifying) the human race in the remote past, and whose hierarchical systems of government closely resemble the Masonic ideal (the Great White Brotherhood) this gives it a semblance of legitimacy. It's not surprising that prominent people in the U.S. would support ideas which accord with the belief systems of the founders of America. Most Americans would also find it easy to accept that the Nine chose to be "channelled" through American contactees since the USA is supposed to represent the current day Atlantis (in a similar fashion many German people were persuaded to swallow the Nazi ideology because it implied the Germans or Aryans were the "master race") It's a very fallible human trait - that folks like to feel superior to their neighbours, and the puppetmasters readily exploit entrenched bigotry and existing divisions within society.

The authors also exposed the connections and personal links between apparently independent groups of people who included scientists, psi researchers, New Age gurus and writers, politicians, millionaires, and members of the intelligence community. Someone called Puharich played a key role in all this as far back as the 50s. Initially a doctor with the U.S army, his psychic research was funded by defence agencies like the CIA, and his skills included advanced hypnosis: he was very familiar with the "instant command technique" used by stage hypnotists, and in implanting post-hypnotic suggestions in the subconscious. People like Uri Geller and others with pronounced psychic gifts, like the "Space Kids" who were tested and trained at P's "turkey farm" were unwittingly exploited to further the agenda of the intelligence community. It was Puharich who brought Geller over from Israel to the U.S in the 70s and who acted as his "handler" - presiding over most of the "channelling" sessions. Some of the kids being experimented on were as young as nine, and they all lived as one big family together with a community of scientists responsible for testing their unusual faculties. They were all caught up in the conspiracy, just as the prevailing youth counter-culture – which started off in a spirit of genuine idealism and a desire to make the world a better place – was hijacked by those who wanted to manipulate this powerful social impetus for their own ends. The New Age movement which showed so much promise in terms of expanding human consciousness, was directed and channelled into military goals.

Puharich was also engaged in carrying out research into hallucinogenic drugs (such as the *amanita muscaria* mushroom used by Mexican shamans or *curanderos*) and psychoactive substances that induce altered states of consciousness – clearly a valuable tool for use in psychological warfare and behavioural control. Some of his medical inventions, like electronic deaf aids, were developed as part of classified army projects and successfully patented. He also invented a miniaturised radio transmitter that could be hidden inside a tooth, which is just one way of *making people hear voices inside their heads* (my italics) In addition to Geller another psychic called Bobby Horne was also used to channel communications from the Nine whilst in hypnotic trance. Horne woke up one morning and discovered that the metal fillings in his teeth had been replaced by compound ones, which he took to be further evidence of the paranormal. The justification given for this liberty was that the "Nine" couldn't channel properly if he had any metal about his person. Doesn't take a genius to work out what's going on here. The only mystery is how supposedly intelligent people could allow themselves to be manipulated in this manner.

To give him his due, Uri Geller pointed out that he cannot vouch for what "the Nine" said through him since he was in hypnotic trance at the time. The tape-recordings of Uri Geller's channelling of the Nine were always mysteriously wiped so that we are only left with P's transcripts of the proceedings. Of course Geller is no fool and remarked in 1972 "I think somebody is playing games with us. Perhaps they are a civilisation of clowns", which echoes Colin Wilson's description of the Nine as "the crooks and conmen of the spirit world" The army chemical centre where P was stationed participated in a programme that aimed to find ways to "program new memories into the minds of an amnesiac subject" This chimes with my own beliefs: I have always thought that many "alien abductees" were in fact abducted by military personnel in black helicopters, and subjected to some form of hypnosis which implanted false memories of "little grey men", of being beamed up into space ships etc. The victims genuinely thought this is what had happened to them when the truth was a lot more prosaic but just as sinister. This way no-one would believe their ravings, and the agents involved used the UFO hysteria as a cover or smokescreen for their research and experimental activities. They couldn't conduct this kind of research openly due to the outcry from civil liberties groups, so popular writers like Whitley Streiber and blockbuster movies like "Close Encounters" etc. were exploited as a means of whipping up UFO frenzy among the population.

Another futurist writer who also worked for the intelligence community was James Hurtak whose alleged "channellings" in his best-selling books *The Keys of Enoch* and *The Only Planet Of Choice* disclosed the following revelations: the only indigenous race on earth who existed prior to the arrival of the visitors from space and who were not "seeded" or genetically manipulated were the blacks – one might ask why? Apparently this was an experiment by the extraterrestrials to see how the "originals" (blacks) would evolve in comparison with the rest whom they colonized and civilised, the latter being hybrids (part human, part god) Hurtak refers obliquely to the "Children of Darkness" and that there will be an imminent battle for the earth (good against evil) Apart from claiming to be the ancient Egyptian godhead the Nine also claimed to be the Elohim, the gods of the Old Testament, which would chime with Jewish belief systems and ensure the latter were brought on board. All sounding a bit suspect, but very clever in that it draws together the major religions and belief systems in the West (Christian fundamentalism including Mormons, Native American shamanistic beliefs, Judaism, freemasonry) in order to broaden its appeal. With so many separate competing belief systems the religious domain is a lot harder to control, so the underlying agenda was to reverse this trend by unifying and absorbing their main elements, in order to create a new global religion for the 21$^{st}$ century.

Once a belief system takes hold in people's minds it is self-generating and takes on its own momentum, and each convert passes it on, so the word is spread. Streiber's *The Secret School* features a group of child abductees including himself at the age of nine, who attended a secret school where they were given nine lessons by their alien abductors. The authors of the *Stargate Conspiracy* have noted the increasing influence the Nine have over key decision-makers and politicians, with a network of leading scientists, best-selling New Age writers, and billionaires who all subscribe to the same philosophy. So what is the hidden message? The prime movers in this "conspiracy" made certain key claims:

- The universe is ruled by a hierarchy of intelligences and numerous planetary civilisations (messengers like the Nine acting as go-betweens)

- They created the hybrid human race and all great technologic achievements on earth were not due to humans but to extraterrestrials. The Great Pyramid was built by the space visitors to act as a physical stargate, channelling energy from cosmic space

- Contact between the human race and the extraterrestrials is imminent, and conspirators are deliberately building up an expectancy in people's minds in order to "soften them up" and prepare them for the return of the Nine

It is notable that the proposed New World Order excludes Muslim beliefs, which a significant number of people in the West would not have a problem with: islamophobia is increasing in direct proportion to the number of terrorist atrocities. Although he was careful not to sound overtly racist Hurtak's implication is that because the black races were not "seeded" they are not part space gods and are therefore inferior in terms of their evolution and degree of civilisation. So it doesn't take a genius to work out who the enemy is, that the great seeding experiment failed, and that the White Brotherhood may have to take some pretty drastic steps to save the planet from destruction, like John Wayne rounding up a posse of "good ole boys" to rid the god-fearing white folk of those "pesky injuns." Hurtak claims that the Nine have informed him that something has gone wrong with humanity's programming, and the superior intelligences who rule the universe are coming to the rescue with a new plan for "upgrading" the human intelligence. Well, Whoopey doo. And does that plan by any chance entail implanted hypnotic suggestions to ensure that any potential dissenters are fully compliant, and do the planners perhaps reside in the U.S (not a million miles from Washington) and not some far-off galaxy? And as for America being the "heir to Atlantis", yeah right. If anybody has a right to lay claim to this pretty outrageous claim, it would be the English who as a society are far more mature, tolerant and civilised than Yankee doodle dandies. Americans are the new kids on the block who never really grew up, and who seem quite incapable of appreciating that modern foreign diplomacy is more than a simple game of cowboys and Indians, and requires something a tad more sophisticated than sheer brawn and military might.

It was a fairly smart conspiracy in that it managed to blend all the most potent modern myths, like alien abduction, with older esoteric and religious systems but not quite smart enough, because it failed to take account of feminism or the fact that people are pretty well-informed these days, with access to the Internet and higher education. It's notable that all this channelling makes little mention of female deities and completely neglects the female principle. As the authors remark "The puppetmasters of the new religion have effectively censored the feminine" For people who claim to be experts in psychic matters, none of this makes much sense in that occult systems all over the world teach of the opposite and equal balance of female and male energies, and that it is only when this fundamental balance is disturbed or out of equilibrium that you get real problems. They might be able to win the hearts and minds of males in the West, some of whom would be only to happy to surrender their freedom and submit to the superior guidance of a hierarchical system of "gods" who can get rid of the Islamic menace (whilst not jeopardising their own position of gender dominance on the planet) but women are not going to willingly submit to the yoke of a white brotherhood any more than they will submit to the yoke of a more oppressive black brotherhood. It's also pretty stupid to claim to be an Egyptian godhead which historically was composed of an equal number of female/male gods, but then neglect to mention the significance of female deities in the Egyptian pantheon in an era where the worship of Isis was widespread: it just smacks of the same old patriarchal obsessions, from which we can infer a human male intelligence at work here and not a superior "godly" one. Women are pretty smart, and they should maybe take that into account next time they dream up some half-baked conspiracy for world dominance.

Nobody denies that the human species is in trouble and things have gone drastically wrong, with certain undeveloped sectors failing to make much progress since Biblical times, but that is because the male has been allowed to take pre-eminence over the female, and any system of governance which fails to address this imbalance is bound to make things worse. The "Great White Brotherhood" is an invention of freemasonry, a quasi-religious organisation which explicitly excludes women, whereas the White Goddess did actually exist and was worshipped worldwide. Robert Graves was one of the few men with the courage and honesty to acknowledge and expose the male conspiracy to censor and suppress the feminine (for which I salute him) and he got a lot of stick from the traditional male academic establishment as a result. At least the brotherhood or "Council of Nine" as they like to style themselves, recognises the threat to civilisation posed by Islamic fundamentalism, but surely it should be obvious to anyone with half a brain that the reason it poses such a threat is because it is based on a quite hysterical fear of women, resulting in a culture of extreme violence, intolerance, and suppression of human freedom. The ideological beliefs of its leaders are so unnatural (since they go against the grain of humanity's collective unconscious) that they have to be imposed by force and terror. Of course there have been times in the past when Christianity succumbed to the same misogyny, when woman-hating priests were accorded too much power – resulting in the Catholic Inquisition and the systematic and bloodthirsty persecution of anyone who challenged their narrow and bigoted views.

So what is actually on the agenda? Probably some form of synarchy (government by secret societies) who operate behind the scenes, which will undoubtedly be male and hierarchical in composition - in other words not much different from the clandestine fraternities already in existence on earth. In 1973 the U.S. government commissioned a report called *Changing Images of Man* which concluded that the spread of the new values (self-realisation and spiritual awareness) with their distrust of authority and the "establishment" - as exemplified by the "tune in and drop out" counter-culture of the hippie era - would radically undermine society. The report recommended the traditions of Freemasonry as being one of the best solutions to contain the social unrest and impetus of the new movement, and to retain control of the masses. And hence the conspiracy was born, though I believe that a lot of the New Age writers who were eventually caught up in it were probably unaware of what was really on the cards. The apocalyptic vision was too narrow, as it detracts from the autonomy of the individual, and undermines the concept of humans being masters of their own destiny.

**From: Cass Ryder**
**To: Leigh Ryder**

No I didn't get the STARGATE attchment
Watching Cassandra the whole time

GOD WHY DON'T YOU GET THE FUCK AWAY FROM ME
FUCK YOU PENIS
Fuck this ugly library youre all such assholes

Keep your4 stinking disability
Youre all losers Youre all so jealous of me You fucking jerk! Why
don't you fuck off

Drugged little shits FUCK ALL OF YOU FUCK YOUR
DISABILITY

Youre such disgusting fuckups>uniformed penis...boring govt.
workers with nothing between their ears...and theirt foul whores

I had no choice but to come here and write....youre assholes God
you look like jerks...Fifty different ways in which smelly sausage
couldn't control women enough  why stink sausage csan fuck off
on planet earth...you totally stink

This is communism and ill be gone soon...at least from this
stinking communist database...and something also google
whatever. Youre jerks..Don't let mentally unstable people on govt
paychecks upset you Cass

Youre going to fuck off WOMEN KILLED YOU WOMEN
MURDERD YOU ..why don't you get your stinking sausage out of
my mind

**From: Leigh Ryder**
**To: Cass Ryder**

Dear Cass,

I just logged in so you must be in the library now. Don't panic –
you probably just typed in the password incorrectly so you couldn't
open the document. Stay where you are, and give me five minutes
to re-send it with the initial password we used before.

Leigh

**From: Leigh Ryder**
**To: Cass Ryder**

Dear Cass,

Were you eventually able to read and open the attached document
entitled "Stargate" which I just re-sent? The reason I ask is that I
intend to organise a Moneygram in time for Christmas, and if I
don't get a response from you fairly soon then I will have to hold
back on sending anything, as I can't be sure you are reading my
communications.

Love,

Leigh

**From: Cass Ryder**
**To: Leigh Ryder**

Yes, I finally opened Stargate attchmt the second time you sent it but someone was in the database earlier and I was angry. The workers have finally gotten some furniture – 2 beds and one table were delivered, but the writer chooses to sleep on the floor because she doesn't like metal springs. They should share an apartment? Why should they? (the "share" is often an operator channel) Writer can find no evidence of the workers being on a social work registry, but recalls the conspiracy theory that covert operatives camouflage as workers in met area social service depts. Donna recently went absent for about a month and has now been replaced by someone called Tracy. The paranoid thought that this might be going on (for example none of them seem to know one another, and there seems to be a very high turnover of staff) Two of the social workers have gotten ill (one with a terminal illness) maybe so they can be replaced with covert operatives: the ones who mean well seem to act as the wife of the giant in the fairytale "Jack and the Beanstalk" in an attempt to get the hero down the beanstalk before he ends up on the giant's plate.

Oh this is paranoia? No it's probably not and they didn't really look into what caused the aids epidemic. The subject had always felt gay men were the answer, and that there had never been an enquiry as to why they died, when the conspiracy theory stated they were viral implanted and bumped off wholesale. Some died, others just spiralled into silence, barely making the bill payments each month. Pretty rough justice. Writer met a woman in the present county, a divorcee with 3 children, who complained of "voices coming out of the walls" so she moves to another townhouse. She has a theory the Lyme disease outbreak in her children was a viral plant by her ex-husband as revenge. She's from New York and there's a conspiracy theory about a Cold Spring Harbour Viral and Biological research station run by Nazis (her ex-husband is German) And of course pink elephants might fly, and that's what the world might turn around and say to the writer but she knows what she's talking about.

Yesterday the subject exclaimed to one of the workers "I'll snap your neck!" She scans the apt in detail each time she enters it, as with hotel rooms….checks cupboards, doors, windows etc. but doesn't seem to realise that anyone could lay in wait in the dark alcove under the stairwell. The John Jay criminal justice college is not responding to a request by M for a transcript of her Master's certificate issued by them, which is pretty backhanded. Some men touch her between her legs when they walk by her…endless thefts of ID…all reasons to feel frustrated. It's possible that mental assault symptoms manifest as an obnoxious attitude, but do you judge someone for having influenza? A person who's been forcefully inebriated cannot be judged for swaying on their feet. For her to have spent 4 years out in the open sleeping on cold metal benches is pretty rough justice when everyone else was having a good day in your face. Writer's observation is YOU try living in those circumstances YOU'D get mad. She seems to be whispering to this Liz under the sheets at night. While recently waking from a dream writer heard a voice say "They will both be thrown out". Damn right. Nightmares, forced OBEs. Writer once experienced a lot of "etheric anal prods" about 5 years ago, extremely irritating and done maliciously with an intent of "Get up on the highway you slut". An exact description is mirrored in a MKULTRA subproject file extracted from an NSA archives located at George Washington university. For example when writer was back in the UK (2000?) she was aware of being perceptually interfered with at the same time the BBC aired a programme about a brother and a sister living together in a coastal town in southeast Kent and interfacing with demons. At the time I had been living in an apt on the third floor of a house in Ramsgate Luke had been renovating. I remember thinking that was weird.

Thanks if you're going to send some money, I'm sure that will come in handy for both of us. The permanent supportive housing comes with some wider support like laundry tokens but how do they expect people to get by without cash? (we sometimes get cash from strangers esp. around Christmas but it's not to be relied on) I delayed on the Soar claim but the worker thinks it would be okay to just submit a psychic disturbance angled claim. No, I would only submit the fact that my muscles are a little bit stressed. Actually I still feel I should NOT make the disability claim and I should HOLD OUT for a better definition, or a chance to find a part time job. But I might have to go ahead with it for reasons I can't go into.But I would much rather have gotten an income from a book publication.

Bye for now. Cass

**From: Leigh Ryder**
**To: Cass Ryder**

Dear Cass,

At least it sounds as though they have got around to providing you with some basic furniture (about time) I trust Madame Serpent's virulent hissing in the vicinity of the opposite sex has abated somewhat. I'm also glad to hear the apartment is adequately heated, and that you're off the streets as I've been hearing about the Big Freeze in NY. I'm hoping this time round that you'll spend the cash I send on *practical* items that will make your day-to-day existence more comfortable. It's worth investing in some thick thermal hiking socks (the sort that are reinforced at the toe and heel for added cushioning) Cheap socks wear out too fast and don't protect your feet from blistering.

Are you any closer to obtaining federal cash assistance? As a homeless person with no source of income you must be entitled to regular payments of some sort, as food stamps cannot cover other basic needs like toiletries, underwear, shoes etc. According to the definition of chronic homelessness "an individual who lacks a fixed, regular, and adequate night time residence" you definitely fulfil the criteria, and could moreover argue that *homelessness itself constitutes a disabling condition* - maybe that is what is actually meant by it being disability-strapped? Remember it is **not your job or your responsibility** to try and puzzle out any seeming contradictions in the terminology (it is the responsibility of government workers to provide an adequate interpretation of the law) As an applicant all you should have to do is prove that you meet the criteria, and your lifestyle is clear evidence that you do! If assistance is not forthcoming then they are in breach of the law, and an attorney could argue your case on a "no win no fee" basis (with no income you would not be liable for legal fees)

I don't know which BBC program you are referring to, but when you were staying in Ramsgate with Luke, he told me you turned up on his doorstep in the middle of the night on at least one occasion in sub-zero temperatures. Apparently he had provided you with a small electric fire, but you had flung it back out onto the landing. He also said he heard growls and other strange noises coming from your room, and when he checked to see if you were OK your facial features were completely distorted. He admitted to me he was so freaked out he actually locked himself in his room, and to this day strongly suspects you were in the grip of something demonic. I am telling you this because if you are still under the intermittent influence of some malign entity, you need to stay vigilant and be constantly aware that it will **fight very hard to keep you isolated**, as this is the only way it can consolidate its power over you. For the same reason it will obviously view me as a threat. Don't let it control you.

I managed to find an excerpt from K. Sullivan's book online (which I have copied below) There were so many eerie parallels with what M has told you about her "missing time" and Mafia connections that I thought you might be interested.

### Excerpt from Unshackled: A Survivor's Story of Mind Control by Kathleen Sullivan

*I performed illegal acts for a network of organizations and agencies. My alter-states knew most of them by code names. Various spook handlers referred to the CIA as the Web, the Agency, the Organization, the Family, and the Company. As a young adult, I met mob members in Chicago and also in Atlanta. (I will not provide any other details about my experiences with any of these individuals) I was taken to meetings of groups known as the Golden Dawn and the Illuminati. They exposed me to a mish-mash of Luciferian and Pagan beliefs. I was also exposed to a mob-connected occult network, headquartered in New York City, code-named Satanic Hierarchy (Again, I will not provide further details* about my interactions with this organization) I repeatedly encountered members of a large, national Aryan Network – The Brotherhood. Alleged CIA handlers referred to male Secret Service personnel as bus boys. Secret Service agents called one of my trained bodyguard alter-states plain Jane. I was also used by members of an international network, code-named the Octopus, that included alleged CIA employees and contractors, members from several Mafia families, and more.

I was taken to numerous U.S. military bases and government facilities over a period of more than thirty years. After our family moved to Atlanta, I was taken to a military base that I was told was Fort Payne. Female teenagers and women were given special training there. I was called a "Golden Girl" and received what was code-named "Black Claw" physical training. At Redstone Arsenal, Alabama I believe I received MKNAOMI biochemical black op conditioning, briefings, and debriefings. At a base called Fort McPherson near Atlanta, a female programmer had forcibly reconditioned me after a failed op (by threatening to shoot me), so that I would continue to do assassinations. The years of programming and conditioning at these government facilities prepared me to become a covert slave-operative. Sometimes I was first taken to a local cult meeting. After the horrific ritual, alter-states were triggered out to be transported. These are some of the activities that my covert op programmed alter-states performed while under the control of professional handlers:

• *Assassinations*
• *Arms smuggling, including transportation of small rockets*
• *Bombings and sabotage*
• *Kidnapping*
• *Taking out snipers*
• *Surveillance*
• *Torture and interrogation*
• *Killing assassin-programmed individuals who had gone out of control and were an imminent danger to those around them.*

*Because they were so dissociated they felt no pain when injured, I was trained to kill them in a particularly gruesome way. Afterwards, I was transported home with no memory of the event. My black op (assassin) alter-states were even more specialized. Through hundreds of repetitive acts, each was conditioned to kill in at least one of the 5 following ways: zip wire, gun, knife, or chemicals.*

*I relived a series of emerging traumatic memories in bits and pieces, starting with a childhood memory of my father driving his chisel into my skin to lift my kneecap – just enough to frighten me. Then he used a drill to wound my feet – again, not enough to leave a lasting scar. In one training session, I held a long sharp knife and plunged it deeply into the front of someone's torso. I was being taught that there were two ways I could do it. I could either do the "T," which was to cut from below the belly button up, and then – at an angle - do the upper stomach and heart, or I could do it with one deep, lower slash from one side to the other, through the intestines. I was taught that either way was extremely effective. The lower slash would leave the person in pain for a while before the actual death, if that was what was intended. To simply kill, the "T" was preferred. Before doing it to live adults, I was made to do it on upright adult cadavers. Each time, I wiped the fatty tissue off my long knife. I was taught that it was important to keep the knife clean, and anyway, I didn't like looking at it.*

*Then I remembered standing in a room with white walls. I saw an intense, slim woman, average height, with short, dark hair and eyes. Other people stood in the room, too. On a table to my right were objects that could be used to attack and kill. I had no choice; the woman held a knife and kept reaching out as if to slice at my forearms. When I finally got tired of parrying, jumping back, and moving my arms away from her, I went after her full-force. I grabbed her knife and cut her neck deeply – from one carotid artery, then right through her throat to the other artery. In the next memory, another adult was fighting me. I grabbed a knife from the table. Unfortunately, because it was dull and serrated, I couldn't use it on the attacker's neck. After I successfully took the attacker down, a slim, friendly, middle-aged man with curly, graying hair took the knife from my hand and pushed it down hard on the victim's fingers – cutting several of them off.*

Is this stuff for real? If so, it's pretty mind-blowing. I left out the last page, which featured Wonder woman Kathleen with a fearsome array of weaponry at some kind of shootout at the OK Corral in a dusty little Mexican town, acting like a robotic psychopath and shooting everything that moved. At this point I was starting to have my suspicions as it all sounded too sensationalist, and why does she keep stating "I will not provide any other details about my experiences with these groups or individuals" if she expects to be believed? If she's revealed this much, and it's out there in the public domain why not go the whole hog and specify details that can easily be verified? You must not believe everything you read, but take most of it with a very large pinch of salt. The best defence against genuine mind control is to keep your critical faculties sharply honed: question EVERYTHING and then some more. I will email you the details you need to collect the cash in another password-protected document.

Bye for now,

Leigh

**From: Cass Ryder**
**To: Leigh Ryder**

My major point about Sullivan's testimony is that I believe it is horseshit, one more example of a disinformation channel. What they do is to throw a monkey wrench into honest relevant debate about the subject matter and offer endless "decoys" SHE IS THE NINE. THE NINE set up the Kathleen Sullivan insert to project that she's "mind-controlled" and to breed discomfort in the mind. SHE'S FULL OF SHIT (she might be a conscious agent or not even exist) She fails to even question the legitimacy of these military bases and the black ops. K Sullivan is CIA or NSA shit purposely inserted hoping I would pick up on it. For instance M also makes stabbing motions in the air. It's a fight tactic that loads of people learn, it's about how to kill... you thrust in a knife and thrust it up and across in a T (she makes a slit motion across her throat ear to ear, bragging this is what's going to happen)

The writer had always had qualms with the concept of a conscious discarnate entity, and tried to understand it in terms of an objective process to do with an invisible media of thought. Not only did MKULTRA take place in the 70s, but a remote surveillance of certain minorities is continued throughout life - all in the quest for mind control. But these people are not the norm, and the majority aren't exposed to that much surveillance, and THAT'S HOW THE HIDDEN ONES GET AWAY WITH IT THEY FOCUS ON A MINORITY ... and meanwhile they keep them separate from one another and deny access to a language to articulate this exposure. They use disinformation from myriad angles...aren't they the most unbelievable bunch of kindergarten playground types compared to the real mafia (equals the Pentagon) The social workers are all retiring and being replaced like the security guards here in this library. Spiderman...how about "shadow nazi"...is watching and interfering, he's just at my elbow. Sausage is getting increasingly upset, but it's not my problem. FUCK OFF to a lunar sausage that white man set up.

Maddy claims she and Alex tried to get through to me. I didn't receive their efforts. My intuition is saying don't write back. I sent them both a batch much earlier with photos and got no response. Explain to Alex that I don't get any replies from her (maybe they had been intercepted) and my cell's been out for a while. I'm wondering whether I should self-publish? It's likely no-one will want to read it anyway.

Cass

**From: Leigh Ryder**
**To: Cass Ryder**

Dear Cass,

Open the attached document with our usual password to access the
Moneygram reference, and email me back **immediately** to let me
know you received it (otherwise I will think shadowman has
intercepted) Please try and spend some of it on useful items such as
fleece-lined thermal trousers or jacket, new boots etc. in the event
of you and M falling out. The apartment is in her name so if she
were to kick you out for any reason you'd have to survive on the
streets again. I agree with you that Sullivan's "confessions" sound
like horseshit, and are quite possibly deliberate disinformation to
discredit honest debate on the subject. You're right, she doesn't
even question the legitimacy of covert black ops.

I will try my hardest to get your book placed with a publisher but
even if we are successful you should be aware that the time delay
between acceptance of a manuscript and commercial publication
can be quite lengthy. Based on my own experience, I would not
recommend self-publishing. For a while I was managing to sell
quite a few books until I became the victim of a campaign of cyber
persecution from a toxic website called "Goodreads" After
receiving a number of very positive reviews from readers, these
were all suddenly and mysteriously erased (only the website
administrators possess the access privileges required to delete
material) When I asked them to investigate this abuse I received a
very rude reply in which they gloatingly informed me that I could
not remove my books from their site even though I own the
copyright! From there things went from bad to worse: some fake
reviewer who had obviously never read my work posted a really
malicious review, and I have since discovered many other
independent authors have been victimised: it's been suggested the
site was set up to promote the work of a handful of third-rate

writers who award their own efforts 5 stars, and routinely trash the work of rival authors they feel threatened by (there is a dedicated website called "Stop the GR Bullies" which exposes their dirty tactics) Unfortunately, most readers are unaware of what is going on behind the scenes, and believe that the fake reviews are genuine. The only reason I mention this sorry saga is because I wish to make it clear that the self-publishing route is doomed to failure unless you have a huge advertising budget. Without extensive media advertising no-one will be aware of your existence. Having said that, I do honestly believe there is a market for your story, which is quite unusual and unique.

Alex did say something about intending to contact you via your cellphone, but if there's no credit on it she won't have been able to leave a message: the battery has probably run down and needs recharging. You can get a cellphone charger which plugs into the mains from any cellphone store or Wal-Mart for a few dollars. Maddy is very sluggish in responding to emails because she doesn't get out to the library that often, and wouldn't know how to open any attachment you sent. The best way to communicate with her is via a simple and personal email with about 3 paragraphs. I am somewhat concerned that all of the social workers who knew you seem to have been replaced recently. Don't give them any more information than you have to. Ironically, it is your natural distrust and suspicion of others that has probably enabled you to survive all these years.

On another note, RAF jets had to be scrambled to intercept Russian bombers off Northern Scotland: just recently more Russian "Bear" strategic bombers were spotted just off the coast of Cornwall (a bit close for comfort!) and two RAF typhoons escorted them away from British airspace. Just the latest of several similar incidents involving Russian military aircraft flying close to British airspace, and the PM has summoned the Russian ambassador for an explanation.

I'm sorry to hear that Sausage is getting upset by our communications. Too bad. Maybe he should stuff his appendage down his throat. Google *"Uroborus"* and you'll see what I mean (yes, you bore us too) Do they honestly think that someone like you – a homeless destitute female - poses some kind of threat to national security? It makes you almost feel sorry for them. Let the asswipes snoop all they want: if they don't like what they read about themselves, the remedy is to stop snooping. As in the old adage "Eavesdroppers never hear any good about themselves"

Love,

Leigh

**From: Cass Ryder**
**To: Leigh Ryder**

What was THE MEANING of the Russian menace WHY DID IT
FLY BY ON HER DOORSTEP in Cornwall? Just when she had
submitted the manuscript to various agents in London?
Something's been stealing my writing from my backpack, sly little
jealous pervert... i had loads of writing that was finished now it's
gone so I'm going to try and get some of it together again today
and send it. Someone is rifling thro my backpack i don't think it's
M ...

The social workers are so physically degraded and evil.. they're
ugly on the inside if they weren't hideous on the outside > they're
basically walking around with a needle and cant wait to force it into
Monica. Kate is a fucking dinosaur .. she never got any of the info I
asked for >> she's a servant of republican fascists. When I sent her
a page of writing I felt hate vibes across my scalp that night >>then
she's going to smile her ugly smile. The other worker Derek who's
leaving the dept at the end of the month is a mouse, he's putting a
black woman Tracy in his place. She'll do the dirty deed like a dog
doing its master's duty. I've seen it over and over again how white
American male sets up black woman to do their dirty deeds.
They're such mice, they're rushing away from this scenario.
Meanwhile they were happy to lap up a lucrative income in an evil
job they didn't have a conscience about. They can't bare any kind
of honesty, can't face that the system is flawed. When Uncle Sam's
got a problem he gets out his ugly servants like he always did,
either as mind controlled religious freaks who unleash their voodoo
onto me, or just plain criminals. White man is on a 3500 year long
drug... they're high on their ego and they are attacking anybody
who is attacking their image. Perhaps what it really represents is a
crisis within men based on race differences, and that right now the
lunar races seem to have grabbed the advantage. It's up to the
Nordic white male elite and his ethnic guard dogs to stop getting

offended by the gender issue, to help themselves get free somehow. But you can't reverse centuries of corruption overnight, and I do not have to carry the cross of their emerging errors.

Subject is completely witchcraft interfered with and has supernormal strength. ..when she claps her hands it sounds like a gorilla clapping. She had mentioned she's able to break concrete with the side of her hand (is she a karate blackbelt?) The occult works like a virus, it gets empowered thro a weakened immune system. They can cause you to walk into a store, they can introduce nightmares into your head, they can drag you out of your body at night. Sat afternoon we took a nap >> she was whispering loudly "mummy mummy" as she was climbing into bed as tho she were a toddler climbing into its mother's arms okay? There's no-one there. Whoever "they" are, they are making out they're her mother as well as her lover but the amour wavelength is the most outrageous. Is this common amongst women? (I have no idea what's normal any longer) Do they consciously invite in demon lovers? Whoever they are, they are trying to get her to attack me >> I think they're going to get her to axe me in the face. I hate this place >> she has caused me to be detained and waylaid here...The smelly little uniformed sausages are trying to say they're going to kill me. IM TIRED OF BEING ATTACKED .. I WANT OUT OF THIS FASCIST DUMP.

The threat to get her on a charge was based on some sausage from the fire dept who stated she said "You fucking bastard". She didn't say it, and I believe she didn't. She went to the local fire dept to get information on 3 house fires in Dec 2010 trying to understand what she was doing there (because she has a memory loss) why there was a fire and why she was back out on the pavement afterwards. She says she was in the house with Claudine, who is now a woman drugged up to her eyeballs who doesn't speak to either of them and is not approachable on the subject. The subject kept parroting Tavistock Road and Canberry Road (both roads do exist – writer checked the map) She apparently lived there with Claudine, and had always said Claudine and Liz had known one another. I went there in person to request clarification and was met with a foia and fee process form (the form never arrived) Later a local gov. personnel guy stated he had gotten a lot of electronic interference in trying to get the fire dept archivist on the phone (the subject's files go missing, and the office worker claims to have no memory of the subject placing the documents with her) As for it's none of my business, can it be imagined how much I'd like to get away from this subject matter and this dump.. Yes it WAS my fucking business if people are spying and didn't have a right to.

The subject told me a lot, sort of held me hostage while making me listen, like a clever insurance policy as though she intuited she would soon not have the mental awareness to convey any of this – in the expectation that I would "catch on" and could use that info by which to help her to retrieve her identity in a bid to save her soul, so it's this former self I'm responding to, not so much the one today. When I took those photographs of her something like a predatory animal came out of her body and her eyes. She snatched up the photos and ripped them up defensively, like it was an entity that didn't want awareness of Monica's face. What I was trying to say to it is "maybe you need to SHIFT OUT of her body" Whether she has an illness or not the health workers are never going to mention the paranormal domain, you can't talk about it. I would never do M the injustice of giving this information to them, she's worth too much for their prying eyes. And the southern med or Italian mafia male hates my guts…her symbolic father no doubt. Liz tried to get her scanned as soon as they crossed over the Maryland VA line 4 years ago. I wouldn't have bothered because I don't believe this military mind control stuff, and covert ops are classified info so it's not something they are able to admit up to. They want these people to get a label of mental illness because it is an integral part of their programme and weaponry. She also told me that Liz's father was a member of the "Knights of Columbus", a Catholic fraternity who are renowned for being extremely anti-gay.

Here's another example, I find it a little odd there are two TV dishes positioned outside her outer wall on the building she's moved into. I had even wondered whether its bugged (I'm certain she's being watched) but this seems like an attempt by the etheric watchdog to concentrate electromagnetic waves in physical proximity to the apt as a means to "cancel out" her verbalizations (they are using electronic media to HIDE their physical body hijacking) I've tried telling you, you're not co-operating with me enough, she is definitely mind-controlled. She hates Africans because she instinctively feels occult interference. Black men do have a crime image, oh of course they are not the only criminals... and eventually it's all an elite control tool by white man to create tension and division within people. But in all honesty it would get on my nerves if I kept hearing that on the floor below (the nigger word she keeps using) These race wars are going on from loads of angles involving loads of people, but with her it's worse because she's been dealing with this gender discrimination her whole life long so she feels like he's attacking her now in her home. So to counter it she just shouts loudly "nigger, spic", and what must that feel like if they can hear through the walls? But what has she really got against "spics"? A clue could be that the ex-FBI cousin is half Columbian. And isn't the "nigger" projection just a self-defence mechanism, like a natural spitting reflex, based on an intuition of what is interfacing with her auxiliary body? She's hissing at them out loud then they try and get back at her thro voodoo. I believe they set up the apt situation thro connections with local govt (the mayor of the county is a black man even though it's a white dominated affluent area) and I feel African witchcraft was used on her (and REMEMBER SPIDERMAN TURNED UP EXACTLY AT THE TIME SHE MOVED INTO THIS APT)

They can cause people to fight, they caused us to fight pretty badly on Sunday. I know one thing her red eye came back, with a bump on her head, and I had a strained right sternum muscle and a slight headache from being sharply slapped in the head (which started it) I SAW A MAN COME OUT OF HER and I've seen him before

315

and it felt like his will that I was going to get a whack in the head. She whipped off her glasses fairly professionally, not before I guess I threw my fist at her and I ended up on the floor. Then she hugged me forcefully...I guess she didn't want me to leave like that because naturally I was heading out at that point. I do not need it .. it gets a bit sickening when it feels that people drag spirits around with them like baggage, so I've not been back. She's actually got a little red mark on her forehead where I positioned my fist after the argument. After hours of boring me and threatening me, having emotionally blackmailed me to go back to the apartment, I began to discreetly eat some chocolate cake powder that I had in my backpack (in a kind of distracted "I'm not bothered" way) when she came up and very calmly and pointedly looked me in the face. Then pretty viciously whacked me in the side of the head. I already have a bad muscle strain in my right rib area, so the brief tussle unthreaded a muscle that was mending there. But maybe my presence has helped to make it worse which is why I didn't go back this week and don't plan to (although she keeps asking me to) I feel our company is being used to fuel arguments so something can say I helped mess her up. "They" always start it and there is definitely an occult force around her that acts like a security guard. I would normally have had much more self-control. I carry a mirror now, and I've promised myself I will look into it before I get very angry again, and will position it around my neck. But so far I'm not going back.

To go back to the point, now they've got a "justified observation" for committal and they're going to get even more of one once Derek ...the archetypal white man in many ways...spider scuttles his way backwards into the inner met area from whence the U.S. military and their black protégés hailed, and is replaced by an African female. You'd think people on a higher level could effect a differentiation in society, a separation between races to stop all the race wars. This is one reason for the current mental illness epidemic, too many conflicting types forcibly integrated into fairly enclosed small spaces. After all, the neighbours aren't exactly royalty, and she needed somewhere detached, like a trailer or detached house. As with ill-fitting clothes, it shouldn't be seen as racial prejudice but that a person has natural preferences and it's more a survival issue (what the writer has discovered throughout her life is that the "liberals" were never really open-minded) It's so-called liberal people who makes these laws but they're sexist to a bigoted degree even worse than the blue collar worker types, because educated women and whites get threatened by African men who are bigger etc. All SET UP by the white male elite and this is the way he keeps control of his people. But she should be able to go some place where she can get along with people. The subject shouldn't be here ...what are the chances that all the low-income apts are mixed racial? What are the chances that she's not going to be able to adapt (big dollops of dog waste here there and everywhere on the grass behind the building and right beneath her apt window) But there are almost no women's communities, certainly none that can be afforded. They don't really exist in any kind of acreage or concentrated area. The most this country has gotten together is 70 acres for lesbians, mostly in the southern states, but that also comes with a "lipstick earring" persona. And guess what, not everyone wants to be called gay who are in the single childless category (like the writer) It's quite probable that women's retirement communities do not accept welfare beneficiaries, and who could really blame them, or the property prices are too high and most people drive a car etc.

The subject can't help it she's perceived as racist, so what? She gets HUGE abuse from black men and that's why she deals it back out, why shouldn't she? Is it racist if a man who burgles your home happens to be black, and you shoot him? No, he's likely to get shot because he attacked you in your home. The subject also conflicted a lot with African men while training at John Jay Criminal Justice College, who were endlessly bragging about their harems of whores and weapons possession and she can't understand why the U.S. is training and employing them. The Democrats didn't help women any more than neo-conservative Republicans. They gave black men the right to smoke joints, and the freedom to fuck their whores whenever they felt like it. The mixed race communities in urban developed areas are full of neurotic people who do not get along but pretend they do. This is a soul attack, the way a political dissident is put in with a bunch of louts in a jail. For instance the writer was assaulted non-stop by African American women in the last three weeks she was in jail for no reason she could understand, unless it was because she happened to be white. The writer strongly advises that a state of emergency be declared in terms of a need for them to get AWAY from each other, and to start orientating around types who are more similar. The concept of separation of race is not new and doesn't need to be viewed as racism. Religion is another big one as in religious believers versus non-believers, and family units versus single individual units, het alliances versus gay alliances. It's a subject matter that very much annoys many people, but the writer would say the subject has a very good reason to be uncomfortable around other races, because black men do prey on women more. And sorry, but it's based on the writer's personal experience after 20 years of being homeless. Writer has also had brush ups with African immigrant males on day jobs, and they're actually not too far from committing murder at any one time. Writer never talked to them because they can get pretty damn obscene. Writer was crashed by the side of the road (though hidden in bushes) and working at apple picking with mainly Haitian workers. One of them walks by her on the bus gripping a knife, and holds it close to her as he walks up the aisle. The writer had NO CHOICE but to work at day labour (needless to say the work only lasted for three days) The writer was once forced to the ground by a black guy, his hosepipe falling out. He was revolting beyond words and had a gun in his hand. He'd had an argument with his whore girlfriend who had tried to lock him out of her car, and then he tried to kill the writer, who was able to administer a pepper spray and talked him out of it.

Writer just kept walking. She could never have adjusted to their housing communities let alone homeless shelters. Lying down like sardines in a can with a bunch of strangers who are looking at you like they want to kill you ... with the cops circling around outside like predatory wolves waiting for a call, for the set-up that justifies their pay checks. They were not sensitive about single apartment units, nor in offering one to the writer who is aware she comes over as very weird, and also has influenza due being out in the open on and off in the last month. Most singles today are surrounded by the "family syndicates" and are being picked on because they don't have the comparatively banal mental level of the younger generation, who have no experience of anything. Personal freedom is less about owning hundreds of acres as it is about not sharing living space with people who don't get along. Actually one could put many singles and gays in a refugee category since the vast majority were targeted with poverty, lunacy level lonerdom, or induced neurosis. The writer doesn't want the permanent supportive housing because she wants nothing to do with the U.S. government (no amount of petty cash can ever make up for the emotional scars ... for being a human circus animal on display) but will go through with the Soar application, though now thinks it's entirely possible they will reject the application as they understand the resultant cash will be used to help the subject.

Cass

**From: Leigh Ryder**
**To: Cass Ryder**

Dear Cass,

So as not to let paranoia get the upper hand here I should point out that the positioning of the TV satellite dishes is perfectly normal. Where a building has multiple occupants, the dishes are usually clustered in the same spot so as to obtain an optimum signal for good reception. And the Russian fly-bys have to be seen in the context of the worsening Ukraine crisis and rising tensions between Moscow and the West. Yes, it was deliberately provocative - like the Cold War all over again - but the official view is that they are "testing our defences."

I agree M would probably have to be a consummate actress if she were a covert agent so I think her outbreaks are probably genuine, but if she is being controlled by some outside agency and can be remotely "triggered" to perpetrate acts of violence then this still places you in a unique situation of danger. You have already been whacked on the head, and could have been knocked unconscious. However if these fights are being "staged" they are in all probability being filmed with the footage being manipulated so that her initial provocation is edited out, and your defensive tactics made to appear as unprovoked aggression. In a court of law, the use of camera surveillance could easily be justified as being for the tenants' own safety since the residents in supportive housing are supposed to be mentally impaired. Your auras are clearly overlapping and the intensity engendered by such close proximity is leading to increased conflict. If we take the idea of occult possession seriously, and if your perception can be relied upon when you claim to have seen a "man" coming out of her, then this indicates the presence of a malign male entity whose power and influence over M is increasing to an alarming degree. If it's demonic in nature then she urgently needs spiritual help, and you need to keep your distance for your own safety. I've read enough literature on the subject of spirit possession to know that once they have taken over your physical body, you become a kind of slave with no will of your own and are powerless to resist any evil or sadistic impulses which can lead to suicide, murder, or other atrocities. Just because she hasn't managed to physically harm you so far is no reason to think you are safe with her. Need I emphasise that you are possibly not dealing with the woman you formerly knew as Monica but a vicious entity who is **becoming stronger and more violent** every day, and who is now able to control her bodily actions. My analysis is as follows:

**Theory One**: I am now starting to think that the entity surrounding M could also be preying on you to a lesser degree, and may even have originated from you, having attached itself to you years ago when you were a teenager, and is seeking a means of re-entry so as to exploit a more vital energy source now that M's immune system is seriously weakened. What you refer to as "self-bio" laid M wide open to this type of possession, not because the act is in itself evil but because it is an addiction like drugs or alcohol (in the same way a lot of men are slaves to their carnal impulses) Something which starts off as quite normal, like the desire for a drink, becomes a craving which completely takes over a person to the extent they are no longer in control, which in turn makes them easy targets for low-level earthbound entities seeking an opportunity to inhabit living bodies.

**Theory Two:** I am inclined to think that her controller is a human male because of the crass assumption lying behind M's provocative remarks which were obviously designed to "draw" you out (the assumption that you are gay when you clearly are not) I'm afraid this bears all the hallmarks of some masculine intelligence, salivating at the prospect of witnessing a pornographic act with cameras trained on both of you. The male sexual impulse has become increasingly depraved and voyeuristic due to the pernicious influence of pornography, and is now completely divorced from the natural procreative impulse which occurs in the animal kingdom.

And because you're not playing ball, the lowlifes who manipulate M's utterances are getting increasingly frustrated, hence the staged fight (using M as bait or provocation so they can get you on a charge of being violent and dangerous) If this is what is happening here then you are quite right to stay away from the apartment. But they have overplayed their hand and there is a now a very real danger of alienating you to the extent you might not return to the apartment, so M is made to appear needy and insecure on her own - a form of emotional blackmail to entice you back into the arena of operations.

There is another small detail you mentioned which immediately caught my attention: "... *she whipped off her glasses fairly professionally...*" Now if a person is in the grip of a powerful emotion like anger would she pause in the middle of a fight to remove her glasses so they don't get damaged? It's about as likely as a marital dispute where the wife is screaming at her husband, then suddenly stops to adjust her makeup in the mirror, before resuming her furious tirade. It's not believable, at least not in the context of a real fight. Such a premeditated act would not even occur to someone in the heat of the moment. Just take a few seconds to think about the implications. You won't like me for suggesting - yet again - that maybe she is an actress playing a prescribed role (but unwittingly betrays herself by these small actions) and that all the conflicts between you are carefully orchestrated, with the goal of eliciting an enraged response from you which will give them the justification they need to get you incarcerated. Like a red flag to a bull you are being goaded. Next time anything like this occurs, do not rise to the provocation, just WALK AWAY and remove yourself from her company. Alright, so maybe she isn't acting on her own initiative, but she is doing someone's else's will by acting her small part in some larger game. It would be very interesting to observe her behaviour when you are not there to witness it: one reason why she doesn't want you there for prolonged periods could be because it's simply too exhausting to keep to the script and to play a role for 24 hours without slipping up. In your absence she can allow the mask to slip and to be herself, until you reappear on the scene.

And all the time people are starting to associate YOU with her more outrageous behaviour - because it only occurs around you - and the conclusion that health workers are meant to reach is that you are a bad influence, and that she is not in any way to blame because she's ill. In a sense this is already happening. A few points I want to make about the nature of friendship and why I think the association between you is a morbid one. Being in the company of M unfortunately does not confer any of the normal benefits of companionship e.g. a true friend is someone to confide in, who will offer the other moral support and encouragement. But M clearly has no interest in your conversation or opinions, preferring you to "shut up" and remain silent in her company, and is either not willing or capable of reciprocating on any level. She does not even recognise you for the person you actually are, confusing you with someone in her past life called "Claudine" whom she obviously didn't like, and with whom she may have been coerced to perform sex acts with for the sick gratification of the usual suspects. I'm afraid it's all negative, and you should take steps to extricate yourself from this situation. In your own words, you have been "waylaid" and "trapped" there for far too long, and she isn't your problem nor is she your responsibility.

If you are no longer staying with M where are you crashing at night? Presumably in a cold weather shelter, as it's not safe to sleep out on your own, and it would be freezing at this time of year. Please let me know if you're OK.

Love,

Leigh

**From: Cass Ryder**
**To: Leigh Ryder**
**Subject: Christmas Message**

Writer is reminded of a Christmas day before she was homeless over 25 years ago of a horrible tragedy which happened when she was working as a part-time aid worker in a privately-funded converted Catholic nunnery for mentally and physically handicapped children in Boston. One young girl who was deaf, dumb and blind had been sexually abused at 10. A white female aid worker was bludgeoned to death on Christmas day by a retarded black man while she was handing him a present. The whole thing was horrible. He used to walk around with coloured lights on a headband like Christmas tree lights: the writer had tried to forewarn staff that this man should not have been mingling with the kids and seemed "unsafe" No-one listened and the staff completely ignored her. The management would hire almost anybody it seemed. The writer left after that, feeling disillusioned and sickened and a little guilty, understanding that these kids needed security and familiarity.

Writer can now see that sister Alexandra and husband are caught up in a devouring materialism and societal phoniness…. addicted to a seemingly never-ending blue sky vision, eternally internationally bound with jet fuel in their nostrils. They basically avoided visiting the writer en route to the airport, hiding behind an overall hypocrisy and Christmas "goodwill" ….as seems to be also happening with the social workers here who wish not to be confronted with something they are uncomfortable with. As for the sister Maddy who is ex U.S Naval personnel and who now lives likes a bum in a room and is eternally on benefits, writer sent her $50 last Christmas, no response. Writer sent her a batch in July or Sept to let her know where writer is, no response. I don't have time to sustain a conversation over the Internet with her esp. in terms of the banal self-projected "little girl" persona she is coming over as, and frankly the writer has nothing in common with her, nor with most women who are unable to sustain honest communication channels. As for they "tried" and couldn't get through, obviously Alex could after she flew to London to attend a wedding in the UK. Possibly something in this county is blocking it, but then sorry that's not the writer. They've had time enough to try and communicate and help, and didn't.

The writer's Christmas observation is that you all needed to look me up… it's not been easy for me to leave…and because you weren't sensitive then fine, don't try and send me Christmas greetings or expect to include me in a biological family. I have good memories and want to end it at that. Yes, homeless for 20 years looks bad, but life's too short to carry the cross of peoples' ignorance. Anyway I had no choice, and a dubious dual national identity was part of the reason, plus 10 years of communication obstacles and no offers of help without strings attached on the U.S. side, and the writer had too much pride to "beg" from the UK authorities.

The poor very much do create their fates in what is (as Jung put it) "an age of the crisis of the soul"

Cass

**From: Adam Ryder**
**To: Leigh Ryder**

Christmas Greetings,

As a point of clarification, my intention was to suggest that perhaps something terrible happened to Cass at primary school. Mention the school to her and see what she has to say about it. Sexual molestation can cause irrevocable hidden damage. Last year an expensive private international school in London was put under the microscope by the FBI for employing a convicted child molester. This particular (married) American gentleman had been drugging and abusing young boys for more than 30 years. Sleeping pills crushed into cookies. So my ruminations about Wincheap were primarily intended to suggest that PERHAPS Cass's condition lies in her childhood experiences. Make no bones about it, and joke if you wish, but Wincheap primary school was rife with abuse.

I had a friend in Canterbury - a former Royal marine - who used to self-harm. His arms, neck, legs, stomach were covered with knife cuts. Really shocking to see. In and out of psych wards all his life. Chronically abused by his step-father. Anyway, I used to tell him about Cass, and almost every time I saw him he would ask about her (never having met her). His advice was for her to be encouraged to get onto an appropriate course of medication. Every time he got off his meds, he would lose it. According to him, every mentally ill person he knew was better off ON their meds than off. Loads of characters who could not ordinarily live any kind of life (without treatment) who were now able to function quite well. The illness accurately diagnosed, medicated against and kept under control. Modern medicine can be a wonderful thing. I only WISH Cass could get some.

Stay on the humorous side, Leigh, without becoming too sharp. Miss the wit and humour. And there is nothing better for you than a good laugh. Beats anything hands-down.

Adam

**From: Staples Copy Centre**
**To: Leigh Ryder**
**Subject: Boxing day message**

That shadow jerk who serves his nazi white master…it's becoming impossible to go to that library. I was beaten up and threatened by him and another black man on the bus 2 days ago….the writer, the subject and an innocent Native American Indian woman. White man does this, he hides behind black man who he gets to terrorize people Rottweiler-style. When you consider how down and dirty they get, and what cowards they are… on the bus he started going on about how these "nasty-assed bitches would get dealt with in DC". The other black man stood up in the aisle and threatened her: the subject stood her ground and he backed down but they're operating through an African witchcraft brotherhood Mafia. Here's another point, as writer stopped by to hand the subject some Christmas cash today that the writer's sister had sent she goes "This is Liz's money" Anyway I'm not in her apartment any more, my presence agitates her.

My writing is being lifted. Please confirm receipt and number of pages. Please transfer each four categories into four files onto a disk. Then attempt to transfer these four separate files into my email address. For some reason am having problems getting this into my inbox at the library.

Cass

**From: Leigh Ryder**
**To: Cass Ryder**

Dear Cass,

Firstly, I am really sickened to hear about the attack on the bus on Christmas eve: however much you might distrust the authorities you do need to ask them for help and protection, and to tell them you are being threatened. This is precisely why I advised you to get your passport re-issued months ago, so that if a situation like this arises you can get the hell out of there fast. Secondly, you need to stop worrying about your writing: it really is not important in the wider context of what is happening to you. Am confirming receipt of 4 scanned attachments sent today:

1) 35 pages
2) 96 pages
3) 83 pages
4) 52 pages

I genuinely don't understand what you want me to do with it - email it back to you as 4 separate attachments? It just doesn't make sense to email you back stuff you've already sent anyway. Instead of trying to carry all of this bulky and heavy paperwork around with you in your backpack, it would be better if you shredded the lot then you wouldn't need to worry about it any more. I have electronic copies stored to disk so it is perfectly SAFE and nothing will be lost.

It's really bad news you can't go to the library any more, though there are Internet cafes you can use for the price of a cup of coffee. As for you sending Maddy $50 at Christmas (presumably with the money I sent you) this was crazy. She receives a regular allowance from the State, whereas you are destitute and need it much more than she does. Your Boxing Day email depressed me greatly, as it just demonstrates that nothing I say or do in the way of advice seems to sink in. The attack was probably provoked by M's offensive racist slurs, so hanging around her is DANGEROUS. For the love of God, get yourself out of this situation as fast as you possibly can. You have a home here with us as long as you need one - how many times do I have to repeat this? I can't think of anything else to say at this point, except to pray for your safety, and hope you have the sense to do what is necessary for your continued survival. I can't go on giving you advice that is ignored, or offering you a solution to your problems if it is rejected. At some point you are going to have make a decision - do you live or die? Which do you choose?

Take care and keep safe,

Leigh

**From: Cass Ryder**
**To: Leigh Ryder**

You dont get it 'He' is everywhere and besides the white man set this one up. And his servant /master is EVERYWHERE  Also the racist verbs are very much mine

You didn't send the attchmts back and you dont give a damn . And as for adam and Alexandra writing to me to say merry chritmsasd they can get lost esp Adam

Youre really phoney  when you kjeep saying 'go back to england ' I HATE ENMGFLAND.I HATE THE US .. you could have met up with me when you were in Canada but didn't.

I dont think  youll be able to do what I suggested with the attachments (theyve got a real problem..its called mind control) and as for england .. what they plan to do is block any meaningful communication channels in and out of britain while they are permitting a certain level of awareness in that country

Cass

**From: Leigh Ryder**
**To: Cass Ryder**
**Attachment: Glasses**

Dear Cass

I'm assuming and very much hoping you weren't physically hurt or "beaten up" but just verbally threatened (?) as you are still able to email. You say you hate England but the USA sounds like a shithole to me, where the homeless are treated worse than rats to be exterminated. Yes, I realise a lot of the bad language and verbs were yours but due to censorship and discrimination laws you need to exercise restraint when using a public Internet service. As for not meeting up with you when we were in Canada, how that would be possible when I had no idea where you were in the States? I had no means of contacting you as you were homeless. The U.S. is a huge country and you could have been literally anywhere. Or perhaps you think I have powerful psychic abilities, and could have tracked down your whereabouts by peering into a crystal ball? I think you are being a little unreasonable. When you placed yourself completely beyond our reach by disappearing off the radar, the onus was on YOU to establish contact - if you wanted it - because we were completely powerless to do so.

I think I know why you aren't getting the attachments which I tried to email back to you as requested: it may be due to a file size limitation. When you have a private email account at home like I do you can receive very large files into your inbox. However, some of your files are HUGE due to the number of printouts with photos from the Internet (text-only files don't take up much space) and when you are using a free public email account such as Yahoo, Hotmail etc. there is a file restriction size imposed on each user. Therefore, although you can send me large files including news clippings and articles with pictures if I try to email them back to you some will fail to transmit properly once the maximum file capability has been reached. And I couldn't split any of the files down to a more manageable size, because your scanned documents are not computer files, but hard copy printouts (like a fax) and therefore cannot be edited. All I can do with them is read them in the format you sent them, or copy out relevant passages and input these into my own WORD documents.

As requested, I have included in your book DF's comments about how she started off in her career by trying to explain occult phenomena in terms of psychoanalytical theory, but ended by having to explain psychological symptoms in terms of the occult: *"I believe that psychology is steadily being forced to the occult standpoint, and that the present generation will see the theories of thought transference and reincarnation incorporated among the body of orthodox scientific doctrines"* If the lesion is on the spiritual plane, nothing but spiritual healing will touch it. She goes on to remark that in certain cases healing may not be possible without recourse to exorcism, the severing of psychic links where a rapport is unhealthy or malign. You need to maintain a constant struggle against negative expression, otherwise it will rebound on you, in accordance with the principal of polarity (which means the function of flow and return of force) The simplest defence technique is to repeat the mantra "I choose life, love, and light" whenever you are angry or fearful, as a form of autosuggestion. Although it may appear trite and ineffectual, the very act of repeating this phrase over and over in your mind will enable it to eventually take root. At which point your subconscious mind will take over and do the rest. In this way you are setting up a powerful opposing force against evil, negativity, and darkness. It may also act as a symbolic link or "signpost" by which to attract positive, benevolent spirits wishing to help. Astral thought forms are channels through which invisible energies work. The power of positive thinking is very real, so give your mind something to work with and it will start to effect a healing process which you are hardly conscious of, and you should eventually see results.

I am attaching another document at the end of this to be opened by the usual password.

**Glasses**

The reason I am sending this separately in a password-protected document is because I'm concerned that some of my recent observations may be angering some "watcher" such as Shadowman (because I'm getting uncomfortably close to the truth?) and he will take it out on you, a scenario I obviously want to avoid. To return to the subject of M's glasses: this may sound overly paranoid but I started watching "Mission Impossible 2" the other night (not for long, I might add) The secret agent played by Tom Cruise wears these dark glasses which enables the agency he works for to communicate with him on a 2-way basis, possibly via a hidden microphone and microscopic earpiece (bear in mind that modern communications are completely wireless which make them invisible) Not only can they pass on instructions but they can also remotely view what he is viewing via a miniature camera embedded in the lens. My imagination may just be running wild here, but the technology is there for a targeted individual to be kept under close surveillance by a covert operative wearing "special" glasses. It occurred to me that when M comes up close and stares at you – as you mention she sometimes does – this could be a way of "zooming in" and bringing you into focus for the benefit of anyone watching the interactions between you from a distance. It would also be an easy way for them to "trigger" her or to pass on instructions like "Remove your glasses now", "Hit her in the face" or "Go to sleep" without you suspecting a thing.

If you have an opportunity to examine M's glasses closely whilst she is asleep it might be an idea to do this. Do you happen to know why she wears them - is she short-sighted or long-sighted? Maybe you could casually ask her why she wears them, without arousing her suspicion, and if her answer is e.g. "I'm near-sighted" you could put this to the test by getting her to confirm the lettering on a store sign from a distance. If she can read it without a problem with no blurring, then it would be fair to conclude she is NOT near-sighted and that they are not normal prescription glasses. Also, if she has been homeless for over 3 years, how has she managed to keep them intact? You would expect them to get broken or lost at least once through sleeping rough or in shelters during that time. For your own safety, I would advise you to keep this little "test" secret, in case she is actually some kind of agent. If this is the case, it would not do to let her handlers know that you suspect what's going on, so as to keep one step ahead of the game and give you the upper hand. Forewarned is forearmed.

**From: Cass Ryder**
**To: Leigh Ryder**

Agreed in retrospect I should have subdivided such an amount into at least eight categories. It's obviously something to do with the public library. I do owe them for prints and I'll try and pay this when I can but no-one's said anything. Or it could be a censorship mechanism on certain subject matters (my intuition tells me that stuff in my inbox is being accessed, that something has my password, whereas they don't have yours) We were corresponding at the time you flew to Nova Scotia (Yeah you had my email because that previous Dec you sent me a $1000 moneygram. Remember? I sent most of it back) In other words it would have been possible for us to meet in Maine over the Canadian border.

No, I haven't had a chance to check her glasses. Writer no longer accompanies her to the apartment, but meets her in a café, mainly because she doesn't want the neighbours to raise a complaint. When she whipped off her glasses during the fight I thought I heard a voice say "look at her eyes, look at her eyes!" (I guess I looked like a wild maniac) But see enclosed information from the Internet on covert communications "bluetooth glasses with spy micro earphone" And her aggressive verbalisations have not let up since moving into the apartment (the negative content that comes out of her mouth is just non-remitting in hourly cycles day and night) She's now on a kind of relentless "Kill, indict and jail them" campaign. Loud whispers in coffee joints, mainly Roy Rogers, where we go for coffee in the mornings and loiter for a few hours because it's close to the apartment. "Cut them up into little pieces…wash the blood off under the shower. Take the car to the carwash" And "rape them up the arse" continually. Maybe she's possessed by a man who had been assaulted whilst in his living body, who only knows. The rape stats amongst males in jails are startling big. Her crude sicko verbalising wouldn't be believed unless it was tape-recorded, besides which she attacked me the one and only time I did record her and she found out. It makes people around her feel uneasy. Yesterday we practically got a trespass notice. My intuition was telling me not to sit inside the govt centre building where the buses go from. She ignores my intuition, gets up and puts her hands around my throat threateningly and then backs down. We go out to get on the bus and a fat female cop comes rushing onto the bus and accuses Monica "You were heard verbally abusing a woman and her children" but there was something "soap operatic" about it as if this had been a tip off. M makes a sarcastic comment, and the cop threatens "I'll issue a trespass warrant" and Monica pretends to salute her and the cop backs down (soon she's barely going to have a defence case because of what she says out loud) It's wiser not to sympathise with her.

After telling the writer "You're of no importance, you're a piece of shit" she still says "I'll see you in the library, or the government centre in the morning" and makes the writer a really good sandwich for lunch each day. But the writer cannot help wondering about the phrase "You can't leave until I can block it and disconnect" or "until I get my money and Liz arrives, then we can go to Malibu to our estate" Another thing she says is "You are not one with me, Liz is one with me, Liz speaks to me through the openings in my body" Her eyes were like those of a person in another world, lost or inebriated. Writer knows people do sometimes have "spirit guides" but consummation with it? Is this normal? (writer thinks not) The wording seems unlike her, and this was just dropped into the conversation completely out of context, in a kind of mechanical robotic way. When she was more coherent she once said "I hated Liz she was a big fat bitch" My belief? She was set up by forces in Long Island for them both to meet then disengage, and for M to then be "drugged" with the imagery association of Liz.

Do men occupy women's bodies? Do entities sit in peoples' bodies like one sits in a chair? Occult skills are a reality, and just as anyone can be forcibly drugged, anyone can be hypnotised or turned into a Manchurian candidate. The "mancan" is like a person

337

who has been planted with a bomb, a walking landmine, and so the most effective way to deal with the problem would be to defuse it. What's sinister is the way this is being directed and exploited, but I'm tired of wrestling with spirit entities who want me dead, who want her to come and choke me at night. More and more people are turning up in mental health depts confessing to being "mind controlled" at military centres. The recent publicized cases show a general tendency for these to be young men as in "Allah inspired" Islamic fanatics (sister's observation that women are less controllable is possibly correct) However the "command buttons" or triggers used in mind control are usually a memory association wavelength of a trauma or an extreme emotion. Perhaps in the subject's case "Liz" is the trigger. But it's not a good sign when someone confuses a real person with a wavelength or a discarnate entity. In the case of Liz it looks like they've attempted to replace the actual relationship with an imaginary one by banking on the subject's mental confusion (Elisabeth or Liz also happened to be her mother's name) THIS IS PRETTY SPOOKY.

If what she told me is true she had a revolving door relationship with psychiatric facilities starting 20 years ago. It's possible she's had traumatic exposure to violence, been beaten up or worse, which would account for her extreme anger. While residing with Liz (2007?) she was out shopping, and can't account for a few days "missing time". Maybe the NY cops hypnotised her. The 2 weeks missing time may be some kind of turning point, in step with a covert war on cpinks. How often has she been picked up? And the memory loss, surely that's something to do with the anti-psychotic injections and the trauma? She recounts how she was given *Mein Kampf* to read, and writer gets the impression she is being branded as a Nazi. M seems to be somehow paying for her cousins' association with the Mafia, which the U.S. govt has warred with on and off in what I now clearly see as a covert warring between rival syndicates. Quite often the subject would refer to the "masters of the universe"(who are DEFINITELY NOT the CIA whoever they are) and today she has been repeating "the 18 levels" (sounds like a secret society type thing)

The government and uniformed crowd now own the subject or think they do, like an invisible leash around her collar. THEY NOW HAVE HER whoever they are, and the social workers hightailed it, like they sense something more going on than just an illness. It seems like something is trying to entrap her here, and then get Cass out of the picture so they can cover up their true relationship with her. They've made her their favourite pastime. It's the kind of "between the legs" thing that criminal syndicates get up to. She's started sticking her butt in the air again, as a kind of "fuck you" gesture to the public, in the expectation of being viewed in a degrading way. Writer had noticed that male supervisors in shelters viewed homeless women as their "animals" to be herded into cots. Her "$7000 for a pop" and finger gun shoots at passing cars and pedestrians is a panic reaction to a subliminal fear of something happening to her. Subject's reactions are like the panic signals of someone in a life-threatening situation (like a rock climber who has slipped and is clinging to a tiny rock crevice) or the camouflage responses of a cornered animal. A psychic operator sets up fear states and then "surfs" the fear, like the Louisiana Superdome evacuees of Hurricane Katrina who hallucinated assaults taking place around them. And homelessness helps the operator since the operator surfs on insecurity, using heightened emotion and panic states as the gateway. Last year at the cold weather shelter she would hover by a window, and when the shelter supervisor asked if she was okay and told her to lower her voice because lights were out, she murmured a few times in terror "They're coming to get me"

In between some beautiful singing this weekend the subject relapsed into a drooling enunciation – like a slowed down speech – exactly how you would expect someone to speak after they had been severely sedated. Sedation could bring temporary relief like chocolate in an energy crisis, but you don't live off chocolate.

These drugs do kill the spirit, and seem to be a way to make people function in isolation. You'd have to be a complete bozo to be offended by her…she is like a frightened or startled animal. That's why they hate me because I'm not offended, I'm just weary of all this but also concerned about her. Writer's key question is if she were to walk away from the subject what's going to happen? Are they going to continue to do this? How long has this been going on? Will she get worse or remain the same? The symptoms are unpleasant, like someone coughing up phlegm, but do you persecute the person because of those symptoms? Whatever the explanation for the symptoms, the disruption is getting so bad it causes misunderstandings from the local community, leading to assault threat scenarios. The subject is really ill, and she wasn't like this 2 years ago, and the writer wonders what she'd be like today if she had gotten help years ago and got out of here like she always said she wanted to do. Anyway enforced injections seems wrong, a Band-Aid approach to a more complex problem in what is a human being not a piece of machinery – why can't they encourage natural diets? This area is in the grip of a mental illness epidemic whereby sleeping tablets, anti-depressants and other chemical prescriptions are daily being serviced up like lunchtime snacks to endless millions. See printout below:

***Dr. Maureen Roberts - Director: Schizophrenia Drug-free Crisis Centre:*** *"The neuroleptic medications prescribed (or forcefully administered) for schizophrenia are not medicines which heal, but rather toxic drugs which can produce permanent disability, irreversible brain damage, even death" and "Alarmingly, over half the people receiving treatment for schizophrenia are being forcefully drugged. In the vast majority of cases schizophrenia is an acute psycho-spiritual crisis which has usually been triggered by a traumatic life conflict"*

Is it a mental health crisis or is it a perceptual interference crisis? The writer has seen enough bug-eyed women in the community (their eyeballs are falling onto the pavement after they've just had long term injections) The orthodox medical system is actually providing the "software" for occult targeting in the form of chemical prescriptions. Wasn't yesterday's trespass notice a prelude to a charge, and an enforced medical? When a person is thrown in jail after being processed and given a jail suit they're then given a medical. We get endless assault threats. With the subject it's an enforced medication threat (with the writer it's a "get on up the road, rabid dog") It seems like they have been trying to get the writer and the subject on a charge on and off over the past 2 years. For instance, last winter some "security guard" tried to stop us from sleeping on a bench at night in the shopping plaza in Sterling, and when the writer called the retail management the next day to confirm whether they were trespassing, the woman she spoke to did not recognise this African guy as a "security guard" (who in any case did not even hand out a written trespass warning) If anything she was trying to be supportive of 2 homeless women who had nowhere else to go, just like one woman was moved to tears (as was one of the female librarians) to see M marched out of Sterling library by cops. The throw-out of Sterling library last year was a uniformed gang-up and was illegal. These pavement level "mafias" do not speak for the mainly white ladies reaching for their wallets, when the reasons given for these throwouts are that they both pose a "threat". One extremely nice wealthy female stops once in a while and flicks something like 200 dollars our way. She says to us "Psychics? Oh that's the devil's work. You shouldn't believe in all that" Subject recounted how a worker in NY had called her the "golden goose", and there is something of Mr. and Mrs. Mallard about her esp. with those fibroids that cause her belly to protrude. Her profile is kind of like a platypus duckbill, and writer had always thought she could have at least starred on a commercial billboard like the Camel man and got money that way. Oh the writer got $30 handed to her by two different ladies in the library and she handed it to the subject... like a kind of phoney crown put on a de-clawed lion in a circus.

The writer has avoided the shelters because she didn't get along with other types in there. Writer once saw a basketful of condoms in a sad day shelter in Martinsburg that the men are encouraged to use, but homeless men don't have girlfriends, so why would they need them? It's not a criticism of the shelters it's just that certain kinds don't survive in these places. The homeless are ugly. One guy just decapitated another one in a shelter the other night. It was in the news. Last night the writer had to fight a strong urge to urinate, but was four blocks away from a restroom…writer must recollect not to drink anything after 12 noon. The writer has been watching her back now for 20 years. The night before last she dreamt a bunch of women were chasing her. One in a dress and high heels brandishes her long nails…she wills herself awake just before they are about to butcher her (their way of saying "we'll get you when you're asleep") Writer is now out in the open, and some of the women around here are generous with cash, and of course I give most of it to M but it's mainly being absorbed on basic living because she won't take foodstamps. One worker who saw me about the SOAR application said "Why would you want this money? Oh, I suppose you could occasionally check into a motel with it…." Just like the fat old Victorian in Oliver Twist "You want MORE FOOD?" (to a starving waif) But she doesn't mind lapping up her lucrative income…why would she want her income paycheck? No, they're busy justifying their incomes and cannot confront most creative criticism let alone honest feedback. Possibly the writer could take the disability cash, and transfer half of it to the subject in monthly remittances. Writer may go to NY. I know you're not going to respond in a relevant way, but compared to other people you have been REALLY incisive and generous.

Cass

**From: Leigh Ryder**
**To: Cass Ryder**

Dear Cass,

The decapitation which occurred in a homeless shelter must have been horrific to witness - I can understand why you avoid those places. There are far too many homeless people with serious mental illnesses (not to mention violent offenders) who wind up in shelters, where they are a danger to others. There should be segregated women-only hostels in every city, staffed by female supervisors: the current setup is a complete disgrace. Please do NOT go to New York. The crime level there is appalling, and it would just be awful if you had managed to survive this far only to end up as some faceless and anonymous Jane Doe in a body bag, so put this thought out of your head. Yes, I do remember we were able to correspond by email briefly before we left for Canada, but either your email address became inoperative or I had a temporary hotmail address whilst travelling which you didn't know about, I can't recall the circumstances. All I know is that I was never able to communicate with you by email again until you made contact in 2013. It was therefore impossible for to meet up with you whilst we were in Canada for 6 months because I had no idea where you were or how to contact you. It really is tragic as I would have given anything to see you again, had I known where you were. I can assure you that nobody in the family had any idea where you were or what had happened to you. By being completely untraceable, I had thought you were trying to "punish" us in some way, though I don't know what for.

When we last saw each other in Bristol you never told me that all your money had been stolen. By keeping such crucial information from family members who could have helped you, in a sense you sealed your own fate. So you do have to take **some** responsibility for what subsequently happened, as none of us had any idea what

dire straits you were in. Had I known what was going on I would
have tried to stop you from leaving the country - but in retrospect
would I have been able to stop you? Somehow I very much doubt
it, so it really isn't fair to keep on harbouring resentment against
me or other family members for a situation we had no control over.
You had it really rough, but I had no idea at the time how rough. I
wasn't even aware that you were homeless in the mid 90s. I
thought you could always come back to the UK if you wanted, and
figured you didn't want to. I now think the family house should not
have been sold so soon after Daddy's death, since this was the
catalyst which forced you into going abroad: what was initially
intended as series of backpacking holidays in far-flung corners of
the globe ended up setting you on the path of homelessness because
you had no "home" to return to. At the time you and Maddy were
both fully adult, and therefore it did not occur to the rest of us that
either of you would be unable to make your own way in the world:
after all, you had managed to hold down multiple jobs
simultaneously in Boston, and Maddy had previously been
employed as a legal secretary there. One of the consequences of
Daddy's death was that we all came into some money – not enough
to set us up for life, but enough to make a difference. We all chose
to spend our inheritance in different ways, and the choices that you
and Maddy made (to spend all or much of it on overseas travel)
were not that wise. It is a pity you did not have access to expert
financial advice, as you were too inexperienced and naive to realise
the long-term implications of not taking some steps to provide for
your future.

This is not a judgement, but a partial explanation of how wrong
choices can sometimes have disastrous consequences. There is
nothing wrong with taking time out to do some travelling if you
come into an unexpected windfall. I did something similar and
journeyed through Central and Latin America. However, I had the
sense to keep most of it back in savings until I was ready to invest
in property, and found a job in I.T. soon after I returned to England.
No, you should not have spent all the money you inherited

travelling the world, or entrusted the rest to a storage locker (a very risky thing to do) you should not have gone to the USA (a country with no welfare safety net) when you had no money, no home or clear destination: it was absolute madness. You should have remained in the UK, you should have contacted family members years ago and asked for their help before it was too late. So many shoulds and should nots. In hindsight, I wish I could turn the clock back, but what's done is done. And many of your problems such as long-term homelessness, destitution etc. do not necessarily stem from occult origins, but from wrong choices made at crucial junctures in your life.

I say "choices" but as no-one can choose the mental makeup they are born with, these cannot really be said to be free choices, since your thought processes determine your behaviour and what actions you take in life. The major difference between you and Maddy was that she has always known "which side her bread was buttered on". Being wholly reliant on the benefits system, she never flounced out of their offices and told them to "Fuck off" when their questions became too intrusive. Which you did, I believe? Your pride would not enable you to tolerate government handouts for long, and so you cut yourself off from your only means of support, leaving you destitute. Maddy has also remained resident in the UK and retained her NI number, so she has full access to the NHS and council accommodation, with all her material needs provided for, whereas you - despite being more intelligent - have nothing. And as far as I can see, you are still seem unable to look after your own interests, and squander your energy and time on people and things beyond your control – all serving as a MAJOR DISTRACTION which keeps you from focussing on what really matters.

I couldn't agree more with your observation about the "basketful of condoms" in a shelter. Surely it would be a damn sight more helpful if they provided free sanitary pads and tampons for homeless women – a basic necessity and not a luxury – rather than condoms! That really angered me. What pathetic dickbrain came up with that idea? Doubtless some pervert who should not be allowed anywhere near the homeless. I looked over the stuff you sent on treatment for the mentally ill, and agree that there is probably a vested interest in misdiagnosis, with many shareholders in the pharmaceutical industry having professions in the mental health industry. Some psychiatrists seem obsessed with "breaking down the defences" during analysis, a process which may well empower the therapist but doesn't necessarily help the patient who has blocked out a traumatic event: the mind often has its own way of healing itself, and the defence mechanisms the psyche creates are possibly done for very sound reasons (in the same way people with severe brain injuries slip into a coma so the brain can heal itself by shutting down) Given that the human psyche has an inbuilt tendency to build up its natural defences or barriers (and paranoia might well be an effective form of defence against unseen aggression, an essential survival tactic) then what is the point of weakening those defences, except to keep the psychoanalyst in a job? A warrior dons armour before going into battle, and where the homeless are concerned, the environment is largely a hostile one and life can therefore be viewed as a battlefield. On the whole, mental heath professionals feel very threatened by strong stoical types. I guess the conclusion to be drawn here is to carry on doing what you are doing. In order to survive a homeless woman needs to avoid most men, and avoid the police and "care" workers since many of them have no interest in protecting the vulnerable, quite the reverse. The deep-seated suspicion and lack of trust exhibited by the homeless (deemed "paranoia" by the medical establishment) is actually quite well-founded and justified.

I am still troubled by various inconsistencies in M's story e.g. was her sister killed in a car crash or as a result of a home invasion? At one point you mentioned she failed her training, so it's hardly surprising if she is currently unable to obtain the certificate which proves she underwent the course. What if she never did train as a cop, but was made to *think* she had (and was instead enrolled in some kind of bogus school which acted as a front for mancan brainwashing), and that she first came to their attention through her aid work in correctional facilities? I see you managed to Google some bluetooth spyware specs. And what's "$7000 for a pop" supposed to signify - the going rate for carrying out an assassination or contract killing? The mind boggles.... Though the finger-gun shoots are probably just a symptom of her illness or a classic "fuck you" gesture to the world. But her constant reiteration of "You're a piece of shit" and other verbal abuse is seriously undermining your confidence, which is NOT what you need at this stage in your life: your self-esteem has already taken a battering and the last thing you need is for your confidence to be further undermined by a constant barrage of negative judgements.

RE the newspaper article you attached about an epidemic of mental illness in Loudoun county, unless the local stats are compared against national levels it's impossible to say whether the incidence of mental illness in the VA area is typical or abnormally high - are you suggesting it's connected to its proximity to centres of power like the Headquarters of the CIA or the Pentagon?

Love,

Leigh

**From: Cass Ryder**
**To: Leigh Ryder**

Shadowman watching at the library - I need to move around a lot more. He was standing right next to me and shouted "See you, Tom" and he did it purposely to upset the writer. White elite man's weapon angled in my face every other day and the BLACK ASSHOLE IS HIS KING. The pan-global pan-racial male homosexual brotherhood are THE DREGS OF THE UNIVERSE. They specialise in black magic assaults, are not very intelligent, and invest all their faith in dense materiality and physical strength. Whilst killing time in a fast food joint during the long night hours to get out of the freezing temperatures where flesh can freeze in 30 seconds, I was forced to watch a disgusting documentary on the TV screen called "Terror at the Westgate Shopping Mall" in Nairobi. Terrorists killed everyone, and horrible things happened. I found them repugnant. They are obsessed with anything that might be a challenge to hosepipe (sorry, an unfortunate observation due to an assault) and use violence to consolidate their neurotic ideals and failed actions, and guess what, small on the inside and big on the outside is their boring little thing.

I'm going to audio record M on the weekend at Roy Rogers. I think it's in her interest at this stage that people know what's going on, and I'm going to air it too. Penises and co set her up to meet Liz, then purposely wrecked the communication channels, had them separated, and repeated the same thing with Claudine. They think they're clever, they set her off in the writer's presence to target the writer like they did with former women (Liz, Claudine etc.) Meanwhile they get M on a drug and are milking her. WOMEN ARE THE MOST UNBELIEVABLE CUNTS ON THE FACE OF THE EARTH. The fact that they are potentially more intelligent does not mean to say that they are. For instance, that bitch Liz dumped Monica on the pavement like a piece of baggage. Liz always had a boyfriend, and later got married, so they were not that close. They were all phallic teased and interfaced with the whole time. Liz worked for CHI which later got incorporated into ARK (a Maryland social services dept) ARK apparently absorbed CHI about 5 years ago. Claudine might well have been connected to ARK, as M always said that Liz and Claudine had known each other. Claudine's apartment was very close to Paxton campus, a place with developmental disabilities which is affiliated with "Ark". THESE PLACES LOOK LIKE FRONTS. It's ALL SHADY…CREEPY AND I'M TIRED OF WAKING AND HEARING THE SOUND OF A BABY CRYING…she's a prisoner in that apartment. More sickening is the idea that she's being sexually exploited and being made to accept culpability along the lines of mediaeval thinking, when a woman was made to pay for "tempting" a man when the crime is his not hers.

Bluntly speaking, I think they get empowered through the self-bioelectrical thing, sick as it sounds. One victim reacted to the threat phase by the insertion of an object, which while inconvenient, worked in terms of muscle blockage. But it matters when she thinks she's with Liz, when it's NOT the embodied Liz it's like a spirit possession. They've hijacked her body. She's now saying all the while she's going to get a Glock and that the CIA tell her they will just "re-provision" her again. The things she's coming out with are sick and sadistic. The subject has gone into depth describing a thing called "trepanning" (drilling holes in peoples skulls?) and how she can have recourse to "blunt tools". The things she has been coming out with "Liz is going to do a tracheotomy on you with rusty tools" etc. are the kind of things a Congolese general or drug-toting mercenary pimp after a night's rampage on a peasant village would brag about, that's what she sounds like and it seems FAKE. From my research I know that trauma is often purposely introduced for mind control purposes, and this endless referencing to "Liz" is a symptom of mind control. A high price to pay for standing by one's principles.

One thing for sure, whoever they are they HATE ME, and I think it's being done to attack me. The writer resonates with cpinks, and that's why she's being set up. Some of the most honest generous types she's ever met were gay women… almost all the women who've ever inspired her were like a beacon of light in a sea of horrors…some of them do seem haunted though. I've spent the last 18 years researching this stuff as best I could whilst being destitute, and I'd like to nail these bastards who are using diabolical means and intents. Let's just face the shit and nail the shit and see it walked off to jail. The subject said "I'm going insane. They do this to me. I have no choice" As though she's anticipating a kind of memory relapse control state which had happened before. Has she been kidnapped, then dropped off in different communities? She also mentioned she'd spent 10 years incognito, apart from her family…sounds like she's being trained to be an agent (has numerous addresses, IDs etc.) It's like a mancan process unfolding.

The first thing she said when she walked into this apt is that it reminded her of the room where she and Liz murdered a Haitian called Falladay in self-defence for his attempt to get M on the ground. Liz walks in and knifes him in the back apparently, and M finishes the thing off by stomping on his face with her little sneakers. Sick? THEY'RE sick... if a man attacks a woman what does he expect? They got her into that apt, they even got her thinking I'm trying to avoid her when I'm not. They get her on her own then they relate to her on the sly in the most sadistic way…a co-mingling of white and African weirdos, and if that's not true then why doesn't white man do something about it all? For instance all that military power he has (yes, and we all know the military are evil too) but why don't they just get to it … knocking them on their woolly heads, viral sterilization of fatsos on welfare with nothing between their ears?? AND PLEASE HURRY UP ABOUT IT.

Cass

**From: Leigh Ryder**
**To: Cass Ryder**
**CC: Alexandra, Patrick, Luke, Adam**
**Subject: Trying to give you moral support**

Dear Cass,

Am writing this in the wee hours of the morning, as I couldn't sleep for thinking of you out in the open. The weather here is horrendous too, with howling winds up to 75 mph and hail slamming against the windowpanes. Being situated on the coast we get the brunt of it during the winter as the winds are blown in off the Atlantic: it sounds really loud out there, a constant roaring.

From the sound of your most recent emails (which mainly consist of 4-letter obscenities and references to the male and female lower anatomy) you are obviously very upset, and clearly suffering from severe sleep deprivation. Rather than trying to while away the night hours in fast food joints - which must cost money, as presumably you have to buy coffees etc. in order to be able to sit there - wouldn't it be better to hit one of the cold weather shelters? I know you don't like these places, but the shelters are there for the homeless in freezing temperatures, so for pity's sake make use of whatever facilities are on offer. You're probably so exhausted you should be able to hit the sack at 10pm and fall asleep immediately (no need to talk to anyone, just get your head down under the covers and try to give your body some much-needed rest) The fluorescent flickering lights and constant noise in fast food joints will only have an adverse effect on your immune system when your serotonin levels are low. At night your brain needs to shut down completely, as this is the only way the body (and the MIND) can repair itself, and the only way you can maintain your health and sanity. If you cannot face the shelter, then you may have to crash at M's apartment again, simply to get out of the cold. Although it's far from ideal, what with her hostile breakouts and noisy tenants partying upstairs, she has to fall asleep at some point so you can at least get a few hours rest, and have a decent breakfast like scrambled eggs on toast.

With ref to the library, I understand that "shadowman" might be stalking you, but when someone says something like "See you Tom" within earshot this is a perfectly harmless remark with no sinister intent, and has no connection whatsoever to our father, Tom being a very common name. There is a fine line between being naturally wary of strangers and letting your paranoia get the upper hand. You're probably not thinking straight right now because you're exhausted, hungry and cold. If you're deprived of sleep and proper nutrients it is no wonder you are continually on edge and suspicious of everyone. Something to bear in mind is that **outer circumstances often reflect inner consciousness.** Have you ever noticed that when you are in a negative frame of mind or filled with thoughts of revenge, obstructions keep cropping up and things go from bad to worse? Another way of putting this is a saying from the Talmud: *We do not see things as they are, but as we are.* Our own perception interprets reality for us, and that perception is by definition subjective and skewed by the circumstances we find ourselves in. If you are tired and irritated, any minor annoyance will seem major and more threatening than it really is. You need to fight the negativity, as negative thoughts rebound on the sender and set up negative reactions in other people. It's like a chain reaction. You need to accept that your thought processes are somewhat muddled, and you therefore need to listen to the advice of others who can think more clearly. If you continue to ignore that advice, then you are on a loser's ticket to nowhere.

The other big mistake you have made is to keep giving Monica money which I sent specifically for you to buy thermal clothing. If she is still refusing to claim foodstamps, that's HER problem, not yours. It is not your responsibility to try and provide for her material needs - she has a warm apartment and you don't. You're out on the streets, destitute, and you **need the cash much more**

**than she does.** And if passing strangers hand you money on the streets, <u>keep it for yourself</u> and don't tell her about it, otherwise you are not going to survive. You cannot bribe or "buy" someone's affection with cash, and I don't think M is capable of true empathy: only her family know the real truth about her, and there may be a very good reason Liz no longer wanted anything to do with her. The fact is she is off the streets now and receiving medical treatment: there is not a lot else the authorities can do, nor is there anything you can do. So JUST LEAVE IT ALONE. I know it must be very hard for you to let go, and I do fully understand how easy it is to become attached to someone whom you spent well over 3 years with 24/7 sharing a bench at night, sharing the terrors of imminent assault etc. Due to years of extreme isolation you have been literally starved of the type of mental and social stimulation that most people take for granted. So when you encountered Maria, with whom you appeared to have certain things in common, this provided a fresh stimulus and interest. Although I know you did not have a "relationship" in the conventional sense, that the two of you didn't even get along that well, nevertheless when you are homeless and alone in the world *any* kind of friendship is like a lifeline. Coming across someone to whom you can relate on some level is like a parched traveller stumbling across an oasis in a desert. It's inevitable that you would have developed some form of emotional co-dependency in these circumstances.

We all need some kind of companionship, and without it the outcome is often psychosis. This is a very basic human need - as basic as the need to eat, drink and sleep- and nothing to be ashamed of. In fact it demonstrates that you are pretty normal, whereas sociopaths tend to be totally self-absorbed and are unable to form emotional attachments. In a relationship such as a marriage which ends in divorce or bereavement, the only way to "move on" with your life is either to meet somebody else or to take up new interests. It's a question of shifting your mental focus. This is one of the chief reasons why I think it would be liberating and transformative for you to leave the States: at the moment your mental processes are stuck in a repeating loop. It's almost as if you are "programming" yourself to remain trapped there like a form of auto-suggestion e.g. "I cannot walk away", "M needs me", "I don't have any choice" etc. You most definitely DO have a choice, and you CAN walk away any time you want.

Love,

Leigh

**P.S.** If anyone in the family is in a position to send Cass anything now is the time to do so.

**From: Alexandra**
**To: Leigh Ryder**

Hi Leigh,

I have tried phoning the number that I last spoke to her on but it doesn't get picked up and there is no voicemail, so I have no idea if it is current or not. I also emailed her before I left the U.S. to say I wanted to send her some money for Xmas, but I didn't get any reply and I have no contact info to send money to. When I sent money last summer, it was to two different places, each with specific instructions from her about where & when to send it. But it was by specific arrangement and she knew to expect it and could go to the designated place to get it with the reference code etc. It's impossible to do that without a prior arrangement….not sure which method you've been using?

I know how awful it feels to go to bed in winter knowing that she is out in the cold… yet it always comes back to the same point – we can't help her unless she lets us and it seems she ensures that it's well nigh impossible to help….that is her illness, clearly, not her real intent. It is also disturbing to know she is still passing on money to this person called Monica. When is the last time you spoke to her? Did you have a number to call her back or did she call you? I can fund a ticket for her to go back to the UK if she will take it. I can give her shelter if she would be willing to accept staying here for a while, but I suspect she wouldn't want to leave that area and come to Texas. I wouldn't feel comfortable opening up our doors to Monica, though. I will be honest and say the idea of having her stay under the same roof does concern me….your message to Cass is directed in a tone that presupposes rationality but she is not rational or well. I don't feel equipped to know how to respond to her illness.

I don't know what to suggest or do – that is why I am mostly silent on the subject. My silence doesn't mean I don't care, and I know that to be true for all of us. If her email address is the same, which it seems to be, I can email her. Does she check it often do you know? Hope everyone is well and that 2015 has started reasonably enough. I think Luke is away on a trip right now.

All for now from a very cold and grey Texas!

Alex xx

From: Leigh Ryder
To: Alexandra
CC: Patrick, Luke, Adam

Dear Alex,

RE Cass's contact details, I haven't spoken to her on the cellphone since the summer, but the email I address I set up for her is definitely operative, and she checks it very frequently (she emails me about 3 times a week) I don't quite understand the circuitous route you used before to transmit money. You do not need to specify any location apart from the country, as she knows perfectly well where she can cash a Moneygram (as with Western Union there are several outlets in most towns) The procedure is simple. You fill in a form stating your name and address and recipient's name and destination country (USA), the amount you are sending and the currency in which it is to be collected, and your signature. You are then issued with a unique reference no. which matches the one inserted on the form. For added security I generally specify a test question to which only she would know the answer and then send Cass an email giving her the reference. This is really the only information you need to supply for her to collect it.

I agree you should have nothing to do with Monica. However, they are now living separate lives, and because the latter is now accommodated in what is called "permanent supportive housing" and Cass is now out in the open on her own again, it's unlikely it will be squandered in 2 or 3 nights at a hotel as before (this was always Monica's choice, not Cass's) Basically she needs cash in order to be able to frequent coffee bars to get out of the cold since she has hours and hours to kill during the day and during the night. Although she is still in receipt of food stamps the U.S. authorities do not provide the homeless with any cash. She has never begged on the streets (in the same way that she will never ask directly for money) but mentions that members of the public occasionally give them handouts, which is what they rely on. She has also mentioned a health bar called "Tropicana" which specialises in veggie drinks, nourishing soups etc. which she would like to visit for health reasons, but cannot afford to. So any money sent would be appreciated.

I have attached her "Christmas message" to you all in this email: I didn't forward it on at the time because the tone is somewhat bitter, as you would expect, and let's face it most of family has not responded to any of my communications concerning her. Cass is extremely suggestible, implicitly believing what she reads or has seen posted on dubious websites, but she is not stupid and I hope the above demonstrates that she IS capable of rational thought (though obviously not all the time) There are times, when she is very disturbed or angry, when her thought processes break down completely and she resorts to abusive language, but this is perfectly understandable in the circumstances. The sense of betrayal and abandonment comes through very strongly, but as you had told her you wanted to send her some cash at Christmas, which never materialized, she naturally feels you are "phoney" because you didn't follow through. It has taken me over one and half years to gain her trust enough for her to communicate with me, and although it's very time-consuming I do it because I don't want her to think she is completely alone in the world. On Boxing Day she and M were threatened with physical violence by 2 men. Fortunately this incident took place on a bus, otherwise the consequences could have been dire, but I include it to further illustrate how vulnerable she is. Anyway, hope this answers your questions.

Leigh

**P.S.** Her charming description of *"fatsos on welfare with nothing between their ears"* who should be "sterilised" could apply equally to great swathes of people in this country.

**From: Cass Ryder**
**To: Leigh Ryder**

Writer was told her other sister Alexandra just got tabbed with a
thing called "red nose" the beginning of a skin cancer or is that kin
cancer? The writer's sister in England helped a lot with comments
on writer's research, but this sister is coming over as rather strange.
She's advising me to take the disability but she herself would work
like the devil not to be dependent on the government. On the
subject of the other sister's "red nose" skin cancer she's just been
diagnosed with wasn't there a nazi called Rudolph, certainly
Rommel. Aren't they calling her a nazi now, isn't this predictable?
RUDOLPH HESS (DEPUTY FUHRER TO ADOLF HITLER) I
recall she went straight back to work when she had her son, that she
always had her own bank accounts/properties, and is an example of
a woman who didn't take a backseat because she became married
… isn't that her deal? I'm almost certain Alexandra's not going to
come up with any help. I don't expect it. Maybe she's some sort of
pervert who tries to mess with my feelings. I can't believe she
honestly wanted to help. And stop trying to force me up to family.
A bunch of weirdos. They're full of shit. One of them could at least
have taken the time to come out to the States for about a year.

Imagine crashing in a ditch or a freezing highway woodlot each
night or being threatened every day, being a slave to the library as a
weather retreat, mouthing "Oh, thank you" when someone hands
over cash, wolfing down sandwiches on cold metal benches, eating
day-old muffins and bagels from Dunkin Donuts bins, keeping
watch on certain characters who have already threatened to beat
you up, being silently hated while people smile in your face. You'd
be obnoxious too. WHAT IS WRONG WITH NEGATIVE
ENERGY? It's a good thing as long as it can be channelled down a
certain route. Negative expression could even be endorsed as
normal, as therapy for people who are continually picked on.
Writer can't stand people, and can't even talk to them. She comes

to this place (the library) like she comes to a jail every day. No one communicates, so she mainly talks to herself or communicates with one sister in England and that's it. As for the subject her will or whatever is not there, she's not able to communicate in any coherent way. The writer's not going to keep coming here and is not going to die beside her in this place. She hates being here and she's miserable all the while. The weather outside is 50 miles an hour winds.

Subject's viewpoints have changed quite starkly in 2 years. Perhaps she's readying herself to be faced with an injection as the lesser of two evils ....as a way to shut up a spirit trading war and force shut an open usage channel, but just the thought of being haunted by a needle… She used to say she could get by with a platonic relationship, but since coming to Leesburg in the last year has gotten a lot more low level and pornographic when referring to Liz or the imaginary Liz. She's laughing right now, devilishly, and saying "I'm a white alpha male god. Me and Liz will soar to greatness" If people saw and heard her esp. anyone versed in psychic matters, they would immediately be able to zero in on the problem. There's no mystery here. The U.S. is like an occult playground as it's obviously full of really stupid people who know nothing. Occult liberty-taking seems to be the future. Another tactic is shit-stirring, turning one prathole against another. The operator channel is a channel where shit-stirring goes on, like oxygen fanning the flames of a fire. But the occult can do nothing without humans, and while fire can be put to good use, something "works through" her, takes control and channels it down destructive paths. The strongest and most positive person would have lost their mind by now. Having an open mind doesn't pay, though that's not even a possibility for most of the younger generation. My generation WERE BETTER. We reached out for more and WE ACHIEVED MORE, and like an endangered species we're going out. There's evidence that quality of life has stagnated or is going down for the majority. And the powers that be on earth seem obsessed with "hot temperature rated" subject matter. They've got deep sexuality hang-ups. On the subject of the 22 lettered a kind of brute force invisible energy invasion took place. Who wants that much closeness to a bunch of invisible bastards?

Why in this huge recent medical overhaul didn't they GET TO THE CAUSE instead of just the symptoms, therefore encouraging the recurrence of mental illness? Different remedies could have included a "special needs with special funding" category for mental assault targets based on an appraisal by persons skilled in ether weaponry. WHY IS THAT SO HARD FOR THEM TO DO? One worker went "Sure it's not something in your subconscious?" almost mockingly. Of course it's something in the unconscious, but just because you have a pile of fertile topsoil in your backyard does that give a neighbour the right to steal it? Just because it's sitting there doesn't mean someone can take it over. The reason why I didn't go to the mental health dept is because I'm very cynical of the establishment generally. Writer doesn't think the subject is that dangerous and has fallen asleep in her presence frequently, and would do so again if a snowstorm started up and she insisted the writer come back with her to the apartment. The writer trusts her.

Meanwhile they're ejaculating with glee over the fact that we're no longer associating with the social workers. They're really nasty. One black cow goes "Last night I locked myself out of my apt and had to sleep in my car" and she's so full of her sense of suffering for that one evening and is actually expecting ME to empathize. People see what they want to see and women are so complacent. Although writer has observed that women get used in lots of ways and are lied to, the conclusion is that they communicate appallingly in a trite shallow way when they do communicate, and are mind-controlled with respect to the systems around them. They clutch fervently and morally to that pocketbook as they go about the business of consolidating their homes. The mainstream married type denies having problems…she sorts it out sensationally. Read the research, no one is more patriotic than they are, or more phoney on religious dogma or belief in the system and it's a perverted one, a warped one, YOU CAN COUNT ON THEM NOT TO TALK. Doubtless the vast majority don't give a shit about their children or their destinies, but neurotically salute something they're not permitted to question. When they do question it they are knocked on the head, and they reconsolidate their compliance in earnest. Then they're praised for being serene, in charge, or whatever; but when they're challenged their egoism completely rebounds in terms of being ill at ease. They deceive themselves a lot. Woman needs to get her hate out into the open...there is a huge gender world war going on where men and women are both guilty of wrong relations, and she is the least likely to admit that she didn't consciously choose her destiny, that she isn't on the right path, and she isn't a winner.

I have not been allowed to talk to the subject in about 12 months otherwise I will literally be physically attacked. She grabs my head or ears and warns me to shut up: "I am a god, I am a billionaire, I am Apollo." The egocentric nature of it is outrageous, "Do not speak or I'll swipe you right across the face" combined with "Stay with me" or "Where are you going?" I tried to audio record her last weekend in Roy Rogers. I re-verified I had it on long distance recording and the volume turned up (I had the recorder up my sleeve resting on my knee on an adjacent table) It had definitely been on but the recording didn't come out. The very next morning Monica says reflectively after coffee "We should probably split up at this stage" This morning just as I'm about to attempt one more time (the third attempt) to tape record her in the cafe where we meet she says "Liz told me that you agitate me and you're part of it and we should not drink coffee together. I'll see you in the library and hand you your sandwich" She's being watched. Oh no? Why did the tape recorder jam the other day? A butch looking lesbian walked in to the café. She looked like she may have been staged to be there, to listen in, and asks us politely if we want breakfast. Here's more proof Monica is channelled. Sat morning she enunciated "Recollect to check the inbox. Your sister (and she did mention the word sister) is about to send some cash" How could she have known? Then she said "it's Liz's money …it's from my mummy".

I tried to get a stupid grocery store job in the kind of place where they employ homeless people and they didn't respond. Writer doesn't want the disability cash, doesn't want the dole either, but certainly can't continue to live unemployed and cashless without secure housing for much longer. And I have what they call a mental disability, it's called an anger issue. But maybe the writer will go back to England just to get revenge on something over here wavelength-wise. But then again the war's been fought and won already. THERE IS NO FREEDOM. There has to be easier ways to live and die, or at least not to get born. The human race is going to die out and go extinct soon, thank god. Lets get straight to the point the biosphere is dead…to mean he and she are not going to inherit it. BUT I'M NOT GOING TO BE AROUND WHEN THE SHIT HITS THE FAN Say you will, Cassandra, you will be around when the shit hits the fan. The writer's view is that they're all losers and it's part of a pan-global elite plan whose covert plans go back decades even centuries, and whose goals only differ as their egos differ.

Cass

**From: Leigh Ryder**
**To: Cass Ryder**
**Attachment:Confidential**

Dear Cass,

Please open the attached password-protected document (entitled "Confidential"), and acknowledge receipt of this by specifying the name of Maddy's school.

Leigh

MONICA OBVIOUSLY HAS ACCESS TO YOUR EMAIL ACCOUNT AND HAS YOUR PASSWORD. WISE UP TO WHAT IS GOING ON HERE. There is no way she could know about the money unless she regularly accesses your account. I have always thought this is the case, and now you've just proved it to me. She is not to be trusted. Surely you must realise that a spirit entity would NOT be able to access an email account and discover the content (the very idea is absurd) The fact that M knew about the Moneygram and specifically asked you to check your inbox proves to me that she knows your password and read my message. If you recall, when I first set up your current email account for you I left the password on your cellphone voicemail, and as you probably share the phone with her, this is how she knows it. She is not being channelled by anything occult – of what possible use would money be to a spirit? You are being manipulated and there is no discarnate entity involved – this is a HUMAN setup. There may be an accomplice in the shadows or she may be acting on her own, but she is definitely involved in the deception. Also, some weeks ago you stated *"Someone is rifling thro my backpack I don't think it's M..."* Who else would it be, considering you left your backpack in her apartment?

It seems very odd that 1) the toilet cubicle in which you peeped over the wall was wrecked soon after receiving my warning of possible hidden cameras 2) that as soon as I suggest you examine M's glasses to see if they are bluetooth spyware she casually tells you that she thinks you both should split up 3) ditto with your attempted recording in the coffee bar.

**From: Cass Ryder**
**To: Leigh Ryder**

Nope, afraid not, you're wrong about Monica, she's genuine. YOURE NOT LISTENING TO WHAT I'VE BEEN TELLING YOU. Ectoplasm represents a kind of bioelectricity looking like a white fluid or stringy glue-like material issuing from people who are channelled (the writer has already recounted how she saw white energy shooting out of the subject's eye once while she was verbalizing) It's called invisible weaponry and it's the world's dirtiest little best kept secret. The spirit world character assassinates people and feeds off vulnerability. F*** Hooker is the name of the damned school. Not even sure I'm talking to you. My test questions to you are 1) pet name you had for Maddy and 2) the Greek island we went to. Have to go now to try and get a feral cat trapped on a bank property relocated to a cat refuge.

Cass

**From: Leigh Ryder**
**To: Cass Ryder**

Dear Cass,

Be assured it's me you're communicating with. RE your test questions: I believe the pet name I used for Maddy was Slipperfoot (it just came to me) and the Greek island we went to back in the 80s was Ios. On the same holiday - during which we slept rough on the beaches - you got a severe case of sunburn and your poor blistered face was like a red beacon when we went to an outdoors disco halfway up a mountain. I keep forgetting that Monica is the only companion you have had in many years so it's only natural you would feel a sense of loyalty towards her. That is a positive character trait in you, but I just wish you could have met someone who was as generous and supportive towards you as you have been towards her. And I'm not really angry about the money. If it makes you happy to give most of it to her, then that's fine. Possibly some agency does read our emails and has become aware that I am getting uncomfortably close to the truth and am "on to them." Maybe you're right and they are trying to cover up the exploitative relationship they have with Monica. But it seems a real shame that M's psyche has disintegrated to the extent you can no longer communicate with her, since it deprives you of companionship.

But imagining that any of us – who are now middle-aged and with numerous commitments – could actually take a year off to live in the United States, shows just how divorced from reality you have become. You cannot just walk out on a job, a partner, a business, a family and expect it all to still be there when you come back. The sensible and obvious solution is for YOU to return to the UK, where I can actually afford to help you out with accommodation, and not for us to keep sending sums of money abroad, or for us to make expensive transatlantic trips. It's precisely because we don't give in to these crazy impulses that we still have some money in the bank. You are undoubtedly right-brain dominant, like a lot of creative and intuitive people, but it means the rational side has suffered. Hence many of your actions appear illogical and incomprehensible to me, but it is impossible to attach any blame, since you are who you are, and I love that person. But that person who you are – the one who rescues feral cats and foolishly gives away all her money to people who are better off than she is, and allows herself to be used by people less worthy than herself – does not have the wherewithal to survive in a material world. I'm not saying that the rest of us are necessarily selfish or callous but we are hard-headed enough and realistic enough to know that the only way to progress in life, or at least keep your head above water is to be practical, to make some provision for the future, and to seize opportunities when they come your way. Vincent Van Gogh was an idealist, his brother was a pragmatist. The latter did all he could to save his gifted brother from self-destruction, and financially supported him throughout his tortured life. He didn't sell a single painting during his life-time and lived in abject poverty and misery for most of his life, so what good did his idealism or his vision do him? Sometimes it's better to compromise a little, in order to live a decent life and enjoy a degree of comfort. These things matter a great deal as you get older and your body less able to withstand privations and hardships. You're right in that poverty does not make you humble, and the poor can be quite intolerant. In *Wuthering Heights* Heathcliff says to Cathy "The tyrant grinds down his slaves and they don't turn against him; they crush those beneath them" There is no freedom in poverty, as you have discovered for yourself.

If you noticed, my most recent email included other family members, and was partially intended as an invitation for others to help you out. As usual I was met by a wall of silence - I really don't know why I even bother writing to any of them. I didn't expect a response from Luke yet, as I'm aware he is abroad (he tries to snatch some time for himself during the winter before the business opens again full-time), no response from Patrick or Adam, and the usual excuses from Alex:

*I have tried phoning the number that I last spoke to her on but it doesn't get picked up and there is no voicemail.... I also emailed her before I left the U.S...but I didn't get any reply and I have no contact info to send money to.....*

Pathetic really, as I've given all of them your contact details on numerous occasions. In my reply I gave her explicit instructions as to how to make a money transfer. Whether this will galvanize her into sending you some cash or not I don't know, but don't hold your breath.

Love,

Leigh

**From: Alexandra**
**To: Leigh Ryder**
**CC: Patrick, Luke, Adam**

Dear Leigh,

I originally set out to reply to Cass but feel it's not fair as she is not in her right mind. It's hard to know what Cass wants and how I can help. I would send some money again if I had the details of where to send, as before, and confirmation that she is able to collect – to do that she needs to communicate as she did before. However, money will not help her cause. She needs proper medical treatment and only she can agree to that.

I won't pretend to understand because I don't, but nor will I be held responsible. I feel it's a shame it's affecting other sibling relationships but it has, and is. Enough is enough. I have copied others (minus Maddy who has her own problems) so that I can say my piece. We have no doubt all suffered varying degrees of discomfort and ranges of guilt at not being able to help Cass. However, we do all have responsibilities in our own lives too that limit each one of us in our potential to contribute to this sad case. I don't see why any of us should be deemed uncaring and to blame.

If any of you has a suggestion for how I can help, please let me know. Otherwise, I think it's best that we do not damage siblings' relationships over Cass's medical condition – I am convinced that if she were in a right mind, she would not want that for us.

I'll email Cass and ask her if she can contact me to arrange for me to send her some more dollars. But I don't see that dollars are the solution and can't do it indefinitely. I'm sorry to sound frustrated but I am. I won't take offense at anything mentioned below (your recent email to her was at the end of her message) but I am just saddened that Cass's mental health is resulting in a siblings fallout....and that is of course what will happen if much more finger pointing goes on. I thought you should all be included in this quick message....I'm sorry if you didn't want to be, and I won't do any more round robins like this again.

On a different and unrelated note, I hope you are all doing fine and that 2015 has started well for you. I'm sorry I'm not in touch more often; my silence is a result of having 10-12 hour days at work more often than not, and then returning to a brain numbing retreat to summon up energy for the next day. As for that choice, it is my own for the present so I'm not complaining, just explaining.

Take care,

Alex

**From: Leigh Ryder**
**To: Alexandra**
**CC: Patrick, Luke, Adam**
**Subject: Can of Worms**

Dear Alex,

I'm deeply reluctant to be drawn into all this, but feel I must because I don't want Cass to suffer the fallout. Firstly, I should like to make it clear she never asked you for any money. You proactively sought her out and sent her an email prior to Christmas stating you'd like to send her some, which she casually mentioned to me. As nothing materialised (and still hasn't, according to her) I took the initiative by adding the postscript "If anyone in the family is in a position to send Cass anything now is the time to do so" as a gentle reminder, nothing else. This produced a curiously defensive response along the lines of how you wouldn't feel "comfortable opening your doors to Monica" etc. So as to allay your completely groundless fears, nothing of the sort was proposed and Cass herself has no desire whatsoever to avail herself of your hospitality or to impose on you in this way. Since you seemed to think it's necessary to have precise contact details in order to arrange a Moneygram I explained how this is not required, any more than you need to know in advance where you can cash travellers' cheques. By expecting Cass (who is homeless) to actually provide you with an address as to "where to send it to" you are creating imaginary difficulties. As long as she has the reference number she could collect it wherever she happened to be in the States. It is the sender's responsibility to notify the intended recipient of the reference, and she has already confirmed to you that her email address is operative and added in a recent message "My cell phone's payment plan went obsolete last fall and that is why no voice messages were relayed"

The second point I wish to make in response to your statement "Nor will I be held responsible" is that nobody, least of all me, has ever once suggested that you or anyone else is to blame or is in any way responsible for Cass's circumstances. I certainly don't consider myself responsible for her mental condition or homelessness, nor do I consider that sending her cash is a solution to her problems. That is not why I do it. I realise people have their reasons for not wishing to get involved, and that is their business. However, all this defensiveness kind of misses the point which is this: I don't think it's fair to email her and say you would like to send her some cash for Christmas, and then fail to follow through. This messes with her head, and further reinforces her belief that people are not to be trusted or are not sincere in their protestations of wishing to help. My remarks concerning "the wall of silence" and total lack of response from family members was not directed at you specifically, and I gave you the benefit of the doubt when I told Cass that you were entirely sincere in wishing to send her something, but first wished to confirm her contact details to ensure it would reach her safely. As for any sibling fallout, it doesn't bother me if anyone in the family harbours resentment towards me. However, it does bother me that any resentment caused by my remarks should backfire on Cass, who is totally innocent in all this. She is not to blame for the postscript I added, which appears to have opened up a can of worms.

Adam, in response to your Christmas greetings, yes of course Cass is ill, but a patient cannot be treated successfully unless their condition is first diagnosed correctly. Medical misdiagnoses lead to inappropriate treatment, which can exacerbate an existing condition and cause irreparable damage. Where the mentally ill are concerned, the prescribed route is enforced injections or chemical prescriptions: their primary purpose is to SEDATE and therefore make it easier for mental health workers or nurses to deal with their patients. In other words drugs like lithium *et al* were not manufactured with therapy or with healing in mind, or to help people with mental disorders get better, but simply to make life easier for the lazy fat asses who administer them. I do not place the same faith that you do in the mental health profession. Good luck to your self-harming Royal Marine pal: I'm glad to hear he has benefited from his "meds" but presumably he is not homeless and can therefore afford to be sedated. People - especially women - sleeping rough on the streets do not survive very long if they have a drug dependency. As Cass remarked *"The writer has seen enough bug-eyed women in the community....their eyeballs are falling onto the pavement after they've just had long term injections"*

And I'm pretty sure Cass did not suffer any molestation on the playground of Sincheap Primary. This is the 70s we're talking about for Christ's sake, and she was a normal, happy, and healthy child - quite boisterous, in fact, and full of mischief - or are you now suffering from selective amnesia? Maybe you'd better lay off those anti-depressants. As it happens, I was molested by my language tutor when I was 15. Because I had missed out on 4 years of French when we were living in the States I was given extra-curricular coaching by this old man who had a chronic case of "wandering hand" syndrome. I smacked him in the jaw and that swiftly put an end to that. At the end of the lesson he said sadly "I suppose now you're going to tell everyone that I'm a dirty old man" I assured him I had no intention of doing any such thing, but that I would not be returning. When my headmistress later asked me whether I could recommend him, I replied "Certainly" but that prospective pupils would be well-advised to turn up in a suit of armour. But this all serves to illustrate that "trauma" - like beauty - is in the eyes of the beholder. A swift smack in the chops is often an effective antidote to would-be gropers, and had he been standing instead of sitting I would have aimed for the goolies (acting under the express instruction of a nanny in Edinburgh, who took it upon herself to advise me in such matters) She also insisted on apprising me of the facts of life at the tender age of 8 when I had no interest whatsoever in the topic under discussion. I did try to halt the flow by saying things like "Look, I really don't want to know how babies are made or about the train in the tunnel" but to no avail...

We grew up in a safe environment, in stark contrast to Brazil where Adam has chosen to reside. A Google search revealed a spate of gruesome witchcraft murders in the district of Maranhao, Brazil over a period of 20 years, stemming from *Macumba* black magic or *umbanda* (voodoo) The victims were bright, promising young boys from the poorer classes who were castrated, brutally sodomised, and drained of blood, and some of the families were offered government jobs or baskets of food to "keep quiet". Most Brazilians are well aware that the country is full of backyard *terreiros* who practice *quimbanda* or *candomble* (an African-influenced cult allied to voodoo) for evil or harmful purposes. A number of Western researchers who were initially sceptical that such practices could actually harm people, and incredulous at what they viewed as the superstitious beliefs of their educated friends, were disturbed by the evidence they uncovered: although uneducated gullible types were often the easiest targets, they also found that Westerners were peculiarly susceptible because their culture lulls them into a false sense of security i.e. "No-one can possibly lay a curse on me because I simply don't believe in all that mumbo jumbo"

It is very difficult for normal people to accept this notion of an invisible world peopled by spirits - it smacks too much of the mediaeval superstitious mindset. Think again. It's a common fallacy to suppose that the material world is the ultimate reality. Just because you don't want to believe in the existence of something it doesn't mean it doesn't exist, or that you are immune from its ill effects. There is some disagreement over just how it works i.e. whether these shamans, witch-doctors, *brujos*, or whatever you want to call them can actually summon up low-level spirits to do their bidding, or whether it works through the occult, that is to say the hidden powers of the human subconscious. But anthropologists and sociologists who have taken the time to really examine the evidence have been forced to concede that it *does* actually work: victims who have been targeted or "cursed" suffer a steady stream of misfortunes and obstacles - ranging from financial to health-related issues, such as bankruptcy, cancerous tumours or strokes, inexplicable depression or suicidal impulses to all-out physical attacks - where all "paths are blocked" Witchcraft as the "poor man's weaponry" - as practised extensively in third world countries - but now increasingly in the developed sector, as members of the intelligence community seize upon the opportunities offered for covert warfare.

Luke, hope you've rested up by now and got the "jet fuel out of your nostrils"

Leigh

**From: Leigh Ryder**
**To: Cass Ryder**

Dear Cass,

It looks as though my most recent email to you was inadvertently copied to Alex (including some of my observations about family members) and she has now forwarded this on to the others, presumably so she can "say her piece" Luke's just got back from 2 weeks in Egypt, and is catching up on his sleep, so was not really aware of the "Moneygate" issue which has been blown out of all proportion. It's entirely my fault, as I took the decision to invite other siblings to help out, when I should have known how it would be received. Oh, how could I have been so wicked as to my put my own flesh and blood through such a trauma? Alex says she is not offended, but I rather suspect she is: didn't you say something about "kin cancer" in a recent email? Anyway, sorry if I've made things worse.

This Liz sounds really suspect. There was clearly no relationship between them since she is straight (and now married) but she just happens to meets up with M a few years ago and offers her a "job" One wonders what kind of job was really on the cards, and whether she is the operator/handler and M the channel. As far as I can determine, the difference between a cobo (covert black ops agent) with a mission and a mancan (Manchurian candidate) with a target is that the former is a *consciously trained* operative and the latter is an *unconsciously brainwashed* candidate. M's obsession with Liz is probably the result of hypnosis, done so that she will slavishly carry out whatever her handler tells her to do. It may be worth recounting here an episode that occurred shortly after our mother's death when I arrived in London in 1989 to start a new job. Feeling at a low ebb and in need of some company, I ventured out to a women's club one evening. Whilst chatting at the bar I noticed that one woman was photographing another group of women sitting at an adjacent table. I casually asked one of the group if they knew who she was and she replied "No idea." This naturally made me suspicious and I made a point of mentioning my misgivings to the organiser, and we jointly kept an eye on her. Later the woman with the camera followed me around and somehow managed to persuade me to give her my phone number. Yes, in hindsight this was stupid, but I figured I could get rid of her any time I wanted and was careful not to give her my address (besides I was curious to see what she was up to, because it there was any undercover surveillance going on I wanted evidence so as to alert other women to give her a wide berth)

She called me the next night and proposed we go to see an open-air production of "A Midsummer Night's Dream" being staged in Regent's Park. She showed up - minus the camera - casually mentioning she had "forgotten" to bring any cash. I bought tickets for us both, and she then said "Look, why don't I write you out a cheque" and grabbed a chequebook out of her bag. I told her I'd rather have the cash, and that if she didn't have it not to bother paying it back. This seemed to annoy her i.e. the fact that I wouldn't accept a cheque: in order to make out a cheque to someone you need their surname, and that once you give out personal information like a surname or birth date, people can find out a lot about you. She had some kind of limp going on with one of her legs, and spent the entire evening whinging - hardly the type of behaviour calculated to impress on a first date. By this time I was pretty sure she was NOT gay (just posing as one) and probably in the pay of some shady agency compiling a database on gays: as you know, I was an IT manager working for a well-known telecomms company, which may or may not be relevant. After this thoroughly boring encounter she called me again several times, asking if she could post me a cheque and badgering me for my address, and each time I made it clear I was busy and not interested in seeing her again. I could hear her getting increasingly frustrated over the phone, and at one point she said "I don't think you're a very nice person" to which my response was "In which case, why keep pestering me?" I didn't trust her as far as I could throw her, and I'm convinced she was on some kind of mission, which I had successfully thwarted. I guess little Miss Supersnoop never got paid for the job she bungled. Maybe she should have brushed up on her woeful acting skills.

And yes, I do think some of M's lewd comments were a crude attempt to "draw out" any cpink tendencies you might have, and in this respect she probably is an "involuntary conscript" just as the butch type who came up to your table in RR was possibly a plant (like the fake feminists who were purposely tasked with infiltrating the women's movement) though I suppose she could have been there quite innocently. I'm going to sign off here because I need a respite from all the sibling emails. Alex has frozen me out, and the others seem to think I've lost my sense of humour – meaning they only feel comfortable communicating on a jocular level (classic case of the ostrich burying its head in the sand) I perfectly understand you have no choice but to spend hours in the library, because it's the only warm place you can go, and that your writing has nowhere to go except my inbox, but why not check out other media in the library - such as music or relaxation tapes - instead of being chained to a computer screen? It might take your mind off M's problems.

Love,

Leigh

**From: Alexandra Ryder**
**To: Leigh, Patrick, Luke, Adam**

Dear All,

I have been racking my brain day & night for what I could do to help Cass that would be more than just a one-off or occasional payment and which would provide some sort of sustainable support and have come up with an idea....though not sure how tech savvy she is.

However, I feel if I could provide her with a mobile device (either the largest screen-sized phone, or something like a mini-sized tablet) and pay for the monthly connection charges she could have internet capability wherever she is, and can basically access almost anything....news, information, entertainment, music etc and she could also access Skype to communicate with any one of us.

I am a great fan of modern technology, not least because of the horizon it opens for people with "disabilities" (sorry, not sure if that is the politically correct term or not and I don't mean to sound patronizing) but also people who are long distances from one another with no hope of immediate physical communication.... frankly, I would be quite a sad mother if I did not have the wonderful opportunity to chat to my daughter who is in England on a regular basis as we communicate on Skype and although it cannot replace sitting down with a cup of coffee and have a good chat, anyone with internet access and a device can make video contact with anyone else anywhere in the world (provided they have a device & internet access too of course)

To be able to provide this to Cass would at least give her the option of keeping in contact and start to re-build a sense of relationship or even a small degree of mental repair....if isolation is one of the causes for mind disintegration. So am thinking about how I can do this. What do you think? Is she capable of keeping a device securely and using it? Would this make Cass a target for theft and hence potentially attack?

I so want to help but have been paralyzed with not knowing what might actually be of use….yes, I could send a payment from time to time….enough to provide a few nights hotel stay which for Cass would only be very temporary shelter, but then she would be back to square one. I have been trying to think of something more sustainable. Let me know what you think….feasible idea or wishful thinking? Worthwhile or not?

Alex (Yes, although I have been known as "Lexie" for over 40 years now by anyone outside of the family, it still feels more familial when writing to family to call myself "Alex" for some reason….or perhaps I have a split personality too !!

Alex

**From: Leigh Ryder**
**To: Alexandra, Patrick, Luke, Adam**
**Subject: Mental Illness**

Dear Family,

Nice to know you're communicating again, Alex, but to be perfectly frank anything that is sent to Cass goes straight to Monica (which is not to say that money isn't always appreciated) So do whatever you think best. I watched a program the other night called "Being Bipolar", which threw up some interesting observations. The researcher began her investigation by taking the novel approach of asking "What is wrong with the **environment**?" instead of the conventional question "What is wrong with this person?" For instance, I do not believe the mass shooting at the elementary school in Sandy Hook in 2012 was caused by guns possession, as some have argued (after all, Americans have possessed firearms since the time of the early settlers and pioneers, but until the last couple of decades people did not go around massacring schoolchildren) it was precipitated by a negative shift in the consciousness of the nation. My feeling is that modern American society causes a great deal of stress in its citizens - and this in turn causes psychiatric problems on a scale never seen before. Cass recently attached a local newspaper article about a mental health epidemic in Loudoun county - posing her own question *"is it a mental health crisis or is it a perceptual interference crisis?"* In other words, are those we label "criminally insane" subject to some insidious form of mental interference and being "drugged" without their conscious consent or knowledge? Whatever the case, a significant number of people are precariously balanced on a knife-edge, and the slightest provocation or perceived slight will tip them over the edge.

There are so many different varieties of bipolar disorder (which is similar to schizophrenia) that it doesn't help to try and label the illness e.g. some sufferers are on the autistic spectrum, meaning they find it impossible to interact with others in a normal way. Autism appears to be on the increase, and prolonged exposure to the Internet may actually be a contributory factor: one of J's nephews who played with interactive video games as a young boy now suffers epileptic seizures, and his mother is convinced this is what caused his condition - he has to take regular medication and is unable to drive. Social media networks like Facebook and Twitter do not connect people in any meaningful way, they only serve to reinforce their herd mentality (the desire to conform and be one of the crowd) and their deep-seated feelings of inadequacy - providing them with an anonymous platform from which they can launch cowardly attacks on others of whom they are envious or whose lifestyles they feel threatened by. I suppose "trolling" is the cyber equivalent of the poison pen note, but the point is teenagers are actually committing suicide because of the malicious postings they read about themselves. The more I learn about this modern scourge the more I am convinced it rots the brain, corrupts the young, and should be avoided like the plague. Socrates would spin in his grave.

*The moving finger writes: and, having writ,*
*Moves on: nor all thy Piety nor Wit*
*Shall lure it back to cancel half a line*
*Nor all your Tears wash out a word of it*

Taken from the Rubaiyat of Omar Khan: he was referring to the ravages of Father Time, but the words are equally relevant to the Internet. Beware of any personal information you post on social media websites, lest it comes back to haunt you.
I distrust cyberspace and I find the whole notion of webcams highly suspect (complete strangers viewing the interior of your home via your laptop screen? No thanks) Maybe it is time to disconnect...

A large survey of randomly selected adults by the National Institute of Mental Health between 2001-3 found that an astonishing 45%

met the criteria established by the American Psychiatric Association for having had at least one mental illness at some time in their lives. In the following 10 years the number of people treated for depression tripled, and about 10% of Americans over the age of 6 now take anti-depressants. The increased use of drugs to treat psychosis is even more dramatic, and the new generation of anti-psychotics, such as *Risperdal, Zyprexa*, and *Seroquel* has replaced cholesterol-lowering agents as the top-selling class of drugs in the US. What is going on here? Is the prevalence of mental illness really that high or are we simply expanding the criteria for diagnosing mental illness? And if these drugs work shouldn't we expect the incidence of mental illness to be declining, and not rising? Instead, the number of children and adults with mental illness has risen at a mind-boggling rate since 1955 and during the past 2 decades - a period when psychiatric prescription medication has exploded: could our drug-based paradigm of care actually be fuelling this modern-day plague?

Most psychiatrists now treat exclusively with drugs. The shift from "talk therapy" to drugs as the dominant mode of treatment coincides with the emergence over the past 4 decades of the theory that mental illness is caused primarily by imbalances in the brain that can be corrected by appropriate drugs: this theory has been broadly accepted by the media. It is now well understood that anti-psychotic drugs and anti-depressants disturb neurotransmitter function with the result that neuronal pathways in the brain are compromised, and the brain begins to function in a manner quite different from its normal state. Because psychoactive drugs affect neurotransmitter levels in the brain it was postulated that mental illness is caused by an abnormality in the brain's concentration of those chemicals e.g. because Thorazine was found to lower dopamine levels in the brain it was postulated that psychoses like schizophrenia were caused by too much dopamine. And because certain anti-depressants increase levels of the neurotransmitter serotonin in the brain, it was postulated that depression is caused by too little serotonin. Thus, instead of creating a drug to treat an abnormality, an abnormality was postulated to fit a drug. Hmmm, I think I'm beginning to get the picture, meanwhile the big pharmaceutical companies are laughing all the way to the bank....

Prozac came to the market in 1987 and was intensively promoted as a corrective for the deficiency of serotonin in the brain. But anti-depressants are worse than useless, conclude Kirsch and Whitaker: *" drugs that increase, decrease or have no effect on serotonin all relieve depression to about the same degree"* i.e. they are no more effective than placebos. *"Today's emphasis on prescription medication will not stand the test of time. They involve a considerable amount of trial and error with benefits being partial or limited, and unpleasant side effects. A fundamental limitation is that psychoactive drugs are foreign molecules that result in an abnormal condition rather than producing normalcy"* Whereas conditions like schizophrenia or depression were once episodic, with each episode lasting no more than 6 months and interspersed with long periods of normalcy (or "lucid intervals") the conditions are now chronic and life-long. Whitaker believes that this might be because drugs, even those that relieve symptoms in the short-term, cause long-term mental harm that continues after the underlying illness would have naturally resolved itself.

Other researchers have published compelling evidence, based on MRI studies, that the use of anti-psychotics (which include tranquillisers) is associated with shrinkage of the cerebral cortex, leading to cognitive decline, and that the effect is directly related to the dose and duration of treatment: *"The prefrontal cortex doesn't get the input it needs, and is being shut down by drugs. Although it may reduce psychotic symptoms it also causes the prefrontal cortex to slowly atrophy"* With long-term use the result *is "substantial and long-lasting alterations in neural function"* according to Steve Hyman, former director of National Institute of Mental Health (NIMH) After several weeks, the brain's compensatory efforts begin to fail, and side-effects emerge e.g. anti-depressants may cause episodes of mania, because of the excess of serotonin, and anti-psychotics produce symptoms that resemble Parkinson's disease because of the depletion of dopamine. As these side-effects manifest they are often treated by other drugs, and many patients end up on a cocktail of drugs prescribed for differing conditions (some patients may take as many as 6 anti-psychotic drugs daily) For instance, episodes of mania caused by anti-depressants may lead to a new diagnosis of "bipolar disorder" and subsequent treatment with a "mood stabiliser" such as *Depokote* (an anticonvulsant) and so on. As medicine is not an exact science and diagnoses are not always reliable, a patient may receive several different diagnoses depending on the doctor he sees e.g. anxiety disorders and depression produce very similar symptoms. Getting off the drugs is very difficult because of the effects when they are withdrawn e.g. when an antidepressant is withdrawn serotonin levels fall precipitously because the presynaptic neurons are not releasing normal amounts and no longer have enough receptors for it (similarly when an anti-psychotic is withdrawn, dopamine levels may skyrocket)

To describe the deterioration of the brain's functioning as an "unpleasant side-effect" (we are talking brain damage here!) seems to me an egregious understatement, but perhaps the pill-popping brigade are now so far gone that they no longer care or have any awareness of what is being done to them in the name of mental health "care." A further disturbing development is that mental health professionals have now moved on from orally administered medication to "long-term injectables": *The goal is long-term disease management of schizophrenia: long-acting injectable anti-psychotics eliminate the need to take medication daily and improve potential for adherence to a treatment program. Aripiprazole, which is a dopamine partial agonist...is administered into the gluteal muscle resulting in sustained concentrations of the drug for more than a month.* Anyone who is diagnosed with a mental impairment can now be forcibly injected with chemicals on a fortnightly basis, and this is what is now happening to Cass's friend Monica, whose condition has progressively worsened since she moved into the apartment and received "treatment". The psychiatric profession is going backwards not forwards, and the practices being promoted today are not so dissimilar from those in Victorian asylums, where inmates were viewed as wild beasts to be physically restrained, with no attempt at counselling or therapy and human interaction kept to a bare minimum. Whilst recognising that Cass has mental health issues and has clearly been damaged by her experiences, I would have to agree with her that the arbitrary association of homelessness with "permanent mental disablement" is definitely something to be very wary of, and the fact that this criteria is being used as the basis for providing any kind of federal assistance to the homeless is deeply worrying. As she herself points out, the only qualifications for eligibility should be that an applicant is homeless and unemployed.

The type of in-depth psychotherapy required in order to integrate a splintered psyche and to arrive at some degree of self-knowledge, is only available to the wealthy. For the poverty-stricken all our society offers is a course of prescription drugs or injections to "shut them up" and stop them being a nuisance to others. It no longer even offers secure sheltered accommodation since most mental institutions have been closed down. Most mystics seem to agree that we are sent to the earth plane in order to evolve spiritually and to achieve a higher state of consciousness, and that this process does involve a certain amount of suffering. Of course most people would rather do without all the suffering and remain at a lower level of consciousness. What person in their right minds would consciously choose to go through what Cass has gone through? However, it's been suggested that certain souls make a conscious choice to take on a difficult destiny before entering the earth plane, either to work through some inherited karma or in order to evolve at a much faster rate so as to rise to a higher spiritual plane. This may be utter and complete bullshit but it might have an element of truth in it. To consciously choose one's life path before being born doesn't make much sense to ordinary people unless you concede that there is a higher purpose to life, and that it's not all about easy options or taking the path of least resistance. I don't pretend to know the truth, but it might explain why some people have a relatively easy ride, whilst others face an uphill battle (but perhaps the latter are the ones who will reap the ultimate rewards)

I agree with Cass that the key to an improved quality of life is simplicity, to divest yourself of superfluous material possessions, and of pointless and unproductive routines, until you are left with only what you actually need. Trite as it sounds, the best things in life are actually free. The next time any of you are feeling down, do yourself a favour, and don't automatically reach for the pill bottle. Have a cup of tea, go for a swim or howl at the moon (if you feel so inclined) It might not solve all your problems overnight, but at least it won't do you any real harm.

Take care,

Leigh

**From: Cass Ryder**
**To: Leigh Ryder**
**Subject: Snowy Wednesday**

I had a forcible OBE the other night where some psychopath is clinging to my back like a wildcat, and making slit throat motions across my neck. As for the bioelectrical they tapped into some reservoir of potential, but not before there was an image of me chasing after a man to "get" him and he gets away. Then I'm inundated with the sound of the motorway spaghetti junctions and I wake up with frozen feet needing to use the loo, and make my way along the windy freezing highway to…where else but MacDonald's? Aside from enforced bioelectricals, they probably introduce hallucinations too – all symptoms of etheric crime in a corrupt system. The etheric prods up the anus are why she's been saying things like "I hope they get raped up the arse" I can personally testify to having had that happen to me on and off for a year or so….it was to do with being in this township and the next one over. It's off the wall…no-one could sustain clarity of consciousness in the context of the type of invisible weaponry that's being used (remote physical capability and perhaps surveillance) Here I am again at the library surrounded on my right by evangelists in suits and ties. I do not belong here … I get so sick of mind-controlled losers which is what most of them are. Perhaps the subject was used to trap the writer here because of her research? But that doesn't make sense because the writer is a nobody, and is not looking for fame. I can't imagine what a drag it would be to be famous, or what a burden it would be to have lots of money. These are other peoples' problems and the writer doesn't like people anymore, or care what they think of her…. since when did I get paid for my views?

They have not been giving out the bus cards, and the weather has been freezing with ice on the pavement. M is supposed to get $10 a week for bus cards but she hasn't been turning up to get them (it costs $2 each day which she doesn't want to waste) They will not deliver them to her or slip them in her mailbox. It's been so cold it's almost impossible to navigate the slippery pavement, and they expect her to touch base with them in person. She has to touch base with the local govt dept at least once a week for socks and laundry tokens etc. which is insane. As for cash one would have thought one was asking for a trip to Jupiter. The miserliness and nastiness level of them was just off the wall. I was trying to get bus cards for her yesterday and "sometimes they have them sometimes they don't" In other words unless she turns up there they won't give her any services. She has ABSOLUTELY NOTHING but the housing utilities paid for (despite her new "billionaire" status that started out as a comparatively humble figure of $200 in mutual or treasury certificates her father possessed and which was supposed to go to her and her sister) Would the British put up with knocking on the door every other day "what have you got for me today Mummy?" She's supposed to spend endless hours doing "song and dances" with these government workers, and even then they don't have to obey the law on providing wider services if they don't feel like it.

Another thing was they mixed it in with bribery and favouritism "If I can see you don't like me you're not going to get any services" (who could possibly like those jerks?) It's cruel to people who can't or DONT WANT to ask for help. They're made to loiter on government property for hours in freezing weather conditions. Meanwhile they bent over backwards servicing wives, mothers, girlfriends and prostitutes. She has no criminal record, has worked a fair amount, keeps her apartment tidy, and doesn't party all hours of the night. Her apartment has no furniture, no computer. Oh they would give her all this? No, they're completely combing it with subtle threats and emotional blackmail (if you're nice to us we'll be nice to you) She hates those people, she shouldn't have to go there. SHE'S GOT A LOT LOT WORSE. And she's still wondering where cash for coffee or grocery supplements, let alone toiletries or transportation is going to come from. They have NO clue. They've never been homeless, they're just such dogs, even the "nice" ones.

Most of them are so wet, so goody two shoes… Once you take up any government benefits you're watched all the time. It's like those "unstable" or "insane" labels attached to political dissidents in totalitarian regimes. Those negative labels just reflect back on the labeller, that's why I don't WANT it, and you can keep your stinking welfare. Meanwhile the bigotry is outrageous. The head of emergency services once said she didn't feel women were any more disadvantaged than men through being homeless. I don't know what the stats are but I would have thought the results of a sexual assault or even the fear of an assault in a woman is much worse than a petty robbery or a beating experienced by a man ... not that homeless men should be exploited either.

The subject is in a foul mood and grabs the writer's collar threateningly, complaining how she has just been made to waste cash on groceries in the awareness that the writer could have paid with her foodstamp card when she noticed me in the store. She then wanted to get a refund but the store clerk won't allow a refund because she's lost her receipt. All the food pantries give out food that's stale and past the expiration date (due to inventory stock workers who don't do their jobs) And it's actually illegal to get on a bus or train with more one than one parcel… how does she get 6 bags of groceries back to her apartment? Apparently she swore at the landlord who she mistook for the plumber. Why was the "plumber" called anyway? I don't think there was anything really wrong with the toilet. The place looks fairly well maintained. She doesn't take baths and probably doesn't shower every day because she's paranoid about running out of hot water. I'm sure all the other female denizens have 2 each day. Anyway I clarified with the social worker that I'm not at the apt any more, and that's fine with me. They initially tried to blackmail us that if we didn't share she wouldn't get the apt (a 1 bedroom apt each should have been offered) The writer's getting feedback tomorrow on why housing wasn't made available to the subject or writer 2 or more years ago when the fed govt introduced a plan to help the chronically homeless with funding about 8 years ago, and whether that's local or federal culpability.

Oh yesterday the writer went for a foot X-ray and a car nearly runs her over, though agreed my protein intake had been down. They were trying to say I had arthritis in my feet. No I didn't, it was continual strain through wearing the wrong footwear, from walking and having to carry a backpack. I had no choice but to continue walking like those Grizzly Adams types in the Rockies. The chiropractor verified the fact that both my feet are seriously strained, but I could have done a full-time sit-down job. I actually applied for a nightshift supermarket shelf-filler job (an African man was sitting next to me gyrating his pelvis non-stop) They're probably going to try and call it an illness, but people who knew me knew that I would jog as late as 1995, though I guess I should feel lucky I still have the use of my legs after sleeping on benches. Homelessness causes all kinds of problems (the writer has emergent gingivitis from flossing with inadequately-stripped twigs) and that's why a lot of people feel distinctive nausea over the disability label, because the system shuns responsibility for causing those conditions, allowing politicians to wash their hands of culpability like Pilate did with Jesus. The system is very much the assaulter, and not some Merlin or "Dark Lord" perched on a mountain crag in Geneva. If invisible weaponry is the "virus" the system is the "vector." They damaged her and should be prosecuted, like the governor of VA who was handcuffed the other day for fraud... perhaps the entire govt on all levels needs jailing.

Last week the writer was in Ashburn and called the county bus dept to get information about commuter schedules: a man answers and gives her a forwarding number, but when the writer calls the number she gets the local mental health dept. She feels it's just another example of private phone calls being tapped into. One of the social workers handed the writer the PSH form for an apt on Friday 13th – just as a black hearse went by. This looked purposely designed to creep her out, which I totally understood to mean it's not necessarily in my favour. I refused it. Keep your sad apartment (don't you mean coffin?) Who wants to live in caged communist compartment in a box? As for elm pollution it suffocates me just to wait at the bus stop inside the apt complex. People in condo complexes are ESPECIALLY BEING BOMBARDED. Writer is balancing it with chemical pollutants like carbon monoxide in clothes and air you get by being homeless and nomadic. I think I'm actually sleeping and focusing better (the woodland songbird scenario is like waking up inside a magnified music box)

M was in a really bad mood this morning in the café (Puccios) where she takes her coffee. Positioned over her head is a TV screen, and there is an image of red-haired and blond children crawling over an embankment with a voiceover "Are your children safe?" That was an example of a beaming that was directed at M in revenge for her sadistic verbalisations. I can't talk about it over the Internet because no-one sees it or hears it except me, and I think they're trying to "deal" with her. The writer has heard voices that sound like the Daleks in that old Dr. Who TV serial or the electronic voice channel used by the physicist Stephen Hawking. When the subject thinks the writer is asleep and is vocalising loudly, the writer hears her voice "speed up" almost like an electronic recording. No time to extrapolate but it looks like a weaponry. When I incurred a back injury while working as a welder for an armaments manufacturer in a Boston shipyard, I was given a cat scan. Apparently cat scans capture the "brainwave fingerprint" which (according to conspiracy theorists) can be archived, enabling sounds and imagery to be remotely transmitted through audiograms and videograms. The cat scan conspiracy theory is almost certainly bullshit but could be a disinformation decoy, so that potential whistleblowers are sent looking for evidence in the wrong place.

Earlier in the library a black female dumped coffee over her head right in front of me, and then ran out. It looked like blood (at the exact time I was scrolling through your reference to Bob the pimp

392

as a "douche bag", which he was) HUGE INTERLUDE. The NSA jerk just threatened Monica: "If you dare say that nigger word one more time...!" Are other people complaining? Nope. He comes across as physically intimidating, and this is arguably an example of sexist behaviour. If he's that perturbed he shouldn't have sat down right beside her and then he wouldn't hear the occasional whisper. That's like making a dog pay for an offensive saying on a billboard someone strapped to its back. It shows tremendous egotism based on perceived offence to blame the dog. Her hand is still shaking, he just raised their anxiety level...but one gets so tired of being preyed on like an animal, and guess what, it's not so easy to stop breathing or to stop walking. He's huge, she's only 5'1 has a mental impairment and justifiable anger issues, and gets preyed on by black men so of course she deals it back out, while he is paid to act with a measure of calm. He's petty and totally non-professional and shouldn't be in the job. He is allowed to intercept anyone's work whenever he wants "Time's up, get off the database!" He acts like he's some sort of despot and this is the African bush.." I won't be going to the library much more anyway. There was a fight outside Rust library where a Latino man bit an African man's ear off. The sister's last email was all about Vincent Van Gogh ...the bastard is noted to have sliced his ear off.

The subject is interfaced with voodoo witchcraft so it's no coincidence that it's an African man behind the intimidation attempt in the library. White people are not good with blades and don't much like bloodshed, so it makes one wonder what race is channelling her. Shadow hosepipe and his white puppet masters make me sick ... After all, white man certainly handed the black man a lot of power over white woman, but one gets the feeling white man isn't in control any more. They're showing their true colours, and this soul tampering is etheric rape...something violent, chauvinist, savage...and is morphing into an inquisition by holding women hostage in the spirit dimension. And because the occult is dominated by men, this puts women at a double disadvantage. The subject can't stand me and I can't stand her on some level ...the spirits around her are insane. But it's almost over, and that in a way is good because something tried to use us both (they use her against me in terms of an emotional neutralizer to try and theft me of my anger) Men are the reason the subject is so messed up. They are arch-bigots and cowards who then slip back into the shadows and cannot confront what's going on. If the subject is a puppet, then a healer would be someone who simply knocks the ventriloquist aside. Subject's father used to call her a "merry mix up" and had a motto "Don't be anyone's bobo doll" (don't let people kick you around) In a jocular self-aware moment M calls herself the "descendant of Caligula".

The other day a man entered the restaurant and sat down practically opposite the writer and subject, grinning maliciously, and bragged audaciously "I kill witches" (this character reminded M of some little pervert she confronted as a correctional facility officer, who had raped his wife) The subject got up as though she's USED to this and stood before him with her tiny fists clenched. They engaged predator/prey for a while then he slunk off, seeming a little mortified. Yesterday I had to plaster across a sign "Physicality fair female and you're free to say F**K off to it" - a massive poster I occasionally put up in case anyone wanted to give a homeless female some cash.

Cass

**From: Leigh Ryder**
**To: Cass Ryder**

Dear Cass,

It wasn't very nice of that woman to pour a cup of coffee over M's head, but I'm sure the latter was not physically scarred or traumatized. It was an irritating incident but nothing more, so put it out of your mind. Crowded urban areas are full of frustrated people who take out their frustrations on other people they accidentally brush up against, and if you over-react to every little thing it will eat you up inside like a corrosive. Dare I suggest that in future you visit the library <u>on your own</u>, without the oh so charming company of she who is the "descendant of Caligula" and whose continual references to "cracking their heads open on the pavement" is a surefire way of getting you both permanently banned. As for your poster "Physicality fair female and you're free to say F**K off to it" this is a brilliant piece of alliteration, but I'm not sure the wording will induce passers-by to reach for their wallets! Don't get overly paranoid about being put through to the local mental health dept whilst enquiring about bus schedules: the county probably provides a range of umbrella services accessed through a central switchboard, and the phone numbers for separate departments may only differ by one digit.

And I have to say I do not believe either she or you were MKULTRA targets. I do not doubt that remote interference and non-lethal electromagnetic weaponry exists, but it's highly unlikely such techniques have been applied to you. It's common knowledge that state sanctioned covert surveillance is going on, hence the Prism project, and there are national security agencies whose job it is to routinely monitor emails and phone calls (how otherwise could they foil terrorist plots?), but it's a mistake to think they would have any special interest in either of you because you do not pose a threat to anyone. Your paranoia is being fuelled by what you read on the Internet. For instance, you describe M sitting in a café beneath a TV screen, and there is an image of children crawling over an embankment with a voiceover "Are your children safe?" To conclude that this is an example of a "beaming" that was specifically directed at M and done purposely to upset her is verging on the absurd.

I received the audio recorder in the post yesterday. Unfortunately most of the tape consists of incomprehensible "white noise" – most likely background interference from the café, so it was impossible to hear the words clearly. I was able to distinguish the following fragments of conversation:

*"Testing, testing.."* (I recognised your voice) Followed by a lot of weird sounding noises like someone eating food very sloppily or slurping their drink. *"I want to see your hand...take your hand out of my pocket NOW!"* (Maria speaking as you were attempting to conceal the recorder?) *"FUCK!", "Hope they kill your children...",* *"If you think you can tell somebody like ME what to do..."* (Maria again?) I then thought I heard your voice again, becoming increasingly frustrated: *"Possession, yes it is...I'm so SICK of it, I really am...every day of my life!...been like this for over 10 years",* *"I've seen the way women are used ....never seen anything like this! They're just so jealous, completely jealous",* *"I don't think it's Maria but some fucking penis in her skin", "Does she have to channel every fucking jerk who walks in?",* etc. Followed by more unidentifiable sounds like clapping or clicking then *"They're such a pack of losers!"* (could be either of you speaking), *"...slit their throats.."* (Maria again) After a while it sounded as though some man was speaking, unless it was the TV, and one of you was heard to say quite politely *"Thank you very much"* (perhaps in response to someone handing you money?) After that Country and Western music cut in over the loudspeaker drowning out all conversation and it was impossible to distinguish what was being said by who. At one point there were sounds like a bird chirping or whistling, which could possibly have been the sound of a coffee espresso

machine. I couldn't make much sense of any of it, but it's clear that anyone overhearing this would think you were both a couple of loonies, and the few snippets of conversation I did hear - not to mention the colourful language - could be quite off-putting to other customers, which is probably why you were both thrown out of RR.

I didn't find any of it offensive, but cafe owners have to make a living and language or behaviour which is offensive or drives away their custom impacts on their business. They seem to have been quite tolerant of your presence up until now, but if they get any complaints from other customers it's inevitable they will ask you to leave. The throwout might not be permanent anyway, but even if it is, it's not the end of the world. Surely you can meet up in some other coffee bar? I forced myself to listen to the tape out of respect for you, but please, please do NOT send any more audio recordings through the post. It's a complete waste of your money as it does not prove anything - sending it to me does not serve any purpose whatsoever. A word of caution – in the scribbled note you say you have retained your own copy but I wouldn't advise giving the tape to ANYBODY to listen to as you sound almost as crazy as Maria (not so the much the actual things you say but the manic tone of voice used) and it could be used against you i.e. as a reason for committal.

I understand that you feel protective towards Maria, but I wonder if she is as vulnerable as you seem to think? I originally flagged up her petite height as being inappropriate for police work, in order to highlight the inconsistencies in her story. For instance, I don't believe she was ever a trained and armed cop. It's a bit like a guy who, for whatever reason, is disqualified from becoming a fire-fighter and can only land an admin office job. Because he works in the Fire Dept (albeit behind a desk) he knows what goes on and therefore sounds convincing to strangers who don't guess the truth. From what you have revealed about M's personality, this perfectly matches a syndrome commonly known as delusions of grandeur.

Most of M's exhibitionist-type behaviour - which has got you thrown out of libraries and almost arrested – is basically an attention-seeking device. In other words, there is a mixture of truth and fantasy in the exaggerated accounts of her past life. I suspect that she may just have worked with criminal offenders in some kind of rehabilitation program which would have brought her into close contact with law enforcement officers. The John Jay Criminal Justice college sounds like an academic institution where the students learn criminal law as part of their vocational training, and this fits in with the kind of career she probably had – as someone who would be expected to work alongside police in a support capacity.

Love,

Leigh

**From: Staples Copy Centre #1094**
**To: Leigh Ryder**
**Attachment: Scan**

In many ways youre the most unbelievable asshole IF this is you speaking and not an impostor (AND FUCK the INTERCE$PTERS)

They the fbi did the towers .. and ..those tv beamings arnt even beginning to touch it (the fronts are numerous here in loudoun county You have NO IDEA .. phone interceptions database intercepts .. hallucinations…James bond gadgetries,viral drops.. fire outbreaks, neurological remote electrical winds mood control that THEY call bipolar .and the mental health workers ARE EVIL. you have NOIDEA .. Monarch mind control started with MKULTRA.

## Psychotronic and Electromagnetic Weapons: Remote Control of the Human Nervous System

*In 1975 a neuropsychologist at the Veterans Administration Hospital in Kansas City unwittingly leaked National Security information. He published an article in American Psychologist on the influence of microwaves on living creatures' behaviour, quoting the results of an experiment described to him by his colleague Joseph C. Sharp, who was working on Pandora, a secret project of the American Navy: "By radiating themselves with these voice modulated microwaves, Sharp and Grove were readily able to hear, identify and distinguish words. The sounds heard were not unlike those emitted by persons with artificial larynxes" That this system was brought to perfection is proved by the document which appeared on the website of the U.S. Environmental Protection Agency in 1997, describing "an innovative and revolutionary technology …using both a low intensity laboratory system and a high power RF transmitter." Numerous military applications exist in areas of security and special operations. In January 2007 the*

*Washington Post wrote:* "*In 2002 the Air Force Research Laboratory patented precisely such a technology using microwaves to send words into someone's head. Where this work has gone since is unclear – the research laboratory refused to discuss it or release other material*"

*We can only stress again that the world media have avoided publishing the full scale of the progress relating to the research of the remote control of the human nervous system. Dr. Robert Becker wrote about the experiment in 1974 by J.F. Schapitz: "...the spoken word of the hypnotist may also be conveyed by modulated electromagnetic energy directly into the subconscious parts of the human brain i.e. without employing any technical devices for receiving and transcoding the messages, and without the person exposed to such influence having a chance to control the information input consciously" In one of the 4 experiments subjects were given a test of 100 questions. Later, not knowing they were being irradiated, they would be subjected to information beams suggesting the answer to the questions they had left blank, amnesia for some of their correct answers, and memory falsification for other correct answers. After 2 weeks they had to pass the test again...the results of the second test were never published. Due to his publications and his refusal to support the building of the antennae for the communication with submarines via brain frequencies, Dr. Becker lost financial support for his research, which meant an end to his scientific career.*

*In the USA at present several hundred people complaining of the remote manipulation of their nervous system are preparing a class action lawsuit against the FBI, the Department of Defence and other agencies, requesting them to release files pertaining to their persons. The Russian politician Vladimir Lopatin, who was working on the Committee on Security of the Russian State Duma, admitted that in Russia experiments on unwitting citizens are carried out. It should be understood that most of these people pass through mental hospitals. Lopatin visited the USA in 1999 as a chairman of the Military Reform Subcommittee of the USSR Supreme Soviet Committee for Issues of Defence and State Security and met with Richard Cheney. At that time he was described as the "leader of a new breed of Soviet dissidents", and then disappeared from the top ranks of Russian politicians.*

**From: Leigh Ryder**
**To: Cass Ryder**

Dear Cass,

It's a little immature and dictatorial to expect people to agree with *everything* you subscribe to, or that if they prefer the voice of sweet reason to paranoia they must be the most "unbelievable assholes" Which is apparently what I am. Afraid you cannot force people up to your viewpoint, unless you happen to be a mad General with an entire army of assassins at your disposal who are trained to liquidate anyone with an opposing viewpoint. Anyway, I Googled the Monarch programme and came up with the following (copied below with my own comments in bold):

*Monarch mind control is a form of mind control which creates a slave by utilising the human brain's trauma response of dissociation to create a form of Multiple Personality Disorder (MPD) wherein various triggers can cause the slave personality to respond to commands given by the "handler." The Monarch designation was originally applied by the U.S. Dept of Defence to a sub-program under the CIA's MKUKLTRA project. However the techniques employed extend further back in time, such as Nazi marionette programming, and can be traced even further back to various generational Satanist families amongst European nobility. The MPD state created by the Monarch programming techniques were used to isolate the personality involved in satanic rituals, who inevitably went insane... The Nazis were using electro-shock and binding to create slaves in the 40s. After WW2 some German and Italian psychologists who were working on Marionette programming were brought to the United States to continue with their research. After the original development of Monarch programming within MKULTRA, it has been adopted by other groups such as the* Illuminati *and the American entertainment industry. Since the 70s the Disney corporation has been involved heavily in Monarch programming. The most commonly used area for enslaving are Colorado, Arizona and the Coachella Valley due to the lack of surveillance in their open lands. Over 1 million Americans have had Monarch Programming applied to them.*

*Monarch programming is achieved through repeated abuse and torture, until the victim dissociates from reality into a fantasy world. When that happens somehow an alternate personality is created, and the handler can trigger this personality or "alternate" at any time. DELTA programming is used to program soldiers and patsies to carry out ritualistic murders. MP is applied when a drone is needed to carry out commands that are of a morally questionable nature. BETA programming is sex kitten programming, used to create "ultimate prostitutes", as well as using celebrities to sell sex in the media to the masses (making it look "cool and awesome" to be sexually abused) They are made to look devoid of all sexual inhibitions* **(this does rather sound like what has been happening to M, wouldn't you agree?)** *It is used heavily in the entertainment industry to create easily manipulated music stars. Many modern female musicians have performed in videos that contain Monarch mind control symbols including Madonna, Miley Cyrus, Rihanna, Beyonce, Lady Gaga, Jessie J. Britney Spears, Christina Aguilera, Katy Perry, Taylor Swift etc. Sex kitten programming aka BETA programming utilises incest or sex abuse to program a woman (or man) as a willing sexual slave. Often the handler in this context is referred to as "Daddy" or "Auntie"* **Didn't you say M refers to this unseen Liz as "Mummy"? And hasn't she also sometimes referred to drones?**

On the subject of "sex kitten" or BETA programming, have you heard of a book called *Fifty Shades of Grey* that topped the best-selling charts in 2011? It is supposed to be about women's masochistic fantasies of being tied up and abused, in other words glorifying a perverted and misogynistic attitude to women. The publicity machine went into overdrive, whipping up a media frenzy with every possible outlet from Waterstones and Smiths to all the major supermarkets being flooded with thousands of copies. It was literally being shoved in your face. According to one or two more intelligent reviewers, the book is badly written and tedious in the extreme, so I was completely mystified as to why were there so many laudatory press reviews claiming that female readers were "lapping it up." Were they really? I somehow doubt it. I mention it in this context because it's a prime example of attempted mind control, i.e. the deliberate manipulation of media channels to influence and mould the public perception, promoting the view that women enjoy being abused and enjoy reading cheap porn, when all the evidence points to the complete opposite: female readers tend to prefer 18th or 19th century novelists like Jane Austen, where there are no explicit sex scenes and the principal characters are portrayed with subtlety, wit and irony. Historical dramas with "gentle" plotlines consistently garner the highest ratings especially with female viewers, much to the frustration of producers who seem hell-bent on force-feeding the public a diet of explicit sex and violence. What's clear is that the big advertising guns are prepared to invest hundreds of thousands of dollars in over-inflated hype in order to ensure that female readers in particular absorb the message, and presumably learn to emulate the behaviour of prostitutes.

E.L. James had a previous career in television and is married to a screenwriter and director, so evidently knows a thing or two about publicity and clever marketing. Prior to *Fifty Shades of Bullshit* she wrote a sexually explicit novel called *Masters of the Universe* dealing with the same themes i.e. bondage, female submission and sadomasochistic practices. **Didn't you say Monica makes frequent reference to the "Masters of the Universe"** Below is a quote from one of your earlier emails: *But what gets me is this continual reference to the NSA and FBI. She would reiterate "masters of the universe" and when I queried her the other day she claimed that had been a reference to the CIA. Back then subject had said an awful lot "they had no right to involve me in their experiments of green cock for soldiers"* And in another email you stated: *"Quite often the subject would refer to the "masters of the universe"(who are DEFINITELY NOT the CIA) and today she has been repeating "the 18 levels" ...sounds like a secret society type thing."* Just another eerie synchronicity or is something more sinister going on here? If there is any substance whatsoever to these claims (of Monarch programming) then it seems to me that those in the know have a moral duty to get this stuff into the public domain and raise awareness. Suggestion is robbed of its power when people know it is being employed. Forewarned is forearmed.

However, I would need to be convinced by hard evidence: a lot of conspiracy theory posted on the Internet is sheer waffle. If some kind of secret occult syndicate exists - whether it be "The Ennead", "Masters of the Universe" or what have you - I'm inclined to agree with you that it does not *originate* with the FBI or the CIA, but that these agencies have been infiltrated and some of their members corrupted or subjected to a form of mind-control, in the same way that the Mafia have successfully infiltrated the police, judiciary etc. For any group seeking to increase and consolidate their powerbase then the American military and intelligence community constitutes a natural arena for their operations - in the same way that political leaders are natural targets for mind-control, and the sons and daughters of the immensely rich are targeted by drug-pushers. The CIA is not only a "control channel" through which occult groups can operate, but it also acts as a convenient scapegoat. And should any scandal arise out of their corrupt practices or criminal wrongdoing be exposed, people just blame the "evil" CIA as usual. The latter are the "fall guys" for puppetmasters behind the scenes whose agenda is, as you have suggested, all-out gender and race warfare.

But who is really calling the shots in this game of double bluff and subterfuge? Whether there is some international shadowy syndicate behind the scenes pulling the strings, I really couldn't say. The jury is still out. But based on the material you've provided, if such an organisation exists their covert agenda would appear to be antidemocratic, anti-female, and anti-Western. Which is not to say that there aren't a small number of rogue males in the West (the "Judas factor" you refer to) who wouldn't collude in this plan, somehow imagining they can run the show and control the outcome (in which belief they are probably mistaken) By definition, chaos is not amenable to any form of control. And savagery and chaos as a way of life is just not natural to the Western mindset. The developed nations have striven for centuries to achieve the complete opposite - civilisation, peace, commerce, and accountable forms of government: it just doesn't make sense that they would want the world to descend into chaos - they have far too much to lose - but when you look at the actions of global terrorists it makes perfect sense. Hence I tend to agree with you as to who the real perpetrators are, and nobody is looking in this direction because they don't want to believe in the existence of black magic. It must also be somewhat humiliating to have to acknowledge that all the technological advances in the world are only just barely keeping pace with what can be achieved by skilled occult practitioners.

As you have noted elsewhere the shamanic experience is closely akin to the mental state produced by the ingestion of psychoactive substances. In *The Stargate Conspiracy* the authors mention a book published by the Swiss anthropologist Jeremy Narby, which explores shamanism amongst the Peruvian Amazonian tribes and the visions/information accessed during trances induced by the natural hallucinogenic substance called *ayahuasca*. He was impressed by their botanical knowledge and medicinal use of rare plants, especially after they cured a long-standing back problem which European doctors had been unable to treat. What was interesting about his research was his observation that certain women are chosen to sit with the male shamans or *ayahuasqueros* during their out-of-body travel whilst under the influence of the drug: the women accompany them to other realms and help them to remember what took place after their return to normal consciousness, but the point to note is that the women are able to do this <u>without</u> taking *ayahuasca*. Which does seem to indicate that women's natural psychic faculties are more evolved than men's. To compensate for this deficiency, men have developed an elaborate system for exploring the paranormal domain, which is based on a combination of chemical aids (hallucinogenic drugs) and technological gadgetry which women have no need of. This might explain some of their resentment of women i.e. not only can the female reproduce with or without the participation of the male (through parthenogenesis) she is also able to enter into the invisible realms by means of her own inbuilt brain chemistry or "stargate". Although men may have convinced themselves they are superior to women on a conscious level, their subconscious – which is older and far wiser – tells them otherwise.

With respect to the attachment on psychotronic weaponry I am aware that such classified projects exist and have long suspected that peoples' thought processes are being interfered with by suggestions/commands being somehow implanted (refer to my earlier emails relating to the criminally insane and the "voices" they hear directing them to kill or maim) But it doesn't necessarily follow that these remote technologies have been applied to you or Monica. As for her weird "electronic-sounding" utterances you admit that *"No-one sees it or hears it except me"* and therein lies the problem. It's impossible to disentangle the psyche from the psychic - particularly when the psyche in question is very disturbed - and it is equally difficult to separate the brain from certain types of technological interference since electromagnetic impulses are a common component of both. People who are sensitive to electromagnetic (elm) pollution experience hallucinations and all manner of sensations, which they interpret as paranormal. The subjective experiences are real enough but that doesn't mean there is a conscious directing intelligence behind them or a sinister intent to control: the various well-documented effects on the human organism and brain are often just an unfortunate by-product of modern telecommunications, and not necessarily evidence of "etheric crime". You have a tendency to confuse vivid nightmares with OBEs or occult attacks: nightmares often incorporate material people have read about or imagery from films they have recently watched or been affected by. Your own mind supplied the "props" or scenery for the resulting nightmare. It is self-evident that a homeless female sleeping rough will be in fear of an imminent physical attack, and this will give rise to the type of nightmare you had recently about the psychopath clinging to your back. Interestingly, the dream also presented an image of you pursuing the guy in order to "get" him, which I interpret to mean that on a subconscious level you do not really see yourself as powerless victim.

The real world is full of complex interrelationships which many of us find incomprehensible, but this is often due to our limited understanding. Sometimes it's wiser to just accept that there are things you do not understand, to admit "I don't really know what's going on here, I am a little puzzled but will keep an open mind" rather than to attempt to offer pseudo-explanations. Although some conspiracy theories are backed up by credible evidence, others are deliberate misinformation (as you yourself suggest) just plain wacko, or the paranoid speculations of gullible people who swallow literally EVERYTHING they read or hear. It's a question of sifting through all the garbage in order to arrive at the truth. I try to provide that balance but in the process I continually run the risk of alienating you if I offer an alternative perspective, or one that you refuse to accept because it doesn't fit in with your preconceptions. That's a risk I have to take - the risk of alienating you - because I believe it is VITAL that someone challenges some of your crazier beliefs, otherwise you are likely to spiral into a frightening and chaotic inner world which is completely divorced from reality. People very much manufacture their own reality and create their own mental prisons.

In connection with her clinical experience in treating patients with psychic problems, Dion Fortune observed: *"Let it never be forgotten that emotions and magnetism are, for all practical purposes, synonymous terms in magic"* She points out that the mind cannot control matter by direct action but the etheric double is the key here, constituting the link between mind and matter: according to occult wisdom, the energy out of which the etheric double is composed is known as elemental or earth energy. This accords with your belief that heightened emotion, such as desire, fear or "panic states" produces the gateway by which extraneous imagery can be introduced. Where energy cannot flow in a natural circuit, this causes a leakage of magnetism or vital force that is dangerous: *"from the magnetism or energy discharged, certain elemental forms are built up"* (she actually wrote a book called *The Circuit of Force* which I have not read) Unless energy can flow in a rhythmic ebb and flow - like the tides - it will become unbalanced, which leads to all kinds of problems ranging from listlessness and depression to the formation of various complexes, neuroses, and psychoses. Wilhelm Reich also stressed that the free flow of this force (which he termed "orgone energy") needs to be uninhibited if both the body and psyche are to remain healthy. So perhaps the next time you experience an "enforced bioelectrical" you should not attempt to block it or fight it, as it is entirely possible that these physiological states are the organism's attempt to re-balance the life-force so as to bring the psyche into equilibrium. They may represent the regenerative and healing powers of the human subconscious, which recognises that something is "out of kilter" and needs re-balancing.

I think it is now time to produce some sort of conclusion to your Memoire so that I can get the MS off to a publisher. Take care of yourself.

Leigh

**From: Staples Copy Centre**
**To: Leigh Ryder**
**Subject: Throwout**

We just got permanently thrown out of the library. When I pointed out Shadowman has no right to intimidate people this way (leaning across Monica's desk) he tried to throw a heavy metal box at me. I called the cops to complain about his threatening behaviour. He basically lied to the cops (he doesn't work for the NSA, he just works for the county library) I can't go back there and now have to pay $5 for 3 mins of email usage via commercial office stores. I can't email as frequently as before. Today the writer really lost it and shouted out loud in the early dawn while making her way to McDonalds "They wank in her body". The writer now has a very suspect aura and persona. They're not going to employ me anywhere in this area – not even for a day – and I need cash to get out. I put up a poster yesterday "any quarters gratefully accepted to assist another homeless woman with" and built a cardboard mailbox they were supposed to slot the money into, and got 20 dollars within an hour, though I've never done this in the past and don't like to.

I sleep in different places every nite in greenbelt areas... writer had to clear cobwebs from her tent today in disgust and woke up with bites from loads of deer mites despite Deet spray. I HATE INSECTS. Today as I'm leaving a park a man tries to hold up a fish in my face he's just gotten from a stream, he made me feel sick...oh and I'm so sick of risking my life and walking with these weirdos. They embrace the criminals, the jerks, the whores, the slobs and abusers. Will send a conclusion in the next attachment but writer's conclusions so far is that the CIA involuntarily contacted "The Nine" when involved in psi/parapsychology research. Western intelligence and global secret societies got together, using private funding and bases, with the complicity of an Arabic oil-centred interest to formulate a planned agenda. These covert plans stink of the Vatican, Catholic men mainly, and evangelists… don't forget Mecca and fatso Saudis. In the US they're covertly undoing anything that's overtly liberal…America specialises in wearing the veil of the "good guy" They have a problem with people who are more free, more so than with those who are more affluent. At current rates in the not too distant future the coverts will be using a genocidal tool angled at people who don't cooperate with the mainstream system. Nowadays companies can't just dump nuclear waste in people's neighbourhoods, so people should be protected against REM process interference assaults, but the prats are obsessed with keeping it classified. They can communicate via the unconscious through an energy-based sympathy wavelength, and influence and control others through PA systems and peoples' voice boxes (using a subtle indoctrination combined with censorship of nonconformist thoughts and behaviours)

It's the writer's theory that a lot of the information about military technological-based mind control is deliberate disinformation propagated to cover up what is really going on. But back to blacks and whites...they need to get away from one another…recognise how much they can't stand one another, recognise the need for race and gender separation and then try and survive. Realise globalisation is a gimmick and a LIE, then try to cooperate in ways that are not dependent on modern man's science and his garbage…his emotional wavelengths that are so command-orientated. But let's not keep implicating men ...how about that wallet/vagina and the expectation of capital, whether it's a silver bracelet or a 10-bedroomed mansion? As for the wife, the matriarch, the goddess consort, it's about wealth and her progeny. The world will always be full of women like that, and she owns this earth. He can't adore her enough, and the cavity-less satellite around her "home", her territory. Women have no right to be obsessed with their egoism when they don't achieve that much, any more than one is entitled to a medal when they don't win the race. The blunt conclusion that the FBI or CIA put *brujos* or whatever the African equivalent is on payrolls, who were given the green light to hound gays, singles, or "nice guys" who aren't interested in forcing women or masquerading as mister macho every other minute. The "bully" today is definitely in the south, if only through being more numerous (the Northern races being on borrowed time) and moreover the southern races seem to be the ones with the invisible energy weaponry (the poor man's weaponry) The south is coming up but rodents and insects are for them to inherit.

Cass

**From: Leigh**
**To: Donna**
**Subject: Have You Seen My Sister**
**Date: 07/03/16**

Dear Donna,

You haven't heard from me before, but I made a note of your email address during correspondence with my younger sister Cass Ryder (who has been homeless for almost 20 years) It's a long story, but we only got in touch in 2013 when she contacted my cousins in Wales. Prior to that I had absolutely no way of contacting her, and it was my dearest wish come true to find out she was still alive. I reside in the UK, and have been desperately trying to persuade her to come back to the UK but she cannot bring herself to "walk away" from another homeless woman she met in a shelter called Monica with severe mental issues and who apparently has now been allocated a PSH apartment. Cass turned down the offer of an apartment due to her paranoia about being "watched" and her fear of being sedated with chemical prescriptions against her will: she has suffered much hardship over the years, and not surprisingly, doesn't trust many people.

Unfortunately, my own circumstances do not permit me to travel to the USA at present, but I am prepared to fully fund her flight back to the UK - where I can ensure she has a roof over her head. She would obviously need to get her passport reinstated, as it was stolen years ago due to her precarious lifestyle. The reason I am writing is to ask you whether you have heard from her recently, and whether you know if she is OK. We have been in fairly regular communication up until about a month ago, since when I have heard nothing. I know she is sleeping rough in a tent, and am naturally worried sick about her. Apart from the cold weather and sub-zero temperatures, as a solitary female she is extremely vulnerable to attack. She has got to be the most courageous and resilient person I have ever met to have survived for so long on her own as a homeless woman, but I fear something might have happened to her. Do you know if she is alright, and where she is? Sorry to trouble you in this manner, but I don't know who else to turn to, and she has mentioned you as being the most decent and caring of all the social workers she has dealings with

Leigh Ryder

**From: Donna**
**To: Leigh**

Thank you so much for contacting me Leigh. Your sister has told me about you and she has the greatest respect and admiration for you. I am out of the office today but now that I know you've lost contact with her I'm going to start putting out the word we need to find her. It's not unusual for her to stay away sometimes over a month at a time. She contacts me when she needs to talk and then another couple months go by. At least she now has her SSI income to get a room if she needs it. Your sister is very special. I feel honored that she has told you about me. Typing on my phone is not easy but I wanted to let you know I received your message and hear your concerns. As soon as I have a confirmed siting I will email you. Due to HIPPA privacy laws I will only refer to her as "your sister" and not use her first name. I will also have her contact you and offer to help with the passport replacement.

Please let me know if you hear from her and I will as well. Donna.

**From: Leigh**
**To: Donna**

Many thanks for your kind and prompt response. That means a lot to me that someone out there cares for her welfare. I guess we can only wait until we hear something. Of course I will let you know if I hear from her before you.

Leigh

**From: Donna**
**To: Leigh**

I talked with the Leesburg Police. One of the female officers actually gave her a ride to the grocery store about one week ago. She is having problems with her foot but otherwise ok. The officer was very kind and is going to check on her today. It was a relief to hear she was not hurt or sick and unable to get help. I now have a good idea where she's been camping. I asked the officer to let her know we're concerned. Will let you know when I talk to her. Thanks again for reaching out. Donna.

**From: Leigh**
**To: Donna**

I'm very grateful to you for having taken the trouble to find this out. She did mention something about her foot, but tends to be very stoical about any medical problems so it makes sense that if her foot is causing her pain she would be unable to get to a public Internet service. How kind of the police officer to give her a ride, as it must be difficult to walk miles to a grocery store in her present condition: she is now in her 50s and not getting any younger (her birthday is coming up soon in March) Once again, thanks for your concern.

Leigh

**From: Donna**
**To: Leigh**
**Date: 08/03/16**

Good morning Leigh,
If you would like, I can attempt to encourage her to return to the UK. Your sister as I'm sure you're aware, is a very strong woman and she doesn't like to feel the idea of someone telling her what she "needs" to do. I've always just been there to listen and allow her to vent her frustrations. After about four stop and starts, she finally allowed me to follow through with getting her SSI payments. It took almost 8 years of short contacts, sometimes months apart. I've never met anyone as strong and determined. She is a survivor but getting older like the rest of us. I always remember her birthday because mine is in the same month. I am hoping she got the message yesterday and will come by to see me. I let the officer know if she only contacts me to set up some regular times and days, I can take her to get groceries and supplies. I just wanted to reassure you I will do everything I can on this end and if she says she wants to go to the UK, I'll help make that happen. It's so good to know she would have someone to receive her should she chose to go. Family is so important to us all.
Have a wonderful day,
Donna

**From: Leigh**
**To: Donna**

Dear Donna,

You are absolutely right in that she is very strong-willed. I agree she cannot be forced to do anything she doesn't want to do, so I use gentle persuasion. I have learned to tread carefully as it's a fine line between a genuine desire to help and what she could perceive as unwarranted interference: you must by now be aware that she is extremely paranoid, but I try to avoid the term schizophrenic as she has never been officially diagnosed and this sends her into a panic. As far as I can ascertain her chief objection to returning to the UK up until now has been her desire to help this other person Monica (who I understand has been diagnosed with lupus and suffers from some kind of aggressive conversational disorder which makes members of the public uncomfortable), but I have pointed out numerous times she is simply not in a position to help anyone else, a fact she finds difficult to accept. There is no shame whatsoever in being homeless - it can happen to anyone - but when she found herself destitute on the streets she did not tell anyone in the family out of a misplaced sense of pride, which meant that none of us could help her or trace her whereabouts. Unfortunately she is the kind of person who will give everything she has to others, and this is one reason why she is in this predicament. She once broke off in the middle of an email saying she had to rush off to rescue a stray cat! She continues to put other peoples' interests before her own, and you could say her innate generosity has been her biggest downfall.

With respect to the passport situation, I'm sure she no longer possesses vital ID documents like her birth certificate, but I forwarded personal information concerning our parents' birth dates and marriage in an attachment to her last year, in the hope that this would assist with getting her passport reinstated. The bureaucracy involved is likely to be very daunting for someone in her circumstances, and she would obviously need help in guiding her through the application process and filling in the necessary forms. I am unfamiliar with the process which could take months - though I may be wrong and it could possibly be fast-tracked in a matter of weeks – but I am prepared to pay for all the necessary admin fees: she would probably have to request a File Search, which is a request in writing that a previous passport record be verified in order to establish U.S. citizenship (costing $150) My difficulty is that I am based over here thousands of miles away, whereas the application has to be made on U.S. soil and I expect she would have to attend one or more personal interviews explaining her unique circumstances. Whatever the case, I don't have the right contacts and don't know which government department she needs to go through. None of this is really your responsibility, and I realise it's not fair to ask you to get involved but I have come to the conclusion that the only way to extricate her from her nightmarish existence is to get her back here, where I am in a position to provide concrete and practical support on a permanent basis. It really is the best solution to her problems, but as you rightly say she needs to understand this herself and consent to let us help her. She has clearly been damaged by her traumatic experiences, but this is a real opportunity to turn her life around. Having finally found her after so many years of searching and heartbreak I am terrified that she might vanish off the radar again.

It's likely she has lost her permanent UK residency status - an added complication which caused her a great deal of anxiety and prevented her from attempting to return to the UK years ago when she was given false and misleading information by library personnel. However, this is an issue I could address myself far more easily once she is over here, by making the appropriate enquiries and tracing her original National Insurance No (the British equivalent to an American social security number) Our mother was English and my sister all of her secondary education in this country so I should be able to sort this out, even if it takes some time. I am prepared to fund her airfare and all travel expenses, and would ensure she is personally met at the airport upon arrival. I am certainly willing to accommodate her in such a way that she can retain a measure of independence. From what I can gather, Monica does not care to see her or even speak to her now that she has her own apartment, so my sister is now very much on her own again, and I view this as a matter of life and death. I honestly do not see how she can continue to survive sleeping rough on the streets as her physical health breaks down. I don't think she quite grasps the urgency as her mental focus is elsewhere, but I foresee a downward spiral and complete mental disintegration if we don't rescue her soon. Yes, she is a true survivor but I never lose sight of the fact that she is also extremely vulnerable, and I dread the thought of her ending up as some nameless "Jane Doe" on a mortuary slab - it gives me nightmares.

Anyway, that's enough for now as I feel I've taken up enough of your time, and you must have a full and busy work schedule with many other clients apart from my sister.

Leigh

**From: Donna**
**To: Leigh**

Hi Leigh,
Thank you so much for the background and your perspective. This will all be very helpful information should she accept my help in replacing her ID and eventually returning home. I also tread carefully and never pressure her to do anything she doesn't want. I can't say anything about her "friend" due to privacy which I'm sure you can understand. I am very aware of the relationship and it's complexities. I'm going out this afternoon to see if I can find her. I will share with her your willingness to help and send you a quick email when I make contact.
Warmest regards,
Donna

**From: Donna**
**To: Leigh**
**Date: 11/03/16**

Hi Leigh,
I'm just checking to see if you've heard from your sister? I still haven't heard anything new and went into the woods to look for her today. I think I've located the spot. She has neatly bagged up trash and secured it with a log and cayenne pepper to keep the animals away. Very smart! Other than the two bags I saw no sign of her being there. As in the past, I imagine she pulls up camp every morning and doesn't set up again until night. I was accompanied by a Leesburg Police officer. He stated he would be working all weekend and would be on the lookout for her. I left her a written message under the log by the two bags so hopefully she'll get it and make contact. Hope you've heard from her. Please let me know if you have.
Best wishes, Donna.

**From: Leigh**
**To: Donna**

Hi Donna,

No, I haven't heard from her and am getting increasingly uneasy. It's unusual for her to go this long without emailing me. She has always had concerns about her personal security - one of the reasons she has survived this long - and if she thinks someone has "tracked" her to her location she is likely to move on. I'm sorry to say that some of her encounters with cops in the past have not always been friendly, despite the obvious good intentions of the ones you are in contact with. With respect to shelters she avoids these places because both she and her friend found them very intimidating and hostile, and women do not feel safe. It's undeniable that some men prey upon the females, and she is therefore constantly looking over her shoulder. She always preferred to camp on her own away from prying eyes but as M refused to sleep in a tent they used to catch the late night bus to the shelters which are inconveniently situated out of town, and these buses were packed with "loud partying men" (at least this is now she described it to me in her writing) They also both experienced the mysterious loss of their personal possessions which were supposed to be kept safe by the staff who supervise these shelters. For all these reasons, she is wary of most authority figures and gives them a wide berth.

I am hoping that if she is well enough to move her possessions to a new location - despite the pain and discomfort in her foot - then at least she hasn't succumbed to sepsis or something life-threatening. But I would imagine that someone who is homeless and in receipt of foodstamps should be entitled to free medical treatment (?) so it might be an idea if she had her feet thoroughly checked out. Is there any reason why she would not have been able to get to an Internet facility to email me - is the weather there very severe at the moment? The reason I contacted you was because I haven't heard anything at all from her and my emails have gone unanswered, which is why I am so worried. Please let me know if you make contact with her, and I will of course let you know immediately if I hear anything.

Thank you for all your efforts,

Leigh

**From: Donna**
**To: Leigh**
**Date: 11/03/16**

Hi Leigh,

I'm sorry to worry you further. I'm sure you would have let me know if you heard something. I have heard the same concerns about the shelters and some of law enforcement from her in the past. At this point I have people from all over this county looking out for her. It is not unlike her to go for months without contacting me. In the past she has been seen over an hour away from here, in all directions. I'm concerned but like I've said, it isn't unheard of for her to head out of the area for a while.

Yes, absolutely I will get her medical care any time she wants it. I have tried to talk her into going for at least a check-up but she isn't trusting of medical professionals either. The female officer who gave her a ride to the grocery store stated she offered to take her to the emergency room when she brought up her foot hurting. She stated your sister declined, that she'd researched it and was treating it through natural methods. That sounds very much like our latest discussion. She recently dropped me off some info on natural medicine for mental health issues about one month ago while I was out of the office.

In terms of internet access, she's had problems at two local libraries and hasn't returned to them. She was going quite a distance to another libraries computers for checking email the last time we talked. Please don't think I'm minimizing your concerns. I would be at my wits end if it were my sister so far away and so vulnerable. I will check my email over the weekend and will forward any word I might get without delay.
Donna

**From Leigh**
**To: Donna**
**Date: 12/03/16**

Dear Donna,

Thanks again. I am reassured that you are doing all you can above and beyond the call of duty. I may be worrying unduly as I am aware she does go for some time without communicating with health professionals unless she has a special concern, but she has been in the habit of regularly emailing me (literally every week, sometimes more frequently) even if it's just a form of talking to herself, or venting her frustration. I am now concerned I may have unwittingly made things worse, because the involvement of others in looking for her - particularly law enforcement officers - may have triggered an attack of paranoia and caused her to bolt like a frightened animal or hunted fugitive. It is sometimes so hard to make her see that people have her best interests at heart when she is apt to attribute sinister motives to the most innocent occurrences and chance remarks.

I know all about the "throwouts" from Sterling and Leesburg libraries, and I received this news with a sinking heart because public libraries are a safe haven for the homeless - not only as a refuge from the cold but as somewhere they have free access to Internet facilities. What I am about to say here concerns her "friend" so I will mention no names in order to protect her privacy, but I am almost 100% sure that my sister would not have been banned had she been on her own. She typically keeps a very low profile in public, and the very last thing she wants is to draw attention to herself. I do not know the full nature of her friend's mental disorder, but there is ample evidence in my sister's factual narration that the former's loud comments and whispering in public places tend to be quite offensive, and are often sadistic in nature. I am not attributing any blame here, as she probably has very little control over this and is completely unaware of what she is saying, but according to my sister an Afro-American male librarian began to "stalk" them, deliberately sitting up close etc. Obviously I don't know exactly what transpired, but I was told the librarian tried to "throw a heavy metal box" at them. My sister predictably sprang to her friend's defence, telling him his behaviour was "threatening", and called the police. The disturbance resulted in their both being permanently banned. I imagine something similar happened at Sterling 2-3 years ago when they were frog-marched out of the library.

Although I am glad my sister found a companion, in many ways the "friendship" has proved toxic for her, and I was concerned that she would be arrested by virtue of her continued association with someone whose behaviour is often misconstrued. Many members of the general public simply do not understand mental illness, and react with fear and hostility instead of compassion. My sister tends to be very protective towards those she perceives as underdogs and liberally shares her foodstamps/cash with this friend, when she scarcely has enough to meet her own needs.

Leigh

**From: Leigh**
**To: Donna**
**Date: 15/03/16**
**Subject: Still Nothing**

Dear Donna,

Still haven't heard a thing. Are you sure the trash bags and cayenne pepper you saw were left by my sister, or could they have been left by some other homeless person sleeping in the woods? At any rate, if it *was* her she did not return to the camp or she would have responded to the note you left. I am trying hard to convince myself that there is a good reason why she has not been in communication with anyone e.g. she may have travelled some distance from where it is impossible to access an Internet facility without transport. However, when she has been unable to use a library service before she has still been able to communicate with me via a commercial print service such as Staples copy centre.

Two possible avenues of enquiry suggest themselves:

1) Would there be any point on asking her friend M whether she has seen my sister recently? Of course the latter may not be *compos mentis* enough to provide reliable answers, since she apparently confuses my sister with other people she has known in the past, namely someone called "Claudine" (?) Despite this, my sister has always remained in intermittent contact with her, if only to assist with cash or groceries

2) Is there any way the issuing authorities can check to see when her last SSI payment was cashed, or when the next one is due? This should give us an idea as to her whereabouts. If it remains uncashed then this would be cause for worry, as she has no other source of income.

I can't help imagining the worst, for instance that she might be lying in some remote spot with a broken leg, or that something else may have happened to her. It seems to me that if various people in the county are keeping a lookout for her she should have been spotted by now, as she is probably a familiar figure to local law enforcement.

Leigh

**From: Donna**
**To: Leigh**
**Date: 15/03/16**

Hi Leigh,

I'm so sorry I know this is hard for you. I can't imagine the worry.

It is possible she is out of this area. You are correct, she is well known in this community and so many people are on the lookout for her. The Leesburg Police assigned a detective and they put out a bulletin to the officers only, requesting anyone seeing her to contact me by my work cell. I check it even in the weekends and evenings but nothing. They talked about putting a notice out for the public but I didn't think that was a good idea yet. She was last seen on 3/5 when the officer gave her a ride to Food Lion, so it hasn't even been two full weeks even though it's been longer since you or I have had contact. I don't want her to feel "hunted" just that we're concerned about her welfare. The police asked if she has a history of depression or if I think she's at risk of suicide. Unless you've heard differently, I told them she's never expressed any thoughts of suicide. Yesterday I did contact the detective to see if they could reach out to area hospitals to see if she was or had been there. Because of privacy regulations, the hospital wouldn't give me that info. I already had my colleague talk to M. She hasn't seen her in several weeks.

I've been thinking about some of our later conversations, in January 2016. She was talking then about leaving this area, the only thing holding her here was her feeling she needed to help her "friend." At that time I asked her if she would please leave me some kind of message if she chooses to leave and she agreed. She receives her SSI money through an automatic deposit to a debit card so she can access the

funds from anywhere. If I remember correctly she got her deposits between the 3$^{rd}$-10$^{th}$ of each month. I can try to find out if there's any activity. If not me maybe the detective can? I won't be able to go into the woods today. I have back to back clients until after dark but I will tomorrow. It's been raining the last few days but tomorrow is supposed to be better.
I will let you know just as soon as I hear something.
Your sister is a survivor and I'm going to try to stay optimistic.
Thanks for staying in touch.
Donna

**From: Donna**
**To: Leigh**
**Date: 15/03/16**

I just got a call from an officer and he is with her at Food Lion! I'm heading over to see how she is and what's been happening.
I'll have her get in touch with you. Whew!!

**From: Donna**
**To: Leigh**
**Date: 15/03/16**

Hi Leigh,
I can't write for long. Have a client waiting but wanted to reassure you she is safe.
She said to tell you she'd be in touch toward the end of the month. She apologized for worrying everyone and wasn't upset at all. I took her on an errand and then back to where she's staying. We made an arrangement to go grocery shopping next Tues and she gave me permission to come out and check on her whenever.
Still has the same concerns and sense of loyalty to her friend.
I really appreciate that she has such a caring sister. I could tell it meant a lot to her when I shared how concerned you were.
Stay in touch,
Donna

**From: Leigh**
**To: Donna**
**Date: 16/03/16**

Dear Donna,

I am enormously relieved and very grateful for everything you've done. I feel reassured that there are people looking out for her. Feel free to contact me at any time you need to.

Kind regards,

Leigh

**From: Cass Ryder**
**To: Leigh Ryder**
**Subject: Ice storm**

Sorry, but I couldn't move around much. My foot isn't being allowed to heal, nor shoulder or back ..my left chest area was recently bruised by accidentally falling on a self-made crutch and I am going to have to keep on moving. Just got death threatened again. I'm on the run metaphorically speaking ..it's related to the incident formerly mentioned and the bastard (s) returned and repeated symbolically with white toilet tissue exactly what they had done before (alias the really offensive object) And of course I haven't been to the woodlot crash site for the last month. The first incident was aimed at me. I'm in another town... I'm not scared but I'm not going back to any place I've ever been and my back doesn't need walking around with a weight. SICK to death of it. Maybe it's just a trespass threat, the point is if it's one of the 'guys on the road' there's real concern because they are almost always ethnic and operate in gangs (I would never keep a tent in one spot because I couldn't move quickly) Thank god it's nearly Spring.

On Valentine's day I wander out in an ice storm, barely able to walk, and a Polish woman stops. She and her little daughter give me a ride to my crash site, but on the second ride round the Shell station a black man turns and looks right into the SUV with a sort of sinister mask-like grin. They drop me off for a lunch at Roy Rogers and later drop off warm clothes and a sleeping bag and a rain tarp (it had holes in it and was threadbare) and asks me if there is anything else I would like. I can hardly walk or move, and I try to point out that if it rains it will be bad news and I could do with a new tarp: my tent site is further away now and I can't even walk to it. She and her 10-year old daughter then disappear and completely ignores my comment "thanks, but this tarp is hopeless" In retrospect I don't think she heard me. She also donated body warmers and a "toe-warmer" which had solidified to stone the next morning (I forgot to take one out from under my sock) and both feet were frostbitten and swollen.

I lay there for 13 days and nights. The occult was going on and taking full advantage of my vulnerability. During that period I had an OBE and something tried to force the writer to do a blowjob on a white male musician who is wailing into a microphone. Writer screams and manages to get back inside her body. She later hears an aristocratic voice say *"Your ordeal is not yet over, Miss Ryder"*. It rained for 2 days and 2 nights ON TOP OF HER (but she survived thanks to a plastic drop cloth) with huge winds blowing straight in her face as she lay on the woodlot ground. She was concerned they might try and take off her toes if she sought hospital help for the frostbite. The writer is not to be blamed for not wanting hospital help. In fact they probably would have thrown her out after a short amount of time because she has no insurance. The defrost pain and strain lasted on and off for about a week intermittently during that 2 month period. After the accident when I fell off a self-made crutch, I pulled an abductor muscle and couldn't move an inch on the pavement. Later the writer has a dream about being in a farmhouse in Maine she once lived in, with river waters rising, and the fear of damp, invasion of water and mould, then this foul family come in and take over, and she's trying to get them out…

I'm not in a bad mood, it's just one more day. As for physiological dysfunctioning and possible mind transference mechanisms I believe it's going on …for example the shit occurred the morning after the night I broke out loud seriously criticising the US system saying I hated it etc. and it seemed like an answer to that (take your shit and go) but does something have the capability to hear me speak out loud to myself? I was just heavily surveilled whilst stalking the shopping aisles. I once shouted at the top of my lungs in Florida "I just GET STRONGER" and yes, I'll devise something if I have to, like I did before. But thank you a lot and sincerely for the help you provided over the last two years. I never blamed any one I had once known for why I have been homeless for 20 years, and I can't begin to say what we would have done without the kindness of strangers. Of course I care about all of you in a remote sort of way and of course NONE OF YOU are WHY I'm homeless because that was going on, the blaming of the family. The writer has described most of the social workers as shits, though the woman right now dealing with the homeless in the county is not such an awful person, and what looks like a conspiracy might be a compassion. Some of the surveillance of the writer and subject might possibly be with benign intent, writer couldn't say. Thanks for the generous moneygram (I just delivered half of it to M and will give her the rest on Saturday her birthday)

Cass

**From: Leigh Ryder**
**To: Cass Ryder**

Jesus wept. I can't tell you how relieved I am that you're alright but could some of this suffering have been avoided? I realise there is no way it is going to be pleasant or comfortable sleeping rough in harsh weather conditions, but it didn't need to be quite so bad if you'd followed my advice about getting a new waterproof tent with a sewn in groundsheet, a goosedown sleeping bag, warm socks etc. at least you would have been warm and dry and might have avoided frostbite. You are not going to survive another winter if you carry on like this. I'm beginning to wonder whether you have some kind of unconscious death wish, which is why you keep giving most of your cash to M whilst neglecting your own far more pressing needs. Did I understand you correctly in that you intend to give Monica EVERYTHING we have sent you? After letting me know that you are so destitute you have resorted to begging we manage to scrape together another $450 in an effort to help you out, only to be told you are giving it all to her. Every single penny? Are you out of your mind? Treating her on her birthday is understandable, but to hand it all over is just….well, words fail me. I first re-established contact with you in March 2013, and I estimate that during that time we have probably sent you between £4000 - £5000 and I have sent you literally hundreds of emails advising you what you should do. It is now May 2016 and NOTHING HAS CHANGED. If anything, your situation has worsened since you are now forced to sleep out on your own, and have to resort to expensive commercial offices to communicate since you've been banned from using two public libraries.

I have tried so very hard to understand you, but I almost have to admit to defeat. It seems you are under some compulsion to immediately throw away or to reject anything that is given to you. I suppose one definition of a mad person is someone who lacks all sense of proportion, and the choices you have made and continue to make are those of someone on a path of self-destruction. *Fugue* is the psychiatric term meaning a flight from one's identity. If you ever do manage to unshackle yourself from the "emotional handcuffs" I will still be here. But right now I'm still stunned by the implications and am fearful for your future. At some point you have to take responsibility for your actions, and to accept that if this is what you choose to do then that choice is going to have very severe consequences for you. Your heart wrenching account of how you spent those 2 winter months shows just what those consequences were. Nobody is forcing you to live like this, like a feral stray dog or a hunted animal. An injured animal living in the wild does not survive for very long, and it seems you are now unable to walk properly. It's unlikely these injuries will heal by themselves, but you don't need to fear going into hospital. Medical staff would not "take off your toes" unless the frostbite was life-threatening and gangrene had set in. It's more likely that they would just bathe and put sterile bandages on your feet and give you a course of antibiotics to knock out any infection, and to enable the skin tissue to recover. Accepting medical treatment doesn't commit you to anything long term, and once you're well then you don't need to go near a hospital again.

The nightmare you describe as an OBE about the musician was clearly influenced by my book report I sent on Alex Constantine's *Covert War on Rock*. Let's face it, a lot of Constantine's writing is nightmare-inducing, so it's hardly surprising your subconscious utilised this material. And as for the other dream about being in a farmhouse with river waters rising and the "foul family trying to take over" was probably your subconscious interpretation of the foul weather you were desperately trying to keep off, and a manifestation of your anxiety about lying out in the rain, being soaked underneath a hole-ridden tarpaulin. Most dreams and nightmares derive from actual circumstances or material you've recently read or been affected by: your subconscious supplies the imagery and content. I doubt whether there were any "occult forces taking advantage of your vulnerability". Your own psyche is perfectly capable of making its own little inhouse movies, utilising whatever stimuli it has to work with. For instance, if the weather had been very hot and dry you might have dreamed about being lost in a parched desert instead of rising river waters. Remember that dreams are always symbolic; that is how the subconscious works, and you don't need to keep frightening yourself by imagining that these nightmares are occult in origin.

If the strains in your feet and back, and the pulled muscle in your thigh get to the point where they prevent you from being mobile you may end up being hospitalised whether you like it or not. If you value your independence then it makes sense to accept whatever medical help is on offer. Quality of life is impossible without good physical health. Surely that should be obvious. Forget the conspiracy theories, forget hounding the social workers about Monica's symptoms (no wonder they are starting to avoid you as they probably view you as some kind of obsessive monomaniac, constantly poking your nose into what doesn't concern you) and instead focus on what is truly important. Who her family is or was, whether she is a raving nutcase or an alien from outer space DOESN'T MATTER, OK? Get your priorities right: the only thing that matters right now is you, and how you are going to survive. For your own safety, try to refrain from saying hostile things about people aloud, as you will only provoke more attacks. Verbal attacks can easily escalate into physical attacks, and you must avoid further injury at all costs. According to Hindu myth there is a river which must be crossed before heaven is reached. Everyone has to find his or her own way across to the far shore. For some it is an easy and quick crossing, for others it is a slow and painful struggle to reach the other side, but everyone gets home in the end.

Love,

Leigh

Writer steps onto the celebrated metro silver line coming out of the Clara tunnel that links the metro exit with the Loudoun county bus transit garage. Adjacent to her on the crowded train are a bunch of people, mainly men, who sound like they're talking Russian. In the middle of them is a woman who looks like she could have been the Subject. She smiles and laughs at what one of them says, obviously her husband. One imagines her home is somewhere in a suburb, maybe has 2 children, is college educated and healthy, has had no problems in her life. Writer has to pause to reflect for a minute. This could have been the subject, and having once seen her nice side and her higher self, the writer reflects what potentially positive qualities she had … a good conversationalist, a good singer and dancer, capable of being sensitive and perceptive, she would also have made a good mother. And reflected on how the powers that be punished certain people - the non-procreators and non-conformists - leading up to really disturbing assaults and trauma exposures to an excessive degree, but why? And how they might have related to her differently had she gone down a conformist route.

The disturbing thought (as the whole thing was unravelling before her eyes) was that it all seems designed… like holding up a patronizing mocking mirror to women who didn't allow themselves to be stewarded into marriage, who are then held up as examples of failures. But it does seem like she's had an abnormally hard life from college years up, and that Society dealt her a really harsh "kick up the butt" card. Meanwhile the above metro journey seems to have been purposely planted in the context of references the writer had earlier made to do with the silver line opening up into the county region.

One thing the writer noticed about Americans is very few of them travel, although she realizes this patriotism wavelength is normal on earth. And people are really influenced by the dominant energy wavelength of their region to the point of being brainwashed. The subject would sometimes say "I've been walking away from people my whole life, people have been walking away from me" or "let me lie in the bed they make" and exuded a deep cynicism (which the writer also experienced) based on a kind of drawn out clandestine persecution that goes way beyond the system, backed up by a major collective of people and its non-capability to confront its culpability. It's a psychic defence ploy like fortifying a castle to keep out the misfits and the alternatives. It's also a citizenry attack, in the same way people in pre-perestroika Russia were KGB mind-controlled and got jailed for their politically dissident views. They both sought to put the blame for their problems onto a minority who possibly did have the answer. Modern man has set it up for a minority of single childless non-conformer types to always be in the company of biological family types, or to have to communicate in a petty tension-strapped way when it's actually about PRIVACY and independence. Made worse by the total idiocy and vulgarity of the people. They're so DUMB it's not true and they can't embrace their stupidity enough as they become more "porn-level" and carnally orientated. To say they are culpable through ignorance is the most unbelievable understatement. ... the covert syndicates are moreover at WAR with them but frustrated, like kicking a machine that doesn't react. They've lost control. As for womb inheritance adjustments they've barely had time before the people completely replicated their behaviour...sorry I don't believe in the "people" or the wealthy. The wealthy have power and the evidence is in the covert successes and what is going to be an imminent takeover.

This researcher's personal experiences are fortified by entrenched cynicism about human nature. The human race is living on borrowed ice age time, and without artificial interference the ice sheets would have covered the north by now, and it would have long gone the way of Walt Disney who became a human popsicle. They don't have the right to keep hanging their problems on the impoverished alternatives and glorying in the advantages of affluence, while most Americans do nothing except consume loads of energy. But we know one thing, they're having a good day and his ten year old son skateboards and dyes his hair purple, and she's romping with her dogs or flashing her new Barbie doll hairstyle at crochet meet-ups and church circle get-togethers. I shouted out loud "foreheads on the ground, wombs generating, legs splayed wide open and noses in the air is the future for women at current rates" and a black female just viciously attacked me (her boyfriend and co in the background) They've got tattoos on their shoulders and wear frocks with their Washington DC "waltz with the guys" connection. They're so suppressed it's sad, they're actually motivated to put up Hilary Clinton, their little puppet, old buck teeth and her multimillion dollar marriage. No I'm not Republican but I'm not you either. Hilary makes me sick…she's such a woman's right abuser you couldn't put it into words. She'll get in the White House but men are behind it and it's just another gimmick (CUNTS WHY DON'T YOU FIGURE IT OUT) American women hate me. We needed a showdown a long time ago.

Let's face it women do have more complexity and possibly more intelligence, but due to their inherited relations with men they're now perverts…afraid so…their emotions are interfered with, they are internally watched and they know it, they are denied a language to describe it. It would take men to change the world for the better. They're not wanting to but they are culpable…not made any better by 'jackhammers on the blink' I don't blame men or the ones in power for being as neurotic as fuck. WHO the fuck could lead this earth today in all honesty? I'm tired of resonating with ugly and judgemental people. Most people walking around today are the rejects of their mother's higher will. All those diplomats flying all over the globe trying to solve the world's problems and oil shortages when the problem might just be the jet fuel they're using when they fly to all those places. Walking on the moon when his legs are broken. The world's panoramic sceneries are being ruined. It's actually possible to argue there's no point in taking a vacation anywhere…family crowds spoil it. The writer messed up earlier in believing that physical wide-open spaces represent freedom. No man is an island and no-one can really live in solitude while the "inside spaces" are so patrolled and surveilled. In this sense a crowded physical space can be freer if it has an internal openness or resonance with a set of symbols that are not in friction with that person's soul. The writer's personal life is testimony that there is an invisible realm, that an etheric watchdog seemed always to have been watching, and was never far off.

The writer is at last beginning to get it, that the world works according to a "give and take" principle and most people operate out of a mutualism called a family. So she was always being judged for not giving either to a relationship, job, or the biological family she was born into (jobs were non-accessible and her family barely accessible) Writer bets someone in her family does know where she is. She knows one thing: they'll never confront the writer, and now it's no longer appropriate. Fine. The writer's not offended. She speaks to one sister right now and to one tentative friend (the subject) and very occasionally to one or two workers. She has a few other siblings that she's not in communication with. Writer doesn't want a relationship, doesn't pretend to like people and doesn't have to, but her unique position is interesting. The writer has been in unemployment most of her life and homeless for 20 or so years at street or woodlot level, but she has good memories of her upbringing and none of her family are to blame for her homelessness. The writer doesn't have to make polite small talk like most people …she struggled through it but not any more. But she also had to reflect on the people who supported the writer in her life. They don't seem too nice or like they really cared about her. But probably they in no way banked on the writer being set up like this…to crash in ditches and sleep on cold metal benches, to be tortured, to be a clown, a lunatic or a criminal … it doesn't necessarily have to mean that.

Maybe the writer is experiencing worse insanity in herself than she gives herself credit for. In the modern era we are in the grip of a mental health epidemic, and you are going to need energy supply backups, going to need to cut your consumer expenditure, get a whisper room for when you flip out, but YOU SHOULD BE ENCOURAGED TO HANG ONTO YOUR RAGE AND THE CRAZINESS and it should be accepted that it's not dangerous nor demonic. The point was never about wanting what everybody else has. I GET STRONGER. Anyway I'm in a good mood and I'm getting all my things wrapped up here. The writer is fairly free of constraints, she doesn't answer to anyone and writes voluntarily. This will be her last book, and is an attempt to offer some sort of appraisal. It probably won't get published and she doesn't want to hurt the feelings of the tiny minority who are hurt enough already. The writer won, a tiny minority of ONE won the war.